CAPTAIN
of the
CARPATHIA

CAPTAIN

of the

CARPATHIA

The seafaring life of *Titanic* hero
Sir Arthur Henry Rostron

ERIC L. CLEMENTS

CONWAY

BLOOMSBURY
LONDON · OXFORD · NEW YORK · NEW DELHI · SYDNEY

Conway
An imprint of Bloomsbury Publishing Plc

50 Bedford Square
London
WC1B 3DP
UK

1385 Broadway
New York
NY 10018
USA

www.bloomsbury.com

CONWAY and the 'C' logo are trademarks of Bloomsbury Publishing Plc

First published 2016

British Library Cataloguing-in-Publication Data
A catalogue record for this book is available from the British Library.
Library of Congress Cataloguing-in-Publication data has been applied for.

ISBN: HB: 978-1-8448-6289-4
ePDF: 978-1-8448-6288-7
ePub: 978-1-8448-6290-0

2 4 6 8 10 9 7 5 3 1

Typeset in Adobe Garamond Pro by Deanta Global Publishing Services, Chennai, India
Printed and bound in Great Britain by CPI Group (UK) Ltd, Croydon CR0 4YY

To find out more about our authors and books visit www.bloomsbury.com.
Here you will find extracts, author interviews, details of forthcoming events
and the option to sign up for our newsletters.

To Julian Clement Chase,
a courageous man

For Barbara Anne Clements,
transatlantic voyager

CONTENTS

LIST OF ILLUSTRATIONS

HERO OF THE *CARPATHIA*

Three weeks to the day after the Armistice that ended the First World War, two distinguished veterans of that conflict, a man and his ship, stood into New York Harbor with the first units of US soldiers returning from Europe. On Monday morning, 2 December 1918, the British troop transport *Mauretania*, Captain Arthur H. Rostron, RNR, commanding, brought 4467 doughboys home, among them 167 wounded in France or Belgium.

After Rostron had invited aboard a welcoming committee led by New York City's mayor and delivered by police boat to the lower bay, *Mauretania* moved slowly up the harbour. She paused briefly for clearance at the Quarantine Station on Staten Island at 9.30am then steamed for her berth on Manhattan Island in the Hudson River. Hundreds of soldiers crowded the transport's decks to take in their homecoming, a few standing atop and even inside of the huge ventilator cowlings that lined *Mauretania*'s uppermost deck. They waved to welcoming crowds aboard other vessels or gathered along the shores of the harbour cheering the progress of their ship. At Battery Park on the southern tip of Manhattan, 'thousands of people who had been waiting in the cold wind since 7 o'clock to see the Mauretania pass ... cheered and waved flags frantically... From the Statue of Liberty to the pier the whistling of harbour craft was continuous.'

Another large and boisterous crowd had been gathering for hours at the foot of West Thirteenth Street outside Cunard's Pier 54 to meet the ship. A fifty-piece band, assembled on the pier, greeted *Mauretania*'s late morning arrival with such sprightly songs as 'When Johnny Comes Marching Home' and 'Hail, Hail, the Gang's All Here.'[1]

Arthur Rostron had assumed command of *Mauretania*, one of Cunard's most prestigious appointments, three years earlier at the relatively young age of forty-six and had seen her safely through most of her war service. Her first postwar visit to New York was not the last time that one of Rostron's ships would be greeted by an expectant city, nor was it the first. Six Aprils previously, the thousands at the Battery and outside Pier 54 had stood subdued in darkness and in sorrow, awaiting the survivors of what would become history's most famous shipwreck. His role in the *Titanic* disaster and rescue have kept Rostron's name alive for a century and is certainly the most obvious reason to write his biography, but just as certainly not the only one.

By the end of the First World War, 'Captain A. H. Rostron, hero of the *Carpathia* … and commander of the *Mauretania*,' as *The New York Times* described him, had served more than thirty years at sea. He made his first voyage in 1887 as an apprentice, an apprenticeship that might as well have been served in the age of Nelson, or even Drake. He spent his early years afloat beating around Cape Horn in sail, subsisting on salted rations and stale water drawn from casks, out of contact with land and its society for months, making annual voyages across the hemispheres aboard ships that advanced at an average of little more than one hundred miles per day.

Seven years as an apprentice and an officer in sail qualified Rostron for a master's certificate – and a career in steamships. By the time the apprentice Rostron unfurled his first canvas, sailing ships were already disappearing over the horizon into history. He, therefore, joined the Cunard Steamship Company, Ltd., at the beginning of 1895, spent twelve years with the line as a junior and senior navigating officer and attained his first command in 1907. His conduct as captain of the *Carpathia* on that night to remember five years later, would win him fame across two continents, numerous official and informal tributes and significant future assignments. He would serve with distinction in the Mediterranean and the Atlantic during the First World War and spend the 1920s commanding Cunard's most prestigious ships.

This biography will tell Arthur Rostron's story, of course, but also, through him, tell of seafaring in his era. Rostron began his career as an apprentice in a thousand-ton Cape Horn sailing ship. He ended it as the most celebrated and decorated master mariner of his generation, commanding a fifty-thousand-ton ocean liner for the world's most famous steamship company on the world's most important seaway. In the forty-four-year term of his career, seafaring evolved from his pre-industrial voyages in sail to employing some of the most advanced technologies and sophisticated organizations of the Industrial Age. The wider history through which he sailed included the evolution of the transatlantic passenger trade, the two wars in which he was involved and some of the celebrated ships in which he served and commanded.

One can only recover such history thanks to the prior labours of other historians and of archivists. The notes and bibliography reveal my debt to many outstanding maritime historians, to whom I am grateful. For their courtesy and assistance I thank the archivists and librarians at the Bolton History Centre, Bolton; the Crosby Public Library, Liverpool; the Guildhall Library, London; the Imperial War Museum, London; the London Metropolitan Archives; the Liverpool Record Office, Central Library and Archives, Liverpool; the Maritime History Archive, Memorial University, St John's, Newfoundland; the Maritime Research Center, San Francisco Maritime National Historical Park; the Merseyside Maritime Museum, Liverpool; the National Archives (Public Records Office), London; the Southampton Archives Office; the Southampton Library and Archives; the Special Collections and Archives, Sydney Jones Library, Liverpool University; and the West End Local History Society, West End, Southampton.

Editor Lisa Thomas and the staff at Bloomsbury Publishing have ably transformed my manuscript into our book. Sir Arthur's grandson, John Rostron, granted this writer an interview upon perfunctory introduction and short notice and sent subsequent, valuable correspondence. My parents, Anna and George Clements and Alan and Vera Patrick, have made my life possible and theirs worth emulating. My sister, Bell Julian Clement, a fellow historian writing her own manuscript concurrently, was source and inspiration for solutions to several writing problems. The Canon Slade School, Bolton, provided, gratis and unsolicited, a copy of John Aldred's history of that institution cited herein. The Conway Club and the publisher Houghton Mifflin Harcourt granted permissions to use materials quoted extensively in the text. Southeast Missouri State University provided the financial assistance that made seven weeks of research in Britain, and thus this book, possible. Thank you all.

Three people merit special mention in association with this project. Its unwitting godfather is the maritime historian John Maxtone-Graham. I met him only once, when I was privileged to attend a series of lectures that he gave in the summer of 2009, but by then he had been a shipmate for decades through his book *The Only Way to Cross*. For a better understanding of the history of the transatlantic liners of the twentieth century, start there. I first read Maxtone-Graham's masterpiece forty years ago and it remains perhaps my favourite work of history. The book before you is not a masterpiece for the simple reason that I am not a master, but if I have written it with a fraction of his skill and grace, I shall be well satisfied.

Before she became my mother, Anna Bell Clements was a doctoral candidate in English in an era when not many women achieved that. Writer, teacher and philanthropist, the last work of her life was reviewing an advanced draft of this manuscript, rescuing us from the worst of my errors. One of her edits gives a glimpse of her character. Describing the bloodletting of 1918, I wrote of 'an offensive that cost Germany more than half a million irreplaceable casualties'. That last word is acceptable usage for the sum of those killed, wounded, missing and captured, but her editing pencil slashed right through it. Above it she wrote: 'men'. She was right, of course; they were men. They had mothers too.

My wife of thirty-three years, Barbara Anne Patrick Clements, provides the inspiration and support for my literary ventures. She helped research and edit this book, flawlessly organized the logistics of our seven-week research trip, has to live with a writer and is ever beloved. She is the reason that I sail as scheduled.

CHAPTER I

A CLASSICAL AND COMMERCIAL EDUCATION

Arthur Henry Rostron was born at Sharples, Bolton, Lancashire, in north-western England, on 14 May 1869, almost precisely the midpoint of Queen Victoria's reign. He was the second child and first son of thirty-year-old James Rostron and twenty-seven-year-old Nancy Lever Rostron, born in nearby Eccles and in Bolton, respectively. James and Nancy married in 1867 and raised five children. Edith was born in 1868 and Arthur came the following year. Fredric arrived in 1870, Beatrice in 1872, Ethel, who survived just two weeks, in 1875 and the couple's last child, George, in 1877.[1]

Located a dozen miles north-west of industrial Manchester and about twice that distance north-east of the world's greatest seaport, Liverpool, the Bolton of 1869 lay at the centre of the Industrial Revolution. The town specialized in manufacturing cotton textiles, with about 150 factories employing twenty-five thousand people to produce medium and fine yarns and cotton cloth products ranging from blankets to fancy goods. 'It is a large and prosperous town and probably ranks second to none in its progress and enterprise,' advised a contemporary business directory. The same publication estimated the number of cotton spindles in the borough at about three million, with the large factories having up to a hundred thousand each. Bleaching, which finished these goods to a bright and uniform whiteness, was 'largely carried on, it being estimated that 6,000,000 pieces of cloth are annually bleached here'.[2]

Bolton's staple industry employed both of Arthur's grandfathers, Henry Rostron as a dyer and Thomas Lever as a cotton-waste dealer. At the time of his marriage, James Rostron, Arthur's father, was also a cotton-waste dealer, which suggests a connection to Thomas Lever and his daughter Nancy. By the time Arthur was born, James had become the manager of the Sharples Bleach Works of George Murton and Company. Arthur's youngest brother, George, followed his father and grandfathers into the trade as a cotton spinner and would later manage Chadwick's spinning mill at nearby Eagley. And if the cotton mills had no appeal, Arthur could certainly have found employment in one of Bolton's 'many extensive machine works ... brass foundries, iron works, chemical works, collieries and other industries,' as did his other brother, Fredric, as a steam engine fitter.[3]

Except that none of Bolton's industry and enterprise interested young Arthur Rostron, who later recalled that he 'never had any ambition other than to go to sea. The spirit of adventure must have lived in some remote ancestor and come down to me; certainly there was in my home no encouragement to set out on long and hazardous trails. Yet at five or six years of age I announced my intention to be a sailor and all that was ever said to dispel that youthful dream – and there was a good deal of quite natural opposition – never had the slightest effect, unless it was to increase my determination.'[4]

This was not a determination that sat well with his parents. James Rostron, though certainly not wealthy, was fairly prosperous and he apparently wished to guide his oldest son through a good education and into a career more secure and less dangerous than seafaring could offer. Young Arthur's desire to roam the planet may also simply have been incomprehensible to his parents, both of whom lived out their lives within ten miles of where they were born. Arthur resisted his father's thinking, however, to the point of running away to join a ship at the age of fourteen, only to be sent home on account of his boyish looks. But Arthur's resolve would eventually force his father's acquiescence.[5]

First, however, came the requirement to gain an education. Arthur initially attended the Bolton Grammar School under headmaster the Reverend Distin Stanley Hodgson. The school, built in 1657, accommodated 116 boys, each of whom was charged one guinea per quarter. Baptized as an Anglican, Arthur next enrolled in the Upper School of the Bolton Church of England Educational Institute, in Silverwell Street. Under the headmaster the Reverend John Worsley Cundey, the Bolton Church Institute, founded in 1846, offered students 'a classical and commercial education, combined with religious and moral instruction in conformity with the principles of the Church of England'.[6]

Besides its preparatory and upper schools, aimed at boys of the middle classes, the institute featured a library and reading room, offered evening classes for adults and, in 1879, opened a girls' school. Classes were 'open to all comers, but it must be distinctly understood that religious instruction is given according to the principles of the Church of England and there is no arrangement whereby the pupils can be withdrawn from such instruction; they are, in a word, distinctly Church of England Day Schools and are the only ones of the class in the town'.[7]

The classical curriculum, intended to prepare students for their university examinations, featured 'Religious Knowledge, English, Modern Languages, Latin, Mathematics and Science,' but the school offered drawing, music and military drill as well. The commercial side of the programme, largely vocational, consisted of a technical school that offered applied mechanics, machine drawing, building construction, principles of mining and such locally useful skills as practical chemistry, dyeing and bleaching, and cotton manufacturing. The institute offered three terms a year, charging fees of two guineas per term for students under twelve years of age and three guineas for those older, although it did offer some competitive scholarships.[8]

On leaving the Bolton Church Institute at the end of 1884, the problem of fifteen-year-old Arthur's career choice resurfaced. Perhaps in compromise – to let the lad test the waters, as it were – James Rostron agreed to enroll his oldest son aboard HMS *Conway*, a merchant marine school ship moored in the River Mersey at Birkenhead on the opposite bank of the Mersey to Liverpool.

HMS *Conway* came into being ten years before Arthur was born thanks to the efforts of the Mercantile Marine Service Association, founded in 1857 to improve the status of Britain's merchant service and its officers. In 1859 the association acquired the surplus 28-gun frigate HMS *Conway* to use as a training ship for merchant officer cadets. The success of the undertaking soon rendered the original ship inadequate and she was replaced two years later by the 51-gun frigate HMS *Winchester*, renamed HMS *Conway*. That arrangement lasted until 1876, when the second ship was replaced by the former HMS *Nile*, a 92-gun, 4875-ton, two-deck, second-rate ship of the line originally built in 1826 and with a steam engine and screw propulsion added in 1854. With her machinery removed and rigging rehabilitated, this third HMS *Conway* would capably fulfill the multiple roles of training ship, campus and dormitory for the following seventy-five years.[9]

Conway shared the river with three other moored school ships. Two were reform schools intended to turn troublesome youths into sailors. The third school ship had the same mission, but her clientele was the orphaned sons of British seamen and other indigent lads. *Conway*'s goal was more exclusive: to train future merchant marine officers. She was, as described in 1883, 'a school for the sons of gentlemen,' intended to develop character as well as craft and 'to this extent … is the same as many another boarding school'. Even if status had not set *Conway* apart from her neighbours, cost certainly did; James Rostron's total expense for Arthur's fees, clothing and extras for his two years aboard *Conway* amounted to £105.[10]

Between reveille at 6am and taps at 9pm, *Conway*'s 170 or so cadets studied and drilled and learned the ropes. The cadets were organized into port and starboard watches, with the watch on deck learning practical seamanship while the watch below attended classes. *Conway*'s academic offerings were both scholastic and nautical, while the cadets also had time for concerts and shows and played their share of sports. *Conway* offered cadets prizes for swimming, rowing, boxing and fencing, held an annual sports festival with nineteen events for 'Running and Jumping, &c,' and fielded its own cricket and football teams. As at other English public schools, cadets went home on holiday between terms.[11]

Rostron enrolled on 1 February 1885. At fifteen years and eight months, he may have joined the ship a term ahead; *Conway*'s academic calendar normally began in September and ended with Midsummer examinations and awards in July. Nevertheless, Rostron had made his mark by the end of his first term. The results of the spring examinations of 1885 put him fourth overall in the second form. Cadets sat for examinations on English history, scripture history, geography, French, arithmetic, algebra, trigonometry and physics, although not all students stood for all subjects. Rostron attained the highest marks in his form in English history and placed second in geography, third in algebra and fourth in arithmetic. Another series of examinations were held for the seagoing subjects of navigation, nautical astronomy and the laws of compass deviation, though students in the second form may only have stood for the first of these. Conway's staff also assessed cadets in a more general review at the end of every term. This evaluation was divided into a 'school report' and a 'naval report', each indicating 'ability', 'application' and 'conduct' and through his first year Rostron's evaluations ranged from 'satisfactory' at worst to 'very good'.[12]

On the Midsummer 1885 Prize List, among the Horsfall Prizes, Rostron won honourable mention from the second class 'For General Proficiency in Geography'. He also received recognition 'For General Proficiency' in the second form under the Clark Aspinall Prizes and was awarded the book *A Voyage in the Sunbeam*, Annie Brassey's 1878 account of her family's circumnavigation of the world by yacht.[13]

Rostron's senior year was even more impressive. He later wrote that he reached the position of head boy, the leading cadet. While he did not attain the highest score scholastically, he certainly did very well. He stood for examination in twelve subjects at the Midsummer examinations for the senior class in July 1886, his total score placing him third among thirty-nine cadets. Rostron scored particularly well in history, dictation, trigonometry and practical navigation. He also took examinations in the academic fields of scripture, geography, arithmetic, algebra and physics, in the vocational topics of nautical astronomy, meteorology and compass deviation and avoided the French exam altogether.[14]

Seniors also faced separate tests in navigation and seamanship administered by an independent examiner from the marine board in Liverpool. These included 'Rule[s] of the Road at Sea, Use of Charts, Signals, [and] Nautical Instruments,' as well as 'the practical work comprised in an Able Seaman's Duties'. Ironically, given his subsequent exploits, Rostron received no special mention or any awards in these nautical subjects.[15]

Rostron's senior-year marks on his school and naval reports were uniformly 'very good', and he repeated his successes at the Midsummer awards ceremony held on *Conway*'s quarterdeck under an awning in pouring rain on 22 July 1886. Rostron placed first among the senior class in English history, second in scripture history, second in physics, third in geography and fifth in trigonometry. He won honorable mention in the competition for the Royal Geographical Society's prize for proficiency in geography and carried off the Torr Prize for the senior class, a barometer, for proficiency in history. He tied for first for the Horsfall Prize for scripture history, receiving a copy of James Macaulay's 1882 book *All True, Records of Peril and Adventure by Sea and Land*. He also came second in the Samuelson Prize for proficiency in physical science, receiving a certificate of merit, and received the only mention 'for Medical Lectures', with a prize, awarded by the school, of Sir Frederick G. D. Bedford's *The Sailor's Pocket Book*, of 1875.[16]

Arthur Rostron concluded his two years aboard HMS *Conway* with an Extra Certificate, issued on 20 December 1886, and the final assessment of: 'Conduct Very Good[.] Ability Very Good.' Four days later, he received an appointment as a midshipman in the Royal Naval Reserve. Rostron later recommended 'that every boy going to sea spend a couple of years on one of the training ships… He will get invaluable ground work and his liking for the life will be well tried.' Cadet Rostron had certainly found his calling. *Conway's* Register of Cadets also noted that Rostron would next join a sailing ship named *Cedric the Saxon*, his first billet in the merchant service and the beginning of his lifetime at sea.[17]

CHAPTER 2

THE BUSINESS OF A SEAMAN

On 24 February 1887, Arthur Henry Rostron, aged seventeen years and nine months, signed an Ordinary Apprentice's Indenture with the Liverpool shipping firm of Williamson, Milligan and Company. In it, Rostron committed to serve an apprenticeship of four years. He agreed to provide his own bedding, clothing and necessities or to see the cost of same was deducted from his wages. He also promised to not 'frequent Taverns or Alehouses … nor play at Unlawful Games'. A final stipulation, handwritten at the bottom, stated that if Rostron's ship were wrecked, the company could cancel his indenture. A third party to the agreement, James Rostron, as surety, was bound to Arthur's completion of the contract at a penalty of forty pounds. In exchange for these obligations, Williamson and Milligan agreed to teach the young man 'the business of a Seaman,' to provide him with 'sufficient Meat, Drink, Lodging, Washing, Medicine and Medical and Surgical Assistance,' and to pay him forty pounds over the four years – five pounds the first year, eight the second, twelve the third and fifteen in the fourth year of his indenture.[1]

Williamson, Milligan and Company, headquartered in the Old Castle Buildings, Preeson's Row, Liverpool, 'engaged in general trade to all parts of the world'. The company owned a fleet of nine ships, ranging from six hundred to twenty-two hundred tons, including one iron-hulled and one steel-hulled steamer and seven sailing vessels, six of iron and one of steel. Rostron's years with the company would be spent in two of the iron-hulled sailing ships, *Cedric the Saxon* and *Red Gauntlet*.[2]

By the time Rostron joined the company, sailing ships had lost the competition with steamers for high-value cargoes on the major sea lanes.

What remained for sailing vessels were long voyages hauling low-value, bulk commodities such as coal, grain, nitrates and timber. These ventures took them to many of the world's outposts on voyages that typically lasted most of a year. Rostron's first ship, *Cedric the Saxon*, was a three-masted, full-rigged sailing ship built at Port Glasgow, Scotland, by J. Reid and Company in 1875. She was 1705 gross tons, with a length of 260 feet and a beam of 40 feet. She had two decks, subdivided by one bulkhead and, as Rostron would soon discover to his discomfort, a freeboard amidships under maximum load of less than five feet.[3]

Rostron joined his new ship at Hull and she sailed for San Francisco on 28 February 1887 under the command of William P. Haines. Born in Birkenhead in 1857, the twenty-nine-year-old Haines passed his master's exam in 1884 and *Cedric the Saxon* was his second command. Haines' officers were first mate George Linden, aged forty-four, and a Swedish second mate named George Peterson. The ship's ratings included a boatswain, carpenter, sailmaker, cook, steward and a donkeyman-seaman who operated the cargo-moving apparatus when the ship was in port. Sixteen able and two ordinary seamen completed the crew. The ship also carried five apprentices, including Rostron, ranging from sixteen to eighteen years of age, one of whom, Francis Williamson, reached the end of his indenture and was promoted to third mate shortly before the vessel reached San Francisco.[4]

Cedric the Saxon's newest apprentice later remembered the first month of the voyage as idyllic, the stuff of the dreams of armchair sailors and enthusiastic cadets. Once the ship reached latitude 40 South, however, the clouds descended – often literally. Fierce weeks of beating slowly around Cape Horn followed as the southern autumn faded toward winter darkness took weeks, the ship relentlessly assaulted by the Horn's 'bitter green water'. The howling fury of an unusually rough passage eventually drove *Cedric the Saxon* four hundred miles south of the Horn on her slog around South America into the Pacific.[5]

'I was to find out that sailing ships meant hard work, sometimes bullying by more or less ignorant officers, great risks and poor food, [and] every sort of discomfort that one can conjure to the imagination… Sleep, rest, food, drink – all gone without through long periods.' Aloft at all hours, in all weathers, he soon learned that even the pretended security of 'one hand for the ship and one for yourself' would not avail in the chaos of a storm, for 'no sail can be furled with one hand while the other is devoted to your own safety'. He was left to wonder, years later, whether ship owners safe ashore 'ever realized what titanic labour and risk went to make their dividends. I fear not. And certainly little of the ship's profits found their way into our pockets!'[6]

This was an era described by one of Rostron's contemporaries, Samuel G. S. McNeil, as 'the bad and hard old days when there were plenty of hard kicks and very few pennies,' particularly for apprentices. McNeil recalled that on their early voyages apprentices 'had to do any kind of dirty job, just the same as the ordinary seaman,' but that the apprentices had their own quarters off watch and were always considered part of the 'after-guard'. One of Rostron's future shipmates, Harry Grattidge, who also apprenticed around the Horn under sail, remembered that the worst of the experience might have been the 'watch and watch' that alternated every four hours. This port-and-starboard regime 'meant that never in all this time could we snatch more than three and a half hours' unbroken sleep... In time you came to hate any emergency as robbing you of those three and a half precious hours... but with the incredible resilience of youth we became adept at carrying out a job while sleeping on our feet.' Even with the dangers and discomforts, however, McNeil saw the value of such an apprenticeship. 'Training in sail taught a youngster to be resourceful,' he found, 'and also taught him to think and act quickly... He learned not only how to lead men, but how to command them.'[7]

Sometimes the sea could at least inflict its hard lessons in grimly humorous ways. One night the new apprentice Rostron was dispatched forward to get hot water for the evening's cocoa. He recalled:

It was blowing fresh with an occasional sea tumbling over the rail. Foolishly I went along the weather side of the deck to the galley, the door of which was abreast of the fore rigging. I had opened the galley door, had just time to see the cook, carpenter, sailmaker and donkeyman sitting on the bench before the fire smoking, when we shipped a lump of a sea. The first thing I knew I was sprawling in the lee scuppers. That sea had lifted me into the galley, swept me right across it, pushed me through the other door and onto the deck again. It had also done much the same for the galley's occupants! We were all mixed up in the scuppers together and you may take it as authentic that the language was neither polite nor complimentary. But I had learned my lesson and on bad nights the weather side of the deck saw no more of me.[8]

Not for the last time in his career, Rostron was lucky. If he needed a horrifying example to caution him further, the sea provided one as *Cedric the Saxon* finally beat her way past Cape Horn and was rounding to the north-west in mountainous seas. At 2.30am on 9 May 1887, a boarding sea caught nineteen-year-old ordinary seaman R. W. Wilkinson on the open deck unprotected and flung him over the rail. He was never seen again.[9]

Cedric the Saxon and her remaining crew finally bested the Horn, only to have the pugilistic Pacific land a last, vicious blow on the trip northward. On 2 June, 'while running in a furious gale from [the south-east, *Cedric the Saxon*] shipped a heavy sea over the stern, carrying away [her] wheel and binnacle; at the same time [the] ship broached to, losing all the sails that were set.' At least that was the dry account of the mishap that appeared in *Lloyd's List*. Rostron remembered that the boarding sea carried away the helmsman and the senior apprentice along with the wheel. 'Fortunately they were caught in the fore part of the poop and regained their feet unhurt.' Unfortunately, the accident also snapped some of the braces securing the ship's masts and *Cedric the Saxon* had to lie to for about thirty hours, while her crew repaired the damage to her helm and rigging and bent on new sails.[10]

Cedric the Saxon arrived in San Francisco Bay on 27 July 1887, after a voyage of five months during which Rostron saw land once between England and the Golden Gate. She tied up at Oakland wharf to unload her cargo of railroad rails. There, nineteen of her crew deserted, including the boatswain, donkeyman, cook and almost the entire forecastle. And it turned out that Oakland had its own hazards; two weeks after her arrival, while lying alongside Oakland wharf, *Cedric the Saxon* was rammed by the steamer *Navarro*. The collision cracked the sternpost and damaged three iron hull plates on the ship. After eight weeks at Oakland, her damage repaired and a cargo of wheat loaded, *Cedric the Saxon* departed for Queenstown, Ireland, on 20 September. Following a less vigorous springtime passage of the Horn, she arrived at Queenstown in the first week of January 1888, remained a week and reached Liverpool on 15 January, completing her round voyage in ten and a half months.[11]

Six weeks later, on 29 February 1888, *Cedric the Saxon* and Arthur Rostron put to sea for San Francisco again. This time the excitement began before the ship reached the high southern latitudes. On the evening of 25 April *Cedric the Saxon* made the harbour at Rio de Janeiro, where she remained for four weeks undergoing repairs after having been 'partially dismasted in a gale'. Rostron later declared that misadventure 'the only happening of importance' on a round voyage that lasted six days less than a year, but even a relatively uneventful voyage produced its share of uncertainty.[12]

Cedric the Saxon had gone to sea again under a new commander, James Veysey, a thirty-four-year-old native of Brixham in Devon. Her officers were first mate Alfred Pope of Liverpool and second mate George Boyd of Belfast. Her midships personnel consisted of a boatswain, carpenter, sailmaker, steward and cook. In her forecastle sailed an able-bodied seaman-donkeyman, sixteen other able-bodied seamen and two ordinary seamen. This gave her a total complement of twenty-seven, consisting of ten Englishmen, three Swedes and a Noah's Ark assemblage of pairs of Scots, Finns, French, Canadians and Americans, plus an Irishman, a Norwegian, a Corsican and a native of the Isle of Man. The ship also carried four apprentices: Virgil Marani, Arthur Clay, William Keiller and Arthur Rostron. Four and a half months into the voyage, Marani's apprenticeship expired and he was promoted to third mate.[13]

As might be imagined of such a polyglot assembly of sailors, their abilities were perhaps as diverse as their origins and their loyalty in the face of hardship was not guaranteed. Excluding the apprentices, fifty-one men signed the articles, eleven of whom – two officers and nine men – completed the entire round voyage from Liverpool. At Rio de Janeiro the ship picked up a new cook, three able-bodied seamen and two boys. Of the five sailors who left the ship there, one departed on account of illness, two deserted and two left by 'mutual consent'.[14]

When *Cedric the Saxon* reached San Francisco on 5 September 1888, more than a third of the crew, ten in all, jumped ship. On 15 October, a day before she sailed for Queenstown, Captain Veysey resigned and the first mate, Alfred Pope, assumed command. Pope was twenty-five years old and had passed the master's exam in his native Liverpool just two years before.

With her new master, a new first mate, a boatswain, a donkeyman, eleven able-bodied seamen and yet another cook signed for the voyage and a cargo of wheat loaded, *Cedric the Saxon* departed for Queenstown on 16 October 1888. She made that port on 14 February 1889 and departed six days later for Liverpool, where Rostron's second sojourn under sail ended on 23 February.[15]

Rostron's third and final voyage as an apprentice began three weeks later. It took him and *Cedric the Saxon* in the opposite direction from the first two, around the Cape of Good Hope bound for Calcutta with a cargo of salt. She departed Liverpool on 16 March 1889, with Veysey back in command, Pope as first mate and William Bond of Liverpool as second mate. The ship arrived at Calcutta three months later, on 20 June. After enduring two months of India's summer, *Cedric the Saxon* departed on 22 August, leaving behind six of her crew due to illness. A two-month voyage brought her to Port Pirie, a grain port in South Australia on the eastern shore of Spencer Gulf, a few miles north of Adelaide. She remained there for more than three months in a more agreeable climate, before sailing for Queenstown, Ireland, with a load of wheat on 3 February 1890. This time she cleared the harbour without one of her able seamen, thirty-nine-year-old John Kennedy of Liverpool, who had died the previous month in the hospital at Port Pirie following an accident. *Cedric the Saxon*'s return passage took four months, with the ship reporting at Queenstown on 4 June to receive orders as to where to deliver her cargo. Those orders were for St Nazaire, on the west coast of France, where the ship unloaded from mid-June until early July. The ship then returned to Barry, Wales, concluding her voyage on 12 July 1890.[16]

After finishing his third voyage in *Cedric the Saxon*, the management of Williamson, Milligan and Company declared that Rostron had completed three and a half years of his four-year indenture 'to our entire satisfaction [and to] that of the captains under whom he has served, who report that they always found him able and attentive to his duties, well conducted [and] strictly sober'. The firm thereupon voided the remaining six months of his apprenticeship, in light of his having passed his second mate's exam, and appointed the twenty-one-year-old Rostron second mate in the company's barque *Red Gauntlet*. As a second mate, his wages increased from the ten pounds a year he averaged over his apprenticeship to a somewhat more reasonable five pounds a month, a sixfold rise in salary.[17]

Red Gauntlet, Rostron's new ship, was a single-decked, iron-hulled barque of 1053 registered tons. Of 205 feet in length and 33 feet in beam, she was built in 1864 at Greenock, Scotland, at the mouth of the River Clyde, by the shipbuilder R. Steele. In this ship, Rostron would undertake his widest-ranging voyage, but his first as a mate was a simple, if lengthy, out and back. *Red Gauntlet* and her new second mate sailed from Barry, south-west of Cardiff, on 10 October 1890. Her master, the Cornishman F. E. Grow, aged forty-six, had also commanded the ship on her previous voyage. The first mate was the thirty-one-year-old George Boyd of Belfast and the ship carried a twenty-one-year-old third mate named H. B. Harvey. *Red Gauntlet* was bound for Port Pirie and made the run around the Cape of Good Hope in twelve weeks, arriving on 9 January 1891. Two months later, on 13 March, she sailed from Port Pirie for Rouen, France, loaded with wheat. The ship arrived in the Rouen River exactly five months later and reached the city itself on 19 August, whereupon Boyd, Rostron, Harvey and fourteen of the crew left the ship 'upon mutual agreement'. After unloading, another crew signed new articles and sailed *Red Gauntlet* to Liverpool on 14 September. Rostron's first voyage as a mate had lasted ten months and nine days, short of the full one year of sea time required to sit for his first mate's certificate.[18]

So Rostron signed the articles again as second mate in *Red Gauntlet* for a voyage that would prove to be his greatest odyssey under sail. The ship departed from Liverpool on 29 October 1891, this time captained by Alfred Pope. Pope and the first mate had been shipmates of Rostron's aboard *Cedric the Saxon*, so, he observed 'the company was pleasant'. *Red Gauntlet* crossed the equator in the third week of November and reached Adelaide on 23 January 1892, after a passage of eleven weeks. From Adelaide, South Australia, *Red Gauntlet* sailed for Newcastle, New South Wales, on the east coast of the continent. On 12 March 1892, after loading coal at Newcastle, the ship departed for Valparaíso, Chile, on the west coast of South America. It was a passage that almost cost Rostron and his shipmates their lives.[19]

Disaster nearly overwhelmed *Red Gauntlet* South of New Zealand. At midnight Rostron had been relieved by the first mate and had just turned in below, when the ship was struck by 'a real southerly buster'. The blow shredded her sails and knocked the ship onto her beam ends, which caused her cargo of coal to shift and the ship to list dangerously. There she lay, her lower lee yards under water and her deck submerged to the hatches, while her crew scrambled to save their ship. For three days they fought to right her, with the watch busy aloft repairing rigging and bending on new sails, while half of the watch below laboriously trimmed coal back to the high side of the ship and the other half slept. Fortunately, the weather moderated sufficiently to allow *Red Gauntlet* to be repaired and righted, as no hope of rescue existed in that wild and empty ocean. Although he would face other crises during his long career, Rostron later declared that this mishap was the closest that he came to dying in his entire forty-four years at sea.[20]

Eventually, *Red Gauntlet* reached Valparaíso and delivered her cargo, leaving port on 27 May 1892, headed 175 nautical miles up the coast to Guayacan to load nitrates. Three months later, on 27 July, she sailed from Guayacan for Portland, Oregon. The nitrates delivered to Portland at the end of September, the next cargo was grain bound for Plymouth, England. *Red Gauntlet* left Portland on 16 October and arrived at Plymouth fifteen and a half weeks later, after an eastbound summer passage around Cape Horn, on 26 February 1893, completing her circumnavigation of the earth in sixteen months. After a month at Plymouth, *Red Gauntlet* departed for London, arriving at the South West India Dock in the first week of April, 1893.[21]

At the end of this epic voyage, Rostron took his leave of *Red Gauntlet* and of Williamson, Milligan and Company. He spent a couple of months back at home where he passed his examinations for first mate. He then landed a first mate's billet, at six pounds per month, with the Liverpool firm of Squarey and Kendall. This posting required a trip to Antwerp, Belgium, to join his new ship. *Camphill* was a steel-hulled barque of 1240 registered tons, a length of 226 feet and a beam of 36 feet. She was built by C. J. Bigger of Londonderry, Ireland, in 1889 and registered at Liverpool. On 19 July 1893, two days after Rostron and the rest of the crew signed on, *Camphill* departed from Antwerp loaded with explosives and bound for Valparaíso.[22]

After many months under the capable command of Alfred Pope, Rostron now found himself under a less impressive master. James Butters was a fifty-five-year-old Scotsman who had commanded *Camphill* on her annual voyages to Australia in 1889, 1890 and 1892. Perhaps the rigours of these long voyages had worn him down for, according to Rostron, upon reaching the South Atlantic *Camphill*'s captain 'became very fond of his cabin – and its contents!' That left the twenty-four-year-old Rostron, assisted only by the twenty-year-old second mate, A. J. McDonald of Deptford, effectively in command of a crew that proved to be almost as dangerous as the cargo.[23]

Camphill carried a carpenter, sailmaker, cook, steward, ten able-bodied seamen, two ordinary seamen and two ship's boys who were making their first voyages. They came from all over Europe, including eight from Scandinavia, but, and perhaps significantly, only three – two Scots and an Englishman – came from Britain. With the master sequestered in his cabin, it appears that the crew decided to test the limits of their young first mate. Whatever the sequence of events, relations between Rostron and the crew deteriorated to the point that he received threats to knife him. 'I quite understood that this was no jest,' he later wrote, 'and in consequence for weeks I carried a revolver, even sleeping with it under my pillow. Never did I approach a man, or let him approach me, unless I was armed.' The revolver established an uneasy truce, but the truce held. *Camphill* rounded the Horn and made Valparaíso on 24 October 1893, 'without anyone being knifed or shot'.[24]

After some reordering of the crew at Valparaíso, *Camphill* sailed on 1 December for Pisagua, a nitrate port in northern Chile. It was on what another English sailor described as 'a bleak, barren coast all right; where trees don't grow and the rain never rains'. She arrived on 9 December, loaded and sailed on 6 January 1894, for 'United Kingdom or Continent'. Her destination turned out to be the Cornish port of Falmouth, which *Camphill* reached on 29 April. After a week there, she sailed for home, arriving at Liverpool on 9 May. Rostron recorded that as *Camphill* approached England, her captain's disposition improved to the point that he had recovered completely by the time she docked.[25]

Whatever *Camphill*'s particular discontents, this was an age when officers, especially in sail, were expected to enforce their orders with their fists, if necessary. Rostron, who had fought before on occasion, would have his last such confrontation on *Camphill*. As he recounted the incident, Rostron was obliged to correct the work of a man who responded first with insolence and then, when called on that, with abuse. 'There was nothing for it,' Rostron believed. 'An officer dare not let a man take the upper hand or all discipline is gone.' The sailor landed the first blow, but it was Rostron who prevailed in the fisticuffs that followed. He thought that 'a fight like that seldom left bad blood, so long as it was a clean scrap.' In his opinion, a brief physical confrontation was a better resolution than entering the man's name in the ship's log, thereby exposing him to formal ship's discipline. In Rostron's experience, a man who had been logged would take his first chance to desert, 'and until then you had to keep your weather eye open, for you were dealing with a man who, with a threat over him, felt he was suffering under a grievance.'[26]

Usually, of course, matters did not come to blows. Rostron's fellow Cape Horner Samuel McNeil believed that 'the mate of a large sailing-ship should be a good organizer,' always on top of the 'hundred and one things to be thought of,' but McNeil declared that 'there is one virtue that an officer in a sailing-ship must have, and that is "courage" – both moral and physical. He has to know what to do and do it without hesitation; he must give his orders in no uncertain voice, and he must have an authoritative manner. The worst of hard-cases will nearly always act decently when given orders by an officer who knows what he wants done and how to set about doing it.' Although not the most physically imposing of men, Rostron had developed into such an officer under sail: competent, authoritative, and a leader. He wrote of his days in sail that during the inevitable intervals 'of stress and messy work … let me say, I was always up to the neck, for I loved the old ship and my work, wanted to be a hundred per cent sailorman and, when leadership and encouragement were required, I never thought of being anywhere save with my men.'[27]

By the time *Camphill* returned to Liverpool in May 1894, Rostron had completed seven years and two months in sail and had demonstrated repeatedly that he could hold his own in tough circumstances. In three voyages as an apprentice, two as second mate, and one as first mate, Rostron had survived fights with discontented sailors, at least seven passages of Cape Horn, *Cedric the Saxon*'s partial dismasting in the Atlantic, and *Red Gauntlet*'s knock down south of New Zealand. He had also personally suffered two significant falls aboard ship, the first from the rigging to the deck during his final voyage as an apprentice in *Cedric the Saxon*, and the second from the deck into the hold at Portland, Oregon, on his circumnavigation as second mate in *Red Gauntlet*. Lithe and lucky, he did not suffer serious injury in either accident.[28]

He had matured into a man about five feet, eight inches tall and weighing about 160 pounds, who would retain somewhat boyish features into middle age. An American newspaper described him at mid-life as 'gaunt of frame and ruddy of complexion, with blue eyes and light hair inherited from the ... Norsemen'. Although a citizen of the world by the time he reached adulthood, a shipmate at the end of Rostron's career remarked that he 'retained quite a marked Lancashire (Bolton) accent' for the rest of his days. Fellow sailor James Bisset, who met Rostron when Rostron was forty, described him as 'of thin and wiry build, with sharp features, piercing blue eyes, and rapid, agile movements. ... In his habits he was austere. ... He did not drink, smoke, or use profanity.'[29]

Rostron had developed those shipboard habits during his days in sail. He dissipated neither himself nor his hard-won wages ashore. Tied up at the foot of Market Street in San Francisco – a port that a fellow Cape Horner declared had 'the worst reputation of any sea port in the world for lawlessness, not excepting New York' in the 1880s – Rostron hardly ventured ashore. He wrote that he 'was perfectly happy and content where I was – on board with my job. For one thing beer was not to my taste and as for the other "attractions" of life in port they had no lure for me.'[30]

This was an attitude that would please ship owners and lead to advancement, certainly, but Rostron held to it for several reasons. One was his belief that sailors were the victims, not the beneficiaries, of their excesses ashore. The beneficiaries were those who preyed upon men just landed after months of danger and privation. He decried the mistreatment of sailors ashore, assailed by 'harpies and sharks ... sometimes to die, always to be robbed, often to be beaten, filled with loathsome liquor and, alas, not infrequently with disease'.[31]

The other foundation of Rostron's personal sobriety was the profound religious faith that he developed during his formative years. It is perhaps a cliché, when discussing sailors and religion, to evoke Psalm 107: 'They that go down to the sea in ships, that do business in great waters; these see the works of the Lord and his wonders in the deep.' But the wisdom of those words fit Rostron's understanding exactly. Expressed in his sailor's vernacular: 'A sailor has his faith; he lives so close to nature, there are times when he feels in touch with the infinite,' or: 'It is so easy watching nature in her vigorous strength and serene beauty, to believe that behind it all there is a destiny shaping our ends.' He once described himself as 'not "religious" in what the ordinary sense of "religion" means, you understand. But, man, nature is with us!'[32]

This was not a faith that Rostron imposed on his shipmates, however. He once observed that 'there is one thing the sailor hates and abhors and that is to see a man coming on board with a Prayer Book in one hand and a Bible in the other. There is no class of men in the whole wide world who have a greater conception, or a greater reverence for the Power that rules over us. Sailors as a rule are not given to saying much as regards religion but they stick to it and they hold it in their hearts. The heart is the place, not the mouth.'[33]

Rostron later admitted that old Cape Horners tended to romanticize their time in sail. He certainly did. At least he did long after his days of losing fingernails to raging canvas or eating salt pork first soaked in sea water to make it 'fresher and more palatable. And this, mark you, is given out with no generous hand.' With such hardships not forgotten but in perspective, Rostron could also write lyrically about days of smooth sailing, when 'we spread our white wings and let the breezes bowl us along with a song in the rigging and music at the prow'. *Cedric the Saxon* would remain the pride of his years in sail. 'She was a beautiful model, taught and trim as a yacht,' he wrote. 'I've known her [to] reel off eighteen knots in a squall with every stitch set ... she just heeled over to it and clipped off the knots... I was on board when she ran 325 miles (nautical) in 22 hours [averaging 14.77 knots] with a hard gale blowing under our stern and heavy seas running.'[34]

Rostron's days under sail were coming to a close, however, at least for the moment. Although *Camphill*'s owners wanted him to remain with the ship as master, his previous voyage in her had left him a few weeks short of the sea time he needed to sit for his master's license. Rostron decided not to make another voyage in sail, which involved investing many months in order to acquire the necessary weeks of sea time. The solution was a shorter passage in his first steamship, *River Avon*, a thousand-ton, single-screw tramper belonging to J. Little and Company and registered in Glasgow. She measured 235 feet long and 33 feet in beam and spent her time knocking around ports in northern Europe and the Mediterranean.[35]

Exactly when and where Rostron joined *River Avon* is uncertain, but if he needed six more weeks of sea time and paid off at Ipswich, as he recalled in his memoir, he would have sailed in her from Newcastle for Bilbao on the north coast of Spain on about 12 September 1894. She arrived at Bilbao on about 20 September and sailed for Swansea after a two-week turnaround, arriving on 4 October. A week later, *River Avon* began a voyage that introduced Rostron to the Mediterranean, a sea with which he would later become very familiar. A passage of twelve days landed the ship at Algiers; a few days after that she headed for Huelva on the Atlantic coast of southern Spain. On 1 November *River Avon* left Huelva, arriving at Ipswich on 9 November, where Rostron took his leave of the ship.[36]

With his sea-time requirements satisfied, twenty-five-year-old Arthur Rostron sat for his master's examinations a month later. He was awarded his Extra Master's Certificate on 17 December 1894, at Liverpool – the 'Extra', the highest possible credential, earned for demonstrating special competency in navigation – and enjoyed the bonus of spending Christmas and the New Year in Bolton with his family. That new year, 1895, would find the recently certified master serving in both sail and steam and entering into another apprenticeship of sorts served during the many years between certification to command and command itself, one that would carry him to new ports and increasing responsibilities.[37]

CHAPTER 3

SMART OFFICER

His Extra Master's certificate in hand, twenty-five-year-old Arthur Rostron hoped to command a sailing ship. 'Those youthful ambitions of mine had always visualised a windjammer; that was the life for a man who wanted to follow the sea. And with all the hardships that had come my way I loved the life.' His taste for sail went back to his months aboard *Conway*. 'In the old days,' he recalled, 'steam was anathema to us.' He once described the remains of Isambard Brunel's giant steamship *Great Eastern*, moored in the Mersey during his time in *Conway*, as a 'mammoth chunk of ugliness,' and remembered that the cadets' preference was decidedly for the sailing ships calling at the port. 'It was the chief delight of the cadets to get "day leave" so that they could mooch round [*sic*] the docks and go on board these ships,' longing for the time when they too could put to sea in sail.[1]

For these reasons Rostron initially resisted serving in steamers. After *River Avon*, which he dismissed as 'a bug-infested old tub,' his next encounter with the breed came at the beginning of 1895. He found his new ship, a Liverpool cargo-cattle steamer on the Boston run, no improvement. He reported aboard, stowed his gear in his cabin and then took a turn about the deck to inspect the vessel. He heard the cacophony of the steam winches hard at work, saw 'everything dirty, everything apparently in disorder,' and inhaled 'the reek of that cattle steamer'. To Rostron it all compared quite unfavourably to the good order, neat lines and quiet manners of a sailing ship.[2]

Beset with doubts, Rostron returned to his cabin, grabbed his gear, lay ashore and telegraphed his regrets to the company. He would find another billet. He later called that impulse 'one of those decisions which affect one's whole life'. That was certainly true, though not in ways that he could possibly have imagined as he walked ashore. On Tuesday, 29 January 1895, Rostron reported, instead, to the offices of the Cunard Steamship Company. He remembered, however, that 'even on the day that I reported to the chief superintendent of the Cunard Line, only half my heart was in the job. I didn't take to the notion of steam.' He was, rather, driven to it – at least if he wished to continue making a living on the sea. Billets in sail, from captain on down, were simply getting harder to find.[3]

So he accepted Cunard's offer of a posting as fourth officer on the passenger ship *Umbria*, scheduled to depart Liverpool four days later on a passage scheduled for five and a third days to New York. She advertised 'superior accommodation at moderate fares for all classes,' which included 500 first-class, 160 second and 800 third. *Umbria* was one of Cunard's four-ship rotation of weekly sailings to and from New York, along with her sister *Etruria*, and *Aurania* and *Servia*, each vessel sailing once every four weeks from Liverpool and New York.[4]

Built in 1884 by J. Elder and Company of Glasgow, *Umbria* was a steel-hulled vessel five hundred feet long and of eight thousand tons. In her day she had been a record breaker in both size and speed, but her day had quickly passed. *Umbria* was, in fact, the last of Cunard's single-screw ships with auxiliary sails. Classified incongruously by *Lloyd's* as a 'screw barque', her profile was dominated by three masts and two well-proportioned funnels. By the time Rostron joined the eleven-year-old ship she had long since become technologically obsolete. However, *Umbria* and *Etruria* – in which Rostron also would log significant sea time as a junior and senior officer – would continue to cross the Atlantic for another decade and a half.[5]

The Cunard Steamship Company, Ltd., had been founded fifty-five years previously on 14 May 1839, when Samuel Cunard, George Burns and David MacIver set up the company as the British and North American Royal Mail Steam Packet Company, a name which precisely declared their purpose. Samuel Cunard was a prominent Halifax shipowner who had considerable previous experience of Royal Mail contracts and of operating steamships along the Eastern Seaboard of North America. He had become convinced of the potential for a profitable transatlantic steamship service and when the Admiralty advertised for one to carry the Royal Mail to Canada and the United States he decided to bid for it.[6]

Cunard arrived in London in February 1839 and the same month offered his bid to the government for a three-ship service to commence the following year. That required the procuring of the necessary ships. The secretary of the East India Company, which Cunard represented in Halifax, introduced him to Robert Napier, one of the leading shipbuilders of the era and a man similarly convinced of the potential of transatlantic steamers. Napier and Cunard rapidly developed ideas for what evolved into an initial fleet of four transatlantic liners each of 1150 tons and with accommodation for about a hundred passengers, aptly christened *Britannia*, *Acadia*, *Columbia* and *Caledonia*. Cunard and Napier signed their first construction contract in mid-March, a month and a half before Cunard won the contract from the British government to provide a mail service from Liverpool to Halifax and Boston for an annual payment of fifty-five thousand pounds.[7]

With the mail contract secured and the ships ordered, Cunard sought additional partners to capitalize the venture. This time Napier offered the introductions, referring Cunard to his associates George Burns and David MacIver. Burns was a Glasgow shipowner who ran coastal vessels to Belfast and Liverpool and MacIver was a competitor in the Glasgow–Liverpool trade operating out of the English city. The partnership entered into in May of 1839 succeeded famously, in part because of a sensible division of labour. MacIver managed the company's British operations from Liverpool, while Cunard ran its business in North America. The Glaswegian Burns oversaw building of the company's ships on the Clyde, then the world's centre for steamship construction. This arrangement worked so well that the company would remain a partnership of the three families for forty years.[8]

On 4 July 1840, exactly fourteen months after signing his agreement with the government, Samuel Cunard departed Liverpool aboard *Britannia* with mail for Halifax and Boston. Her thirteen-day crossing to Halifax inaugurated the era of the steam-powered transatlantic liner that lasted for the next century and a quarter. In 1848 Cunard's company began calling at New York, in part because it remained ice-free year round. In 1878 the heirs of the original owners reorganized the firm as the Cunard Steamship Company, Ltd., offering its shares to the public for the first time in 1880.[9]

By then Cunard's fleet had grown sevenfold, to twenty-eight vessels aggregating more than sixteen times the tonnage of its original four and operating in the Mediterranean as well as the North Atlantic. The fleet's evolution entailed more than number and scale, as iron hulls succeeded wooden ones and the screw propeller replaced paddlewheels for propulsion. These improvements were outmoded in turn by steel hulls in the 1880s and twin screws in the 1890s.[10]

Much of this innovation took place under competitive duress, for the company in those years tended toward technological conservatism. With its mail contract providing a significant competitive advantage, Cunard's managers were inclined to let other companies wager their solvencies on the virtues of the latest technologies, preferring to adopt significant innovations in hulls, engines and propulsion only once they were tried and trusted. And for a generation that strategy worked, as Cunard's company saw off such early competitors as Britain's Great Western Steamship Company in the 1840s and America's Collins Line in the following decade.[11]

By the time Rostron joined the company in 1895, however, Cunard had been forced to abandon this approach due to competitive pressures. In 1884 the company introduced the record-breaking *Umbria* and *Etruria*, each a single-screw, steel-hulled vessel with a speed approaching twenty knots. The company built no new ships from 1885 through 1892, however, and while it remained inactive those eight years, its competitors did not. The American-controlled Inman Line countered *Umbria* and *Etruria* in 1889 with *City of New York* and *City of Paris*, twin-screw beauties that were the first Atlantic liners to exceed twenty knots. Britain's Oceanic Steam Navigation Company, better known as the White Star Line, topped that briefly in 1890 with *Majestic* and *Teutonic*. In 1893 Cunard rejoined the competition with *Campania* and *Lucania*, a hundred feet longer and a third larger than *Umbria* and *Etruria*. These new twin-screw racers established their supremacy by adding a knot to a crossing's average speed. They enjoyed a four-year reign as queens of the Atlantic before Cunard faced renewed technological and financial challenges.[12]

Such matters were not the concern of a junior officer intent on making his living, however. So when informed that he was not eligible for promotion after five round voyages in *Umbria*, Rostron returned to his old employers, Williamson, Milligan and Company, and headed for Antwerp for a reunion with an old friend on 24 June 1895. In his last voyage under sail, *Cedric the Saxon* once again carried Rostron around Cape Horn, this time with David Rees as master. Born at Burry Port, Wales, in 1838, Rees did not pass for master at Liverpool until fifty years later. Fifty-seven in 1895, Rees had assumed command of *Cedric the Saxon* in 1891 for the voyage after Rostron left her.[13]

Cedric the Saxon departed from Antwerp for San Francisco on 5 July 1895, on Rees' fourth voyage in command. Rostron, then aged twenty-six, signed as her chief mate at the rate of eight pounds a month. *Cedric the Saxon* carried a crew of twenty-eight on this voyage, consisting of Rees, Rostron, a second mate named Bullock, a midships complement of a carpenter-donkeyman, boatswain, sailmaker, cook and steward and a forecastle of sixteen able and four ordinary seamen. The vessel also carried one apprentice, Edgar Ackroyd, who served out his term in the seventh week of the passage and re-signed the articles as third mate. *Cedric the Saxon* arrived in San Francisco on 8 November after a passage around Cape Horn that had lasted eighteen weeks. Her sailors seemed more satisfied with their lot than usual, as the ship only had to sign a new cook and two ABs at San Francisco. She sailed for London at New Year, tying up at the West India Dock in the Thames, after seventeen weeks at sea, on 28 April 1896.[14]

On that day Rostron had unknowingly paid off for the last time in sail. He returned to Cunard, while Rees remained with *Cedric the Saxon*. Williamson, Milligan and Company sold the ship to Robert Barr and Company, which re-registered the vessel in Glasgow. At the beginning of July *Cedric the Saxon* put to sea from London in her new service, with a crew of twenty-three and four apprentices. After loading her cargo at New York, she sailed for Padang, Sumatra, on 19 September 1896, was sighted south-east of Long Island by another ship the following day and then … disappeared.[15]

No clue to the ship's demise was ever discovered. *Lloyd's* simply posted her missing on 12 May 1897, 234 days after she sailed from New York. But it is not difficult to imagine the fate of a sailing ship, even an iron-hulled one like *Cedric the Saxon*, carrying a cargo of thousands of cases of petroleum. Rostron was convinced throughout his life 'that there is a Providence which shapes our ends,' but he also acknowledged such a thing as good luck. He may have thought both were working for him when he missed *Cedric the Saxon*'s voyage to oblivion.[16]

Rostron returned to the Cunard fleet in the spring of 1896 to sail as third officer in *Aurania*. The year before, after she suffered a fractured steam pipe at sea and arrived in New York two days late, a correspondent to *The Times* in London described *Aurania* as 'one of those old slow ships by which the British Post Office delights to send mails to New York'. She was thirteen years old by the time Rostron joined her crew. Built in 1883 by J. and G. Thomson of Glasgow, the steel, single-screw, 7,269-ton *Aurania* measured 470 feet in length and 57 feet in beam.[17]

Rostron soon came to see some advantages to serving in Atlantic mail ships, even old, slow ones. 'Though once I had been inclined to look askance at the modern liner as not a sailor's job, I had to confess that there was something to be said, after the wild days and wilder nights in a wind-jammer, for a comfortable cabin, a warm bunk, steam heat and electric light, not to mention good food and as much of it as you wanted.' But those improved living conditions came at the price of hard work aboard ships worked hard.[18]

Being an officer in steamships was certainly safer and more comfortable than life under sail, but it still had its rigours. The languid pace of one annual sailing voyage, with its weeks laid up in ports, was replaced by the fast passages and rapid turnarounds of the North Atlantic liner. On that most competitive of oceans, owners did their best to maximize the value returned by both vessels and crews. *Umbria* had already introduced Rostron to these cold, wet realities. 'That first trip in a liner [in February 1895] was a winter crossing of the Atlantic and brought me a new experience. We bore into the heavy seas and I was staggered at the speed that was maintained in spite of the damage the weather was causing to the ship. But in those days speed was the be-all and end-all of the crack ships... Steamers were driven for all they were worth.' He watched his early ships 'run up bills of thousands for damages in order to save a few hours'.[19]

The deck watch suffered along with the ship, since the liners of that era featured minimal accommodation for watch standers. Usually the wheelhouse was just that – an enclosure large enough to house the wheel, the binnacle and the helmsman. In bad weather it offered some necessary protection to that sailor, but none to the junior or senior officer of the deck, who stood their watches on the exposed bridge. On the liners in New York service during Rostron's early years with Cunard, that bridge was only about forty feet above the waterline. Rostron's contemporary Samuel McNeil remembered watch standers being constantly doused with heavy spray on all but a few summer voyages, describing those ships as 'just like half-tide rocks'. In the worst weather, the problem changed from comfort to survival. 'Time and again,' wrote a watch officer with a rival line, 'I have seen the ship driven into a huge green wall of water crowned with that wicked, curling breaker, which it seemed utterly impossible for anything to withstand. An immediate dash is made for an iron stanchion and, gripping this with might and main, one awaits the crash.'[20]

If the duty was especially arduous in storms, the hours were long no matter what the weather. Cunard watch officer James Bisset doubted 'if there is any calling in the world in which men work such "broken time" and have so little regular sleep, as men in the seafaring profession'. That was certainly true of sailing ships, with their watch and watch below, but it also applied to junior officers in liners, who stood port-and-starboard watches. 'In consequence,' remembered McNeil, 'more than three hours' sleep at any one period was impossible.'[21]

Even setting aside the problem of sleep deprivation, a mailboat officer worked long hours. Rostron claimed that he once went four years as an officer in a liner without ever enjoying forty-eight consecutive hours of leave, an observation seconded by McNeil, who wrote that 'it was a hard life for the officers ... and I had many voyages when, during her stay in Liverpool, I was never away from the ship for thirty hours'. Despite the long, sometimes strenuous hours, appointment to an officer's billet on an Atlantic liner was the pinnacle of service in the British merchant marine and thus, wrote another officer, 'despite the rigorous conditions and the powers of endurance one has to exhibit, there is never a word of complaint'.[22]

Rostron served in *Aurania* for about six months in mid-1896 before reporting to Portsmouth for reserve officers' training with the Royal Navy and deployment to the fleet, an assignment that lasted from November of 1896 until July of 1898. He returned to Cunard and to *Aurania* in August of 1898, with a promotion to second officer. This assignment lasted only one or two voyages before Rostron transferred to *Umbria*'s sister ship *Etruria* in October 1898. He served as second officer in that vessel for over a year and a half, to the end of May 1900. Now a senior officer, the bridge was his during his watch and the responsibility with it. Of the weight of that responsibility, Bisset observed that 'what makes a ship's officer seem so cheerful when he is off duty, or ashore, or retired from the sea, is the very fact that at those times he is off duty! That same man on watch on the bridge, secluded from the passengers in his care, is usually grim, severe and intensely concentrated. He is two personalities in one skin – off watch and on watch. It could scarcely be otherwise.'[23]

Rostron assumed the duties and demands of the Atlantic express liners, first as a junior and then a senior officer and prospered in Cunard's service. He impressed his superiors aboard liners as he had impressed others in the past. Cunard's captains submitted evaluations of their subordinate officers to the company at the ends of June and December. Cunard asked its masters to evaluate their officers on their abilities as seamen and navigators, their diligence and sobriety, their general conduct and their health and eyesight. Evaluations of Rostron were uniformly positive. With the exception of one captain, who marked Rostron 'satisfactory' across the board, Rostron rated good to excellent as a seaman and navigator. Under diligence, his captains described him as 'active' and 'most attentive'. Sobriety, general conduct and health all drew favourable marks, while Rostron's eyesight rated from 'good' to 'perfect'. In his June 1904 evaluation, Captain William Cresser summarized Rostron tersely: 'Smart Officer.'[24]

Such positive evaluations brought promotion, increased responsibility and better pay. Perhaps it was the rising affluence that came with a senior officer's salary that permitted Rostron to marry a woman whom he had first met several years before. As he himself told the story, just before departing for China Station on naval service in March 1897, he returned home on leave from Portsmouth. At a concert in Bolton he ran into an old acquaintance named Stothert, whom he had not seen in fourteen years. Invited to stay at the family home a few days later, Rostron was charmed by Priscilla and Richard Stothert's youngest daughter, twenty-three-year-old Ethel Minnie Stothert. Ethel, four and a half years younger than Arthur, was born in 1873 in Atherton, four miles south-west of Bolton. Of course, any immediate interest was checked by his departure for China two days later, but Ethel and Arthur began to correspond while he was in the Far East and their relationship developed from there.[25]

Ethel Stothert and Arthur Rostron were married at St John the Baptist Church in Atherton on Thursday, 14 September 1899, the vicar, William Nuttall, presiding. Arthur was then thirty years old and Ethel twenty-five. Arthur's mother, Nancy Lever Rostron, did not live to see him married; she had died eleven years before, on 8 April 1888, while he was outbound on his second voyage as an apprentice. The witnesses included his father James, his twenty-seven-year-old sister Beatrice and his twenty-two-year-old brother George. Arthur Rostron, second officer on *Etruria* at the time, was soon enough back on the transatlantic run. Although Arthur and Ethel's marriage inevitably suffered the long separations that seafaring imposes, it would contentedly endure until death parted them forty-one years later. 'You ask for an account of some of my achievements,' Rostron replied to an interviewer a dozen years into his marriage, 'the greatest of them was my good fortune in being able to win my wife.'[26]

His marriage required something Rostron had not needed since he left Bolton for HMS *Conway* fifteen years before: a home ashore. By the end of 1900 the newly-married couple had moved into a red brick, two-storey terraced house on Ashdale Road in Waterloo, one of Liverpool's northern suburbs. Ethel and Arthur lived there for the next decade along with their growing family. Three of the Rostrons' four children were born at Ashdale Road. The first, Harry Maxwell Rostron, arrived on 31 December 1900. Robert James Rostron followed two years later, on 11 January 1903 and Arnold Richard Rostron was born on 30 August 1907. Their fourth child, a daughter, Margaret Ethel, was born on 12 January 1915.[27]

Eight months after his wedding, at the end of May 1900, Rostron reunited with *Aurania* as first officer and put to sea bound for an entirely different theatre and purpose. *Aurania* was five years older and as slow as ever, but could capably transport soldiers to South Africa. Long-standing tensions between Dutch colonists in the Transvaal and Orange Free State and British settlers in the Cape Colony and Natal had erupted into the South African or Boer War. Convinced that war was inevitable, the Boers invaded Natal and the Cape Colony in October 1899, besieging the settlements of Ladysmith, Mafeking and Kimberley. By the time Rostron became involved seven months later, British and imperial forces had lifted those sieges, invaded the Dutch colonies and captured Bloemfontein, the capital of the Orange Free State. The British would wind up this second phase of the war by capturing Pretoria, capital of the Transvaal, on 5 June 1900. By then, with the Boers' conventional armies bested, the Dutch and British had already embarked on a brutal guerrilla war that would last another two years.[28]

The men and supplies that Britain required to fight a major war at the opposite end of the planet could only be deployed using the ships of the British merchant marine on the long sea route between England and the Cape Colony. From 1899 to 1902, Southampton witnessed almost nine hundred arrivals and departures of transports carrying more than half a million soldiers.[29]

Aurania was one of six Cunard mail steamers the British government requisitioned to serve as transports. Rostron recalled that the South African War presented no danger to those afloat; 'a troop ship in those days was little more than an onlooker at war. We took out the fit to fight – and brought back the invalids.' *Aurania* had returned from South Africa on the latter mission only a few days before he joined her, discharging 610 patients, of whom 217 were wounded and the rest down with diseases, such as typhoid, caused by contaminated water and poor hygiene in camp or on campaign. Within two weeks *Aurania* had embarked soldiers at Southampton and was outbound again, calling at Queenstown on 7 June 1900, for an additional eight officers and 450 men of the Dorset and Shropshire regiments and the Royal Munster Fusiliers. She brought back the invalids from Cape Town at the end of July, carrying forty-one officers, 620 men and ninety-four other passengers. And so it went until Rostron left the ship before the end of the year. He would earn the South African Transport Medal for his war services, but 'neither had cause nor opportunity to do any fighting'.[30]

Upon returning to civilian service, Rostron continued his climb up the ranks at Cunard. In April 1901 he was assigned as chief officer, the second in command, aboard *Cherbourg*. He made at least six round voyages to the Mediterranean and one to the Baltic in 1901 and 1902 aboard this 1614-ton, 251-foot, single-screw cargo ship, built in 1874 by J. and G. Thomson of Glasgow.[31]

Rostron then returned to the passenger fleet, serving as first officer in *Saxonia* in 1903, in *Campania* for two voyages at the beginning of 1904 and then as chief officer of the new liner *Pannonia* in Mediterranean service to

New York starting that May. The year 1905 and most of 1906 found him back on the transatlantic run as chief officer of *Etruria*. Starting in November of 1906, he made several voyages to the US as chief officer aboard *Campania*, the last of which departed Britain at the beginning of April 1907. After he completed that voyage, Rostron was reassigned as chief officer to yet another vessel, this one the talk of the maritime world.[32]

CHAPTER 4

A PRIDEFUL OCCASION

In the dozen years after Arthur Rostron joined the line, the Cunard Steamship Company, Ltd., faced one of its most rigorous periods of competition. A technological challenge to Cunard emerged in the Atlantic trade, while financial manoeuvrings threatened the very existence of the company.

The recently unified, modernizing, industrial nation of Germany presented the technical threat. Aspiring to an international position to match its economic one, the country embarked on an ambitious naval building programme in the 1890s. Less worrying to the British but just as irksome, the great German shipping lines – Hamburg-Amerikanische Packetfahrt-Actien-Gesellschaft, known as HAPAG, and Norddeutscher Lloyd – had determined to dominate the Atlantic passenger trade. These companies had a geographic advantage over Cunard in attracting European emigrants, particularly people from southern and eastern Europe who were beginning to dominate immigration to the United States.[1]

One of the ways for competing steamship companies to win both favourable publicity and passenger traffic was to hold the 'Blue Riband', the earnestly coveted symbol of the fastest ship on the Atlantic. Until the mid-1890s, this garland was generally passed back and forth between British companies – Cunard, White Star, Guion, and Inman – with Cunard having the last word with the twin-screw, 12,950-ton sisters *Campania* and *Lucania* of 1893. But supremacy in speed shifted suddenly and decisively to the government-subsidized German companies in 1897. First Norddeutscher Lloyd's *Kaiser Wilhelm der Grosse*, then HAPAG's *Deutschland* and Norddeutscher's *Kronprinz Wilhelm* and *Kaiser Wilhelm II* locked up the speed records in both directions for a decade, a situation completely unsatisfactory to British seafaring at its supremacy. In June 1904 *Kaiser Wilhelm II* established a record average crossing speed of 23.68 knots.[2]

If this German challenge was irritating, the American threat was alarming. In the early years of the twentieth century, the American financier John Pierpont Morgan attempted to form a transatlantic shipping cartel primarily at the expense of British interests. J. P. Morgan and Company's first encroachment on Britain's merchant marine came in April 1901, when it gained control of Frederick Leyland and Co., popularly known as the Leyland Line. The following year, the Morgan group brought nine other steamship companies under one holding company called the International Mercantile Marine, capitalized at $120 million.[3]

Among the assets IMM acquired were such former British flags as the Leyland Line, the National Line, the Dominion Line and, most disturbingly of all, financial control of Cunard's main competitor, the White Star Line. The Morgan consortium also made at least five approaches to Cunard's shareholders from late 1901 into the spring of 1902. After failing to capture Cunard, the IMM embarked on an Atlantic rate war that ran from 1903 into 1904, before entering a rate alliance with the German lines at the end of 1904.[4]

Thanks to German technological and American financial advances, Cunard was certainly under duress by 1903, but by then both technological and financial solutions to its problems were developing. Neither Britain's politicians, nor her naval and maritime interests, nor her populace had any desire to see their country's merchant marine rank second to Germany's in prestige or become an American subsidiary. Cunard's chairman, Lord Inverclyde, used both Norddeutscher Lloyd's possession of the Blue Riband and the real possibility that IMM would either consume or destroy his company as leverage to negotiate significant financial assistance from the British government.[5]

In September 1903, the government agreed to loan Cunard £2.6 million at 2.75 per cent interest so that the company could purchase two large, fast liners. The loan was to be repaid over twenty years, with collateral being Cunard's existing assets. The government also agreed to provide an additional £150,000 annual operating subsidy for these vessels beyond what they would earn from government mail contracts. In exchange, Cunard guaranteed to order two ships capable of sustaining an average speed of 24.5 knots in moderate weather and designed to carry twelve six-inch guns. The company also agreed to remain British-owned and controlled, from the boardroom to the ships themselves, and to permit the government to conscript any Cunard vessel into its service in a national emergency.[6]

The technical solution to propelling these significantly bigger ships significantly faster had been developing for more than a decade. It came from the English inventor Charles Algernon Parsons, who had been refining the steam turbine power plant since the 1880s. Parsons had originally used his much more powerful, efficient and quiet engines to generate electricity ashore, but in 1894 he incorporated The Marine Steam Turbine Company at Newcastle and that same year launched a 104-foot, 44-ton prototype vessel named *Turbinia*.[7]

For three years, despite some promising preliminary results, Parsons' experiments on the Tyne failed to draw much attention from the Admiralty. Ignored by the navy, Parsons decided to make his case audaciously. The forum he chose was Queen Victoria's Diamond Jubilee Fleet Review, held at Spithead, off Portsmouth, on 26 June 1897. His argument consisted of brazenly sprinting *Turbinia* through Prince Albert's review of the fleet at the previously unheard-of speed of thirty-four knots. After the admirals recovered from their displeasure at being upstaged at their own review, their awakened interest quickly begot destroyers HMS *Cobra* and HMS *Viper*, the first turbine-powered warships, in 1899. Seven years after that, in 1906, HMS *Dreadnought* entered the fleet as the world's first modern battleship and, not coincidentally, the first propelled by turbines.[8]

The combination of size and speed required to best the German liners demanded that Cunard use Parsons' revolutionary – in both senses – engine. Before making the final decision, however, the company undertook an experiment on a slightly smaller scale, producing the twenty-thousand-ton liners *Caronia* and *Carmania*, then the largest ships in Cunard's fleet. Known as 'the pretty sisters', both ships were completed in 1905 by John Brown and Company, Clydebank, and were 675 feet in length, 72 feet in beam and of almost identical tonnage and horsepower. However, in their vitals they were not sisters; *Caronia* was a twin-screw vessel powered by quadruple expansion engines, while *Carmania* was a triple-screw ship driven by Parsons' turbines. Trials and trips soon demonstrated *Carmania*'s superior speed and efficiency. 'The departure has proved eminently successful,' boasted Cunard in September 1907, 'especially as regards freedom from vibration and as a consequence the two mammoth Cunarders, the *Lusitania* and *Mauretania*, are both [to be] driven by turbine machinery.'[9]

Mauretania was laid down at Swan, Hunter & Wigham Richardson on the Tyne at Wallsend in August 1904, and *Lusitania* at John Brown & Company at Clydebank in Scotland in May 1905. *Lusitania* was the first into the water, launched on 7 June 1906, with *Mauretania* following on 20 September. Fitting out these 32,000-ton, quadruple-screw vessels took another year, but if their profiles were incomplete at launching, their purpose was already transparent. At *Lusitania*'s launch luncheon, Sir Charles McLaren, deputy chairman of John Brown, told his audience that national issues were at stake and asserted that none of his listeners wanted Germany to hold the record for Atlantic liners in either size or speed.[10]

After he returned to Britain in April 1907 from his last voyage aboard *Campania*, Rostron joined *Lusitania* at Glasgow as chief officer. After weeks spent superintending completion of the ship and the loading of essential supplies and equipment, the next problem facing Captain James B. Watt and his officers and crew was moving their enormous new vessel safely down the constricted Clyde. She left the fitting-out pier at John Brown at 11.50am on Thursday, 27 June 1907 accompanied by several tugs and excursion steamers, while ashore 'great crowds watched her progress down the river'. *Lusitania* reached Greenock on the Firth of Clyde without incident two hours later.[11]

From Greenock, she proceeded to dry dock in Liverpool. Floated out on 22 July *Lusitania* steamed back to Scotland five days later and made a series of test runs on the measured mile at Skelmorlie on the Firth of Clyde, generating sixty-eight-thousand horsepower and 25.6 knots. That evening, 27 July, the ship departed with invited guests for a trial cruise around Ireland that included fuel consumption tests at 18, 21 and 23 knots. Her passengers included Cunard's chairman and directors, officials of John Brown, the Admiralty and the merchant marine and Charles Parsons himself.[12]

Lusitania landed most of her guests at Liverpool on Monday morning, 29 July, then returned to sea for the most rigorous set of tests she would face.

These included crash turns and stops at Skelmorlie before the programme culminated with a midnight departure on a two-day, full-power run. The chosen racecourse was a 304-mile stretch of the Irish Sea between Corsewall Point at the southern end of the Firth of Clyde and Longships Lighthouse off Land's End in Cornwall. *Lusitania* ran the course twice in each direction to nullify the effects of winds and tides. The test consumed 2200 tons of coal in fifty hours and produced an average speed of 25.4 knots, almost exactly a knot greater than the Admiralty's requirement. *The Times* declared the tests and *Lusitania* herself, 'an unqualified success worthy of the best traditions of the Cunard Company and of the builders, John Brown and Co. (Limited), Clydebank'. Victory within reach, the ship anchored at Greenock for a last round of adjustments before steaming back to Liverpool at the end of August and entering service in September 1907.[13]

'Amidst scenes never before equalled in the annals of Liverpool,' declared *The Times*, 'the great Cunarder *Lusitania*, which is destined to win back for this country the Blue Ribbon of the Atlantic, sailed from the Mersey for New York on Saturday night,' 7 September 1907, with 2200 passengers aboard. *The Times* estimated that several hundred thousand people assembled to witness her departure just after 9pm. Their cheering combined with the whistles of steamers in the river to provide a spirited send off for the queen presumptive. Twelve hours later *Lusitania* called at Queenstown, greeted by a flotilla of small craft and witnessed by untold numbers who had been gathering since dawn along the bluffs overlooking the harbour. After clearing Queenstown harbour at noon, *Lusitania* dashed to Sandy Hook, at the entrance to New York Harbor, in four days and twenty hours.[14]

'England again holds the blue ribbon of the Atlantic,' claimed *The Times'* reporter aboard for the voyage, 'and holds it easily with considerable power in reserve.' The correspondent reported that 'the reception of the *Lusitania* in New York Harbour is tremendous. A crowd as great as that which assembled in Liverpool at the departure of the vessel is present here to welcome her on her arrival.' *The Times* declared *Lusitania*'s performance 'a magnificent achievement for a first voyage'. Norddeutscher Lloyd disputed this first boast of supremacy on grounds of average speed, but within the month that company's manager had to concede that *Kaiser Wilhelm II* had been bested. *Lusitania* was the fastest merchant ship on the seas.[15]

Although a key participant in the preliminaries, Chief Officer Arthur Rostron was not party to *Lusitania*'s achievements on the Atlantic. By the time *Lusitania* sailed on her initial voyage, Captain Arthur Rostron had already been at sea for a week. On 30 August, the day after *Lusitania* arrived at Liverpool to prepare for her maiden voyage, Rostron had been promoted to command *Brescia*, a small Cunard cargo ship. He sailed from Liverpool for the Mediterranean the following day. At first he suffered the disappointment of missing the historic voyage and even questioned the virtues of being named master of a vessel half the length, a third of the speed and a tenth of the tonnage of the mighty *Lusitania*. 'But only for a day or so. Then I was at sea with my own ship and – well, one's first command is a prideful occasion; the larger vessels could wait.'[16]

Rostron's first command, the 3235-ton cargo steamer *Brescia*, was built in 1903 by J. L. Thompson and Sons, of Sunderland, England, in the three-island design popular in her day. The ship's raised forecastle and poop housed quarters for sailors and enginemen, respectively, while the centre island contained the officers' quarters and bridge. The well decks forward and aft of the island each had two cargo hatches, providing access to *Brescia*'s four holds. She could carry four thousand tons of cargo worked by derricks attached to her two masts. The ship measured 345 feet in overall length and 45 feet in beam and her triple-expansion steam engine and single screw drove her at a speed of eight to ten knots.

Brescia was certainly no queen of the seas, but neither was she a tramp. She worked her regular circuit as part of Cunard's Mediterranean cargo service, which carried goods from Britain to the ports of southern Europe, northern Africa and the Middle East, loaded raw materials for home from those same ports and fed cargoes to Cunard's larger passenger-cargo liners that linked the Mediterranean to New York. James Bisset joined *Brescia* at the beginning of 1909 as third officer and made four round voyages under Rostron's command that year, beginning a professional association that would encompass four ships over twenty-three years. Bisset found *Brescia* – outfitted with furnishings and fittings acquired second-hand from one of Cunard's earlier passenger liners – to have accommodations 'of a quality seldom seen in cargo-steamers'.[17]

The British and North American Royal Mail Steam Packet Company had not been incorporated to deal in matters Mediterranean, but in 1849 one of its partners, Charles MacIver, had chartered a ship for Mediterranean service on his own. The success of his venture convinced George Burns and Samuel Cunard to buy in and the partnership commenced a three-ship Mediterranean service from Britain in 1851. This venture operated from 1855 as a separate company named the British and Foreign Steam Navigation Company. The service produced its own profits, but also added value by feeding passengers and cargo to the partnership's North Atlantic service. To better coordinate their operations, the two companies were merged by the three families in 1867 as the British and North American Steam Packet Company. By 1880 nine of the combined company's twenty-eight ships were committed to Mediterranean service.[18]

During Rostron's first decade with the company, Cunard ordered five single-screw cargo ships of approximately three thousand tons to handle its Mediterranean traffic, starting with *Pavia* and *Tyria* in 1897. *Cypria* was delivered in 1898 and *Veria* the following year. *Brescia*, the last of them, arrived in 1903. These five ships, supplemented originally by the smaller and much older *Saragossa* and *Cherbourg* – replaced by *Phrygia* and *Lycia* in 1909 – maintained a six-ship service of fortnightly sailings. Their voyages distributed cargoes around the Mediterranean, Bisset remembered, 'comprising almost everything of Britain's immense variety of industrial production, from salt and chemicals to textiles, pottery, machinery, iron and steel, fancy goods, whiskey, salt fish, or re-exported goods such as baled cotton and wool, sugar, rum, metal ingots, ores and everything else ... that was handled in the many warehouses of that thriving emporium city, Liverpool'. *Brescia* and her sisters would also call outbound at Swansea, Wales, to add coal, tinplate or copper sulphate to their manifests.[19]

Once a ship reached the Iberian Peninsula the service became, in Bisset's words, 'a laborious sequence of entering ports, handling cargo and clearing out of ports in rapid succession, for week after week, with short runs from port to port'. The ships gathered cargoes of all kinds from ports around the Mediterranean, Adriatic, Aegean and Black seas. Depending on the season, homebound cargoes might include raisins, currants and figs from Greek ports on the Mediterranean and Aegean; coffee beans or tobacco from Constantinople; figs from Smyrna, Turkey; wheat from Kherson on the Black Sea in southern Russia; cotton, cotton seed or onions from Alexandria, Egypt; or casks of wine from Leixões, Portugal.[20]

Rostron's first complete voyage in command certainly fitted this pattern. It started with *Brescia*'s departure from Liverpool on 31 August bound for Swansea, where she arrived the next day. She left Swansea on 5 September for a brief stop at Leixões and then called at Lisbon on the afternoon of 9 September. Two days later *Brescia* sailed from Lisbon for Gibraltar, arriving the following evening. The next day she entered the Mediterranean, bound for Genoa, Italy, which she reached on 17 September. After that *Brescia* worked her way down the west coast of Italy, calling at Leghorn (Livorno) on 20 September and departing on the 22nd for Naples, which she reached the following day. *Brescia* left Naples on 24 September, passed the Straits of Messina, rounded the toe and heel of Italy into the Adriatic and called at Bari, on Italy's east coast, on 26 September. Rostron's ship then worked north up the Italian coast to Ancona, where she called for five days starting on the 28th. *Brescia*'s tour of Italy concluded at Venice, which she reached on 3 October.[21]

From Italy, *Brescia* steamed back down the Adriatic and across the Aegean to ports in the Austro-Hungarian and Ottoman empires. Departing Venice on 7 October, she arrived in Fiume (now Rijeka) the following day. Eight days later *Brescia* commenced a six-day passage to Smyrna (now Izmir), Turkey, where she arrived on 22 October and remained for five days. She sailed on 27 October and called at Patras, Greece, which she left on 2 November. At dusk on 4 November *Brescia* called at Malta. She steamed for home the following morning, passed Gibraltar on 9 November and tied up at Huskisson Dock, Liverpool, on 16 November 1907, completing her round voyage from Liverpool in exactly eleven weeks. Twelve days later, *Brescia* and Rostron sailed for Swansea and their next circuit of the Mediterranean.[22]

In the summer and autumn of 1907 – while Rostron orbited the Mediterranean in *Brescia* and first *Lusitania* and then her sister *Mauretania* raced to and from New York – Cunard's transatlantic rivals, including the White Star Line, had to decide how to react to the triumph of Cunard's turbine-powered twins. The answer was not still greater speed, which was too expensive a proposition without a substantial subsidy that an American-owned, British-flagged enterprise like White Star was unlikely to win from either government. The answer was scale and opulence. A *New York Times* article discussing *Mauretania*'s trials that September mentioned rumours of a White Star liner of 840 feet with a power plant combining reciprocating engines and turbines. The article called such speculation 'to put it mildly, premature,' but the idea matured rapidly at White Star and its shipbuilder, Harland and Wolff, of Belfast.[23]

The plan called for a class of three ships, each half again as large as *Lusitania* and *Mauretania*, to operate a weekly service from Southampton via Cherbourg and Queenstown to New York. In 1908, *The Times* reported that the first of these new liners would be named *Olympic* and the second probably *Titanic* and that their speed would 'not be high in a record-making sense'. White Star would offer no speed competition to Cunard, but, so the strategy went, wealthy passengers would not begrudge White Star an extra half day at sea spent aboard enormous and comfortable ships featuring luxurious staterooms and such amenities as gymnasiums, swimming pools, steam baths, squash courts and à la carte restaurants.[24]

Olympic's keel was laid at Harland and Wolff on 15 December 1908 and the vessel launched on 20 October 1910. 'The Cunard Company has proved what can be done in expedition,' observed *The Times*, 'and the White Star Line [will] now demonstrate what can be done in the way of capacity.' *Olympic* sailed from Southampton on her maiden voyage on 14 June 1911, arriving at New York early on the morning of 21 June, crossing in five days and sixteen hours at an average speed of just over 21 knots.[25]

Three weeks earlier, on 31 May 1911, Harland and Wolff had launched *Titanic* 'in brilliant weather and in the presence of thousands of spectators'. The launch had been 'personally supervised' by the shipyard's chairman Lord Pirrie and witnessed by White Star's chairman, J. Bruce Ismay, and by J. P. Morgan, owner of the International Mercantile Marine. 'Today, a floating city; tomorrow, a floating island,' *The Times* had opined six months before. 'No other word is spacious enough for the gigantic ships now coming into existence.'[26]

During all of this time Arthur Rostron had remained on Cunard's Mediterranean cargo circuit. He completed ten Mediterranean voyages in *Brescia* in twenty-eight months, from August 1907 until December 1909, when he was transferred to *Veria*, an almost identical vessel in the same service. He commanded that ship on two Mediterranean voyages through May of 1910 then sailed once as relief to the regular master of *Saxonia* in July. *Saxonia* was a different kind of ship altogether, being forty per cent longer and almost four-and-a-half times the tonnage of his previous commands. This voyage was also Rostron's first in command of a passenger vessel and his first visit to the United States as captain. After that taste of commanding the big ships, he ended 1910 as master of *Pavia*, a freighter very similar in tonnage, dimensions and service to his first two commands.[27]

Rostron left Cunard's cargo service for good in January 1911, when the company assigned him to command *Pannonia*, a vessel in which he had served as chief officer when she was new seven years before. He spent all of 1911 as master of *Pannonia*, a 9851-ton ship, 486 feet in length and 59 feet in beam, working in Cunard's 'New York–Mediterranean–Adriatic Service'. By that summer, his fifth as a master of Cunard's ships, Rostron had established his style of command. Bisset characterized him as 'not the burly type of jolly old sea dog. Far from it.' In civilian clothing, Rostron, with his penetrating blue eyes, high cheekbones and slightly upturned nose and outturned ears, still exuded a faintly boyish appearance although by now in his early forties. In uniform, however, he exuded authority and resolve. Lacking physical bulk, Rostron infused his personal energy into his leadership. Ships' crews often give their captains nicknames. These generally derive from some physical or character trait and are not necessarily complimentary. Rostron's was 'the Electric Spark', which, in Bisset's opinion, 'fairly described his dynamic quality'.[28]

By the time Rostron paid off from *Pannonia* at the end of 1911, he and his family were doing well. In 1908, the increased affluence of a ship's captain had allowed Arthur, Ethel and their sons Harry, Robert and Arnold to relocate just north from the terraced house on Ashdale Road in Waterloo to occupy one half of a large semi-detached house on Victoria Road in Great Crosby. His annual salary of £275 as master of *Brescia* in 1907 had increased to £300 at the beginning of 1909 and he received two more raises in 1911, to £350 in January and £400 in October.[29]

In February 1912 Arthur Rostron completed twenty-five years at sea with appointment as master of another, still larger, passenger liner in the

Mediterranean service and promotion to commander in the Royal Naval Reserve. All of these successes were tinged by the passing of his father, James, who died at Bolton on 15 November 1911, aged 72. Although James Rostron had seen his wilful eldest son, the one who had only ever aspired to go to sea, rise to command passenger ships for one of the world's most prestigious steamship companies, he did not live to see Captain Arthur Henry Rostron celebrated across two continents only six months later.[30]

CHAPTER 5

A COMFORTABLE AND FRIENDLY SHIP

On 6 August 1902, Swan and Hunter's shipyard at Wallsend-on-Tyne launched another in a series of medium-sized, passenger-cargo steamers introduced to Cunard's fleet in the first years of the twentieth century. Following her sea trials in the last week of April 1903, the new ship, christened *Carpathia*, spent her initial summer on the North Atlantic before joining the company's new Mediterranean emigrant service at the end of the year.[1]

Cunard first entered the steerage trade in 1860, when Liverpool dominated the business. The city was the last British port for many Irish emigrants and it also drew numerous emigrants from northern Europe, who crossed the North Sea to Hull and then crossed northern England by rail to Liverpool. By 1870 four British steamship lines, Cunard among them, carried ninety-six per cent of passenger traffic to America, replacing the American sailing packets that had controlled the trade twenty years before. But Liverpool's advantage was short-lived. By the 1880s the sources of American immigration were shifting from Ireland and north-western Europe to central and southern Europe. This broke the British monopoly and, by the turn of the century, transferred the advantage to the Continental lines, particularly the German companies HAPAG and Norddeutscher Lloyd.[2]

Cunard reacted to these changed circumstances in two ways. One was to begin to compete aggressively in the new emigrant markets, particularly in the Adriatic. In the spring of 1904 Cunard and the Austro-Hungarian government signed a transportation agreement, which quickly evolved into a profitable service for the company. Cunard's vessels called for Austro-Hungarian passengers at Trieste and Fiume at the head of the Adriatic Sea and carried Italians chiefly from Naples and Sicily. But emigrant traffic was more varied than that. Rostron remembered that emigrants 'came from all the countries round the Mediterranean – Italians, Croats, Hungarians, Austrians, Greeks, Bulgarians, Rumanians'.[3]

Carpathia was originally built as a two-class ship, with accommodation for two-hundred second-class and as many as 1,700 third-class passengers. As those proportions suggest, her primary purpose was to carry steerage passengers. To entice them to sail in its vessels, Cunard's second strategy was to substantially upgrade third-class accommodation and meals on its new emigrant ships, such as *Carpathia*. Cunard hoped to capture the patronage of Italian and Hungarian emigrants with low fares and by endowing *Carpathia* with, in the words of *The Times*, 'a scale of comfort to which third-class passengers are strangers'. On *Carpathia* gone were the days when a steerage passage meant just that: a bunk in a dormitory room crammed either down aft in proximity to the ship's steering gear, engines and screws, with the associated noise and vibration, or far forward, with its pronounced pitching and jolting in rough seas.[4]

Aboard *Carpathia*, steerage passengers were quartered on the two highest decks within the hull, most in dormitory accommodation, but up to six hundred in two-, four- or six-berth cabins. Men berthing in steerage had their own smoking room and bar while women had a 'ladies retiring-room'. All had access to a dispensary, ate their meals in shifts in a 300-seat, wood-panelled dining room and enjoyed the use of 'a large covered promenade' rather than the exposed well decks that steerage passengers endured as outdoor space on many ships. *Carpathia*'s superstructure, which ran almost exactly half the length of the ship, contained the ship's second-class accommodation and public rooms, navigating and wireless stations, lifeboats and officers' quarters.[5]

A good-sized ship at her launch, *Carpathia* measured 558 feet overall, with a beam of 64 feet and a registered tonnage of 13,603. She carried four masts and a single funnel that towered 65 feet above the boat deck slightly forward of amidships. Her bridge and pilot house were set well aft, between the mainmast and funnel almost 220 feet from her bow, to provide room for the four cargo hatches forward of her superstructure. These hatches and four more located aft provided access to the ship's seven main holds, which had capacity for 12,500 tons of cargo. The professional journal, *The Marine Engineer*, reported that *Carpathia's* 'facilities for rapid loading and discharging of cargoes are up-to-date and very extensive. Fourteen steam winches and eighteen cargo derricks are fitted on the shelter deck.' *Carpathia's* cargo facilities included considerable insulated refrigerated space on her 'tween decks forward of the boilers, for carrying chilled beef.[6]

Steam to drive the cargo winches and the ship herself came at 210psi from seven single-ended, forced-draft boilers. Underway, these boilers supplied the two quadruple-expansion engines that spun *Carpathia's* two propellers, producing nine thousand horsepower and a cruising speed of about fourteen knots. *The Times* told readers that 'although she is not a very fast vessel, she is decidedly comfortable and cheap'.[7]

Carpathia sailed for Boston on her maiden voyage from Liverpool on 5 May 1903. She transferred to the New York service on her next voyage, but after spending six months on North Atlantic routes, Cunard reassigned *Carpathia* to the Mediterranean trade that would employ her for most of her career. Although the ships in Cunard's Mediterranean passenger fleet still called Liverpool their home port, Cunard operated the service out of New York. Ships stayed on the circuit for a year, calling at Gibraltar, Naples, Trieste, Fiume and other ports around the Mediterranean and sometimes also stopping at Madeira, the Portuguese island in the Atlantic six hundred nautical miles south-west of Gibraltar, before returning to New York. Each round voyage lasted between six and seven weeks, so it required four ships, which Bisset characterized as 'comparative slowcoaches and more serviceable than stylish,' to maintain a fortnightly service at speeds of twelve to fourteen knots. Each year, after completing seven voyages, each ship returned to Liverpool for refit and crew rest and reassignment. After a month of rehabilitation, each would sail back to the Mediterranean to begin the circuit anew. Working in this service thus meant that Rostron and his fellow sailors would be away from England, home and family for almost a year, much as he was in his days in sail.[8]

Due chiefly to tariff barriers, cargoes on the Mediterranean circuit consisted mostly of raw materials. Cargoes arriving in New York 'included dried vine-fruits and figs, olives, olive oil, wines, sheet cork … cases of oranges and tangerines and casks of fresh grapes'. Goods outbound from the United States consisted of 'bagged wheat, baled cotton, tobacco, bagged ore, pig-iron, ingots of copper and other metals and lumber'. These ships also carried mails between the Mediterranean and the United States, as well as a few first- and second-class passengers. These travellers were usually Britons or Americans cruising the Mediterranean or else former emigrants returning to visit their home countries after some years in America.[9]

The main purpose of and profit from the Mediterranean service, however, came from moving emigrants from south-eastern Europe to the United States. That emigrant traffic boomed in the decade before the First World War, with approximately two million Hungarian and Austrian immigrants and a like number of Italians sailing to America. *Carpathia* did her part. On 17 April 1906 *The New York Times* noted that 850,632 immigrants entered that port in 1905 and predicted that 1906 might bring a million. The newspaper reported that Ellis Island had processed 5233 immigrants on the previous day, with another 18,301 on ships in the harbour awaiting their turn. That previous day's arrivals included eight vessels that swelled the total by almost 13,000: Hamburg–America's ships *Prinz Oskar* and *Moltke* from Naples and *Algeria* from Marseilles; Holland–America's *Nieuw Amsterdam* from Rotterdam; Red Star's *Zealand* from Antwerp; White Star's *Republic* from Naples; the French line's *La Bretagne* from Le Havre; and Cunard's *Carpathia* bringing, claimed the newspaper, 2197 emigrants from Naples.[10]

For a fare of ten pounds for the trip from Trieste or Fiume to New York, third-class passengers received room and board for a westbound passage that could last three and a half weeks. The three daily meals in steerage consisted of familiar foods prepared by cooks and served by stewards of the same nationality as the emigrants. Cunard also hired Italians and Hungarians to serve as doctors, purser's staff and ship's police. Women passengers were quartered forward and men aft, a segregation strictly enforced after lights out at 11pm. During the day and evening they mingled and socialized in the third-class public rooms and deck spaces.[11]

Although order usually prevailed, the ship's ethnic police force existed for good reason. James Bisset noted that Cunard was careful to fill a ship with either Italian or Hungarian emigrants exclusively, in order to avoid conflicts between nationalities. While Rostron described most steerage passengers as 'being quiet to the point of almost pathetic docility,' he wrote that occasionally disputes erupted into conflict and even degenerated into knife attacks. 'We had to treat these offenders with a certain amount of severity,' he recalled. 'That usually consisted of making them spend a night down in the forepeak [tank in the very bow of the ship] with the rats and the pitchy dark for company and to the tune of the pounding seas against the hull they learned the reasonableness of better behaviour.'[12]

Each emigrant received a medical examination before embarking to prevent those infected with diseases barred by US immigration rules from taking passage. When an immigrant ship arrived at New York, her first stop was to anchor off Staten Island at Quarantine for a preliminary health inspection. This examination of all of the ship's passengers consumed several hours before she was cleared to proceed to her Manhattan pier. Immigrants who failed the health inspection would be removed by launch at Quarantine and detained to await repatriation to their countries of origin at the shipping company's expense. They would be inspected once more at Ellis Island, with the same fate awaiting those who failed the examination.[13]

Given the limits of the science of public health in that era, it is not surprising that, despite the initial health inspections, these crowded ships were vulnerable to outbreaks of disease, sometimes leading to death. Such a tragedy befell Mrs Joseph Farkas, travelling from Austria to New York with her two children in the autumn of 1910. Crossing in *Carpathia* to be reunited with her husband at South Bethlehem, Pennsylvania, her eleven-month-old baby fell sick with the measles. He was removed from the ship at Quarantine and taken to the immigrant hospital on Hoffman Island, where he died. The following June, *Carpathia* suffered an outbreak of fifty cases of measles among the 1100 immigrants she brought from Naples. On that occasion the health inspector detained *Carpathia* until the sick were removed to a hospital and about 150 other people were kept under observation. *Carpathia* was allowed to dock and discharge her cabin-class passengers only after she was 'thoroughly disinfected'.[14]

If immigrant ships like *Carpathia* suffered illness and even death, they also served as the means for beginning new lives. Hungarian immigrant Petra Kozkowska arrived in New York aboard *Carpathia* in May of 1910 to meet and marry a miner she had never met, as arranged by his mother back in Hungary. Having cleared immigration at Ellis Island, met the man and visited a minister, she departed for Colorado as Mrs Andrew Maller. Rostron also recalled that crews on emigrant ships of that era anticipated one or more births on every westbound passage. Parents sometimes planned their ocean voyage to coincide with the end of a pregnancy, knowing that if they reached port their child would be born an American. But giving birth at sea had other advantages. The mother would be assured of the cost-free attention of the ship's doctor, an amenity rare among the poor in the old country or the new. The parents would usually also benefit from a collection taken up by the other passengers and crew and the newborn might be showered with gifts. Sometimes, in commemoration, parents named their child after the ship.[15]

Thus began the life of Irene Carpathia Bodher, born in the mid-Atlantic to Hungarian-emigrant parents a week before the ship arrived in New York in November 1907. The new passenger elicited much interest in both the steerage and cabin classes. Helen Floyd-Jones, a Californian debutante returning from a year abroad, was selected as godmother; Captain H. M. Benison, *Carpathia*'s master, named godfather; and three priests and many cabin passengers attended the christening in the steerage hospital. Irene Carpathia Bodher went ashore accompanied by a trunk filled with clothing and other presents donated by passengers, while her father pocketed the fifty dollars raised to start her on her own voyage.[16]

As the presence of a Californian debutante aboard *Carpathia* indicates, Cunard sought Mediterranean revenue from tourists as well as emigrants. The company quickly turned the necessity of a ship's positioning voyage to the Adriatic into the virtue of a Mediterranean pleasure cruise. 'AN OPPORTUNITY,' advertised the line in September 1905, 'Special Trip from LIVERPOOL – SATURDAY, OCTOBER 14th – to Gibraltar, Naples, Trieste, Fiume, by the magnificent twin-screw steamer CARPATHIA, 13,603 tons.' In order to accommodate wealthy clientele for these 'yachting cruises', Cunard reconfigured *Carpathia*'s upper decks in 1905 to accommodate 150 first-class passengers, reducing the second-class accommodation from 200 passengers to 50.[17]

First- and second-class tourists departed Liverpool, enjoyed a cruise to Gibraltar, Italy, or Egypt and then returned to the United Kingdom aboard one of the company's homebound vessels or through arrangement with another shipping line. Cunard soon offered such cruises from New York to the

Mediterranean and also expanded its offerings beyond these ships' regular Italian and Adriatic ports of call. In 1910 *Carpathia's* February positioning voyage added stops in Spain and along the North African coast as far east as Alexandria, Egypt, with 'sufficient time being allowed at each port to enable visitors to see the principal places of interest'. The ship then worked the Adriatic before calling at Naples. There her winter-cruise passengers transferred to *Caronia* for their return to Liverpool, while *Carpathia*, back in the immigrant trade, steamed for New York.[18]

Carpathia capably made her rounds for a decade in Cunard's Mediterranean service. Harry Grattidge, who sailed in her as a junior officer just before the First World War, described *Carpathia* as 'a proud ship: clean, well-rigged, scrupulously run'. James Bisset, who joined *Carpathia* as second officer when Rostron took command, found her to be 'a comfortable and friendly ship'. Rostron's posting to *Carpathia* on 18 January 1912, after a year in *Pannonia*, represented a charge of modestly-increased size but a continuation of his previous duty as a captain in Cunard's Hungarian-American passenger-cargo service.[19]

Joining *Carpathia* in the spring of 1912 in the four-horse harness of Cunard's 'Hungarian-American fleet' were Rostron's former command, *Pannonia*, and *Ivernia* and *Saxonia*, all of similar type. Each steel-hulled ship carried four masts and a single funnel and each was a twin-screw vessel driven by reciprocating steam engines. *Ivernia* and *Saxonia*, built for Cunard and delivered in the spring of 1900, measured 14,278 and 14,297 tons respectively. The slightly mismatched 9851-ton *Pannonia* was laid down for another company in 1902, but purchased on the ways by Cunard for its Mediterranean service. Rostron would eventually command them all.[20]

After loading coal at the Canada Brand dock along with general cargo and 120 saloon-class passengers at Huskisson dock, *Carpathia* departed Liverpool under Rostron's command at 4.30pm on 10 February 1912. She arrived at Gibraltar four days later, sailed the day after that for Algiers and arrived there at the end of her first week, on the morning of 17 February. Twelve hours later she was underway for Malta and after touching there on 20 February, for Alexandria, where she arrived on the morning of 22 February. On the evening of 24 February, *Carpathia* departed Alexandria for Constantinople.[21]

Forty-eight hours was enough to do *Carpathia*'s business at the capital of the Ottoman Empire and she departed Constantinople on the morning of 29 February bound for Trieste, the principal port of the Austro-Hungarian Empire. This passage from the head of the Dardanelles to the head of the Adriatic consumed exactly four days. *Carpathia*'s call at Constantinople had marked the end of her eastbound voyage; from there she would switch from primarily discharging cargo and passengers to receiving them.[22]

At Trieste the ship took on 595 tons of cargo over three days and one first- and one second-class passenger and 149 third-class passengers before departing for Fiume on the evening of 6 March. *Carpathia* reached Fiume, 110 miles down the east coast of the Adriatic, after an overnight passage. There she spent another three days loading 300 more tons of cargo and boarding 754 passengers, 37 in second class and 717 in steerage, before departing on the evening of 9 March. Her next call was at Messina, Sicily, at midday on 11 March. Before departing at dawn on 13 March, *Carpathia* had received 1 first-class and thirty-six second-class passengers and loaded another 382 tons of cargo. She called at Palermo that afternoon and evening to pick up fifty-eight second-class passengers and arrived at Naples at noon the next day to load 424 tons of cargo and twenty-eight first-class and sixty-two second-class passengers. *Carpathia* departed Naples at daybreak on 15 March and reached Gibraltar, her twelfth port of call on the voyage, three mornings later.[23]

After a four-hour stop, at 10am on 18 March, she sailed for America, having added three first-class, three second-class and 22 third-class passengers to the total. 'It was then that the fun really began,' Bisset remembered of Atlantic crossings, 'as the majority of our passengers saw the mighty ocean for the first time in their lives and what they saw displeased them'. He remembered that, while most initially became seasick, 'they were a brave, hardy and sturdy people and soon adjusted themselves'. *Carpathia* took eleven days to cross the Atlantic in March of 1912. She arrived off Sandy Hook at 4am on 29 March and, following her health inspection, tied up at her Manhattan pier five hours later.[24]

Twelve days later, while *Carpathia* lay alongside her New York pier, a far more celebrated ship sailed for that harbour. In the autumn of 1911 the White Star Line had announced that *Titanic* would leave Southampton on her maiden voyage on 10 April 1912. True to the company's schedule, her sea trials and provisioning completed, the 'largest vessel at present afloat' cast off at noon on that second Wednesday in April. She called at Cherbourg that evening and arrived at Queenstown just before noon the next day. Passengers, baggage and mails quickly transferred to and from the ship by tender, *Titanic* departed Queenstown at 1.30pm, 11 April, for her first Atlantic crossing with, as *The Times* had the figures, 1390 passengers, 903 crew and 3814 sacks of mail. The newspaper noted improvements to *Olympic*'s propellers since her introduction and commented that 'it will be interesting to see whether the *Titanic* … will show still better results'.[25]

Three-and-a-half hours later, at noon in New York, Rostron ordered *Carpathia* to cast off and backed her into the Hudson. Two hours after that she dropped her pilot at the mouth of Ambrose Channel and stood out to sea on another 3194-mile voyage to Gibraltar, carrying 122 first-class, 41 second-class and 571 third-class passengers. On Saturday, 13 April, the shipping section of *The Times* reported: '*Titanic*, Southampton for New York, signalled Brow Head [on the south-west coast of Ireland] 3.46am [Friday], 250 miles west… *Carpathia*, for Mediterranean, left New York 2pm Thursday.'[26]

CHAPTER 6

WE WERE ALL ON
THE *QUI VIVE*

In the first few minutes of Monday morning, 15 April 1912, Captain Edward J. Smith of *Titanic* learned the awful truth: his ship could not survive the night. Twenty minutes earlier, lookout Fredrick Fleet had sighted 'a black mass' in the water about a quarter of a mile away. Fleet rang the crow's nest bell three times to warn of an object dead ahead and then telephoned the bridge with the warning 'iceberg right ahead'.[1]

First Officer William Murdoch reversed *Titanic*'s engines and ordered her helm hard over to try to avoid a collision. In the forty seconds or so that it took to reach the iceberg, *Titanic*'s bow did swing about twenty degrees to port, which cleared the ship's stem but fatally exposed her starboard side. Scraping and ripping along a third of the length of the hull, the iceberg holed in quick succession *Titanic*'s forepeak tank, first, second and third holds and sixth and fifth boiler rooms. The largest ship in the world then drifted to a stop and began to sink, imperceptibly at first.

Captain Smith arrived on the bridge immediately. He dispatched Fourth Officer Herbert Boxhall to inspect the ship. Boxhall's brief examination turned up nothing, but soon bad news began to inundate the pilothouse like the water inexorably filling the ship below. This being the liner's maiden voyage, Smith had aboard the expertise of Thomas Andrews, the principal designer of the ship. Smith and Andrews made a rapid inspection of the forward end of the vessel and Andrews realized that with six of her sixteen watertight subdivisions opened to the sea, *Titanic* was doomed. After Smith returned to the bridge and ordered the lifeboats prepared for launching, Boxhall asked him 'Is it really serious?' Smith replied, 'Mr. Andrews tells me he gives her from an hour to an hour and a half.'[2]

At about that time, *Titanic's* plight was broadcast as far as her wireless signal would carry. *Titanic's* first distress message was transmitted at 12.15am, but was not received by the vessel that would come to the rescue. About sixty miles to the south-east, *Carpathia* steamed eastward at her standard fourteen knots on the fourth day of a voyage remarkable until then for nothing save its unusually fine, cold weather. Second Officer James Bisset, who assumed the watch at 8pm that Sunday night, found a smooth sea and no wind under a clear, moonless, star-filled sky, with the aurora borealis flickering to the north. He remembered later that 'the air was intensely cold'.[3]

At midnight First Officer Horace Dean assumed the watch and Bisset retired to his cabin. In *Carpathia's* wireless shack on the raised lifeboat deck aft, the ship's only wireless operator, Harold Cottam, was also preparing to turn in. He had worked a long day and had been up most of the previous two nights. As part of winding up, Cottam took a summary of the day's wireless traffic to Dean on the bridge shortly after midnight, thereby missing *Titanic's* first distress call.[4]

Having delivered his report, Cottam returned to the wireless shack and resumed listening, awaiting confirmation of a message he had sent earlier to *Parisian*. With that ship not answering and knowing from listening to Cape Cod that *Titanic* had wireless traffic backlogged at that station, Cottam decided to contact *Titanic* at 12.25am. He was shocked when his cheerful salutation to *Titanic's* wireless operator Jack Phillips was interrupted by: 'Come at once. We have struck a berg. It's a CQD O[ld] M[an]. Position 41.46N 50.14W.' Having confirmed both *Titanic's* distress and her position, Cottam hurried to the bridge and informed First Officer Dean.[5]

Rostron had retired for the night and though not asleep was getting there. He was thus none too pleased when Dean and Cottam came crashing through the cabin door by the head of his bunk unannounced at 12.35am. But the message instantly absolved the messengers. 'You can imagine,' Rostron wrote, 'I was very soon wide awake and, to say the least, somewhat astonished.' He immediately dispatched Dean back to the bridge with orders to steer north-west while Rostron worked up the exact course. Before he did so, however, he turned to Cottam and twice confirmed the incredible news.[6]

While Cottam returned to the wireless shack to inform *Titanic* that *Carpathia* was on the way, Rostron summoned his chief engineer and headed for the chart room. When Chief Engineer Alexander Johnstone arrived, Rostron ordered another watch of stokers turned to and all possible speed made. After Johnstone left, as Rostron finished dressing he worked up the exact course needed to reach *Titanic* and dispatched it to the bridge: North 52 West (308 degrees) True.[7]

Rostron calculated that *Titanic* was fifty-eight miles away. *Carpathia* would cover that distance in just less than four hours and ten minutes at her normal cruising speed of fourteen knots. But with the watch below tumbling out and hurrying to the stokeholds to help fire her and with steam diverted from the ship's heating and hot water systems into her engines, *Carpathia*'s speed soon climbed through fifteen and sixteen knots.[8]

Meanwhile, the first-class surgeon Frank McGee, Purser Ernest Brown and Chief Steward Evan Hughes had appeared in answer to Rostron's summons. Once they assembled in his cabin, he issued the stream of orders necessary to prepare their departments for the rescue. Here Rostron's experience of twenty-five years at sea and almost five in command manifested itself on what he later called 'the most drastic and memorable night of my career'.[9]

Rostron's orders to his subordinates, later listed in testimony, stand a century on as a monument to organization and decision under duress:

English doctor, with assistants, to remain in first class dining room.

Italian doctor, with assistants, to remain in second class dining room.

Hungarian doctor, with assistants, to remain in third class dining room.

Each doctor to have supplies of restoratives, stimulants, and everything to hand for immediate needs of probable wounded or sick.

Purser, with assistant purser and chief steward, to receive the passengers, etc., at different gangways, controlling our own stewards in assisting *Titanic* passengers to the dining rooms, etc.; also to get Christian and surnames of all survivors as soon as possible to send by wireless.

Inspector, steerage stewards, and master at arms to control our own steerage passengers and keep them out of the third-class dining hall, and also to keep them out of the way and off the deck to prevent confusion.

Chief steward: That all hands would be called and to have coffee, etc., ready to serve out to all our crew.

Have coffee, tea, soup, etc., in each saloon, blankets in saloons, at the gangways, and some for the [*Carpathia*'s] boats.

To see all rescued cared for and immediate wants attended to.

My cabin and all officials' cabins to be given up. Smoke rooms, library, etc., dining rooms, would be utilized to accommodate the survivors.

All spare berths in steerage to be utilized for *Titanic*'s passengers and get all our own steerage passengers grouped together.

Stewards to be placed in each alleyway to reassure our own passengers, should they enquire about noise in getting our boats out, etc., or the working of engines.

To all I strictly enjoined the necessity for order, discipline and quietness and to avoid all confusion.[10]

After the surgeon, purser and chief steward departed, Rostron climbed to the bridge just after 1am, received an update on *Titanic*'s situation from Cottam and issued the orders necessary to prepare the deck to Chief Officer Thomas Hankinson and to First Officer Dean as officer of the watch:

Chief and first officers: All the hands to be called; get coffee, etc.

Prepare and swing out all boats.

All gangway doors to be opened.

Electric [light] sprays in each gangway and over side.

A block with line rove hooked in each gangway.

A chair sling at each gangway, for getting up sick or wounded.

Boatswains' chairs, [p]ilot ladders and canvas ash bags to be at each gangway, the canvas ash bags for [lifting] children.

Cargo falls with both ends clear; bowlines in the ends and bights secured along ship's sides, for boat ropes or to help the people up.

Heaving lines distributed along the ship's side and gaskets handy near gangways for lashing people in chairs, etc.

Forward derricks, topped and rigged, and steam on winches; also told off officers for different stations and for certain eventualities [such as the need to use *Carpathia's* boats].

Ordered company's rockets to be fired at 2.45am and every quarter of an hour after to reassure *Titanic*.

Rostron also arranged to pour oil down the forward lavatories on both sides of the ship, should it be necessary to calm the seas and he issued one final order:

As each official saw everything in readiness, he reported to me personally on the bridge that all my orders were carried out, enumerating the same and that everything was in readiness.[11]

'All this, quickly spoken in Captain Rostron's clear and steady tones within less than a minute, roused men still drowsy to a pitch of intense alertness,' remembered Bisset, who had rejoined the proceedings on the bridge. Bisset, who had exceptionally keen eyesight, was one of the officers that Rostron told off for different stations. Rostron stationed him on *Carpathia's* starboard bridge wing with orders to devote his whole attention to keeping lookout for lights, flares and especially for ice. Rostron also placed extra lookouts in the crow's nest, on the bow and on the port bridge wing.[12]

Carpathia's captain was 'fully conscious of the danger my own ship and passengers were sharing' in her all-out dash; danger from icebergs and especially from growlers, large but low-lying chunks of ice that were just as dangerous but much more difficult to see. As Rostron later observed, 'I knew the *Titanic* had struck ice. Therefore, I was prepared to be in the vicinity of ice when I was getting near him… I went full speed, all we could … [but] doubled my lookouts and took extra precautions and exerted extra vigilance. Every possible care was taken. We were all on the *qui vive*.'[13]

Below decks, *Carpathia's* stewards, cooks and medical staff were hurrying, as quietly as possible, to implement Rostron's orders. Steward J. W. Barker said that 'all of the stewards were assembled, [and] the storeroom was ransacked. Blankets, brandy, medicines and bandages were gotten out and the dining room tables were laid to provide a large and extra fine meal for the rescued'. Arpad Lengyel, *Carpathia's* Hungarian steerage doctor, turned out in response to Rostron's call for all hands and took charge of the aid station set up for survivors in the third-class saloon. He remembered that as the crew swung into action, 'the lights were all turned on and the ship became a brilliant mass of light'. Rostron's order to prepare coffee for one thousand people also impressed the doctor.[14]

Having issued his orders, Rostron stationed himself on the bridge, manoeuvering his ship and receiving progress reports from the various departments. Chief Engineer Johnstone reported first, at around 1.30am, that all hands were at work below and doing all that they could. Reports from the wireless shack were much less encouraging. First came word at about 1.30am that *Titanic* was 'putting the passengers off in small boats,' followed fifteen minutes later by an ambiguous but ominous report of her 'engine room full up to boilers,' which Rostron regarded as 'a case of all up'. That signal was Cottam's last contact with the sinking liner, though he continued to try to communicate with her. At 3.15am he flashed: 'If you are there, we are firing rockets.'[15]

Titanic was not there. By then she lay scattered on the floor of the Atlantic. Fifty-five minutes before, passenger Mahala Douglas, in *Titanic*'s lifeboat number 2, had watched her sink, 'and the last picture to my mind is the immense mass of black against the star-lit sky and then – nothingness'. In the hour that followed, the sinking itself and the frigid Atlantic killed fifteen hundred people in what *Titanic*'s Second Officer Charles Lightoller, who swam among the shipwrecked, described as 'an utter nightmare of both sight and sound'. The surviving 705 passengers and crew rowed or drifted in the darkness on the flat-calm ocean aboard *Titanic*'s twenty lifeboats. But Fourth Officer Joseph Boxhall, commanding boat number 2, was working on their rescue. He had brought with him a box of green flares and he lighted eight or nine of these at intervals to signal to the other lifeboats or to approaching rescue ships.[16]

As Rostron remembered the night, Dr McGee climbed to the bridge at about 2.35am to report everything in readiness in the medical department. Rostron was conversing with McGee at 2.40am, 'when quite suddenly – and only for a couple of seconds – I saw a green flare' about five degrees off *Carpathia*'s port bow. Given *Carpathia*'s distance from *Titanic*'s position at that moment, Rostron thought that this had to be a signal from *Titanic* herself, which eased his concern over the worrisome wireless reports.[17]

Five minutes after Rostron saw the first green light, Bisset spotted something more sinister by the light of a star, an iceberg three-quarters of a mile ahead on the port bow. Rostron altered course to starboard and reduced speed to half ahead. Once satisfied that he had cleared the danger, he resumed course and speed and continued his charge, but that was only the first of about a half-dozen icebergs that *Carpathia* encountered during her dash to *Titanic's* position. 'Icebergs loomed up and fell astern,' he remembered, '… sometimes we altered course suddenly to avoid them. It was an anxious time with the *Titanic's* fateful experience very close in our minds… [*Carpathia's*] lives, as well as all the survivors of the *Titanic* herself, depended on a sudden turn of the wheel.'[18]

Every time they spied another of Boxhall's green flares, Rostron answered with a rocket of his own and, as *Carpathia* closed in, with Cunard's company night signal to identify his ship. Rostron said that with green flares to chase and icebergs to dodge, 'you may depend on it, we were keyed up pretty tight and keeping a bright lookout'. Bisset recalled that 'the sudden bursts of light from our rockets added to the difficulties of lookout, but they were an imperative procedure in the circumstances'.[19]

At about 3.30am, the purser and chief steward came to the bridge and reported all in readiness in their departments. Five minutes later, knowing that he must be nearing the distress position, Rostron rang *Carpathia's* engine telegraph to standby, alerting her engineers to be ready to manoeuvre instantly. At about the same time, the occupants of *Titanic's* lifeboat number 13 sighted one of *Carpathia's* rockets. A flash low on the horizon followed by a faint boom, as passenger Lawrence Beesley described it. 'And then, creeping over the edge of the sea where the flash had been, we saw a single light and presently a second below it and in a few minutes they were well above the horizon and they remained in line!' That meant that *Carpathia* was headed directly toward him. The survivors in Beesley's boat lit torches out of paper, both to be seen and to avoid being run over.[20]

It was another of Boxhall's signals, however, that guided *Carpathia* to the end of her race. Knowing he must be near the position, Rostron stopped engines at about 4am and *Carpathia's* way fell off a couple of knots by 4.05am. At that moment Boxhall lit another flare. Rostron knew from its position in the water ahead that it must be a signal from a boat, though he could not see the boat itself in the darkness. Only then did *Carpathia*'s watch spot yet another small iceberg, this one floating 'right ahead' a quarter to a half of a mile away. The position of the berg made it impossible for Rostron to manoeuvre *Carpathia* to windward of Boxhall's boat. Rostron went hard over to miss the ice and full astern, but *Carpathia* overshot Boxhall's boat, which, with only one other sailor aboard, could hardly manoeuvre. So Rostron backed *Carpathia* down, bringing the boat along her starboard side at 4.10am, and the recovery began. Rostron ordered Bisset to board the boat with two seamen, secure it alongside and assist the survivors aboard. Bisset found its occupants numbed and 'in no fit condition' to climb the Jacob's Ladder to the gangway door on C Deck. He used the boatswain's chair and canvas bag to recover adults and children one at a time.[21]

As *Carpathia* manoeuvred to recover Boxhall's boat, Beesley watched from lifeboat number 13 as 'she slowly swung round and revealed herself to us as a large steamer with all her portholes alight. I think the way those lights came slowly into view was one of the most wonderful things we shall ever see.' But a survivor in another boat, sixteen-year-old Mary Conover Lines, was struck by how *Carpathia* 'looked so small in comparison to the tremendous *Titanic*'.[22]

Rostron summoned the last of the occupants of lifeboat number 2, Boxhall, to the bridge. He confirmed what Rostron had feared – that *Titanic* had foundered two hours before. By then daylight was breaking, which revealed a new problem. The disorganization that had characterized *Titanic*'s abandonment had extended to her lifeboats. Some boats had been sent away with orders to remain in the vicinity of the ship, perhaps with the idea of using them to load additional passengers through *Titanic*'s gangway doors. Others had been ordered to row for the lights of a ship visible to the north. Still others were lowered away with no orders at all; these rowed or drifted depending on the decision of the sailor in charge or, in several cases, the will of their passengers.[23]

Thus, a breaking dawn found *Titanic*'s lifeboats scattered over several square miles of ocean, the farthest being four to five miles from *Carpathia* in Rostron's estimation, 'some in groups of two or three, others singly, pulling in toward a common centre – the *Carpathia*'. Seaman George Hogg, in charge of lifeboat number 7, spotted *Carpathia*'s lights in the distance. 'It is all right, now, ladies,' he said. 'Do not grieve. We are picked up. Now, gentlemen, see what you can do in pulling these oars for this light.' While every lifeboat that could do so rowed for his ship, Rostron 'was dodging about all over the place to pick them up'. *Carpathia* eventually recovered the occupants of eighteen of *Titanic's* boats; survivors aboard two waterlogged collapsible boats were recovered by other lifeboats that then made for the safety of *Carpathia*.[24]

Beesley's lifeboat number 13 came alongside at about 4.30am. Safe in *Carpathia's* lee, occupants of the boat held lines at 13's bow and stern passed down from the rescue ship, while survivors embarked through gangway doors. 'Women went up the side first, climbing rope ladders with a noose round their shoulders to help their ascent; men passengers scrambled next and crew last of all. [A] baby went up in a bag with the opening tied up.' That was one of the ash bags that Rostron had ordered placed at each gangway, which he later reported as being 'of great assistance in getting the infants and children aboard.' Beesley reached the deck 'grateful beyond the possibility of adequate expression to feel a solid ship beneath [me] once more'.[25]

Rostron, Beesley and Bisset later all declared the striking feature of the rescue to be its silence. 'There was absolutely no excitement,' remembered Rostron, '... as though the disaster were so great it silenced human emotion.' Beesley thought it 'just the quiet demeanor of people who are in the presence of something too big as yet to lie within their mental grasp and which they cannot yet discuss'. Bisset agreed, recalling that 'the rescue operations proceeded in a deathly silence. Except for an occasional working order, no one was capable of saying anything that would be adequate to the occasion.'[26]

The rescue of the occupants of the eighteen lifeboats took time, however. As day broke the wind and waves began to pick up, making the long pulls of the last few, overcrowded boats harrowing experiences. Passenger Eloise Hughes Smith remembered that 'the sea had started to get fairly rough by the time we were taken on the *Carpathia* [from lifeboat number 6, one of the last to arrive] and we were quite cold and glad for the shelter and protection. I have every praise for the *Carpathia's* captain and its crew, as well as the passengers aboard,' she continued. 'They were kindness itself to each and every one of us.' Passenger Emily Ryerson agreed. Her lifeboat, number 4, came alongside at about 8am. 'Very soon after we got on board they took a complete list of the names of all survivors. The kindness and the efficiency of all the arrangements on the *Carpathia* for our comfort can never be too highly praised.'[27]

The dawn also revealed a sight to give a ship handler pause. 'It looked like the North Pole to me,' survivor Emma Schabert wrote shortly afterwards, 'miles and miles of ice white and silvery in the sun.' A large ice field lay about three miles north-west of *Carpathia*, while twenty-five large icebergs and innumerable smaller ones surrounded the rescue ship. Rostron reflected a few days later: 'I can confess this much, that if I had known at the time there was so much ice about, I should not [have run under a full head of steam]; but I was right in it then. I could see the ice. I knew I was perfectly clear. There is one other consideration: Although I was running a risk with my own ship and my own passengers, I also had to consider what I was going for ... Of course it was a chance, but at the same time I knew quite what I was doing ... and that I was doing perfectly right in what I did.'[28]

With 'unbounded relief', Charles Lightoller guided the last lifeboat, number 12, into the safety of *Carpathia*'s lee at around 8.30am. It had been a long, hard pull through increasingly choppy seas for the sodden passengers of that overloaded boat. 'Fortunately,' he wrote, 'none of them realized how near we were to being swamped.' Once alongside *Carpathia*, 'quickly the bosun's chairs were lowered for those unable to climb the sheer side by a swinging rope ladder and little enough ceremony was shown in bundling old and young, fat and thin, onto that bit of wood constituting the "Boatswain's Chair". Once the word was given to "hoist away" ... up into the air they went. There were a few screams, but on the whole, they took it well, in fact many were by now in a condition that rendered them barely able to hang on, much less scream.' Lightoller, the last person rescued, stepped aboard *Carpathia* at 8.39am that morning, four and a half hours after the recovery began.[29]

Carpathia recovered most of *Titanic*'s boats along with all of her survivors. Passenger Archibald Gracie noticed as his boat approached *Carpathia* that 'ranged along her sides were others of the *Titanic*'s lifeboats which had been rowed to the Cunarder and had been emptied of their loads of survivors'. As the ship slowly cruised about, her forward cranes lifted six of them onto the forecastle. As it became evident that *Carpathia*'s own boats would not be needed, these were swung inboard and secured, their falls detached and *Carpathia*'s davits used to hoist seven of *Titanic*'s boats, which were lashed outboard. Rostron abandoned the five remaining lifeboats that had reached *Carpathia*, including both of the collapsibles.[30]

In the meantime, the cargo-passenger ship *Californian* arrived in *Carpathia's* vicinity. She had been stopped for the night to the north at the edge of the ice field, less than a third as far away from *Titanic's* position as *Carpathia*. *Californian's* sole wireless operator, Cyril Evans, had attempted to warn *Titanic* about the ice field, but had been cut off by *Titanic's* operator, Phillips, who was busy working commercial traffic with Cape Race, Newfoundland. Shortly after that exchange and only a few minutes before *Titanic's* collision, Evans shut down his set and retired for the night.[31]

Evans had been roused from his bunk at about 5.30am by *Californian's* chief officer, George Stewart, who was concerned about the meaning of the rockets that the ship's second officer had seen fired through most of his mid-watch. The wireless operator in the steamer *Frankfurt* informed Evans of the disaster and Stewart told *Californian's* master, Stanley Lord, the news. Lord got his ship underway and steered her cautiously through the ice field for two or three miles, then steamed south along the western edge of the ice field at full speed, crossing back through the field and reaching *Carpathia's* position from the south-west by 8.30am.[32]

As the rescue concluded, Rostron decided that it would be appropriate to hold a service of prayer for the victims and thanksgiving for the survivors of the sinking. Still involved in the rescue himself, Rostron asked one of *Carpathia's* American passengers, an Episcopal minister, to conduct the service. While the service occupied the survivors gathered in *Carpathia's* first-class lounge, the ship slowly cruised the debris field in a futile search for additional survivors. Satisfied that none existed, Rostron decided not to recover the one body sighted, thinking it a sight too hard for the survivors to behold, or to go looking for others.[33]

By 8.50am locally, 7am New York time, Rostron had seen enough. 'The sea was rising and I was anxious to get well away from that danger zone in good daylight.' Asking *Californian* to continue the search, he ordered *Carpathia* steered south-west to work her way around the ice field. At 9.30am local time, Cottam advised all stations that they need no longer stand by *Carpathia* and fifteen minutes later he informed White Star's *Baltic*, one of the ships until recently steaming to the rescue, that *Carpathia* was 'proceeding to Halifax or New York full speed… Have about 800 passengers on board.'[34]

Rostron had decided to abandon his voyage to Gibraltar. Even if his ship's provisions held out, which was doubtful, hauling *Titanic*'s survivors back across the Atlantic seemed pointless and cruel. He did not yet know the physical and mental condition of the survivors and heading east would put *Carpathia* completely out of wireless contact with any land station for almost a week. 'I knew from the gravity of the disaster that it would be best to keep in touch with land stations as best I could.' Steaming west gave him a choice of landfall at Halifax, Boston, or New York. Halifax was closest, but in sailing there *Carpathia* would encounter much field ice and many icebergs, 'and I knew very well what the effect of that would be on people who had had the experience these people had had'. He also did not know if Halifax had sufficient accommodations for the survivors and landing at either Halifax or Boston would require overland rail transportation to New York, making additional complications for the survivors and their families.[35]

No, New York would be the best, in Rostron's view, 'the only port possible under the circumstances'. Although it would require the longest voyage, Rostron would deliver *Titanic*'s survivors to their intended destination, then re-provision and resume *Carpathia*'s Mediterranean voyage. Within an hour of getting underway and after clearing his decision with Bruce Ismay, chairman of the White Star Line and among the disaster's survivors, Rostron composed a message to be transmitted to Cunard: 'AM PROCEEDING NEW YORK UNLESS OTHERWISE ORDERED, WITH ABOUT 800, AFTER HAVING CONSULTED WITH MR. ISMAY AND CONSIDERING THE CIRCUMSTANCES. WITH SO MUCH ICE ABOUT, CONSIDER NEW YORK BEST.'[36]

Rostron then wrote three additional messages to be dispatched to Cunard, White Star and the Associated Press in New York. Identical in their essentials, the one sent to the Associated Press read: 'TITANIC STRUCK ICEBERG SUNK MONDAY 3AM 41.46N 50.14W CARPATHIA PICKED UP MANY PASSENGERS AM PROCEEDING NEW YORK ROSTRON.' Despite Rostron's efforts, confirmation of *Titanic*'s sinking would not reach White Star's New York office for another ten hours. Word came not from any of Rostron's messages, but from one sent by Captain Herbert Haddock of the *Olympic*, which began serving as a communications relay for *Carpathia* late Monday afternoon. Haddock's message arrived at White Star's New York office at 6.16pm on Monday evening. It informed Philip Franklin, IMM's vice president, that *Titanic* had sunk, indicated the sinking's time and position, reported all of her boats accounted for and estimated 675 survivors. The distraught Franklin quickly broke the news to the assembled press, confirming the worst of the rumours that had circulated throughout the day.[37]

Sixteen hours had passed between the time *Titanic* sank and the time definitive confirmation of her sinking reached New York. That delay was but the beginning of three and a half days of chaos and vexation for wireless operator Harold Cottam, Cunard's *Carpathia* and the transatlantic world.

CHAPTER 7

IS THERE A CENSOR ON
THE *CARPATHIA*?

By the time Captain Rostron set *Carpathia*'s course for New York, the first reports of *Titanic*'s distress had already reached the streets of the city. The wireless station at Cape Race, which *Titanic* was working when she struck the iceberg, picked up her first call for assistance at 10.25pm New York time. Her last signal, heard by the steamer *Virginian*, ceased abruptly at 12.27am New York time. These first ominous transmissions allowed the city's morning papers to publish preliminary accounts of the accident. Nothing horrifying appeared on Monday morning, 15 April. Reports simply indicated that *Titanic* had struck an iceberg and was launching lifeboats and identified various vessels thought to be steaming to her assistance. *Carpathia* did not appear in these early bulletins.[1]

Throughout that Monday various rumours circulated as to *Titanic*'s situation. *The Times* correspondent in New York reported to London that 'the conflicting early morning reports bewildered every one'. His own newspaper testified to that. Using various press reports, the Tuesday morning edition of *The Times* informed England that *Titanic* had sunk with many lives lost, had sunk without loss of life, was proceeding to New York under her own power and was being towed to Halifax by the steamship *Virginian*.[2]

The true situation was best understood aboard *Carpathia*, of course, but her transmitter was too weak to reach the wireless station at Cape Race, about 350 miles north-west of the site of *Titanic*'s sinking. Help was rapidly approaching from the west, however, in the form of the lost liner's sister. *Olympic* had departed New York on Saturday afternoon, 13 April and by

7.45am New York time on Monday morning was three hundred miles west of *Carpathia* making for the scene of the disaster at full speed. That meant that the two ships were closing on each other at a speed of about 35 knots. At that rate they would come within wireless range of each other by early Monday afternoon and would cross paths between 4pm and 4.30pm New York time.[3]

Olympic had the most powerful wireless transmitter in the region and once she got within range *Carpathia* used her to relay messages ashore throughout the rest of the day. After they established contact at 2pm New York time, *Carpathia* passed an unofficial 122-word account of the situation to *Olympic*. This information was conveyed at once to *Olympic*'s master, who responded by asking for further details of the disaster, about ice conditions in the region and asking if there was any point to *Olympic* searching *Titanic*'s position the following morning. *Carpathia* responded at 4pm, sending 'absolutely no hope [in] searching Titanic's position,' giving advice on the ice situation and providing a brief summary of the disaster. At 4.35pm *Olympic* relayed to White Star via Cape Race *Carpathia*'s information, most of which quickly appeared in the newspapers. Fifteen minutes later, at 4.50pm, *Olympic* asked *Carpathia* 'can you give me names [of] survivors [to] forward?' *Carpathia* replied 'will send names immediately we can, you can understand we are working under considerable difficulty. Everything possible [is] being done for [the] comfort of survivors. Please maintain stand by.'[4]

Within minutes, *Carpathia* began to reveal her grim truths, starting with a private message dispatched to *Olympic*'s master at 5.45pm New York time: 'Captain, chief, first and sixth officers and all engineers gone. Also doctor, all pursers, one Marconi operator and chief steward gone. We have second, third, fourth and fifth officers and one Marconi operator on board.' Following that message, *Carpathia* immediately began sending the names of 322 first- and second-class survivors – a process that consumed an hour and fifty minutes – and promised to send lists of third-class and crew survivors later. *Carpathia* then sent *Olympic* the messages drafted that morning for transmission to Cunard, White Star and the Associated Press.[5]

With the distance between them rapidly opening, *Olympic* lost contact with *Carpathia*'s weak signal by 8.45pm New York time on Monday night, whereupon *Olympic*'s operator turned his attention to transmitting ashore *Carpathia*'s lists of first- and second-class survivors. *Olympic* had her own difficulties reaching Cape Race due to poor atmospheric conditions, but finished transmitting the names at 2.30am on Tuesday morning, New York time, followed by *Carpathia*'s service messages. Within the hour, with Tuesday's sunrise, *Olympic* lost contact with Cape Race for good.[6]

Thanks to *Olympic*'s wireless relay, by the time that sunrise reached New York City, the extent of the disaster had been acknowledged on both sides of the Atlantic. *Titanic* had sunk with a catastrophic loss of life. The *New York Times* of that morning estimated that 1250 had died; the Hearst syndicate's *New York American* speculated that the toll might be as high as 1800 lives. Once the sinking and the scale of the disaster became official, the *American* reported that 'a veritable torrent of telegraphic messages, seeking information, poured into steamship and newspaper offices all day'. The newspaper likened the anxiety displayed 'to that which followed some great battle of the Civil War, where thousands had been reported killed and the list of those dead and wounded was received slowly'.[7]

By Tuesday Rostron's ship had been identified as one of the rescue vessels and perhaps the only one, although ashore hope remained that the Allan liners *Virginian* and *Parisian*, the Leland Line's *Californian*, or even a tramp steamer or fishing vessel without wireless might have recovered survivors. 'Cunarder Carpathia Rushing to New York with the Survivors,' *The New York Times* announced, somehow increasing *Carpathia*'s original estimate of 'about 800' survivors to 866. But the paper also printed *Olympic*'s warning that 'grave fears are felt for the safety of the balance of the passengers and crew'. No word came directly from *Carpathia* herself, out of wireless contact on the broad Atlantic.[8]

In the absence of facts about the sinking, newspapers indulged in some creative reporting. On Tuesday morning, 16 April, the tabloid *New York American* published on its front page a doctored photograph of *Olympic* charging straight into a mountain of ice and claimed in print the following day that 'the impact almost rent the ship asunder. It cut decks, sides and bulkheads from [the] bow nearly to amidships. It smashed boats and upper works to pieces.' In London, *The Times*, presumably more responsible, was almost as sensational. Its Tuesday morning coverage described *Titanic*'s passengers as 'awakened and terrified by an impact which crushed and twisted the high bows of the liner and broke them in like an eggshell'.[9]

Without information upon which to build newspaper stories about *Titanic*, the story quickly became *Carpathia* herself. As Tuesday wore on, attention shifted entirely to Rostron's ship, as messages from *Olympic*, *Virginian* and *Parisian* confirmed that the disaster's only survivors were aboard *Carpathia*, which had accounted for all of *Titanic*'s lifeboats. As to the number of survivors, some accounts went as high as 868, while others gave a figure of 675. *The Times* declared that 'there is little hope, however, that the disaster will not prove to have been the most awful in the history of the sea'. The paper anticipated that *Carpathia* would soon be within range of shore stations and would be able to send the particulars of the tragedy, but admitted that as of Tuesday evening in New York, 'no definite authoritative details are available regarding the disaster itself'.[10]

A lack of details did nothing to stifle the story. *The New York Times* posted bulletins about the city 'in hotels, clubs, office buildings, public buildings and large stores'. The newspaper issued five of these between 5.30am and 6.30pm on Tuesday, but still found its offices 'overtaxed with enquiries… Telephones rang constantly with seekers after information.' The White Star Line's New York office received hundreds of visitors and telegrams, as well as telephone calls from all over the United States and Canada inquiring after people who had been aboard *Titanic*.[11]

As *Carpathia* became the focus of the story on Tuesday, Cunard's New York offices were also overwhelmed with crowds seeking news, of which the line's officials had none to give. The company's frustrated New York general manager, Charles P. Sumner, told the press that he had repeatedly asked *Carpathia* to furnish a complete list of *Titanic*'s survivors. 'I have sent five orders to the captain and they apparently are not delivered,' he said. Sumner thought *Carpathia* should be in contact with New York via shore stations at Cape Race or Sable Island, or through ships at sea. Asked when the ship would arrive at New York, Sumner 'said with much feeling that he could not even find out where she was'.[12]

Unbeknownst to Sumner, *Carpathia* had regained contact with the outside world at about noon on Tuesday. This time her conduit was the Atlantic Transport Line's fourteen-thousand-ton passenger-cargo liner *Minnewaska*, which had departed New York for London on Sunday morning, 14 April. *Minnewaska*'s captain, aware of the world's demand for knowledge, asked

Carpathia for the number of survivors aboard and for a complete list of them. A reply at 12.40pm assured *Minnewaska* that *Carpathia* was 'only too anxious to get all names to shore[;] doing all possible'. Having already dispatched the names of first-class and second-class survivors via *Olympic*, *Carpathia* used *Minnewaska* to send ashore the more than two-hundred names of *Titanic*'s surviving crew.[13]

Some of the mystery lifted late on Tuesday afternoon, when the complete list of *Titanic*'s first-class and second-class survivors reached the Eastern Seaboard. But even this information did little to allay the excitement, as the list was only a partial accounting of the survivors and many of the names were so garbled that they did not match those on published passenger lists. Worse, the pathetically small number of saved was disquieting in itself. 'It is now thought – feared would be the better word – that this list is now practically complete,' said *The Boston Globe*.[14]

Shortly thereafter, at about 5pm on Tuesday, *Carpathia* made her first wireless landfall through the Canadian government's station on Sable Island, located about 120 miles south-east of Halifax, Nova Scotia. *Carpathia*'s course from the wreck site to New York barely brought her low-power signal within range of Sable Island, which reported her transmissions to be quite faint. 'Details of the disaster, it is now hoped, will therefore be soon forthcoming,' said the *Globe*, but the great range, combined with poor atmospheric conditions, limited contact and increased frustrations ashore. A *New York Times*' headline Wednesday morning reported, 'Vain Attempts All Day [Tuesday] to Reach Her for Details of the Disaster.' Late Tuesday night Rostron did manage to advise Cunard that his ship would arrive in New York by 11pm on Thursday, 18 April. *Carpathia* then disappeared into the wireless gap between Sable Island and shore stations in Massachusetts for most of another day.[15]

One man unwilling to wait for *Carpathia* to steam within range of shore stations and able to do something about it was US President William Howard Taft. Concerned about the fate of *Titanic*'s passengers, among them his friend and military aide Major Archibald Butt, on Tuesday evening Taft dispatched two US Navy scout cruisers to establish wireless contact with *Carpathia* and to relay ashore, in the words of *The New York Times*, 'every particle of information they could as to survivors and the circumstances of the disaster'. USS *Chester*, at sea testing equipment east of Nantucket Shoals, was directed to steer east to intercept *Carpathia*, while USS *Salem*, at Hampton Roads, Virginia, was ordered to steam for the Nantucket Lightship and, once there, to relay messages between *Chester* and navy shore stations. Shore stations were instructed to forward any information received to the Navy Department, which would release it to the public.[16]

It was not the US Navy, however, but another Cunard ship that reestablished contact with *Carpathia* on Wednesday morning, 17 April. The liner *Franconia*, which had departed Boston on her scheduled voyage to Liverpool on Tuesday, established contact with *Carpathia* at 6.10am the following morning. From *Franconia*, through Cunard's New York office, the world learned at midday that *Carpathia* was about five hundred miles east of New York Harbor at 9am that morning, with an estimated arrival time of 8pm on Thursday. *Franconia* also established the actual total of survivors aboard *Carpathia* as 705 and relayed a number of their messages to Sable Island. The *Globe* reported, however, that 'the most anxious requests for particulars [of the disaster] from the captain of the *Franconia* and other captains have been unanswered by the captain of the *Carpathia*'.[17]

USS *Chester* established contact with *Carpathia* at about 1pm on Wednesday. The *Globe* informed readers that with the cruiser's arrival, 'a full list of saved and details of the Titanic's collision with the iceberg is hourly expected'. No further details of the sinking emerged, however. That afternoon *Carpathia* dispatched her last list of survivors, the third-class passengers, through *Chester*. *Chester* relayed the list to *Salem*, which began transmitting the names to the naval wireless station at Newport, Rhode Island, just before midnight. By then *Carpathia* herself had established direct contact with the United States through the Marconi Company's Siasconset wireless station on Nantucket Island.[18]

In New York City, the anxiety only intensified on Wednesday. 'Crowds haunt the White Star and Cunard offices, hang round the bulletins of survivors posted at various places and snap up successive editions of the newspapers, which are almost wholly devoted to the disaster,' reported *The Times'* New York correspondent, although a *Boston Globe* headline that morning admitted that 'Carpathia's list of saved [is] the only real news'.[19]

Thursday morning found the press and public 'as distressingly in the dark as yesterday'. *Carpathia* passed the Nantucket Lightship, two hundred miles east of New York City, at daybreak. 'With the exception of some driblets of information,' however, she continued to dispatch survivors' messages. A suspension of wireless transmissions along the Eastern Seaboard and *Carpathia*'s proximity to the Marconi stations on Nantucket and Long Island improved communications somewhat Thursday, 'but no word came to the repeated requests for details of the accident'. Ashore, the excitement increased. 'The Custom House has been flooded with requests for passes,' *The New York Times* reported Thursday morning, 'and one of the greatest crowds that ever met a steamship is expected to be on and outside the pier when the rescuing liner arrives to-night'.[20]

Unwilling to wait passively while *Carpathia* churned her way slowly to New York, two newspapers had already put to sea to seek her out. The *New York American* chartered the seagoing tug *Mary F. Scully*, which departed from Newport, Rhode Island, at noon on Wednesday with Jack Binns aboard, ready to intercept *Carpathia*. Binns, employed by the *American* in 1912, was the former wireless operator of the White Star liner *Republic*, who became a hero manning his transmitter when that vessel sank after a collision in fog off Long Island in 1909. The *American*'s idea, which the Marconi Company endorsed, was to have Binns put aboard *Carpathia* to relieve her exhausted operator – and, not incidentally, to transmit exclusive stories to the *American*. Poor visibility thwarted the rendezvous and transfer, however, even had *Carpathia*'s captain been willing to permit it. Binns and the *American* had to be satisfied with monitoring *Carpathia*'s communications, Binns reporting that the rescue ship was sending wireless messages, 'but news of how Titanic struck must wait till private messages are off'.[21]

The Boston Globe tried a dual approach. It also chartered a seagoing tug, *Salutation*, installed a wireless set aboard and dispatched her from New London, Connecticut, shortly after midnight on Thursday morning, hoping to meet *Carpathia* off Montauk Point, Long Island. The *Globe* had previously put a reporter named Winfield Thompson aboard *Franconia*. *Salutation* had no better luck than *Mary F. Scully* finding *Carpathia* in the fog – or getting her to communicate – and had to settle for meeting the liner at Ambrose Channel and describing her entry into New York Harbor. Thompson did a little better after *Franconia* made contact with *Carpathia* early Wednesday morning. His signal success came in ascertaining the official number of survivors aboard

Carpathia, 705, and having that fact transmitted back to Boston before *Franconia* steamed out of range. Thompson's newspaper ballyhooed the figure as a great scoop and a fitting reward for its initiative, saying 'the *Globe* took the chance, sent Mr. Thompson and got what it desired to get – the truth. In the meantime,' the paper added, 'Mr. Thompson is on his way to Liverpool.'[22]

Lacking any eyewitness accounts, however, newspapers continued their creative writing. On Thursday morning, the *New York American* estimated that 150 of the *Titanic*'s crew, 'peacefully sleeping in the forecastle head, were instantly smashed to death' when she hit the iceberg. Later the same day *The Boston Globe* described *Carpathia* herself as 'a floating house of horror, with at least 250 people seriously hurt or desperately ill'. In the same issue, however, the *Globe* admitted that 'it is doubtful now if any definite details of the disaster will be obtainable until the Carpathia reaches port,' while the *American* complained that 'the Titanic, herself in ten thousand fathoms [*sic*] of water, did not hold her secrets more firmly than the Carpathia, steaming doggedly and silently toward New York'.[23]

Attempts to extract information from the rescue ship as she neared New York also came from officials on high. A signal from Cunard's general manager, Charles Sumner, reached *Carpathia* at noon on Thursday asking for the status of half a dozen of *Titanic*'s passengers, as well as for *Carpathia*'s arrival time at Ambrose Channel. That evening a telegram arrived from IMM's besieged vice president, Philip Franklin, addressed to Bruce Ismay: 'CONCISE MARCONIGRAM ACCOUNT OF ACTUAL ACCIDENT GREATLY NEEDED FOR ENLIGHT[EN]MENT PUBLIC AND OURSELVES THIS IS MOST IMPORTANT.' Early Thursday morning, Guglielmo Marconi himself had demanded that *Carpathia*'s operator 'WIRE NEWS DISPATCHES IMMEDIATELY TO SIASCONSET OR TO NAVY BOATS; IF THIS IMPOSSIBLE ASK CAPTAIN GIVE REASON WHY NO NEWS ALLOWED TO BE TRANSMITTED.'[24]

At noon on Thursday, 18 April, *Carpathia* reported ninety-five miles east of Ambrose Light in New York's Lower Bay, steaming through a heavy haze that had dogged her since 8am, and indicated that her wireless was working unsatisfactorily. Across the Atlantic that same day, *The Times* published an article from its correspondent in New York. While acknowledging communications problems, the writer complained that 'even when communication has been established with the *Carpathia*, no details other than the list of survivors have been forthcoming'. The correspondent declared *Carpathia* 'unaccountably silent', and reported 'some grumbling about a possible censorship which is felt to be cruelly tantalizing'. An exasperated *New York Times* went that idea one better, bluntly asking: 'Is there a censor on the Carpathia?'[25]

There was, actually; his name was Arthur Rostron.

CHAPTER 8

THOUSANDS GATHER
AT THE PIER

'It was all too terrible the scenes and sadness we lived in for the next four days and nights on the darling *Carpathia*,' wrote *Titanic* survivor Laura Francatelli. 'Oh but they were so kind to us.' Aboard the unheralded rescue ship – anonymous the day before, but soon the focus of the world's attention – *Titanic*'s survivors and *Carpathia*'s crew and passengers settled in Monday morning for the three-and-a-half-day return voyage to New York.[1]

Carpathia's crew and passengers spent the first day accommodating the survivors in a manner that they sincerely appreciated. Archibald Gracie swam away from the sinking *Titanic* and spent the rest of the night standing in the freezing cold on *Titanic*'s overturned collapsible boat B before being rescued by lifeboat number 12. He recalled that 'nothing could exceed the kindness of the ladies, who did everything possible for my comfort' after he climbed aboard *Carpathia*. 'All my wet clothing, overcoat and shoes, were sent down to the bake-oven to be dried,' while he lay on a lounge in *Carpathia*'s first-class dining room under rugs and blankets. Friends from New York aboard the rescue vessel kept him supplied with hot coffee and cordials which soon 'dispersed the cold'.[2]

Lawrence Beesley's experience of floating about in a lifeboat all night was far less traumatic. Of the survivors' arrival aboard *Carpathia*, he wrote that 'they asked us politely to have hot coffee, which we did; and food, which we generally declined – we were not hungry – and they said very little at first about the lost *Titanic* and our adventures in the night'. Beesley may have been more dispassionate, but he, too, remembered being received aboard *Carpathia* 'with a welcome that was overwhelming in its warmth'.

Upon reaching New York, Beesley offered the press a statement that said 'there is not a member of the *Titanic* survivors who feels capable of expressing in adequate terms his gratitude for the attentions showered upon us by the captain, officers, crew and passengers on board the *Carpathia*... Hot meals, blankets and berths were provided for each as they came on board. Clothing and money was supplied individually by passengers. Berths were given up by men, who slept on the smoke-room floor or anywhere else that a corner could be found... The catering arrangements, in charge of the purser and stewards, have been so admirably organized that it would not be possible to be better served had we been regular passengers aboard our own ship.'[3]

Beesley's observations were affirmed by another statement issued to the newspapers by a committee of survivors that read in part: 'The officers and crew of the *Carpathia* had been preparing all night for the rescue work and for the comfort of the survivors. These were received on board with the most touching care and kindness, every attention being given to all irrespective of class. Passengers, officers and crew gladly gave up their state rooms [*sic*], clothing and comforts for our benefit. All honour to them.' *Carpathia*'s steward J. W. Barker recalled that 'we slept in the steerage or anywhere we could in order to make room for the strangers'. Rostron yielded his cabin to Madeleine Astor, Eleanor Widener and Marian Thayer, the new widows of millionaires John Jacob Astor, George Widener and John Thayer. Where Rostron slept during *Carpathia*'s return to New York – if he lay down at all – went unrecorded.[4]

While making the rescued as comfortable as possible, *Carpathia*'s stewards assembled and confirmed lists of survivors of *Titanic*'s three passenger classes and crew and distributed telegraph forms so that those recovered might send word of their rescue free of charge. As the survivors settled in and *Carpathia* concluded the rescue, Second Officer Bisset assumed his regular forenoon watch after his sleepless night. Leaving the scene of the wreck before 9am, *Carpathia* spent the remainder of his watch sailing south-west two to three hundred yards from the ice field. During Bisset's watch she 'passed dozens of icebergs in the first three hours [underway], frequently changing course to avoid colliding with them'. Rostron recorded that it took almost four hours and 'quite fifty-six miles' to clear the ice pack before he could set course for New York after noon.[5]

That same afternoon, a few minutes after establishing contact with *Carpathia* at 2pm, New York time, *Olympic*'s captain, Herbert Haddock, wired *Carpathia* with his ship's position and suggested the two ships meet, presumably to transfer *Titanic*'s survivors to her sister ship. By the time *Olympic* transmitted Haddock's message, the vessels were about seventy nautical miles apart. That would have permitted a rendezvous late that afternoon, but Haddock's idea unsettled Rostron for several reasons. One was the thought of another mid-ocean transfer for people who had seen quite enough of lifeboats for one lifetime; another was the psychological trauma that *Olympic*'s resemblance to her sunken sister might produce. Rostron replied to Haddock: 'Do you think it advisable *Titanic*'s passengers see *Olympic*? Personally I say not.' The decision was removed from either captain's jurisdiction once Rostron consulted Bruce Ismay aboard *Carpathia*. He agreed with Rostron and ordered *Olympic* to remain out of sight.[6]

On Tuesday morning Dr McGee reported to Rostron that all of the survivors were in good health and that same day they began to mobilize to help their own. Some of those rescued met in *Carpathia*'s saloon and organized a survivors' committee of seven members that included the Wall Street attorney and noted tennis player Karl Behr. 'We were occupied mainly with the steerage passengers,' he remembered, 'obtaining clothing, blankets and arranging places for them to sleep'. The committee also helped gather the names of third-class survivors for transmission ashore and ascertained their addresses and circumstances. *Carpathia*'s passengers collected about seven thousand dollars for the committee's relief fund and donated and made clothing for survivors. Rostron himself had little contact with passengers throughout the voyage, speaking to only a handful on Tuesday afternoon, he said, presumably in connection with the relief efforts.[7]

Carpathia's return voyage began with cold and ice on the first day and gradually warmed, with some rain, as the ship approached New York. She encountered fog every morning and most of her last day at sea, although the ocean remained fairly calm. The worst weather, a violent thunderstorm with heavy winds, awoke Karl Behr late Tuesday night or early Wednesday morning. He was asleep on a table in *Carpathia*'s forward smoking room, when 'suddenly there was a terrific crash. I jumped off the table, sure we had collided with another ship or iceberg. I rushed out the door on to the deck...

As I hit the deck it was pouring rain – suddenly a flash of lighting almost knocked me down. It was followed by another crash of thunder. I turned back to the Smoking Room; never had a violent thunder-storm been more welcome.' Amidst this excitement, at 11pm Tuesday, *Carpathia* reported her position to Cunard as 596 miles east of the Ambrose Channel lightship.[8]

Wednesday morning found *Carpathia* about five hundred miles east of Sandy Hook at 9am. Mildred Brown, one of *Titanic's* passengers, described the survivors' shock and lethargy, writing that day that 'ever since I've been here I've felt in a stupor, everything seems too much trouble and I can't bother what happens to me'. Brown slept on the floor of *Carpathia's* dining room the first two nights. She noted in her Wednesday letter 'a most awful thunder storm last night and today it's … foggy,' concluding 'I shall be glad to be on *terra firma* again'.[9]

Survivor Gladys Cherry confirmed the prevailing sense of shock, writing the same day that 'it has all been too ghastly and I seem still dazed'. She shared a cabin with three others, but was 'so thankful to be in anything'. She spent Wednesday morning 'cutting out garments for the steerage [and second-] class children, some of whom had no clothes at all, we made little coats and legging[s] out of the blankets and etc.' She also took charge of a child who had lost its father 'every day for a bit while the mother rests. I love to do something,' she wrote, 'it stops one thinking.'[10]

Lawrence Beesley spent his Wednesday thinking and writing about the disaster, composing 'in odd corners of the deck and saloon of the *Carpathia*' a letter to *The Times* concerning *Titanic's* sinking. He also drafted an account of the disaster for distribution to the press upon landing 'to calm public opinion and to forestall the incorrect and hysterical accounts which some American reporters are in the habit of preparing on occasions of this kind'.[11]

By Thursday morning, off Nantucket and due to reach New York that evening, patience was fading aboard *Carpathia*. 'The ship is dreadfully crowded,' wrote survivor Emma Schabert, mentioning that 'we have not been out of our clothes, sleeping in the smoking room or library'. She added that 'it is pitiful to see so many young widows sitting about weeping'. Outside, the bad weather continued. Gladys Cherry worried that 'this fog will prevent our getting in tonight and I can't stand another night on the sea'. She wrote that while 'all the crew, Captain, passengers and stewards have been perfectly sweet to us,' she was struggling with her memories. 'The doctor save[d] me a little Bromide last night and I slept a little better, but one wakens up terrified, which is very silly, as we have nothing to grumble at in comparison with … the poor widows, oh it is too dreadful to see them.'[12]

Ashore, meanwhile, 'world-wide interest demanded of the Cunarder … the long withheld secret of what took place on the *Titanic*'s decks when it became known that the doom of the great liner was sealed. But that word was not spoken.' To *The New York Times*, *Carpathia*'s failure to provide details of the disaster had become a mystery 'beyond even the mystery of how the mammoth *Titanic* met her fate'. Other newspapers offered conspiracy theories. The *New York American* postulated that Thursday that the long delay in announcing *Titanic*'s sinking was to provide 'ample time for insurance gamblers to reinsure cargo and express packages'. *The Boston Globe* suggested the same day that *Carpathia*'s 'reticence is due to the influence of J. Bruce Ismay, manager of the White Star Line, who is among the saved on board the *Carpathia*'.[13]

In fact, neither insurance gamblers nor Bruce Ismay had a hand in *Carpathia*'s communications problems. People, as well as circumstances, did conspire to limit *Carpathia*'s utility as a news source, however. The trouble began with her overwhelmed wireless operator. When *Olympic* first contacted *Carpathia* on Monday afternoon and asked for all of the details on *Titanic*, Harold Cottam replied, 'I cannot do everything at once. Patience, please.' In the same exchange with *Olympic*'s wireless operator, Ernest Moore, Cottam also mentioned that he had not eaten in twenty-one hours. Cottam began transmitting his first list of survivors to *Olympic* late Monday afternoon with the caveat 'please excuse sending, but [I] am half asleep'. This was not news to Moore, who recorded in his log that 'during the transmission of the names it was evident that the operator on *Carpathia* was tired out'.[14]

Monday afternoon was only the beginning of Cottam's ordeal by wireless. He later estimated that he slept for a total of about ten of the eighty-six hours from when *Carpathia* left the scene of the sinking until she tied up in New York. That after already having been awake for about twenty-four hours thanks to the rescue and working into the early morning several nights before that. Cottam reached his breaking point very early on Wednesday morning, when he simply fell asleep at his key for about three hours, awakening at dawn to go at it again. At that point, *Titanic*'s surviving operator, Harold Bride, resting in *Carpathia*'s sickbay suffering from frostbitten feet, was asked if he could help. Carried to the wireless shack, Bride relieved Cottam, 'from Tuesday night until the time of docking ... watch and watch'. They thus got at least some rest, but seldom left the wireless cabin, their meals being brought to them.[15]

Even with fresh operators, *Carpathia* would still have suffered the limits of her wireless set. 'It worked satisfactorily for what it was,' Cottam would testify later, 'but it was hardly satisfactory. He estimated the maximum range of *Carpathia*'s relatively old, low-powered transmitter was 250 miles in ideal conditions. Rostron said that the apparatus had a range of about 200 miles in good conditions and 150 miles in normal conditions, but that 'fog, mist, haze, snow, or any other unfavourable weather conditions make it so that we may not get more than 90 to 100 miles'. *Carpathia* would encounter everything but snow returning to New York. Cottam remembered 'wet, foul weather all the time'. Poor atmospherics, especially the severe electrical storm on Tuesday night, masked *Carpathia*'s own electric sparks and made communicating exceedingly difficult.[16]

With the exception of *Olympic*, the steamers *Carpathia* encountered were usually only slightly better equipped than she was. Worse, not only did other wireless operators often fail to provide a solution to *Carpathia*'s communications woes, they sometimes became part of the problem, their own sending obscuring *Carpathia*'s signal. The jamming of *Carpathia*'s transmissions began at the site of the wreck. Cyril Evans, *Californian*'s wireless operator, having been off the circuit since just before midnight, returned to the air at 5.30am. Evidently a morning person, he then chattered away with nearby vessels, exasperating Cottam and other exhausted operators trying to transmit information about the rescue operation.[17]

Gilbert Balfour, a travelling Marconi supervisor who happened to be aboard the White Star liner *Baltic*, made numerous entries in his log that morning noting that the jamming caused by Evans' 'long, irrelevant conversations' made it impossible to work. After two hours of this, the exasperated Balfour flashed Evans: 'Stand by immediately. You have been instructed to do so frequently. Balfour. Inspector.' But three hours after that Balfour recorded that, '*Carpathia* is trying to send me a message but communication is out of the question owing to *Californian*.'[18]

Later that afternoon Cottam managed to transmit the names of the *Titanic's* first-class and second-class survivors and Rostron's bleak service messages through *Olympic*. But even with her powerful, modern wireless set, *Olympic* had her own problems communicating. At 10.55am, New York time, *Olympic* picked up Cape Race weakly at about 350 miles, but suffered considerable interference from several vessels while trying to work that station. *Olympic's* operator logged that he had 'told the *Berlin* that it would be a serious matter for him if he kept on interfering'.[19]

The opposite end of the wireless communications system was also quickly disrupted and almost as badly. News of the disaster spread across a fogbound New York Harbor on Monday evening, with ten passenger ships lying off Ambrose Channel waiting to enter. Passengers aboard those vessels inundated the wireless system with messages asking after those on *Titanic*. This heavy local traffic of Monday evening completely obscured the faint signals from Cape Race. Not until after midnight, when the ships off Sandy Hook complied with a request to cease transmitting, could New York reestablish contact with more remote stations.[20]

The situation did not improve significantly after *Carpathia* made direct contact with North America. Her signal being too weak to be received by Cape Race, *Carpathia's* wireless first reached land through Sable Island, Nova Scotia. From there, Cottam and Bride worked Marconi's Siasconset station on Nantucket Island, Sagaponack at Southampton on Long Island and Seagate at the entrance to New York Harbor.[21]

All of *Carpathia's* potential points of contact along the Eastern Seaboard of the United States intensified rather than resolved the communication problems and frustrations, however. *The New York Times* noted that 'the very number of [stations] who sought communication with the rescue ship was a handicap. Atmospheric conditions were good … but the maze of wireless flashes which darted from every station formed a hissing mixture from which scarcely a complete sentence could be picked up by any receiving station.' The traffic that did get ashore intact indicated to the newspaper that survivors had first priority, 'for the messages … all had to do with the private affairs of people aboard the liner'.[22]

Carpathia and Marconi's chain of stations also had to contend with interference from amateur wireless operators. *The Times* reported legitimate wireless traffic disrupted by 'private telegraphists, who have filled the air with irrelevant messages'. That paper urged 'civilized nations ... to combine to put down these freaks of private vanity, or levity, or ostentation'. Of her attempts to contact *Carpathia*, USS *Salem* reported, 'conditions very unfavourable, with many stations interfering with each other'. All of this chatter easily overwhelmed *Carpathia*'s weak apparatus.[23]

USS *Chester* did establish contact with *Carpathia* on Wednesday afternoon, but that only introduced further exasperation and recrimination due to the differences between the Marconi Company's Continental Morse and the navy's American code. Tasked with transmitting the names of *Titanic*'s third-class survivors to *Chester*, Bride 'had to repeat these names, nearly 300 in all, several times ... taking up nearly a couple of hours of valuable time, though I sent them in the first place slowly and carefully'. *Chester* then transmitted the list to *Salem*, which started sending it to the naval wireless station at Newport, Rhode Island.[24]

The cruisers' signals also masked *Carpathia*'s transmissions. Siasconset's operator reported the 'system paralyzed on account of [the] navy,' with 'Chester sending long lists of names'. *Carpathia* had no choice but to remain silent during *Chester*'s lengthy transmission. The Newport, Rhode Island, naval station, with a signal that sometimes reached Panama, could not reach *Carpathia* directly 'because of the interference of small wireless stations and of a myriad of steamers[,] each of which persisted in trying its own wireless for a word from the *Carpathia*'. The station commander eventually asked all stations within range to cease transmitting to permit *Carpathia*'s traffic to be relayed through *Chester* and *Salem* to Newport.[25]

In an effort to reduce this chaos, on Wednesday afternoon the Marconi company and the US Government agreed to silence all government stations north of Norfolk, Virginia, including *Chester* and *Salem*, and all commercial stations, except a few designated Marconi stations that lay along *Carpathia*'s course to New York, to give the rescue ship 'an uninterrupted field for sending news'. The silence order, transmitted at 4.34pm, instructed the designated Marconi stations – which included Siasconset, Sagaponack and Seagate – to handle only traffic with *Carpathia* or the government ships sent to meet her.[26]

Even without exhausted operators, poor atmospherics and jamming, however, the rudimentary wireless network of April 1912 would have been overwhelmed by the *Titanic* disaster. Its system of bucket-brigade relay from ship to ship and again several times once ashore was completely inadequate to douse the communications conflagration ignited by *Titanic*'s sinking. Thus what today would be inconceivably long delays occurred. Rostron's original message announcing *Titanic*'s sinking and his own intentions, dated 7.55am New York time Monday, arrived at Cunard's New York office at 7.20am on Tuesday. This situation never improved much. Rostron's Tuesday-night message advising Cunard of *Carpathia*'s anticipated time of arrival took nine hours and forty-five minutes to reach the company.[27]

Titanic's survivors also contributed to the traffic jam. Most of the messages they sent ashore were not as succinct as that of *Titanic*'s third officer, Herbert Pitman, who had 'SAFE BURT' flashed to his relatives in England. Generally each survivor's telegram ran a sentence or two, all had to include the names and addresses of the recipients and the transmission of each was usually repeated. That took time. Cottam did as much business with *Olympic* as possible, consisting of service traffic and the lists of first-class and second-class survivors, before she faded out of range on Monday night. After that he and Bride prepared hundreds of messages for transmission as soon as *Carpathia* came within range of a shore station. Sable Island, the first such possibility, was quickly inundated from landward with messages 'from all quarters from relatives of passengers craving for news,' in what *The New York Times* gently characterized as 'a congestion of enquiries'. And if Cottam and Bride did not always cooperate with the demands of the shore stations, the reverse was also true. Cottam said that he established contact with Sable Island, but 'when I offered him about 250 [messages] he ignored me altogether'.[28]

The increasingly frantic activities of the American press added to the turmoil. With at least a dozen daily newspapers in New York City alone, the ferocious competition to get the scoop quickly compounded *Carpathia*'s communications backlog. The scramble began before anyone even knew for certain that *Titanic* had sunk or that *Carpathia* had recovered her survivors. On Monday afternoon the *New York World* told *Olympic*'s wireless operator Ernest Moore 'WE WILL PAY YOU LIBERALLY FOR STORY OF RESCUE OF TITANIC'S PASSENGERS ANY LENGTH POSSIBLE FOR YOU TO SEND EARLIEST POSSIBLE MOMENT.' Moore quickly 'received seven or eight messages to the same effect' from the *World*, the *New York Herald* and the *New York Sun,* among others. He thereupon informed the operator at Cape Race 'that it was no use sending me messages from newspapers asking us to send news of *Titanic,* as we had no news to give'.[29]

Once *Carpathia* came within range of shore stations on Wednesday 17 April, this torrent rained upon Cottam and Bride. The newspapers' queries were full of helpful suggestions. 'Mention prominent people,' advised the *New York World.* The *New York Herald* wanted as 'many facts as possible'. *The New York Times* asked Rostron to allow Cottam 'to wireless full details [of the] *Titanic* including narratives by some well-known passengers'. *The Boston Globe*'s Winfield Thompson wanted Cottam to get the 'most promising man[,] preferably Frank D. Millett or Maj. Butt' to write that paper's exclusive, while the *New York American* asked Cottam to 'please tell Stead and Furtrelle[,] *Titanic* passengers[,] to send [a] wireless story quick' – unaware that all of those men were forever beyond writing newspaper articles.[30]

And everyone besieging *Carpathia*'s operators – from relatives to newspapers to government officials to Cunard, White Star and Marconi Company officials and others important or self-important – considered their traffic 'extremely urgent'; 'rush answer', 'answer quick', 'rush messages', 'Marconi quickly', 'every moment precious', they insisted. Many of these messages claiming priority demanded that Cottam or Bride confirm the loss of prominent people whose names did not appear on the lists they had already laboriously transmitted. And many of the recipients of one of the hundreds of survivors' messages they sent felt compelled to reply, clogging the network even further with such heartfelt trifles as: 'VERY HAPPY YOU ARE SAVED LOVE TO BOTH PAUL.'[31]

Cottam and Bride did their best to ignore the distractions and transmit survivors' messages. Bride believed that the pair sent between four hundred and five hundred personal messages to land stations. Cottam estimated that he sent more than five hundred messages during the return voyage, about half of them service traffic and the other half survivors' messages. Bride said that they got off 'quite seventy-five per cent' of the survivors' messages, but that left up to two hundred messages unsent. Absorbed in his work, Bride continued to transmit even after *Carpathia* tied up, only desisting when Guglielmo Marconi himself entered the wireless cabin and cut him off with: 'Hardly worth sending now, boy.'[32]

Given all of these circumstances, Cottam and Bride shut out the press without misgivings, mostly for practical reasons. Bride wrote that 'when we established communication with the various coast stations, all of which had heavy traffic for us, in some cases running into hundreds of messages, we told them we could only accept service and urgent messages, as we knew the remainder would be press and messages inquiring after someone on the *Titanic*. It is easy to see we might have spent hours receiving messages inquiring after some survivor, while we had messages waiting from that survivor for transmission.' Beyond that, the operators found the aggressiveness of the press irritating. Asked by Marconi himself if he had sent press messages, Bride answered: 'Not a word, Sir, not a single word. Whenever I started to take their queries they sounded so out of keeping with the suffering, so curt and so demanding in tone that I shut them off and went ahead sending our personal messages.'[33]

Above and beyond all these technological circumstances and personal factors, however, stood Rostron's orders. *The New York Times*, in reporting that 'a censorship appeared to exist on the *Carpathia* which prevented any response to enquiries', mentioned that 'the wireless operator on the *Carpathia* is an officer of the Cunard Line and therefore subject to the ship's commander'. The newspaper was half right; wireless operators were actually Marconi employees assigned to a ship, but they were completely subject to their captain's orders.[34]

Cottam, who neither transmitted news nor responded to Marconi's message demanding it, said that 'the captain's order was that no traffic was to go through and no message was to be executed otherwise than official messages and passengers' traffic. I had more than I could handle with the passengers' traffic without this other stuff.' Survivor Charles Stengel said that Rostron had a large notice posted announcing that rumours circulating aboard *Carpathia* that the press was occupying the ship's wireless were untrue. In it Rostron said 'I wish to state emphatically that there have not been but 20 words sent to the press,' and he assured the survivors that *Carpathia*'s wireless was at their service.[35]

Although neither Rostron, Cottam, nor Bride ever exuded much sympathy for the newspapers, standard wireless protocol also put press traffic last and least. It had fourth priority behind emergency messages, service messages sent in the captain's name to other ships or shore stations concerning navigation or company business, and paid wireless traffic – which included the hundreds of survivors' messages awaiting transmission. So, for Cottam and Bride to suspend their other activities in order to satisfy the needs of the press – if that were even possible – would have required them to defy Rostron's orders, international wireless protocol and the dictates of their own consciences.[36]

Rostron and Cottam could also be forgiven for thinking that they had satisfied their obligations to the press. Upon completing the rescue, Rostron dispatched the essential details to the Associated Press as quickly as possible. Cottam also 'informed the *Baltic* of the whole catastrophe' at mid-morning on Monday and sent *Olympic* his own 122-word informal summary of events and Rostron's official messages about the disaster that afternoon. These became the basis of *Olympic*'s 4.35pm Monday telegram informing White Star and the world of *Titanic*'s demise. With the essential information sent ashore, Cottam, and later Bride devoted the rest of the voyage to handling ship's traffic and survivors' messages, as per Rostron's orders.[37]

Of all of the messages, back and forth, sent and unsent, one especially rankled the American press. Relayed by *Chester* to *Carpathia* on Wednesday night, this signal asked on President Taft's behalf about the survival of, among others, his friend and military aide, Major Archibald Butt. To this Cottam made no reply at all, which set some American newspapers to buzzing about an insult to the president. 'Carpathia Refuses Information Even to President Taft,' announced *The Boston Globe* the next morning.[38]

Cunard officials immediately assured the public that *Carpathia* had intended no disrespect to or neglect of the president. Cottam later stated that he had missed the significance of the message because it was sent over the name of *Chester*'s captain, Benton Decker, not that of President Taft. Thus it became simply one more among the mountain of messages to be answered when time permitted. Upon arriving at New York on Thursday evening, Rostron said that Cottam 'never reported such a message to me'. The next day, however, he remembered a signal from *Chester* with 'something in it about the President … being anxious about the passengers, if [I] remember right'. But the telegram's importance did not register with Rostron either because he 'was rather worried at the time, as it was foggy and these messages came up to me on the bridge. I had my hands full.' And Rostron admitted that he, too, was extremely fatigued, telling a reporter upon tying up: 'I have had virtually no sleep in the last four days.'[39]

Rostron, exhausted, isolated on the bridge and immersed in *Carpathia's* problems, and even Cottam and Bride, overwhelmed in the wireless cabin, simply failed to comprehend that the *Titanic* disaster was not just a shipwreck, it was *the* shipwreck – 'a catastrophe of unparalleled magnitude, even in the catastrophic annals of the sea,' as *The Times*, normally understated, expressed it. That point was driven home emphatically when *Carpathia* loomed out of the haze near Sandy Hook at 6.10pm on Thursday evening, 19 April. She was greeted by a flotilla of more than fifty tugs, launches, yachts and other small craft, many bearing newsmen and photographers, waiting to escort her up the harbour to her Hudson River pier.[40]

The New York press would gain no more satisfaction from *Carpathia* or Rostron close aboard than it had in the days leading the ship to the Lower Bay. Charles Sumner, Cunard's New York general manager, had wired Rostron: 'If any vessel attempts [to] put newspaper men aboard claiming [to] have authority from me, it is false.' In the same cable he instructed Rostron 'to proceed [to dock] with all dispatch consistent with safety,' and informed him of the US Government's suspension of customs and immigration rules to hasten *Carpathia's* arrival. Sumner also did what he could to limit reporters and forbid photographers on the pier where *Carpathia* would tie up.[41]

It was left to Rostron to decide whether to allow reporters aboard his ship. He had been receiving wireless requests from newspapers asking permission to board the ship at Sandy Hook, but he decided that he did not want survivors confronted by reporters on his ship. Rostron therefore ordered that no one but the pilot would board *Carpathia* at the mouth of the harbour. Second Officer Bisset recalled that when reporters in the small boats crowding around *Carpathia* learned of the prohibition, 'pandemonium broke out'. Boats came alongside, with some reporters shouting questions, some waiving money to bribe their way aboard or get stories from those lining *Carpathia's* rails and others trying to scramble aboard the liner. *Carpathia's* crew stood to to repel boarders. Five reporters came alongside on the pilot boat, intending to follow the pilot up the ladder. They were only persuaded to remain aboard the pilot boat by the fists of Third Officer Eric Rees, the officer in charge of the pilot ladder, who climbed down to the deck of the pilot boat to defend it. He restored order long enough to permit the pilot to board, Rees to follow and the ladder to be drawn up immediately behind him. *Carpathia* then stood up Ambrose Channel to the sound of the reporters on the pilot boat, in Bisset's words, 'putting on a remarkable exhibition of profanity'.[42]

Carpathia reached quarantine off Staten Island at 7.35pm. The usual procedures waived, she merely slowed to pick up health officers before continuing into the Upper Bay. Rostron's ship was headed for a reception that dwarfed the demonstration at Ambrose Light. 'The interest in the arrival of the Carpathia is intense,' reported *The Times*' New York correspondent. 'Never, perhaps, in its history has the city been so terribly impressed. The gloom is heightened by the rain.'[43]

A thunderstorm had broken over New York Harbor, adding its own booming clatter to the human cacophony attending *Carpathia*'s advance up the bay. The *New York American* reported that men in the boats crowding around *Carpathia* 'used megaphones or yelled insanely up at her silent throng in frantic efforts to get some first word'. Gladys Cherry described *Carpathia* as 'having a dreadful time coming up the river, with all the newspaper tugs that wanted to put Pressmen on board but of course our Captain would allow no one to board us but the Pilot'. To the tumult of the storm and the bedlam of enquiries, news photographers added their exploding flashes – 'magnesium bombs,' Beesley called them – to capture images of *Carpathia*'s night-time arrival.[44]

At about 7.50pm *Carpathia* passed the Statue of Liberty and met a tug chartered by Cunard to assist the liner into her berth. With the tug came instructions from Captain Roberts, Cunard's marine superintendent in New York, that *Carpathia* was to proceed first to White Star's piers, about a half mile farther up the river than her own, to discharge *Titanic*'s lifeboats. *Carpathia* passed the Battery at the southern end of Manhattan Island at about 8.10pm. A silent crowd *The New York Times* estimated at ten thousand people watched her steam into the Hudson River. Half an hour later, at 8.40pm, *Carpathia* arrived off of White Star's Twenty-first Street pier and began lowering *Titanic*'s thirteen recovered lifeboats. That solemn duty discharged, Rostron swung *Carpathia* about in the river with what one reporter described as 'nerve-destroying leisure', and stood her down toward Cunard's Fourteenth Street pier.[45]

After consulting with White Star officials, Roberts had decided to land *Titanic*'s survivors at *Carpathia*'s regular pier. Beyond the problems of excluding press photographers and limiting reporters, as Cunard's general manager directed, the company was besieged by requests for passes from relatives and friends of survivors. With the city braced for anything in the absence of news, the pier also had to accommodate doctors, nurses, 'scores of white-clad hospital attendants with stretchers', representatives of the coroner's office, at least a hundred customs officials, members of the Salvation Army, a committee from the New York Stock Exchange which brought $20,000 to the pier to distribute to the needy, and members of the city's recently organized *Titanic* relief committee. 'Thousands Gather at the Pier', *The New York Times* reported. Roberts stationed more than 150 Cunard and White Star employees about the pier, while on the streets outside the city deployed over 200 mounted and foot police to keep order in anticipation of 'turbulent scenes'.[46]

Events quickly justified these precautions. A crowd of two thousand massed on Manhattan's Pier 54 itself, while on the adjacent streets the police struggled to control a crowd variously estimated at ten to thirty thousand that jammed Thirteenth, Fourteenth and Fifteenth streets for two blocks back from the waterfront to Ninth Avenue. 'Frequently the crowd tried to break the police lines and were driven back by the policemen with their nightsticks.'[47]

By 9.30pm Rostron had manoeuvred *Carpathia* into the north side of Pier 54; the first gangway went down at 9.35pm and she was all fast two minutes later. Most of *Carpathia*'s passengers and *Titanic*'s crew remained aboard the rescue ship, but *Titanic*'s rescued passengers began to disembark almost immediately. Cunard had directed the more than five hundred relatives of survivors admitted to the pier to stand behind the customs letters corresponding to the last names of the survivors they had come to meet. Cunard and White Star employees placed portable fencing around each gangway, formed cordons to hold back the crowd and directed each survivor to the proper letter. Steerage survivors not being met were registered by customs officials as quickly as possible and assisted by relief volunteers.[48]

Once more, initially at least, 'a solemn silence marked the assemblage of the throng'. That decorum dissolved, however, as the survivors came ashore.

The New York Times characterized the crowd's reaction to the first survivors as 'a low wailing sound … wild and weird, [that] grew steadily louder'. Soon 'there was no cessation of the wailing cries'. Gladys Cherry believed that sensational news reports had 'quite unstrung [hundreds] of men who were meeting people [and] some of the women went quite out of their heads and shrieked'. *The Times* reported that 'many of those present were weeping'.[49]

As the survivors dispersed many had their first encounter with journalists, who conducted interviews on the pier. Lawrence Beesley was uninspired by the experience, writing that 'the first questions the excited crowds of reporters asked as they crowded round were whether it was true that officers shot passengers and then themselves; whether passengers shot each other; whether any scenes of horror had been noticed and what they were'. But having reached New York, Rostron could no longer shield *Titanic*'s survivors from international scrutiny.[50]

And despite his best efforts to keep the press at bay, two reporters had been aboard Rostron's ship before she docked. One was there legitimately. *Carpathia*'s passenger Carlos Hurd was also a reporter for the *New York World*. He gathered stories during the rescue ship's return to New York which he assembled into a bundle that he managed to drop onto the deck of a tug chartered by the *World*. By the time *Carpathia* tied up, Hurd's stories were being typeset for his newspaper's final extra of the evening.[51]

The second reporter was an uninvited interloper who managed to gain *Carpathia*'s deck before being apprehended and taken to the bridge. Second Officer Bisset had been detailed to help lower *Titanic*'s lifeboats off White Star's piers, but when he returned to his normal harbour station on the bridge he found the man standing next to Rostron. Busy manoeuvring *Carpathia* toward her berth, Rostron told Bisset that the reporter was aboard without permission, ordered Bisset to make sure that the reporter did not leave the bridge and instructed Bisset to present him to Cunard's marine superintendent for disposition once *Carpathia* docked.[52]

'I sized him up,' wrote Bisset. 'He was twice as big as me and I wondered what would happen if he decided to leave the bridge to get more stories.' The journalist, however, was perfectly happy to remain on *Carpathia*'s bridge as she docked – an exclusive story indeed. Once docked, Bisset managed to find Captain Roberts at the gangway, but before Bisset could hand him over the reporter 'charged down the gangway like a bull moose' and disappeared into the throng waiting on the pier. It was good riddance, in Roberts' opinion, as Cunard and *Carpathia* had many more urgent matters to address than the case of a trespassing newsman.[53]

Bisset later identified his giant journalist as being from the *Globe*, but he actually worked for the *New York American* and exacted some revenge for his handling through an anonymous article that appeared in that paper the next day. In it the reporter said that he boarded *Carpathia* from a tug off Lower Manhattan. In his more cosmetic account of his apprehension, 'a number of the crew were at hand to impede his way, but the reporter finally reached the bridge,' there to accost Rostron righteously about the 'news suppression'.[54]

The article portrayed Rostron – usually spelled 'Rostrom' – as uncooperative, defensive and petulant. In the piece Rostron threatened to put the *American*'s reporter in irons, dodged any responsibility for *Carpathia* not transmitting news and refused to let the reporter see or interview any of *Titanic*'s survivors. The article contained an extended dialogue unlikely to have occurred between a journalist and a captain in the midst of manoeuvring an ocean liner in the Hudson River and described Rostron as 'suffering from a great load of anxiety'. The reporter suggested that this anxiety stemmed from Rostron's being 'conscious of the fact that he had subordinated his position, advisedly or otherwise, to more powerful influences and had realized the error of having remained mute up to this time'. The melodrama ended with Bisset escorting the reporter to meet Roberts at the second-class gangway, allowing the journalist to conclude the article with an exchange with Roberts that portrayed the *American* as the courageous defender of the public interest.[55]

Before resuming *Carpathia*'s interrupted Mediterranean voyage the following afternoon, Rostron produced a report on the rescue for Cunard which he also released to the newspapers, declaring it to be his first and only statement to the press. But Rostron forgave the *American*'s reporter his trespasses, shipboard and literary, writing years later that 'he made a jump that risked his life and landed on the deck. This was reported to me and I had him brought to the bridge. I explained my reasons for not having anyone on board and that I could not allow the passengers to be interviewed. I put him on his honour not to leave the bridge under certain penalties and, I must say, he was a gentleman. After we had docked and the passengers had left I know he made a good story out of his exploit, being the only man to get aboard and I believe he got complimented – which, after all, he deserved for his temerity.' Rostron could afford to be generous; that reporter's article was the only bad press that he would ever receive.[56]

CHAPTER 9

HE DID THE VERY BEST
THAT COULD BE DONE

'As they landed,' Rostron wrote months later of *Titanic*'s survivors, 'we all felt such a relief as only those experience who have for days been under a great strain – keyed up to the highest pitch of anxiety all the time. With such anxiety for the safety of so many people placed in my care under such heart-rending and tragic circumstances, on their landing I was thankful.' In some ways, however, *Carpathia*'s arrival in New York was the beginning rather than the end of the matter. As the survivors dispersed into the crowd gathered on the pier to receive them, others boarded the ship. Guglielmo Marconi arrived to talk to his operators. The International Mercantile Marine's vice president and general manager, Philip Franklin, came aboard to consult with the consortium's president, Bruce Ismay. Various Cunard officials crossed the gangway, as did newspaper reporters chasing stories 'until after midnight'. Two US senators also appeared, seeking facts about *Titanic*'s demise.[1]

On Wednesday, 17 April, with *Carpathia* still five hundred miles out at sea, the United States Senate unanimously authorized the creation of an *ad hoc* subcommittee of its Committee on Commerce to investigate the disaster. The subcommittee was empowered to summon witnesses and gather evidence and was charged with investigating the cause of the wreck, to the end of either writing legislation or reaching an international agreement on regulating safety at sea. The Committee on Commerce met the following day, appointed seven senators to the *ad hoc* committee and named Michigan's William Alden Smith its chairman.[2]

Smith, the author of the original Senate resolution establishing the investigation, immediately named his own subcommittee of three senators – himself, Francis Newlands of Nevada and Jonathan Bourne of Oregon – to travel to New York that evening to meet *Carpathia*. Smith intended to summon witnesses before they departed from the rescue ship and he brought the Senate's sergeant-at-arms with him to serve subpoenas to compel their testimony. He was particularly interested in examining White Star Chairman and IMM President J. Bruce Ismay. Smith had learned from the navy of wireless messages it had intercepted from *Carpathia* indicating that Ismay intended to return to England immediately, perhaps to avoid answering such questions.[3]

When Smith and Newlands arrived at New York's Penn Station at 9pm on Thursday night, they were informed that *Carpathia* was at her pier. Intent upon securing the testimony of every important witness, the senators immediately hired cabs and 'upon arriving at the pier … served subpoenas right and left'. Rostron was among those served. The senators also met with Ismay and Franklin aboard the ship for about half an hour, found them forthright and cooperative and announced that the hearings would commence at the Waldorf-Astoria Hotel at 10am the following morning.[4]

Thus began for White Star, its officials and its employees what *Titanic's* senior survivor Charles Lightoller described as 'that never to be forgotten ordeal carried out in Washington[,] repeated again in England and finally concluded in the Law Courts'. He was most critical of the US Senate's enquiry, declaring it years later 'a colossal piece of impertinence that served no useful purpose,' thanks to its lack of coordination and its 'abysmal ignorance of the sea'. Lightoller believed that 'with all the goodwill in the world, the "Enquiry" could be called nothing but a complete farce'.[5]

Conducted by politicians rather than maritime authorities, the American enquiry sometimes wandered into side issues, but despite Lightoller's unsparing criticism, the Senate's investigation had several advantages over those that followed it. One was immediacy. Smith began taking testimony at the Waldorf-Astoria within thirteen hours after *Carpathia* tied up. Another was the testimony of a range of indiviuals, eighty-two in all – survivors and witnesses, White Star employees and passengers of various classes, British and other nationalities – unavailable to or unsolicited by the British Board of Trade's subsequent investigation.[6]

Captain Arthur Rostron was the second witness examined by the senators, his testimony almost entirely overshadowed by that of the first, J. Bruce Ismay. Attacks upon Ismay's conduct and that of his company had begun before *Carpathia* landed, so his demeanour and testimony were closely scrutinized by the American press. *The New York Times* reported that Ismay had 'been subjected to a great deal of criticism … of a sort calculated to completely unnerve a sensitive man,' but found him 'cool and debonair' when taking the stand to answer questions about his business and his behaviour. *The Boston Globe*, in contrast, characterized Ismay as 'visibly nervous' as he prepared to testify.[7]

Rostron testified on Friday, 19 April, while his crew took on coal and provisioned *Carpathia* to resume her interrupted voyage. No questions of conduct surrounded his behaviour. Praised by Senator Smith for his performance and thanked for his appearance before the committee, Rostron first answered the committee's questions about his career to date and the particulars of his service in *Carpathia* up to the moment of receiving *Titanic*'s distress message. Asked about his actions after receiving the news, Rostron presented to the committee a typewritten copy of the list of orders that he had issued concerning the rescue and then recounted *Carpathia*'s run to the scene of the tragedy and return to New York. 'Captain Rostron was asked many questions,' *The New York Times* reported the following day, 'but he knew how to tell the story and he told it in his own way.'[8]

Senator Smith questioned Rostron closely about *Carpathia*'s communications difficulties. Smith and Rostron discussed the capabilities of *Carpathia*'s wireless equipment at some length and Smith asked Rostron directly: 'Was there any attempt made by anyone to influence you in sending or receiving wireless messages?' Rostron responded:

From the very commencement I took charge of the whole thing
and issued orders that every message sent would be sent under my
authority and no message was to be sent unless authorized by me.
My orders were: First of all, the two official messages … to the Cunard
Co. and the White Star Co., as regards the accident, telling them
that I had got an approximate number of passengers aboard and was
returning to New York... After those two messages were sent, I sent a

press message to the Associated Press, practically in the same words…
After these messages were sent, we began sending in the names of the
first-class passengers. This was by the *Olympic* on Monday evening.
We got the first, and I think all the second [class passengers' names]
off by the *Olympic*. Then we lost touch.[9]

The one time that Rostron did deny responsibility was when questioned
about the telegram from the White House asking after Major Butt. When
Rostron said he had no knowledge of 'the attempt of the President of the
United States to communicate directly with your ship,' Smith continued:
'I gather that there was no intention whatever of either ignoring his message –'

'My word, I hope not, sir,' Rostron interrupted.

'Or neglecting it?' Smith added.

'Absolutely no intention of any such thing, sir,' Rostron reaffirmed.

Smith then asked again if anyone had attempted in any way to censor
Carpathia's wireless traffic, at which Rostron reassumed the mantle of
responsibility. 'Absolutely no censorship whatever,' he replied, meaning
censorship by any higher authority. 'I controlled the whole thing, through
my orders. I said I placed official messages first. After they had gone and
the first press message, then the names of the passengers. After the names
of the passengers and crew had been sent, my orders were to send all private
messages from the *Titanic's* passengers first, in the order in which they were
given in to the purser; no preference to any message.'[10]

Those points clarified, Rostron's testimony was otherwise that of a
friendly witness. After covering *Carpathia's* background and her activities
during the rescue, Smith and Newlands questioned Rostron about standard
practices at sea, including a captain's authority and international steaming
routes. When questioned about lifeboat capacities, even the normally astute
Rostron missed the lesson of the *Titanic* disaster. Asked by Smith why
the Board of Trade required *Carpathia* and *Titanic* each to carry twenty
lifeboats, though the latter was more than three times the size of the former,
Rostron replied that 'what it has to do with is the ship itself. The ships
are built nowadays to be practically unsinkable and each ship is supposed
to be a lifeboat in itself. The boats are merely supposed to be put on as a
standby. The ships are supposed to be built and the naval architects say they

are, [to be] unsinkable under certain conditions.' When Senator Newlands observed that 'that expectation was not realized in the case of this ship', Rostron could only offer: 'It has been an abnormal experience as regards the *Titanic*.'[11]

When questioned directly by the senators about the specifics of *Titanic* and her operation, however, Rostron avoided answering through the simple and honest expedient of professing ignorance of the ship, the collision, or the operating practices of Captain Smith or the White Star Line. Asked by Newlands how many additional lifeboats he thought *Titanic* could carry, Rostron replied: 'I have not the faintest idea, sir, what the *Titanic* was like. I believe she is a sister ship of the *Olympic*. I have seen the *Olympic* once, when she was at the end of our dock. I have no idea of her construction.' When Smith asked Rostron if he had 'any kind of knowledge at all' about the force of *Titanic*'s collision with the iceberg, Rostron replied: 'I know nothing about it, sir. I have not asked any questions about this kind of business. I knew it was not my affair and I had little desire to make any of [*Titanic*'s] officers feel it any more than they did… From the officers I know nothing. I could give you silly rumours of passengers, but I know they are not reliable, from my own experience; so, if you will excuse me, I would prefer to say nothing.' With that, Rostron concluded his testimony before Smith and Newlands at 1.20pm on Friday afternoon, 19 April, and cast off *Carpathia* for the Mediterranean two hours and forty minutes later.[12]

Rostron, who testified on the first day of the American investigation, appeared on the last day that the British enquiry into the disaster took evidence. He was temporarily relieved of *Carpathia*'s command at Naples on 18 June, during her second circuit of the Mediterranean after the rescue, so that he could return to London to testify. Although Britons besides Lightoller thought the American investigation both an impertinence and a farce – five days into the proceedings *The Times* opined that 'the American enquiry, if continued upon present lines, may be interminable and that its futility may be nearly as great as its length' – that did not prevent British officials from seeing the need for their own examination.[13]

On Monday, 22 April, the government announced that John Charles Bigham, Baron Mersey of Toxteth, would preside as wreck commissioner for an enquiry by the Board of Trade, a decision 'received with great approval' in the Commons. Mersey was a seventy-one-year-old Liverpool native and successful barrister and judge, much experienced in commercial and maritime litigation. Called to the Bar in 1870, he was created a Queen's Counsel in 1883, appointed to the Bench in 1897 and was a former president of the Probate, Divorce and Admiralty Division of the High Court.[14]

Lord Mersey's enquiry commenced on 2 May, at Scottish Hall, Buckingham Gate, Westminster, London. It ultimately examined ninety-seven witnesses at thirty-seven public sessions lasting through the third week in June. Mersey was assisted by five assessors – experts in naval architecture, engineering, and navigation – several of whom had long experience of maritime enquiries. Sir Rufus Isaacs, the Attorney General, served as lead counsel for the Board of Trade and the principal examiner of witnesses.[15]

If the British enquiry had greater expertise among its officials than the American, it had a similar advantage among its witnesses. The wreck commission not only drew testimony from survivors, but also examined British sea captains, shipping company officials and officials of *Titanic*'s builder, Harland and Wolff. Although some British newspapers might have been reluctant to admit it, the British enquiry also had the benefit of the American enquiry that preceded it. Mersey and counsel at the Board of Trade's investigation repeatedly referred to testimony given at the US hearings, using it to focus or extend their own queries.

The Board of Trade's examination operated within the limitations both of vested national interests to consider and of conflicts of interest in the enquiry itself. Chief among the latter was a Board of Trade wreck commission sitting in judgment of the efficacy of the Board of Trade's safety regulations – the Board of Trade appearing 'as both defendant and plaintiff', as one British journalist expressed it. 'Hence the whitewash brush', in Lightoller's opinion.[16]

Rostron arrived in London on the evening of 20 June – his first appearance in England since early February – and testified at Scottish Hall the following morning. First things first, however; a few questions into the examination, Isaacs stopped to tell Rostron 'on behalf of His Majesty's Government how deeply grateful we are to you for your conduct and for the great number of lives which you were instrumental in saving'. Sir Robert Finlay, representing White Star, concurred, as did Lord Mersey on behalf of his fellow commissioners and 'these remarks were heartily endorsed by the applause of those in court'.[17]

With these pleasantries concluded, Isaacs took Rostron through his account of the disaster, from *Carpathia* receiving the initial distress call through her recovery of *Titanic*'s boats. Lord Mersey and the several counsellors examining Rostron did not ask him a single question about *Carpathia*'s communications difficulties and only two about *Carpathia*'s return to New York, but did examine him closely about icebergs and his practices in the vicinity of ice. The enquiry wished to know what icebergs looked like at night and the best ways to sight them, as well as how many lookouts Rostron posted and where about his ship, and who among the watch keepers was most qualified and likely to spot an iceberg. In effect, Mersey and his associates had Rostron testify as an expert witness as to practices *Titanic* should have employed, without questioning him directly about *Titanic*.[18]

The one point over which Rostron's answers elicited some surprise came toward the end of his testimony and concerned the matter of speed in proximity to ice. Asked what precautions he would take in regions with icebergs or ice fields, Rostron replied that 'a great deal would depend on the weather and the atmospheric conditions'.

Mersey stipulated *Titanic*'s situation: 'Suppose it is perfectly clear?'

Rostron answered that 'if it is a perfectly clear night and I was sure of my position and everything else, unless I knew there was a lot of ice about, I should feel perfectly justified in going full speed'.

Isaacs led Rostron to agree that if there were much ice about, he would not do this, but Rostron reaffirmed that 'for one or two bergs I should feel perfectly justified in going full speed'. Mersey then suggested that this was a matter for the captain's judgment, to which Rostron replied: 'Absolutely.' When he finished testifying, Rostron received Mersey's thanks and shook hands with Isaacs and Finlay. Rostron would remain in England for another six weeks, enjoying honours, home and family, before rejoining *Carpathia* at Fiume on 7 August.[19]

By then both the British and American enquiries had issued their reports. On 28 May, Senator Smith addressed the Senate on the findings of his committee. In that florid rhetoric common to Edwardians and United States senators, Smith compared Rostron's performance with Captain Lord's. After condemning Lord for *Californian*'s drowsier approach to seafaring, Smith continued:

> Contrast, if you will, the conduct of the captain of the *Carpathia*
> in this emergency... By his utter self-effacement and his own
> indifference to peril, by his promptness and his knightly sympathy,
> he rendered a great service to humanity. He should be made to realize
> the debt of gratitude this Nation owes to him, while the book of good
> deeds, which had so often been familiar with his unaffected valor,
> should henceforth carry the name of Capt. Rostron to the remotest
> period of time... It falls to the lot of few men to perform a service so
> unselfish and the American Congress can honor itself no more by any
> single act than by writing into its laws the gratitude we feel toward
> this modest and kindly man.[20]

The committee's official findings, though less effusive than Smith's speech, were just as complimentary. After reviewing Rostron's actions, the final report reprinted his flurry of orders, 'which the committee deem[ed] of sufficient importance to quote in full'. Having done so, *'Titanic' Disaster: Report of the Committee on Commerce, United States Senate* said of *Titanic*'s rescuer:

> The committee deems the course followed by Captain Rostron of the
> *Carpathia* as deserving of the highest praise and worthy of especial
> recognition. Captain Rostron fully realized all the risks involved. He
> doubled his lookouts, doubled his fireroom force and notwithstanding
> such risk, pushed his ship at her very highest limit of speed through
> the many dangers of the night to the relief of the stricken vessel. His
> detailed instructions issued in anticipation of the rescue of the *Titanic*
> are a marvel of systematic preparation and completeness, evincing
> such solicitude as calls for the highest commendation.[21]

The committee's praise of *Carpathia*'s captain did not extend to her wireless operators. Smith became convinced that the absence of information from *Carpathia* in the days after the disaster indicated a conspiracy between the Marconi company and *The New York Times* to monopolize news of the disaster.

In reality, such thoughts of conspiracy suggest a degree of organization that did not exist either afloat or ashore. Captain Herbert Haddock of *Olympic* had a better sense of it. When Senator Smith absolved him of responsibility for the communication delays, blaming instead 'those who failed to give you the information', Haddock replied: 'I do not think that anybody failed to give us the information. The *Carpathia* had at that time a terrible job on her hands.'[22]

The committee could not accept the straightforward explanations offered by Haddock and Rostron, but it relieved Rostron of responsibility through the expedient of blaming the 'information withheld' on *Carpathia's* preposterously overworked and under-slept wireless operators, Harold Cottam and Harold Bride. The committee concluded that Cottam did not show 'proper vigilance in handling the important work confided to his care after the accident'. The report went on to suggest obliquely that Jack Binns' example may have caused Cottam and Bride to withhold information in the hope of profiting thereby and that the Marconi Company and Mr Marconi himself at least acquiesced in the practice, which the committee concluded should be prohibited.[23]

With Rostron thus exonerated, the committee's call 'for the highest commendation' of his actions took the form of a congressional joint resolution introduced to the Senate by Smith at the conclusion of his remarks, passed without dissent by that body on the same day, 28 May, and by the US House of Representatives a week later. The resolution extended the Thanks of Congress to Rostron and through him to *Carpathia's* officers and crew, for 'heroically saving the lives' of *Titanic's* 705 survivors. As a token of its gratitude, Congress authorized President Taft to present to Rostron 'a suitable gold medal, appropriately inscribed, which shall express the high estimation in which Congress holds the service of this officer,' and appropriated a thousand dollars to create the medal. With its thanks, Congress also granted Rostron the rare privilege of entering the chambers of the House and Senate, which he did during a visit to Washington in December of 1912. Rostron was escorted around the floor of the Senate by Smith and 'received with great enthusiasm'.[24]

Across the Atlantic, Mersey's report – dated 30 July and concurred in by the commission's five assessors – found that the collision that doomed *Titanic* was 'brought about by the excessive speed at which the ship was being navigated'.

In the face of testimony by several ship captains, including Rostron, that they maintained full speed in clear weather in the vicinity of ice, Mersey declined to rule *Titanic* lost due to negligence. Rather, the report found the error in common practice. It therefore declared that this loss was not negligent, but that the next would be. The report summarized *Carpathia*'s involvement in one paragraph. Not inclined to Smith's grandiloquence, Mersey concluded simply: 'The Court desires to record its great admiration of Captain Rostron's conduct. He did the very best that could be done.'[25]

CHAPTER 10

WE HAVE A HERO
HERE TONIGHT

Many people on both sides of the Atlantic shared Lord Mersey's admiration for Rostron, but the *Titanic* disaster haunted a number of the other individuals involved ever after. On landing in New York, White Star's chairman Bruce Ismay found himself denounced as a coward and a criminal on the floor of the US Senate and scalded by the American press. His treatment did not improve much when he returned home. Horatio Bottomley, MP and owner of the weekly paper *John Bull*, assailed Ismay as 'primarily responsible for the scandalous condition of affairs which the *Titanic* disaster has revealed,' and one of Ismay's inquisitors at the British enquiry said in his presence, in essence, that he did not deserve his own life.[1]

Ismay's reputation never recovered. The *St Louis Post Dispatch* editorialized with some sympathy a week after the disaster: 'Until we forget that such a person as J. Bruce Ismay ever lived, there are probably at least 50,000,000 readers … in this country, Canada and Great Britain whom no evidence hereafter will convince that he would not be much more respectable if dead… He has become the scapegoat against whom public sympathies, excited by a great tragedy, focus in reproach… Poor Fellow. He needs to be allowed to get out of sight as soon as possible and get his nervous system as nearly back to its normal stage as it can ever be hereafter' – which is essentially what happened.

Although absolved of misconduct in Lord Mersey's report, Ismay resigned as president of IMM in 1913, which he had intended to do before the disaster, and as chairman of White Star, which he had not. He spent his last twenty-four years, if not a recluse, certainly withdrawn from public life.[2]

Titanic's four surviving navigating officers saw their careers stalled because of their association with the tragedy. Second Officer Charles Lightoller bore no responsibility for the sinking, did his duty effectively during it and then took his chances in the frigid ocean. As senior survivor, he resolutely defended his captain and company at the two enquiries, particularly that of the Board of Trade. Nonetheless, Lightoller never achieved command of a White Star ship, nor did any of the *Titanic*'s junior officers.[3]

Captain Stanley Lord of the *Californian*, condemned by both the American and British enquiries, carried the stigma of that night for the rest of his life. Unlike Ismay, however, Lord has had his defenders, who believe he absorbed wrath that should instead have been directed at the *Titanic*'s Captain Smith. But the lethargy of the *Californian*'s watch officer and captain in the presence of 'rockets or shells, throwing stars of any colour or description, fired one at a time at short intervals,' the international signal for distress at night, was indefensible. Lord lost his command of *Californian* and his employment with the Leyland Line; he spent his remaining fifteen years at sea commanding nitrate freighters loading on the west coast of South America.[4]

Of all of those associated with the disaster professionally, one reputation was enhanced and another made. The reputation enhanced was Guglielmo Marconi's. Although he faced some pointed questions about his company's operations at the Senate enquiry, the public would not have it. If the *Titanic*'s sinking had cost 1500 lives, Marconi's invention had played a crucial role in saving more than seven hundred. At his first public appearance following the sinking, a speech to the New York Electrical Society, the audience cheered Marconi for at least two minutes at his introduction, cheered him again following the reading of a congratulatory telegram from Thomas Edison, and his 'every reference to the adaptability of wireless to rescues on the high seas brought forth [more] applause'.[5]

The reputation made, of course, was Rostron's. He emerged the undisputed hero of the tragedy in an age that took its heroism seriously. The first suggestion of his new role as '*Titanic* Hero' came when *Carpathia* cast off to resume her Mediterranean voyage at 4pm on Friday afternoon, 19 April. In the nineteen hours *Carpathia* had been tied up at New York, Rostron got some sleep, testified at the Senate's enquiry, met with Cunard officials, wrote a report on the rescue for his company which he also issued to the press and received a loving cup presented by a survivors' committee chaired by Samuel Goldenberg. Meanwhile, his ship had taken on coal and had received fresh laundry. As *Carpathia* backed into the Hudson, people standing on the pier cheered. Rostron tipped his cap in acknowledgement, but he could not have realized that this demonstration was only the beginning. *Carpathia's* seven-week loop through the Mediterranean became something of a victory lap for the ship, her crew and her captain.[6]

During her stops at Gibraltar, Naples, Trieste, Fiume, Messina and Palermo, *Carpathia* was visited by more than 100,000 people, all curious to see the suddenly famous rescue ship. She was greeted at Naples, on 2 May, by a flotilla of ninety sailing vessels and six days later, at Fiume, the mayor and a representative of the president of Hungary welcomed Rostron. 'At each port of call on our run to the Mediterranean and Adriatic,' Bisset wrote, 'Captain Rostron was feted and hailed as the hero of the Titanic disaster.' After calling at Gibraltar westbound on the evening of 18 May, *Carpathia* steamed for America with 1531 passengers.[7]

She arrived in New York Harbor shortly after midnight on Wednesday morning, 29 May. If Rostron had not yet comprehended the magnitude of his new celebrity, this second return to New York, which lasted until the afternoon of 4 June, made it clear. Awaiting *Carpathia's* captain were a dozen sacks of mail that included thousands of letters and hundreds of parcels in Bisset's estimation. Rostron assigned to his second officer the job of sorting these by priority, a task that took Bisset several days. He found the parcels filled with gifts of 'all kinds of things which the Captain already had, or did not need: but all the letters and gifts had to be answered in common courtesy – a task which occupied the Captain's spare time (when he had any) for many weeks thereafter'.[8]

Carpathia hosted hundreds more visitors during her one-week layover in New York. 'Many of the rescued passengers,' recorded the *New York American*, 'applied for permission to board the steamer to thank Captain Rostron again for his bravery.' Rostron and his crew were celebrated afloat and at numerous engagements ashore. The first morning, after her Mediterranean passengers had departed, Rostron ordered all hands who had been involved in the rescue to muster in *Carpathia's* first-class dining saloon at 10.30am. There the *Titanic* survivors' committee also gathered – headed by the committee's secretary,

Frederick W. Seward, and including Karl Behr, Margaret Tobin Brown and several other survivors – to recognize and reward the Cunarder's sailors.[9]

The committee had ordered gold, silver and bronze medals to be created to honour *Carpathia*'s captain, officers and crew. These featured a bas-relief of *Carpathia* recovering *Titanic*'s lifeboats amid icebergs, with King Neptune arrayed above and dolphins and an anchor below. The reverse was inscribed: 'Presented to the Captain Officers & Crew of R.M.S. "Carpathia" in recognition of gallant & heroic services from the survivors of the SS "Titanic" April 15th, 1912'.[10]

Seward made a brief address, in which he 'spoke in glowing terms of the high regard all the survivors felt for Capt. Rostron ... and said that but for his heroism they might not be alive today'. He next pinned one of the gold medals on Rostron's chest and presented him with two framed resolutions of thanks to the entire crew from the *Titanic*'s male and female survivors. The committee also presented Rostron with a fifteen-inch silver loving cup on an ebony base and 'a purse of gold'. The cup was inscribed: 'Presented to Captain A. H. Rostron, RNR, commander of the R.M.S. Carpathia. In grateful recognition and appreciation of his heroism and efficient service in the rescue of the survivors of the Titanic on April 15, 1912 and of the generous and sympathetic treatment he accorded us on his ship. From Survivors of the Titanic.' The purse contained $4500 that had been pledged by first-class and second-class survivors before *Carpathia* reached New York. This money was distributed among the ship's officers and crew, with Rostron receiving $500.[11]

The *New York American* recorded that, in thanking the committee, Rostron said 'I tried to do my duty as a sailor ... [and] toward suffering humanity. But I will not take the credit for the achievement of that night, when we went to the aid of the people of the Titanic. I do not deserve that credit. My crew deserves it and to them I want to give my heartfelt thanks for their loyalty, valor and fidelity to the trust that was imposed.' He also offered his thanks on behalf of himself and his family and the newspaper reported 'both cheers and tears as Captain Rostron concluded'. Seward then thanked and presented medals to each member of the crew. As the ceremony concluded, Rostron, with the loving cup, posed with Mrs Brown for press photographers and also sat for several group photographs with his officers.[12]

If that ceremony were not enough to establish Rostron as the '*Titanic* Hero,' the following evening certainly did. Rostron, *Carpathia*'s first-class surgeon Frank McGee and three of the ship's junior officers went to see Al Jolson perform at the Winter Garden Theatre. During the performance, Jolson stopped the show, announced 'we have a hero here tonight,' and pointed out Rostron seated in one of the theatre's boxes. 'At the mention of the name of the Captain and the ship every person in the big audience stood up and cheered, shouting Captain Rostron's name and asking for a speech' quoted *The New York Times*. After the cheering subsided, the theatre's orchestra led the audience through choruses of 'The Star-Spangled Banner,' and 'God Save the King,' the latter sung by the two English members of the cast. That failed to quell the demand for a speech, however, so Rostron rose and thanked everyone for the honour shown to himself and *Carpathia*'s officers and crew. His remarks 'were applauded again and again'.[13]

The next day, 31 May, Rostron and McGee visited the widowed Madeleine Astor for a lunch at her Fifth Avenue mansion, her first social function of any kind since the disaster. Marian Thayer also attended and Rostron and McGee later accompanied her in a private railroad car to a dinner held that evening at her home near Philadelphia. The following day, 1 June, they attended another lunch, hosted by Eleanor Widener at her residence in Philadelphia. These three women had shared Rostron's cabin on *Carpathia*'s voyage to New York. Rostron and McGee returned to New York on the afternoon of 2 June, in part to attend a memorial benefit band concert commemorating *Titanic*'s musicians held at the Moulin Rouge Theater. Again a box at the theatre was reserved for Rostron and his officers, who were applauded once more upon entering.[14]

This round of honours for Rostron culminated at 11am the following morning, 3 June, when the editor of the *New York American*, John Temple Graves, presented him with a cheque for ten thousand dollars in yet another ceremony held before the ship's company aboard *Carpathia*. The money had been raised through a subscription drive launched by the *American* on 28 April. 'The Brave Captain Rostron Should Be Fitly Rewarded,' said the paper, lauding 'the good name and the great heart of Rostron, of the *Carpathia*' in its call for donations. 'It seems to the New York American,' the article continued, 'that some substantial recognition is due THE MAN WHOSE COURAGE

AND EFFICIENCY SAVED 705 LIVES [*sic*]… Let the fund for the captain of the Carpathia equal the gratitude which the name of Rostron arouses.'[15]

The *Titanic* survivors' committee was already raising a cash award, which it rendered to Rostron and his crew when *Carpathia* returned to New York on 29 May. The committee's secretary, Frederick Seward, told the *American* that the committee would cooperate with the newspaper, however, saying 'nothing is too good for that gallant sailor'. Seward told the *American* that the committee had continued to receive donations after *Carpathia* reached New York and would consider contributing something to the newspaper's sum. He asked those donating to the survivors' committee in the future to designate all or a portion of their contribution, should they wish, 'for the Rostron Purse Fund'.[16]

In the ensuing weeks the paper published the names of contributors to the Rostron fund. The largest donation, $2500, came from the widowed Eleanor Widener. 'No mere contribution can express the gratitude and admiration which Mrs. Widener feels for the kindness and consideration shown by Captain Rostron to the survivors of the Titanic,' said a telegram accompanying her donation. Several other *Titanic* survivors contributed amounts from five hundred dollars on down, the great New York impresarios Levi Schubert and George M. Cohan each contributed a thousand dollars and the *American*'s owner, William Randolph Hearst, added five hundred.[17]

In his presentation speech before the mustered ship's company, editor Graves briefly extolled the Cunard company and *Carpathia*'s crew. Then he turned his attention to the ship's master:

> Captain Rostron, you have done this country and your own a great
> and signal service and we know it. You have saved seven hundred
> human lives… You have written in epic axiom that the only thing
> upon the ocean that justifies the risk of human life is the duty of
> saving other human lives… You have made plain that real heroism
> rests not only in the single act, but in the sustained devotion to cause
> and deed… You have taught in better things than words, to make and
> direct heroes in the future tragedies of land and sea. For this reason
> your history should live that other men may read as they go out upon
> the ocean. Other Titanics may sail and sink. Other Carpathias may go

bravely out to rescue and to save. But the prompt courage with which they go and the wise and tender judgment they display will take lesson and inspiration from the Arthur Rostron way![18]

After his rhetorical onslaught, Graves handed Rostron the *American*'s 'practical memorial of ten thousand dollars'. Accepting the cheque from Graves, Rostron, as was his habit, complimented his subordinates: 'What we were able to accomplish was accomplished not through any special merit in me, but because I received from my entire crew a loyal support such as no other captain in the mercantile service has ever known. From the moment I gave the first order until we had the last survivor aboard not one member of the *Carpathia*'s crew ever waivered.' He thanked the newspaper for the reward, remarking that the money meant more than friendship to him, 'for it gives me a feeling of greater security for the future of my wife and children'. In an interview with the *American* the day before the ceremony, Rostron had observed that 'men in my business have neither time nor opportunity to accumulate wealth and generally we leave our families poor and not adequately equipped to carry on the struggle alone after we are gone'. He said that the money meant that he could afford to buy a home, send his three sons to college and secure his wife in her old age.[19]

A day after Rostron's reward ceremony, on sailing day, 4 June, the festivities concluded with the presentation of *Carpathia*'s final garland. Rostron was presented with 'Captain', a six-month-old black cat, on *Carpathia*'s bridge by two young women. They had attended the Winter Garden's show on the same night as *Carpathia*'s officers and had decided that the rescue ship needed a mascot. Rostron thanked the ladies, promised that Captain would have a berth in his cabin and posed with the cat for yet another press photograph. That final tribute rendered, *Carpathia* departed at 2pm, again to the enthusiastic cheers of those assembled, which Rostron once more acknowledged from the bridge.[20]

The accolades continued for most of another year. Rostron travelled to Washington, DC, in December 1912, visited both houses of Congress and called upon President Taft, who presented him with a letter of thanks. 'From associations and lifesaving societies in all parts of the United States and Great Britain tokens of appreciation of his skill and seamanship poured in,' *The*

New York Times recalled years later. Among these were a gold medal from the Lifesaving Benevolent Association of New York and another gold medal presented to Rostron by the Bolton Grammar School Old Boys' Association on 12 February 1913.[21]

Rostron had a final gold medal coming, the one authorized by Congress on behalf of the US Government and people, but that ceremony had to await the creation of the medal itself. This greatest of Rostron's American honours has often been misidentified, even by Rostron himself, as the US Congressional Medal of Honor – the highest commendation for valor against the enemy awarded to members of the US military – an award for which he was not eligible. What Congress approved to accompany the Thanks of Congress to Rostron and his crew was a Congressional Gold Medal, a civil award uniquely created for and presented to Rostron in his honour.[22]

In August 1912 President Taft invited selected artists to submit designs and Taft chose the winner. Rostron's medal was designed by New York sculptor John Flanagan and struck by the Medallic Art Company of Danbury, Connecticut. The medal featured Rostron's left profile, in uniform and cap. The use of Rostron's likeness required that he pose for a portrait, which he did when *Carpathia* arrived in America in December. He sat for several sessions in New York before sailing *Carpathia* to Boston, where the portrait was completed. The obverse was also crowded with the inscription: 'FOR THE HEROIC RESCUE OF THE SURVIVORS OF THE TITANIC LOST IN MID-ATLANTIC THE THANKS OF THE CONGRESS OF THE UNITED STATES TO ARTHUR HENRY ROSTRON'. The reverse bore the date 'APRIL XIV MCMXII' and an allegorical scene showing two men in a boat, one throwing a line to a man in the water. The medal, two and three-quarters inches in diameter and of twenty-four karat gold, weighed eight and a half ounces.[23]

As befitted the importance of the award, Cunard detached Rostron from his regular duties and he and Ethel departed Liverpool on 16 February 1913, as passengers aboard *Carmania*. They arrived in New York on Monday, 24 February and in Washington, DC, that Friday. The ceremony took place on Saturday, 1 March, in the East Room of the White House. In one of his final acts as president, William Howard Taft decorated Rostron, accompanied by Ethel and in the presence of Britain's ambassador to the

United States, James Bryce, *Titanic* survivor and widow Eloise Smith and other guests. Taft made brief remarks praising Rostron's courage, care and kindness. 'It was a record,' he said, 'worthy of the best traditions of England's seafarers.' Rostron, in turn, thanked the president, Congress and the American people.[24]

After the White House ceremony, the Rostrons visited the British Embassy, where Ambassador Bryce decorated Rostron with the American Cross of Honor and commended him for his bravery and gallantry. That medal, with blue ribbon, featured an American eagle atop a circular badge, with 'A C H' and '1906' appearing below. The American Cross of Honor Society presented this award annually 'to the person who has performed the most heroic act in the saving of life'. An unusual feature of this award was that the Society's members consisted exclusively of people who had themselves saved lives and been decorated for it by the US Government.[25]

'My wife and I had a royal time for a few days,' Rostron recalled. They returned to Liverpool aboard *Mauretania*, which left New York on 5 March. Eight weeks later, on 29 April 1913, at Liverpool, the Austro-Hungarian government tendered Rostron a final honour, a gold watch: 'In recognition of his services in rescuing certain Austro-Hungarian subjects on board the steamship "Titanic", on the occasion of the loss of that vessel, 15th April 1912.' The watch bore the royal coat of arms of Emperor Franz Joseph and contained the inscription inside.[26]

Britain's reaction to Rostron, while certainly positive, was more subdued than that of the rest of the Atlantic world. His most significant public recognition came from the Liverpool Shipwreck and Humane Society five days after he testified at the British enquiry. In a ceremony held at Town Hall on 26 June 1912, the Lord Mayor of Liverpool, Lord Derby, presented Rostron with the Society's gold medal and 'an illuminated and framed copy of the resolution of the Liverpool Shipwreck and Humane Society, expressing thanks, for "praiseworthy and humane service in rescuing 705 survivors" of the Titanic.' Ethel Rostron attended, as did, among others, Cunard's chairman, Alfred Booth, Lionel Fletcher representing White Star and seven members of the Mercantile Marine Service Association, which superintended HMS *Conway*. The Lord Mayor said that Rostron should understand the award to express not just the thanks of the Society and the city of Liverpool, but of the whole of the Empire, to 'you, your officers and ship's crew, for the magnificent work you did at that terrible disaster'.[27]

The Liverpool Echo reported that 'Captain Rostron, who was warmly received, said he felt deeply honoured at coming there and deeply gratified that the Lord Mayor should have mentioned the remainder of the ship's company.' Rostron then lauded *Carpathia*'s crew not only for the rescue itself, but for its conduct on the ship's return to New York and thanked the Lord Mayor for recognizing the crew's efforts. The ceremony concluded with Rostron calling for three cheers for the Lord Mayor, a salute rendered to Rostron in return.[28]

Rostron and his crew had received another kind of reward earlier in June, when the White Star Line announced that, with Cunard's permission, it had awarded one hundred guineas to Rostron, fifty guineas each to *Carpathia*'s Surgeon Frank McGee, Purser Ernest Brown and Chief Steward Evan Hughes and a month's pay to every other member of *Carpathia*'s crew. White Star also offered to pay all of the expenses Cunard had incurred in making the rescue. This Cunard officials declined, saying their company had been privileged to help. They also doubtless realized that those costs had been more than recouped in good publicity.[29]

That, however, would be the extent of direct British recognition of Rostron's role in the rescue. He did not receive Lloyd's Medal for Saving Life or any other recognition from the insurance company, nor was he officially recognized by the British government. In mid-June 1912, two weeks after Rostron's whirlwind layover in New York, the president of the Board of Trade was asked in the Commons if he were aware of the various honours Rostron had received in the US and whether he intended to propose anything 'to secure adequate recognition' of Rostron and his crew in Britain. He replied that while the board knew of the honours extended to Rostron and his crew and certainly appreciated their efforts, it was not the board's practice 'to grant rewards for services of this kind when rendered by one British ship and crew to another British ship and crew'. Rostron and his crew had done their duty and that was that.[30]

Except, for Rostron, that was never really that. Mention of the *Titanic* rescue was invariably appended to anything written about him throughout his life thereafter and he was dined and decorated for it for the remainder of his career. Society figures continued to invite Rostron to meals or holidays during his calls at New York and a number of his later honours made specific mention of the rescue. Presenting Rostron with his organization's silver medal in 1929, the president of the Cherbourg Chamber of Commerce declared that it signified, in part, 'the public recognition of those who have brought help to their fellow men in times of distress and danger. What greater proof of merit could there be than that which you gave on the fateful night of April 15, 1912, when the *Titanic* sank beneath the waves?'[31]

For his part, Rostron agreed with the Board of Trade's view of the circumstances. Upon landing *Titanic's* survivors in New York he told a reporter that 'I am not entitled to any more credit than would have been due any other man of the sea, had the opportunity for the service my ship rendered been afforded to others.' He also said 'that every member of the crew deserves just as much credit as is being given to me so generously by people everywhere... Every man of them appreciated as fully as I did what our duty was and every man of them did his duty without urging or repeated instructions.'[32]

Arthur Rostron never said publicly how he felt about 'Capt[ain] Rostron, of Undying Fame,' but some evidence suggests his initial discomfort with his celebrity. 'When I see my name in the headlines and my picture in the newspapers,' he said seven weeks after the disaster, 'I scarcely recognize either as belonging to me.' He found the outpourings of American enthusiasm for their newfound hero pleasant, but also unsettling. While gratified by his ovation at the Winter Garden Theatre, 'it was also rather embarrassing, he said, to a shipmaster to be suddenly thrust in the limelight before a large audience'. He wrote years later that 'only modesty, not lack of appreciation, forbids me enumerating details of the amazing cordiality of my reception when in company with my wife I was the recipient of many honours and guest at many celebrations following the rescue of the *Titanic*['s] passengers'. But whether or not Rostron desired his new role as '*Titanic* Hero' was beside the point to the press and public that had found in him an exemplar to redeem an otherwise forlorn story.[33]

'His face an Inspiration,' gushed the *New York American*, which declared that 'in appearance and manner he is reminiscent of the most heroic tales of the sea ever written,' and predicted that 'his exploits will take their place in history alongside of the finest narratives of modern heroism'. The same newspaper described Rostron as modest to the point of shrinking from the acclaim, saying that 'Captain Rostron is extremely shy in talking about himself. "Whatever you may write about me," he pleaded, "please be careful not to exaggerate anything."' Newspapers less melodramatic than the tabloid *American* joined the parade of praise for Rostron the Hero. He was often described as modest or as emotionally affected by events surrounding the rescue and its rewards. *The New York Times* reported that Rostron 'seemed overcome' by the remarks and applause accompanying the presentation of the medals and loving cup by the survivors' committee, while *The Boston Globe* portrayed him as 'in tears' and *The Washington Post* said that 'Rostron wept' while recounting *Carpathia*'s exploits at the Senate enquiry.[34]

In at least the *American*'s case, such flattery was partly self-serving. That paper could claim that its Rostron fund discredited the idea that its trampling of Bruce Ismay, Stanley Lord and the Board of Trade was simply anti-British venom. 'We would like you to carry back to your great country, Captain Rostron,' said editor Graves when presenting the *American*'s check, 'the message that if the American press and the American people have made sharp criticism of Englishmen who feared or failed to do their duty, they have given unstinted love and praise to a great Englishman who has done his duty'. Whether or not that alibi was legitimate, the American public's celebrations of Rostron, such as at the Winter Garden, were genuine and affectionate. These effusions also demonstrate that Rostron the *Titanic* Hero was not a British invention created to distract from the embarrassment the *Titanic* disaster had inflicted on British shipbuilding, seafaring and the Board of Trade.[35]

Coming from newspapers, frequent mention of Rostron's modesty could be dismissed as part of the formula – a popular hero could not be a swaggering braggart, after all. But others who knew or met Rostron characterized him as a soft-spoken, modest man. A pious man as well, he may also have had misgivings about gaining from a disaster that killed fifteen hundred people, though he was certainly cognizant of doing so. In the dedication to his memoir, published at his retirement nineteen years later, Rostron credited wireless operator Harold Cottam's alertness with making possible the rescue that 'firmly planted my feet on the ladder of success'. He had made steady and significant but fairly typical progress with Cunard through 1912. Rostron joined the company in 1895 with his extra master's certificate and eight years of sea time. He served twelve years with Cunard working his way through the officer ranks, then spent three years commanding small freighters and two years commanding medium-sized passenger-cargo ships in Cunard's secondary Mediterranean service.[36]

In October 1913, only ten months after he left *Carpathia*, Rostron served as the relief captain of *Lusitania*. In October 1915, three and a half years after the *Titanic* rescue, he was assigned as the regular master of *Mauretania*, among the most prestigious commands in the British merchant service.[37]

Carpathia, meanwhile, continued her unglamorous though profitable circuits of the Mediterranean until the First World War broke out twenty-seven months after *Titanic* sank. The crisis of August 1914 found her involved in another rescue of sorts: ordered to Naples to carry fleeing Americans home to New York, where she arrived on 2 September. *Carpathia* spent the First World War carrying cargoes, munitions, passengers and soldiers from North America to Europe, meeting her end carrying out that role four months before the Armistice.[38]

On the morning of 17 July 1918, *Carpathia* was the largest ship in a convoy west of Ireland, fortunately westbound with only fifty-seven passengers aboard. At around 9.15am a torpedo smashed into her boiler room portside, killing three firemen and two trimmers. A minute later another exploded against her engine room. Fifteen minutes after that a third struck farther aft. With her fate sealed, *Carpathia*'s 215 surviving passengers and crew escaped in her lifeboats quickly and in good order, to be rescued just after noon and returned to Liverpool by the minesweeper HMS *Snowdrop*. At about 11am *Carpathia* sank stern first, ending a career that consisted of fifteen years of faithful service and one legendary three-and-a-half-hour dash.[39]

CHAPTER 11

IN GOVERNMENT SERVICE

As *Carpathia* sailed towards New York Harbor with *Titanic's* survivors, she flew not the red ensign of the British merchant service, but the blue ensign of the Royal Naval Reserve issued to her on 1 February 1912, after Rostron assumed command. The Admiralty authorized a passenger liner to fly the blue ensign when her captain and a sufficient percentage of her officers and ratings served in the Royal Naval Reserve. Cunard encouraged its officers to join the reserve, established in 1861 to provide naval training to merchant sailors and to give the navy a force upon which to draw in emergencies. Beyond the blue ensign's prestige, Cunard's managers realized that substantial reserve membership by the company's officers and crews would ease the transition of its liners, subject to Admiralty requisition during wars. At the start of the First World War, 139 of Cunard's 163 navigating officers were commissioned reservists.[1]

Rostron had been appointed a midshipman in the Royal Naval Reserve on Christmas Eve of 1886, upon graduating from HMS *Conway*. Rostron was promoted to acting sub-lieutenant in April 1893 while still in sail and to sub-lieutenant in March 1896 during his last voyage on *Cedric the Saxon*. His naval training began in earnest, however, in the autumn of 1896, when he took leave from Cunard's service to enroll for four months of torpedo and gunnery training, followed by a year's deployment with the fleet. Named an acting lieutenant on 31 October 1896, at the age of twenty-seven, Rostron reported two days later to HMS *Vernon*, the Royal Navy's torpedo training school at Portsmouth, for two months of training. He followed this with two more months at HMS *Excellent*, the navy's gunnery school at Portsmouth, through the end of February 1897.[2]

He returned to sea after a month's leave. In those years before the submarine, torpedo training suggested assignment to cruisers. Rostron was initially posted to HMS *Edgar*, a 'first-class protected cruiser', for an orientation that began on 28 March 1897. He was then reassigned to the smaller and older armoured cruiser HMS *Undaunted*, which delivered him to China Station, where he transferred to the receiving ship HMS *Victor Emmanuel* at Hong Kong on 28 May. On 15 June he joined HMS *Grafton*, in which he would serve his tour in the Far East.[3]

HMS *Grafton*, an Edgar-class cruiser, was a twin-screw vessel of 7350 tons and a complement of 544 officers and men. Built by Thames Iron Works, Blackwall, London, *Grafton* was laid down on New Year's Day, 1890, and completed in May 1893. She had an overall length of 387 feet, a beam of 60 feet, a top speed of twenty knots and a cruising range of ten thousand miles at ten knots. She carried two 9.2-inch main guns, ten six-inch quick-firing guns, another seventeen secondary guns of smaller calibres and four submerged 18-inch torpedo tubes. The class featured two tall funnels and fore and main masts of exaggerated height, with yards, all set well aft and a rather large pilothouse forward of the foremast. Despite a somewhat ungainly appearance, 'in service they proved to be very good seaboats and exceptional steamers'.[4]

On 6 May 1898, after eleven months of service in *Grafton* on China Station, Rostron transferred at Hong Kong to HMS *Pique*, an Apollo-class, second-class cruiser, for his return to the United Kingdom. *Pique* was another twenty-knot ship, but with about half of *Grafton*'s tonnage and crew. She featured a main battery of two six-inch guns and had a range of about eight thousand miles at ten knots. Before her homeward voyage, *Pique* made a brief round voyage to Manila Bay just days after the US Navy's devastating attack on the Spanish fleet there opened hostilities in the Spanish–American War. HMS *Pique* then returned to home waters via Suez and Rostron detached on 20 July 1898. A month later he was back in Cunard's service.[5]

As he had done in his merchant career, Rostron impressed his naval superiors. His service record noted of his training in HMS *Edgar* his 'sobriety, diligence & attention,' and described Rostron as 'a zealous officer who has done the regular duties of a Lieut[enant]'. On China Station aboard HMS *Grafton* he was 'regularly employed as OOW [Officer of the Watch],' and judged a 'very good and trustworthy officer'. Homeward bound aboard HMS *Pique* he was again considered 'V[ery] G[ood] as O. of W'.[6]

Rostron emerged from his training and deployment with the reserve rank of lieutenant, issued in August 1898. As he worked his way up Cunard's ranks over the next fifteen years, he resumed active naval duty several times for requalification. In October 1902 he returned to HMS *Excellent* to take a one-month gunnery course. In June 1910 he spent a week at HMS *Eagle*, the reserve training station in Liverpool – 'A V[ery] G[ood] test & drills very well indeed' – followed by three weeks of requalifying in gunnery at HMS *Vivid*, the naval barracks at Keyham in Plymouth. On 9 November 1909, Rostron, twenty-two years a reservist and still a lieutenant, was awarded the Reserve Decoration, created the previous year and issued to officers with at least fifteen years of reserve service. On 19 January 1912, just before he assumed command of *Carpathia*, he was promoted to commander in the Royal Naval Reserve.[7]

His years of reserve service and training notwithstanding, Rostron would never see action with the regular navy. By the time Britain entered the First World War, Rostron was simply too valuable as a merchant captain of large passenger liners to employ in some subordinate role as a naval officer and probably too inexperienced as a naval officer to be granted command of a significant warship. During the last year of the war he did command a vessel flying the Royal Navy's white ensign, but she was a most unusual warship indeed.[8]

Before the start of the First World War, Rostron had left Cunard's Mediterranean service for its North Atlantic routes. He paid off *Carpathia* on the last day of 1912, after her annual return to Liverpool. Although some thought was apparently given to sending him back to the Mediterranean in command of *Saxonia*, he had, in fact, left the company's Mediterranean operations for good. Instead, he departed immediately for the US aboard *Caronia* in relief, returned to England in *Campania* and then made one round voyage to America in *Carmania*. Beginning at the end of April, he completed seven round voyages to the US in six months in command of *Campania* and then received two significant votes of confidence from his superiors. The first, at the end of October 1913, was the round voyage as relief captain of *Lusitania*. The second, immediately after that at the end of

November, was Rostron's assignment to command a newly-built ship on a route new to both himself and his company.[9]

Always searching for ways to strengthen its competitive position on the competitive North Atlantic and to diversify its services, Cunard acquired several other steamship companies in the first decades of the twentieth century. The first of these purchases, of the Thompson Line in 1911, gave Cunard access to Canadian ports on the St Lawrence River. Cunard established a weekly cargo service and a fortnightly passenger ship schedule to Canada, with their eastern terminus initially at Liverpool. This was later relocated to London to serve both English and French channel ports.[10]

The Canadian service's western terminus presented a more complex problem. Cunard delivered passengers and cargoes to Canada via one of three routes, depending upon the season. In winter, with the St Lawrence River frozen, Cunard's ships called first at Halifax, before continuing to the American ports of Portland, Maine, Boston or New York. Halifax had the advantage of year-round access, but the profound disadvantages of fog, ice and innumerable fishing vessels working the Grand Banks, making the waters south of Nova Scotia among the most hazardous on the Atlantic.[11]

The St Lawrence usually thawed in mid-April and remained open through November, but the river had to be approached by different routes at different times because of the danger of ice at sea. In the spring and early summer, ships steamed south of Cape Race, Newfoundland, then through the Cabot Strait into the Gulf of St Lawrence and the river from the south. During late summer and autumn, the voyage could be shortened by about half a day by passing north of Newfoundland and into the gulf through the Strait of Belle Isle. Ships navigated 290 miles up the St Lawrence before picking up a pilot at Father Point and proceeding another 158 miles upriver to Quebec. From there, a different pilot would guide the ship the remaining 139 miles to Montreal. With a passage of about a dozen days in each direction, depending upon circumstances, a round voyage to Montreal usually took a few days less than a month, with an added layover of a week or so in the ship's home port.[12]

The company profited from its new Canadian services, but if the Thompson Line's routes proved satisfactory, its ships did not. Cunard therefore resolved to have three purpose-built ships constructed for its new service. The first two, *Andania* and *Alaunia*, emerged from Scotts' Shipbuilding and Engineering

Company, Greenock, built very much along the lines of Cunard's previous intermediate-sized passenger-cargo liners, such as *Carpathia*. Fourteen-knot, quadruple-expansion, twin-screw steamers of 538 feet and 13,405 tons, they could accommodate five hundred second-class and fifteen hundred third-class passengers in cabin accommodations. *Andania* entered service in July 1913 and *Alaunia* four months later with Rostron as master.[13]

By then Rostron had commanded Cunard ships for six years. During that interval his salary had continued to climb. He received a significant increase from his £400 annual salary of 1912, to £600 in 1913. With his income more than double that of his early years in command, the Rostrons left their semi-detached house on Victoria Road and settled in a substantial detached house on Park Avenue in north Crosby in 1914.[14]

Rostron entered Cunard's Canadian service on 24 November 1913, but his ship would not visit the St Lawrence River for another six months. He joined *Alaunia* at the Huskisson Dock at Liverpool, where she had lain since arriving from Greenock on 11 November and spending a day in dry dock. Rostron took her to sea on 27 November, called briefly at Portland, Maine, on the morning of 6 December and finished the crossing at Boston the same afternoon. Five days later *Alaunia* ran the route in reverse, arriving back at the Huskisson Dock on 20 December. This set the pattern for the ship's winter voyages of January, February and March 1914, sailing from Liverpool and Queenstown with calls at some combination of Halifax, Portland and Boston.[15]

On returning to Britain from those ports in March, *Alaunia* stopped first at Plymouth before arriving at her new home port of London on the last day of the month. A week later, Rostron had her underway on her April voyage to Queenstown, Halifax and Portland, returning to London on 5 May. Her next voyage brought *Alaunia*'s introduction to the St Lawrence. She departed London on 12 May, embarked more than a thousand passengers the following day at Southampton, added another thirty-five in a one-hour call at Queenstown on the evening of 14 May and then sailed for Montreal with 243 second-class and 816 third-class passengers. Six evenings later *Alaunia* passed Cape Race headed for Cabot Strait. She called at Quebec at 4am and Montreal at 7pm on 24 May, completing her transit in half an hour less than ten days.[16]

If Rostron needed any sobering lessons about the dangers of navigating the St Lawrence, he received not one but two on his first voyage up the river. In a telegram dated 26 May, *Lloyd's List* reported information from Montreal that *Alaunia* had arrived 'damaged by ice. Will be surveyed today.' *Lloyd's* did not publish the results of that survey, but the damage was insufficient to prevent *Alaunia* from sailing for Plymouth and London with 660 people four days later. By then, the river had staged a second and much harsher demonstration. On 29 May 1914, the Canadian Pacific passenger steamer *Empress of Ireland*, having just dropped her pilot at Father Point outbound for London, collided with the inbound collier *Storstad* at 2am in a dense fog. *Storstad* suffered a crumpled bow; *Empress of Ireland* went to the bottom in fourteen minutes taking a thousand passengers with her.[17]

An exponentially more appalling calamity, the First World War erupted two months later. *Alaunia* was tied up at Montreal handling cargo when Britain declared war on Germany on 4 August 1914. The war certainly complicated Rostron's departure from the St Lawrence and return home through the English Channel. *Alaunia* left Montreal on 8 August and Quebec the following day. Reports would emerge a week later of British liners dodging German cruisers to reach the St Lawrence to deliver thousands of Canadian and American tourists home from Europe. Rostron, forewarned of the cruisers, had a similar experience eastbound. The trip outbound through the Gulf of St Lawrence, conducted at full speed in fog, had been an adventure in itself, Rostron and *Alaunia* taking their wartime chances. After one near miss with an inbound ship, *Alaunia* reached the open sea, where visibility improved off Cape Race. At dusk the watch sighted what Rostron identified as a German cruiser. Once darkness fell, Rostron transmitted his course in the clear, then altered course and, running blacked out, eluded the other ship. *Alaunia* reached Plymouth on 19 August, ten days after she left Quebec, and arrived in the Thames the following day.[18]

Alaunia made another civilian voyage under Rostron a week later, departing London filled with repatriating Canadians. She arrived at Montreal on 6 September and moored there for almost three weeks before shifting to Quebec on 24 September. She remained at Quebec until the end of the month, when she began her new career as a troop transport. On 30 September *Alaunia* departed Quebec, her sailing recorded tersely in Cunard's movement log as:

'Left – Transport.' She joined a thirty-seven-ship convoy that carried more than thirty-five thousand Canadian soldiers to England, making Plymouth on 16 October and London two days later.[19]

Alaunia and Rostron departed London 'in Government Service' on 24 October 1914, on a voyage headed east from Britain. She called at Southampton for three days before steaming for India, via the Mediterranean, on 29 October, with two battalions of the home division to replace regulars destined for the war in Europe. Rostron's ship lay at Port Said, at the northern entrance to the Suez Canal, from 9–12 November and reached Bombay, India, on 1 December 1914. After her soldiers disembarked, *Alaunia* took aboard 2400 women and children for the return voyage, while the rest of the convoy carried troops of the 29th Division, destined ultimately for the Mediterranean theatre. Rostron was not happy with this arrangement, finding the civilians too prone to complain about the limitations of wartime transportation. *Alaunia* reached the Suez Canal on 22 December, arrived at Avonmouth, at Bristol, England, on 11 January 1915 and Liverpool on the evening of 14 January. *Alaunia* then returned to civilian service for one voyage, departing Liverpool on 19 January with a grand total of eight passengers, calling at New York on 30 January, Halifax a week later and arriving back at Liverpool on the evening of 14 February 1915.[20]

A month later, Rostron and *Alaunia* returned to troop carrying and to the Mediterranean to contribute to the Allied build-up for the opening of a southern front against the Central Powers. By the spring of 1915 the war in Western Europe was mired, literally, in brutal stalemate. The Allies sought some way to outflank Germany, but since the western trenches extended from the English Channel to Switzerland their flanking manoeuvre would have to be strategic rather than tactical. They chose to attack the Dardanelles, the narrow passage leading from the Aegean Sea to Constantinople, capital of the Ottoman Empire, one of the Central Powers.[21]

At best, capturing the Dardanelles would knock the Ottoman Empire out of the war and open the route from the Mediterranean to the Black Sea and Russia. At worst, so the thinking went, an attack at the Dardanelles would relieve Turkish pressure on Russia in the Caucuses, threaten the Austro-Hungarian Empire from the south and perhaps even divert German resources from the Western Front. The first plan was to capture the strait by a naval assault. If that failed, the next attempt would try to pry it open with landings on Gallipoli Peninsula. In January 1915, the Admiralty began deploying elderly battleships for the naval operation and developing plans to occupy the Greek island of Lemnos – located about fifty miles west of the entrance to the Dardanelles at the head of the Adriatic Sea – should an invasion prove necessary.[22]

The Allies opened their naval attack on the Dardanelles on 19 February 1915, intending to use minesweepers to clear mines and warships to destroy forts as they advanced north along the strait toward Constantinople. This initial probe was repulsed and a month later, on 18 March, the Allies returned with a bigger hammer – twelve British and four French battleships, preceded by numerous minesweepers. Again, the passage proved impenetrable; the minesweepers could not clear the minefields laid in the narrows of the Dardanelles while under fire from shore batteries and the battleships could not get close enough to reduce the shore batteries without the minefields being cleared. Three Allied ships sunk and seven damaged sufficed to end the naval assault five days later and to convince Allied commanders that a landing would be necessary.[23]

Working from their closest bases, on Malta and at Alexandria, it took the Allies another month to achieve sufficient strength to launch an amphibious assault on the Gallipoli Peninsula. The Allies occupied Lemnos on 7 March and began to develop a forward naval base and supply depot on the island around the harbour at Mudros. Staging from Lemnos and leading the attack would be the British Twenty-Ninth Division, regular soldiers which *Alaunia's* convoy had redeployed from India at the beginning of the year.[24]

In mid-March *Alaunia*, with Rostron in command, sailed from Avonmouth for Mudros crowded with soldiers destined for Gallipoli. One was Fred Odhams of the 1st Lancashire Fusiliers, 86 Brigade, 29th Division. His unit arrived at Avonmouth at 6am on 15 March 1915. *Alaunia* sailed unescorted on the evening of the next day and, Odhams wrote home, passed a German submarine that midnight, which she escaped at 17 knots. Rostron's ship passed Gibraltar at midday on 20 March and reached Malta at 10am on 23 March. She began loading coal that afternoon and remained for two days, joined by twelve other transports. *Alaunia* departed from Malta at 7am on 25 March, escorted by one destroyer, with the remaining ships to follow the next day. Odhams wrote that a 'French Dreadnought gave us a good send off[, the] band playing as we sailed past her'.[25]

Alaunia entered the Aegean on the following afternoon, but received new orders by wireless that night diverting her to Alexandria, where she arrived at noon on 28 March. Odhams and his fellow soldiers disembarked the following day and marched to a camp about ten miles outside of Alexandria. He wrote to his mother and sister that he expected to get into action at Gallipoli in a week or so. He did not know where Gallipoli was, except that it was in Turkey, but confided that 'we expect to have a rough time there because the Turks … are not going to let us have it all our own way, I think myself that this will be our hardest job'. A tragically prophetic prediction in Odhams' case; he was killed at Gallipoli at the beginning of June.[26]

The 29th Division went ashore at five points on the southern tip of the Gallipoli Peninsula on 25 April 1915. Two miles off shore, Rostron 'stood on the bridge that dawn and watched it all'. After her detour to Alexandria, *Alaunia* had arrived at Mudros to find about fifty ships crowding the harbour, not counting heavy warships. *Alaunia* loaded her share of the Twenty-Ninth Division and, with two hundred other merchant ships and the battle fleet, manoeuvred into her position off the beaches under cover of darkness. The fleet opened a one-hour bombardment at 5am in a light mist, then small vessels towed landing launches loaded with men from *Alaunia* and the other transports to the beaches. Meanwhile, five miles up the west coast of the peninsula, the Australian and New Zealand Army Corps – consisting of the First Australian Division and the Australian and New Zealand Division – were landing at what became known as Anzac Cove.[27]

Within two weeks the Allied advances had been thwarted. The Gallipoli Peninsula consists mostly of steep cliffs with only a few places suitable for landings, circumstances not lost on its Turkish defenders. Having ceded surprise with their February and March naval assaults, the Allies met an enemy well disposed and supplied. Even those few shores where beach landings could be carried out were usually backed by cliffs, up which the invading soldiers were obliged to advance against entrenched infantry and artillery. By the end of the first day, the Allies had suffered four-thousand casualties among thirty-thousand men landed.[28]

The Gallipoli campaign would later be roundly criticized for its lack of organization, particularly as concerned the treatment and evacuation of Allied wounded. Originally, the Allies used the same transports that had carried the soldiers to the invasion to remove the sick and injured. Those ships – called 'black carriers' because their hulls were painted black to avoid detection at night – proved slow and unsanitary. The same vessels, that had so recently transported soldiers and even their livestock, were quickly reorganized into hospital ships, or 'stinking dens of infection' as one historian described them. They removed casualties from Gallipoli to Lemnos, where the Australians established several field hospitals, or to Egypt or Malta, but early shortages and delays in the medical train caused many deaths.[29]

Alaunia, a better class of black carrier than most, immediately converted to this mission without sufficient resources. She had scarcely disgorged the soldiers she had transported to the landing when casualties started streaming back to her. They arrived in launches and small vessels, many directly from field stations. 'It was no small task to turn a troop ship into a floating hospital at an hour's notice,' Rostron remembered. *Alaunia*'s surgeon was the only medical officer aboard and the ship carried no nurses. The purser was pressed into service as anesthetist, *Alaunia*'s stewards acted as orderlies and her wards were improvised. Rostron also took the precaution of ordering red crosses painted on the ship's sides and having a red cross flag made up to fly. 'I did not imagine these would be [of] the slightest use, actually, but ... it gave [the wounded] a feeling of security.' Rostron's lack of faith in these security measures came from his suspicion, retained long after the war, that submarines of the Central Powers actively hunted Allied hospital ships.[30]

Once loaded with casualties, *Alaunia* sailed for Alexandria, where she acquired several army medical officers and nurses. At the beginning of June, 'after two months knocking about between Gallipoli, Alexandria and Mudros carrying wounded, stores and so on,' *Alaunia* was ordered back to England. She departed Alexandria on 6 June 1915, carrying about two thousand sick and wounded soldiers. She sailed first for Southampton, where she unloaded her casualties and then headed for Liverpool, where she arrived on 26 June. *Alaunia* remained in Liverpool for only ten days before she steamed for Plymouth to load more soldiers and return to the war.[31]

This time she was bound for a place called Suvla Bay. In an effort to break the stalemate on the peninsula, the Allies decided to land yet another force several miles north of Anzac Cove to threaten to trap Turkish Army units to the south and thereby break the stalemate. Among those who sailed for Suvla Bay in *Alaunia* was a Sergeant H. Elliot of the 13th Casualty Clearing Station, Royal Army Medical Corps. His unit reached Devonport and boarded *Alaunia* on the afternoon of 10 July 1915 and she sailed under escort two hours later. The escorts detached the following morning and *Alaunia* reached Gibraltar on the morning of 14 July. She arrived at Malta three mornings later to be greeted by 'swarms of vendors with various kinds of merchandise [who] crowded round the ship in small boats,' as well as 'boys diving for coppers'. Elliot purchased fifty Egyptian cigarettes and a book of views from a vendor, but the cigarettes 'had a distinct aroma of india-rubber [sic],' so he gave those away. With refuelling completed, *Alaunia* departed at 6pm on 17 July, headed for Alexandria.[32]

She arrived at Alexandria early on the morning of 20 July, to find 'many transports and two hospital ships. Our ship appeared to be the best and largest,' according to Elliot. *Alaunia* fuelled and departed that evening. Elliot, finding the atmosphere below decks 'stifling', decided to sleep on A Deck, which proved cooler but entailed being awakened at 4.15am by a sailor wanting to wash down the deck. *Alaunia* maintained a zig-zag course through the Greek Archipelago, a precaution against submarines operating among the islands, and arrived at Mudros on 24 July to find the harbour 'full of all classes of shipping'.[33]

The following day *Alaunia* departed from Mudros with Elliot and his unit still aboard, headed south-east for Mytilene on Lesbos, which she reached that evening. Rostron's ship joined many British and French warships in the harbour. 'Our transport was evidently the first to arrive,' wrote Elliot. 'The sailors gave us a ringing cheer which we answered with great enthusiasm.' Four days later, on 29 July, Elliot's unit transferred from *Alaunia* to a smaller ship and departed Mytilene. Ten days after that, on 8 August 1915, the Thirteenth Casualty Clearing Station went ashore at Suvla Bay. There Elliot and his comrades spent the following four months enduring the terrors of enemy fire and the torments of dysentery, malnourishment and bad weather.[34]

Rostron and *Alaunia*, meanwhile, had delivered other soldiers to Suvla Bay for the initial assault, on 6 August 1915, but did not linger this time to see it take place. The ship had been ordered back to Mudros the previous evening to lie in readiness to transport casualties to England. These followed quickly. Within three days of the landing, Ottoman forces succeeded in isolating Suvla Bay and turning it into yet a third savage stalemate.[35]

Three weeks later, *Alaunia* sailed for England loaded with sick and wounded soldiers from Gallipoli. She departed Malta on 28 August and discharged her casualties at Southampton on 9 September. Two days later she arrived at London, where, on 23 September 1915, Rostron took his leave of *Alaunia* after twenty-two months of service in the Atlantic, the Mediterranean and the Indian Ocean. His next assignment, though not as varied geographically, would bring Rostron a significant increase in profile.[36]

CHAPTER 12

MEMORIES OF WOUNDED

To meet the shipping requirements of its eastern Mediterranean operations of 1915, the British government employed some of the country's largest and fastest liners as troop transports and hospital ships. Cunard's *Mauretania* served in both capacities. She had spent most of the First World War in harbour until then. She left Liverpool for New York in the final days of peace and was diverted to Halifax after Britain declared war. *Mauretania* returned to Liverpool on 19 August 1914, made three more transatlantic voyages in civilian service and then was laid up at Liverpool by Cunard from the end of October 1914 to mid-May 1915. The company cut its New York sailings by half due to decreased wartime demand, the service being provided by *Lusitania* until she was destroyed off the south coast of Ireland on 7 May 1915.[1]

Mauretania was recalled to service a week after the sinking of *Lusitania*, not to replace the lost liner on the New York run, but to carry soldiers to the Mediterranean during the build-up to the August landings at Suvla Bay, Gallipoli. The *Lusitania* disaster demonstrated that the great liners were too valuable to risk in civilian service during the war. Their range was too limited and they were too fuel hungry to be useful for gathering soldiers from around the Empire to fight in Europe, as *Alaunia* and other smaller ships had been doing. And for all of these reasons they proved ineffective at wandering about looking for trouble as the 'armed merchant cruisers' as which they had been conceived.[2]

At Gallipoli, however, the great liners found a purpose. *Mauretania*, *Aquitania* and White Star's *Olympic* and later *Britannic* proved very effective for moving large numbers of men back and forth at high speeds between Britain and the eastern Mediterranean, a distance roughly equivalent to a transatlantic voyage. On 16 May 1915, *Mauretania* was chartered by the War Office for conversion into a merchant troopship. Most of her fittings and furniture were removed and bunks and hammocks substituted, doubling her capacity from two thousand civilian passengers to four thousand military personnel.[3]

Mauretania departed from Liverpool at 1.30am on 20 May for the first of three trooping voyages to the Mediterranean. Carrying 3400 soldiers from three Scots regiments, she arrived at Mudros on 29 May and then returned to Liverpool on 22 June. She left Liverpool on her second trooping voyage on 9 July carrying 4554 people, consisting of 3644 soldiers of the 10th (Irish) Division, 60 nurses and 850 crew members. *Mauretania* reached Mudros on 16 July and returned to Liverpool on 3 August. Her third voyage began three weeks later, on 25 August, with a one-day passage to Southampton, where she took on soldiers. Departing from Southampton on 28 August, she reached Mudros on 3 September, but did not return to Liverpool for more than a month. She called first at Spezzia, Italy; Toulon, France; and Gibraltar in search of enough coal to reach Liverpool. On these three trooping voyages, *Mauretania* transported a total of 10,391 soldiers to the Mediterranean theatre.[4]

Mauretania arrived back in Liverpool from her third voyage on 5 October 1915 and entered the Gladstone dry dock. She returned to service two-and-a half weeks later a very different vessel. Having used its large liners as troopships to carry Allied forces to Gallipoli and the Balkans, Britain would use them as hospital ships to bring the sick and wounded home. *Mauretania* emerged from the yard painted white, with a three-foot green band around her hull twenty-five feet above the waterline, interrupted on each of her sides by three large red crosses. Workers painted her stacks a buff colour, laboriously scraped off all of the black paint that they had applied to her portholes and windows for her trooping service and rigged floodlights about her decks. His Majesty's Hospital Ship *Mauretania* would sail carrying the hospital flag at her masthead and brilliantly illuminated at night.[5]

Mauretania's interiors were also reconfigured, this time to accommodate 2500 patients, up to 350 medical staff and her crew of 850. Lounges, smoking rooms and some of the ship's dining rooms were converted into wards, as was the promenade deck, which was glassed in and equipped with two hundred cots on each side. *Mauretania* was no converted 'black carrier'. 'Oh, she was a beauty as a hospital ship,' Rostron told a reporter just after the war. 'Never saw anything like it afloat… She was not only a hospital ship. She was a hospital, complete in every way. There were big rest and recreation rooms, wards, private rooms, two big operating theatres, X-ray laboratories, everything.' The ship's medical staff, under Colonel Frank Brown of the Royal Army Medical Corps, consisted of thirty doctors, about seventy nurses and two hundred orderlies. *Mauretania*'s crew provided the navigation, engineering, maintenance, catering and housekeeping.[6]

One last significant change occurred before HMHS *Mauretania* departed Liverpool for the Aegean Sea on the evening of 22 October 1915: Arthur Rostron assumed command. Being assigned as master of one of Cunard's most valuable vessels was a significant affirmation of his company's trust in Rostron. 'I was proud to have her,' he wrote of his new ship, 'though I had not then guessed how great a part of my life she was destined to become.' Unlike *Alaunia*, *Mauretania* did not carry Rostron close to the action; she was simply too valuable to risk manoeuvring close to a hostile shore. Instead, *Mauretania* called at Mudros to embark patients delivered to that harbour by smaller ships or transferred from hospitals on Lemnos.[7]

Samuel McNeil, Rostron's fellow Cunard captain, worked the other end of this poignant delivery system, commanding the converted Channel steamer *Reindeer*. McNeil recorded that *Reindeer*'s typical round began with a 10pm departure from Mudros loaded with replacement soldiers and ammunition. She anchored off of her assigned beach at Gallipoli at 3am. Two hours later, at first light, small vessels began to come alongside to transfer the new soldiers ashore, while *Reindeer* discharged the ammunition into a barge moored to her opposite side. At 9am tenders began to arrive with sick and wounded soldiers. At about noon, her decks covered with stretcher cases, *Reindeer* departed Gallipoli for Mudros, which she reached at 4pm. She first went alongside the harbour's command ship to receive the orders that dispatched her to one of the hospital ships in the harbour, where she discharged her casualties. Then she returned to loading ammunition and soldiers for her next 10pm departure, a rotation, McNeil recalled, that allowed for 'little rest or sleep'.[8]

From Mudros, hospital ships evacuated the wounded to Alexandria, Malta, or, in *Mauretania*'s case, directly home to England. Although not deployed to the front as *Alaunia* had been, *Mauretania* was still sailing into war and Rostron was well aware of the potential consequences. James Bisset had joined *Mauretania* as first officer in July 1915, before her second trooping voyage. He recalled that on the day before *Mauretania*'s first departure under Rostron, with her crew about to sign the ship's articles, her new captain, 'being an extremely conscientious man,' ordered all hands mustered in the third-class dining room. There, Rostron read the Articles of War aloud to them, emphasizing the penalties for disobedience and paying particular attention to the capital offenses. Bisset remembered that Rostron concluded: 'Now, men, that will give you something to think about! Sign on, or not, as you please, but never let me hear any complaint that you didn't know what you are invited to sign!' According to Bisset, all hands signed.[9]

In fact *Mauretania* had already had her closest brush with death. Because of her great speed, the liner steamed unescorted except in proximity to her ports. Returning from Mudros alone on her second trooping voyage, she was attacked by a submarine off the island of Skyros, about sixty miles south-west of Lemnos, on 23 July 1915. *Mauretania* was zig-zagging southbound at twenty-five knots when one of her lookouts spotted a periscope about sixty degrees to starboard and half a mile away.[10]

Captain Daniel Dow, on the bridge at the time, reacted by ordering the helm hard over, turning his ship toward the submarine only seconds after it launched two torpedoes. His manoeuvre skidded *Mauretania*'s stern out of the path of the torpedoes, both of which passed a few feet astern. This crash turn to starboard had the added advantage of threatening the submarine with ramming, forcing that vessel deep. Once the torpedoes passed, however, Dow went hard over the other way, reversing his course to present *Mauretania*'s stern to the submarine's position, offering the smallest target and bringing his only weapon, her stern gun, to bear. Dow then called down for emergency power and *Mauretania* disappeared into the dusk at 27 knots, a speed no submarine of the era could approach.[11]

Even without the harrowing experience of a torpedo attack, Rostron's time in command of His Majesty's Hospital Ship *Mauretania* provided him with his most vivid memories of the First World War. 'To me,' he wrote fifteen years later, 'very largely, memories of the war are memories of wounded.' Rostron sometimes toured *Mauretania*'s wards with Colonel Brown, the chief medical officer, 'and was always amazed at the cheeriness of even those who were in [the] most wretched plight. Disablement, pain, misery, seemed outside their consideration; the only thing that occupied their minds was that they were going home – home to Blighty and all that Blighty meant.'[12]

Mauretania made three voyages to Mudros as a hospital ship, gathering the sick and wounded from the Allied campaigns on Gallipoli and in the Balkans and bringing them home. She left Liverpool on her first voyage at 8pm on 22 October. In her new role, she sailed unescorted, did not zig-zag and was brightly lighted. *Mauretania* called at Naples on the morning of 28 October and departed for the Aegean the following day. She arrived at Mudros on 31 October. With no wharf in the harbour able to accommodate her, she lay at anchor for four days while 2312 wounded and sick, principally suffering from dysentery, were brought aboard. Casualties came by barge from shore facilities or arrived directly from Gallipoli aboard smaller hospital ships. These tied up alongside and both walking wounded and stretcher cases crossed over through *Mauretania's* gangway doors. Stretcher casualties arriving by barge were hoisted aboard in a sling by one of *Mauretania's* cargo cranes.[13]

On 4 November 1915, near her hospital capacity, *Mauretania* departed from Mudros. She called briefly at Naples before sailing for Southampton, where she arrived on 11 November. Ten of her patients, all dysentery cases, died in transit and were buried at sea. Southampton replaced Liverpool as *Mauretania's* home port while a hospital ship, both to reduce her transit time by a day and to land her closer to the large military hospitals established in southern England to receive casualties from France.[14]

Mauretania left Southampton just before noon on 23 November on her second hospital run to Mudros. Tensions ran higher than usual on this voyage, due to accusations published in the German press that the British were using their hospital ships to transport soldiers or war materials in violation of the rules of war. Rumours circulated that *Mauretania* would be stopped and searched at sea. In response, Rostron ordered his ship scoured for anything that might be construed as contraband material, going so far as to order 112 copies of a board game called 'The Road to Berlin' to be tossed overboard as being too provocative. The game, brought aboard to amuse the patients, concluded when the winning player rolled a cannonball into the Kaiser's mouth and Rostron worried that a German boarding party would not see the humour in it.[15]

Fuel-hungry *Mauretania* generally called at Naples at some point in her round voyage to avoid having to refuel at Mudros. On her first hospital voyage, she was inspected for possible contraband, a process carried out by neutral consuls. When *Mauretania* called at Naples on her second voyage, on 28 November, Rostron took this inspection process a step further. The neutral Swiss, Danish and American consuls signed a document the next day certifying 'that at the request of the Commanding Officer of the ship, we have this day visited and inspected H.M. Hospital Ship *Mauretania* and are satisfied that there are no combatant troops or warlike stores in her and that the rules of the Geneva Convention are being observed in every way'.[16]

The diplomatic necessities attended to, *Mauretania* sailed for Mudros on 30 November, collected another 2021 patients, returned to Naples on 8 December and then brought the boys home for Christmas, arriving at Southampton at daybreak on 14 December. *Mauretania*'s third and final hospital voyage to the Aegean, a quick one, began on 7 January 1916. She called briefly at Naples five days later, returned to the Italian port a week after that with 1974 patients aboard and reached Southampton on 25 January, after a round voyage of two and a half weeks. True to Cunard's motto, in her three hospital voyages *Mauretania* had evacuated over six thousand casualties from the Aegean theatre with 'speed, comfort and safety'.[17]

Mauretania idled for two weeks at Southampton, where her medical staff and most of her crew left the ship, before shifting to anchorage in Cowes Roads off the Isle of Wight. After two weeks there, she departed on 24 February for yet another refit at Liverpool. Four days after she arrived, on 29 February 1916, Rostron relinquished command of the ship.[18]

Two months earlier, while *Mauretania* lay at Southampton between her second and third hospital voyages, the 13th Casualty Clearing Station withdrew from the Gallipoli Peninsula on the night of 19–20 December. Sergeant Elliot noted that 'the evacuation was a complete success,' as was the entire Allied withdrawal from Gallipoli, which concluded on 8 January 1916. But the brilliance of that retreat contrasted starkly with the failures that compelled it. The Gallipoli campaign did not open a route to Russia, threaten Constantinople, take pressure off Serbia, or divert the resources of the other Central Powers, although it had tied down a third of the best Turkish divisions.[19]

Such paltry results could never justify their cost. The Allies suffered over a quarter of a million casualties at Gallipoli – about half of those deployed – the Ottoman Empire perhaps more. Estimates of Turkish losses are as high as 350,000, with 86,000 killed. The Allies lost approximately 58,000 killed or died and another 228,000 wounded or sick. Empire forces – British, Australian, New Zealander, Indian and Canadian – suffered about 205,000 casualties: 115,000 killed, wounded, or missing and another 90,000 evacuated sick, usually wracked with dysentery or typhoid. Australia suffered 7594 dead and 18,500 wounded and sick, while New Zealand lost 2341 dead, with 5230 wounded and sick. Britain bore the brunt of Gallipoli, however; her portion of the carnage came to about 43,000 dead and 162,000 wounded and sick.[20]

Political recriminations over Gallipoli's conduct began in Britain a month into the campaign and criticism of the operation has not abated. One historian observed that at Gallipoli the Allies learned 'some military lessons ... which should not have been needed – the importance of proper planning and secrecy, the need for adequate medical and health services, the hazards of the opposed landing, and the tactical unwisdom of daylight attacks against entrenched infantry'.[21]

Rostron, among others, anticipated the historians; he attributed the 'fiasco' of Gallipoli to a lack of secrecy, poor planning and lack of organization. Rostron described Lemnos as 'haunted by spies', and believed that transmitting the information they gathered required merely an overnight passage by small boat between Lemnos and Gallipoli. Indeed, the espionage system may not have been even that complex; Turkish aircraft began flying over Mudros and observing the Allied build-up almost daily beginning two weeks before the first landings.[22]

Within his own bailiwick, the transports, Rostron found mismanagement symptomatic of 'weak organisation' characterized by 'wastage everywhere'. To one fresh from the competitive Atlantic, 'trained to waste nothing and especially [not] time ... it was irritating to see the lack of method that grew up under the inefficient emergency control'. He found it 'pitiful to see the ships – dozens of them – lying up in Alexandria when they were urgently needed at home for trooping'. McNeil concurred, writing that 'for some reason, Mudros

Harbour remained in a chaotic condition for months. There must have been chaos in England, too, because store-ships would arrive and the Navy in Mudros would know nothing about them.'[23]

The temper of the naval reservists and merchant sailors manning the transports was not improved by what Rostron regarded as 'unnecessary arrogance in the Transport Offices' of Britain's naval bureaucracy. In his experience the navy 'definitely looked on us [merchant marine officers] as inferiors'. He recalled seeing British merchant captains, presumably with better things to do, idling in the outer offices of Naval Transport waiting to see some official. Rostron believed that 'only towards the end of hostilities did the Navy wake up to the fact that we [in the merchant service] knew our business far better than they knew it … [since] their experience did not include the running of a big liner with all its complicated organisation'.[24]

The naval establishment's attitude toward merchant officers extended to naval reservists, who, as in Rostron's case, were often the same individuals. McNeil recalled that early in the war, even senior naval reserve officers 'were just tolerated and this attitude continued to the end of 1917. It was the cause of so much bitterness and friction.'[25]

Such frictions only compounded the operation's logistical problems, serious enough by themselves. Every Allied soldier landed on Gallipoli had to be supplied by sea over thousands of miles. The main support base for the operation, Alexandria, was eight hundred miles away by sea. The Allies' forward operating base at Mudros completely lacked wharves, warehouses and fresh water before the campaign began. This extended and disorganized supply chain caused much privation on the peninsula. In Bisset's succinct summation, 'muddle prevailed'.[26]

Even though the Allies withdrew from Gallipoli at the beginning of 1916, they remained active in the Aegean and eastern Mediterranean, as did Rostron. The Allied misadventure at Gallipoli encouraged Bulgaria to side with the Central Powers in September 1915 in an attempt to win territory from Serbia. That small country thus found itself set upon from both the east and north. If the Central Powers could defeat Serbia they could implement the Allies' Gallipoli strategy in reverse, physically connecting the Central Powers with the Ottoman Empire through Serbia and Bulgaria. Serbia could not remain in the war without Allied assistance, so in October 1915, after

Bulgaria mobilized against Serbia, five British and three French divisions landed at the Greek port of Salonika, located on the western side of the head of the Aegean, about 150 miles west-north-west of Lemnos. The Allies used the port to maintain their divisions afield, but the Serbian army's defeat at the end of 1915 turned Salonika into another disease-ridden cul-de-sac for the Allies.[27]

Throughout 1916, however, the war in the northern Aegean continued. Following a month ashore after paying off from *Mauretania*, Rostron left Liverpool on 19 April 1916, in *Ivernia*, embarked soldiers at Plymouth and sailed for the Mediterranean on 23 April. *Ivernia*, akin to *Carpathia* in type and purpose, was a quadruple-expansion, twin-screw steamer, 598 feet long and of 14,067 gross tons. Rostron spent the rest of the year commanding *Ivernia*'s eastbound trooping voyages between Toulon or Marseilles, France, and Salonika and returning westbound via Alexandria carrying Australian and New Zealand soldiers bound for France. Rostron wrote that while in *Ivernia* he experienced a torpedo attack in foggy weather on one of her voyages to Salonika, 'just a breathless minute and we knew the projectile had lost itself somewhere. Then the fog closed in again.'[28]

Rostron went ashore once while at Salonika to visit the Allied front lines opposite Bulgarian positions close to the Saar River 'about a forty-mile motor run' from the ship. While at Salonika, he discovered that the navy held no monopoly on underestimating the importance of logistics. Rostron was hosting several army officers at dinner in his cabin, when one of them dismissed the non-combatant merchant ships as unimportant. '"Who brought you here?" I asked him. "Who brought those men fighting on the peninsula? Who carried their supplies, fed them on the route out? What would you do with your wounded if there were no merchant ships?"'[29]

Ivernia returned to England only once under Rostron's command, spending the second half of August 1916 in Liverpool. On 28 August she departed Plymouth under Rostron once more for the Mediterranean, from which she would never return. *Ivernia* and he spent the next three months trooping about the Mediterranean. Rostron left the ship at Marseilles on 27 December 1916. He was relieved, only four hours before she departed on another trooping voyage to Salonika, by William Turner, the captain who had survived *Lusitania*'s destruction in 1915. Turner would also survive *Ivernia*, torpedoed fifty-eight miles south-east of Cape Matapan, Greece, on New Year's Day 1917, with the loss of 120 soldiers and 33 of her crew.[30]

After a period of leave, Rostron's next assignment involved a brief reunion with *Mauretania*. With the Gallipoli bloodletting concluded and her services as a hospital ship no longer required, the great Cunarder had been reconfigured yet again as a troopship over the summer of 1916. While Rostron sailed the Mediterranean, *Mauretania* made voyages to Halifax in October and November, bringing 6214 Canadian soldiers to Liverpool. Back in the Mersey on the last day of November, she returned to idleness. She spent most of the next two months alongside Gladstone Dock or moored in the river before the authorities decided to move her to Greenock on the Firth of Clyde, where she could lie inactive in greater security. Rostron commanded her relocation voyage, which proved neither short nor simple.[31]

As Rostron later recounted, on 24 January 1917, he shifted the ship from her buoy in the Sloyne to anchor nearer the mouth of the river to await darkness and a favourable tide. At about 7pm, with a gale blowing up the river, he was attempting to weigh *Mauretania*'s port anchor when its cable parted. The Mersey pilot tried to turn her downstream and to hold her Rostron ordered the starboard anchor let go. That also carried away. *Mauretania*'s crew next managed to pass a hawser to an accompanying tugboat, but that snapped as well. In Rostron's telling, the climax of this chaos found *Mauretania* being driven helplessly back up the Mersey, broadside to a 7-knot tide.[32]

Fortunately, rather than striking any other river traffic, underway or anchored, the great liner drifted onto a bar. Tugboats refloated her without injury and wrestled her bow downstream. Rostron then had no choice but to stand out of the Mersey and cruise about until daylight afforded the chance to re-enter the river and tie up, since *Mauretania* could not proceed to Greenock without anchors. The ship spent three weeks at Gladstone Dock waiting for her anchors to be retrieved from the river bottom and returned to her. She finally departed from Liverpool on the evening of 19 February, arriving at Greenock just after noon on the following day, the only complication this time being dense fog. Secure at Greenock, *Mauretania* would remain inactive for almost a year.[33]

After manoeuvring *Mauretania* into the safety of the Clyde, Rostron spent several weeks enrolled in what he described as 'a submarine course at Chatham' Dockyard. He next went to sea on 14 March for a single voyage in command of *Alaunia*'s sister ship *Andania*. She arrived at New York on the afternoon of 25 March carrying two thousand sacks of mail but only seventy-seven passengers. She left New York on 6 April 1917, the same day that the United States declared war on Germany, and arrived back in Liverpool eleven days later. Rostron left *Andania* before she sailed for America again on 1 May. The ship continued on the Liverpool–New York run, calling at Halifax on her return voyages, until she was torpedoed and sunk in January 1918.[34]

At the beginning of June 1917 Rostron took command of *Saxonia* and would remain master of that ship for the rest of the year. Built by John Brown and Company, Clydebank, in 1900, *Saxonia* was a twin-screw, quadruple-expansion steamer of fourteen thousand tons and 598 feet in length, constructed at the same time and to similar design as *Ivernia*. She spent most of 1915 and 1916 in Cunard's civilian New York service. The British government assumed control of *Saxonia* in 1917 and kept her on the same route, moving cargoes and American soldiers to Europe after the US declared war. *Saxonia* usually called at Halifax on her return voyage to England to collect Canadian troops and cargoes. Rostron made four round voyages to the United States in *Saxonia*, sailing from London in June and July and from Liverpool in September and November.[35]

Rostron's last voyage in *Saxonia*, which commenced on the afternoon of 19 November 1917, proved the most memorable. He brought his ship into busy and crowded Halifax harbour on the morning of 30 November and departed for New York twenty-two hours later. *Saxonia* reached New York on the afternoon of 3 December and remained there for seventeen days. She cleared Ambrose Channel at about noon on 22 December and returned to Halifax at Christmas to behold a city in shambles. 'Half the town was blown to bits,' in Rostron's words. On the morning of 6 December, the explosives-laden freighter *Mont-Blanc*, standing into Halifax harbour, had been rammed by an outbound vessel. Set alight during the collision and hastily abandoned by her crew, *Mont-Blanc* drifted ashore at Halifax, where she exploded at 9.04am, killing more than two thousand people, injuring another nine thousand and obliterating much of the city's waterfront.[36]

Saxonia returned to Liverpool on the morning of 7 January 1918. Rostron relinquished command of her ten days later and took charge of the *Carmania* on 30 January. This command, like that on *Andania*, lasted Rostron just one round voyage. *Carmania* sailed from Liverpool on 3 February, lay over at New York for three days, called at Halifax for four days and returned to Liverpool before the end of the month. Rostron paid off at the beginning of March to assume the command that he would hold for the rest of the war.[37]

By 1918 the Americans were finally mobilized and massed in numbers sufficient to make a significant difference on the Western Front. But first they had to get there. They could not reach Europe without transport from the British merchant marine. This gave the great Atlantic liners another chance to operate in the service for which they had always been intended: hauling large numbers of people medium distances at high speeds. With the Americans crossing in numbers to justify it, *Olympic* and *Aquitania* were pressed into this service, as was that other famous liner, which had spent the previous year idled in the Firth of Clyde.[38]

The *Mauretania* that greeted Rostron in March 1918 had been reconfigured once again. This time she flew the white ensign as the commissioned Royal Navy armed merchant cruiser HMS *Tuber Rose*, a *nom de guerre* largely ignored, save by officialdom. Harder to ignore was her new colour scheme – a dazzle-painted arrangement of chequerboard patches stood on end on the fore part of the ship and a hodge-podge of disjointed stripes down aft, in black, blue, grey and white – a garish livery intended to befuddle the optical rangefinders of enemy warships in those days before radar. If an engagement became inevitable, however, HMS *Tuber Rose* at least had some answer in the form of six six-inch guns mounted at points about the ship.[39]

Rostron's assignment to command HMS *Tuber Rose* came with his promotion to Acting Captain in the Royal Naval Reserve on 6 March 1918. It also completed a set for Rostron, who believed himself to be 'the only captain who sailed under all the four ensigns – the White of the Royal Navy, the Red of the Merchant Service, the Blue of the RNR and the Admiralty of the hospital ships' during the war.[40]

Mauretania made seven round trip voyages to New York under Rostron from March to November of 1918. She transported 33,339 American soldiers to Europe, a total only exceeded by *Aquitania* and *Olympic*, which made eight and nine such trooping voyages, respectively. *Mauretania*'s round voyages averaged seventeen days, including a five-day layover in New York. Except in the vicinity of land at each end of a crossing, she steamed unescorted, finding safety in a speed that averaged 22 to 23 knots.[41]

Mauretania's only excitement during this time occurred when, early one morning, a submarine was sighted about two miles away. Thomas Royden, later Cunard's chairman, happened to be aboard for that voyage. He remembered that 'though the Watch [*sic*] was extremely keen to have a shot at it, Rostron refused to allow any firing'. Royden wrote that Rostron's decision not to engage prevented a panic among the green troops aboard in the opinion of their commanding officer. Rostron's decision to use his speed to escape rather than to employ his potentially superior firepower against the submarine also suited his – and doubtless the Admiralty's – general strategy: 'Our motto was to get there and not look for trouble.' In that he succeeded. 'In the course of seven trips we only lost one soldier and he committed suicide.'[42]

Rostron and *Mauretania* had just begun their seventh return voyage with another group of American soldiers, when word came by wireless on 11 November 1918 that the Armistice had been declared. The ship delivered the soldiers to Liverpool and then reversed the process. After the hostilities ended, the United States Navy chartered *Mauretania* to help bring men home from England and France. On 30 December *Mauretania* arrived in New York on her second repatriation voyage with 3707 soldiers, including 237 injured and ill. She crossed from Brest, France, in less than six days at an average of 22 knots, a passage highlighted by a Christmas Day turkey dinner for 'nearly 5000', followed by a concert with carols from the ship's glee singers. *Mauretania* and Rostron would continue these repatriation voyages until the ship was discharged from government service in May 1919.[43]

The British merchant marine had played the most significant part in bringing North America's military potential to bear against the Central Powers. Of the 2,027,914 Americans transported across the Atlantic during the First World War, fifty-three per cent sailed in British ships, twenty-eight per cent in confiscated German ships employed by the American Overseas Naval Transportation Service and nineteen per cent in American-owned vessels. Cunard by itself transported about 900,000 soldiers and moved ten million tons of cargo during the war, operating 180 ships on the North Atlantic under the British government's direction. By war's end the company owned or controlled through its various subsidiaries 558,380 tons of shipping, with another 426,800 tons under construction.[44]

Rostron had done his part and then some in the British merchant service during the four terrible years of the First World War. He had spent 971 of the 1561 days of the war away from Britain, usually steaming in harm's way. His six ships had carried over one hundred thousand soldiers during the war and lost only the one to suicide. 'I was jealous of my record,' he wrote later, 'tremendously glad of it and, if I may add, put much of it down to ... my belief in a divinity that shapes our ends.' Rostron would be suitably recognized for his contributions. To his Sea Transport Medal, awarded for his service as first officer in *Aurania* during the South African War, he could add the 1914–15 Star, awarded for service in any theatre during those years; the British Mercantile Marine War Medal, awarded by the Board of Trade to merchant sailors who had sailed in war zones; the British War Medal, awarded to those who served in a theatre of war from August 1914 to November 1918; and the Victory Medal, issued to holders of the 1914–15 Star or the War Medal.[45]

In addition to these four decorations, awarded to many people with similar service, Rostron was recognized individually for his conduct, both within the service and publicly. He was commended in his service record by the Lords of the Admiralty 'for valuable services rendered in evacuating sick and wounded from Gallipoli Peninsula in course of operations at [the] Dardanelles'. His name was specially mentioned by the director general of medical services in Egypt and also in a report from the War Office, for his 'courtesy and assistance shown to Officer Commanding troops on board the "Mauretania" which conveyed wounded from Mudros to Southampton'. In May 1916 Commander Arthur H. Rostron, RD, RNR, was mentioned in naval dispatches 'for good services whilst employed on Transport duties at the Dardanelles' when commanding HMT *Alaunia* the year before.[46]

With the war won, Rostron received two significant rewards. Effective from 31 December 1918, he was promoted to the permanent rank of captain in the Royal Naval Reserve. At the same time, 'in recognition of valuable services rendered in connection with the War,' he was appointed a Commander of the Military Division of the Most Excellent Order of the British Empire.

One final, signal military honour came five years later, on 2 February 1924, when Rostron was appointed Royal Naval Reserve Aide de Camp to the King. Rostron retired from military service three months later, on 14 May 1924, his fifty-fifth birthday, at the rank of captain.[47]

Recognized he was, but Arthur Rostron and his generation paid a high price for their citations and decorations. Almost 15,000 sailors in the British merchant and fishing fleets were killed during the First World War. Cunard Steamship Company alone lost twenty-two ships of 220,444 gross tons, comprising fifty-six per cent of the company's prewar tonnage. The company's heaviest losses came from among the medium-sized passenger-cargo ships that Rostron spent most of the war commanding.[48]

Rostron's experience reflected that of his company. Six of the fourteen Cunard ships he had commanded since he became a captain in 1907 were lost in action during the First World War, including three of his six wartime commands. First and most notoriously went *Lusitania* – 'whose brutal and unnecessary loss was so much deplored by every decent person' in Rostron's opinion – sunk off the south coast of Ireland with the loss of 1198 lives on 7 May 1915. Rostron's second command, the small cargo steamer *Veria*, lasted until that 7 December, when she was torpedoed a few hours before she would have reached Alexandria, Egypt. *Alaunia* sank on 19 October 1916, the victim of a mine off Eastbourne in the English Channel while returning to London from New York. Ten weeks later, on New Year's Day 1917, *Ivernia* sank after her torpedoing south of Greece. A year after that, on 27 January 1918, a submarine torpedoed *Andania* off the north coast of Ireland bound from Liverpool to New York and she went ashore and was lost during a salvage attempt. *Carpathia* went down west of Ireland on 17 July 1918, the sixth and last of Rostron's former commands lost to the enemy during the First World War.[49]

Rostron not only survived all of this carnage, he was never involved. Each of these vessels met her end after Rostron had left her. Rostron acknowledged in his memoir that 'the fortunes of war favoured me in that respect, for though many of my old ships came to disaster, I was lucky throughout and thus my memories of the war, while those of one in the arena, are not coloured by actual personal hurt'.[50]

That was a half-truth, however. Rostron's family was to suffer the tragedy of the First World War through the loss of his youngest brother, George, godfather to Arthur and Ethel's first child, Harry. George Rostron, age thirty-nine and unmarried, enlisted as a private in the 3rd Cheshire Regiment in June 1916. On 26 January 1917, he was commissioned a second lieutenant in the 59th Battalion, Machine Gun Corps. His unit arrived in France on 6 February 1918 and deployed at Bullecourt, about nine miles south-east of Arras, five days later. He was killed in action thirty-eight days after that, on 21 March 1918, at the age of forty.[51]

George Rostron vanished at the point of attack on the first day of the German spring offensive of 1918. After Russia, wracked by revolution, officially withdrew from the war on 3 March, the German high command shifted most of its army to the western theatre and launched an all-or-nothing effort to break the Allied front and either roll up the British Army against the Channel or capture Paris before the United States could bring its strength to bear. The British and French front bent before the German onslaught, in some places badly, but it did not break. By June the Allies had stalled an offensive that cost Germany more than half a million irreplaceable men. Germany launched one last sputtering drive toward Paris in mid-July, but by then Arthur Rostron and his fellow sailors were delivering a quarter of a million Americans to France a month, swinging Germany's temporary numerical advantage back to the Allies. In August and September the French, British and Americans launched their own offensives, driving the German Army back over the contested ground and draining it of the last of its vitality. On 11 November 1918, Germany capitulated, ending the First World War.[52]

CHAPTER 13

THE MOST BEAUTIFUL LINER AFLOAT

'More than a score of ships have been home to me,' Rostron wrote at his retirement, 'and of those vessels the pride must always be the *Mauretania* … in my eyes the most beautiful liner afloat; the vessel that seemed a living thing to me.' Some liners of her era were larger; some were more opulent. None was faster. Blessed with an extra turn of speed over her Clyde-built sister *Lusitania*, *Mauretania* established the fastest eastbound passage of the Atlantic in 1907, set the westbound mark in 1909 and then held the record in both directions for the next twenty years. While *Lusitania* is now remembered mostly for her terrible destruction only seven years into her career, *Mauretania* survived the war to become Cunard's signature ship of the first third of the twentieth century.[1]

Rostron served as *Mauretania's* master from October 1915 to February 1916 and from March 1918 until July 1926, a total of eight years and nine months. He was the sixth of her nine regular masters, but commanded the ship for a third of her years in service and for nearly twice as long as any other captain. During Rostron's years in command the only serious challenges to *Mauretania's* speed records came from herself.[2]

The ship was world famous long before Rostron took charge in 1915. Laid down in the autumn of 1904 at Swan, Hunter & Wigham Richardson's yard on the north bank of the River Tyne at Wallsend, Newcastle, the vessel was launched two years later, on 20 September 1906, by the Dowager Duchess of Roxburgh. *Mauretania* had an overall length of 790 feet, a beam of 88 feet and was designed for a maximum draft of 34 feet. *Lusitania* and *Mauretania* were half again as big as the world's next largest ship, Norddeutscher Lloyd's twenty-thousand-ton *Kaiser Wilhelm II*. *Mauretania*, at 31,938 gross tons, was the larger of the pair by three hundred tons.[3]

To propel a vessel of that size at the Admiralty's stipulated 'minimum average ocean speed of 24.5 knots in moderate weather' – and thereby also to best *Kaiser Wilhelm II* – would require seventy per cent more horsepower than the German liner produced. If *Mauretania*'s upper works were devoted to public rooms and staterooms for first-class passengers, her lower decks were mostly occupied by the enormous power plant that drove her.[4]

In the ship's four boiler rooms forward, twenty-three double-ended and two single-ended boilers devoured the thousand tons of coal a day fed to them by a force of 204 firemen and 120 coal trimmers. Those boilers delivered steam at 195psi to the ship's enormous turbines, originally rated to develop 68,000 horsepower. Because their designers believed it unwise to exceed twenty thousand horsepower per shaft, the sister ships were propelled by quadruple screws, the first Atlantic liners so equipped. Since a steam turbine cannot be rotated in reverse, six turbines had to be jammed into the ships' engine spaces. Steam from the boilers drove two high-pressure turbines linked to the ship's outboard shafts, then fed into two low-pressure turbines that turned her inboard shafts, to which the ship's two reversing turbines were also connected. While Charles Parsons' firm built the turbines used in *Lusitania*, *Mauretania*'s machinery and boilers were constructed by Wallsend Slipway and Engineering Company – in which Swan Hunter had a controlling interest – working in cooperation with Parsons' company, which lay adjacent to it along the Tyne.[5]

In addition to her engineering department of 393 officers and men, *Mauretania* had a deck force of nine officers and sixty men, while 476 of the crew, including twenty women, worked in the 'Victualating Department', as a ship's hotel and restaurant staff was known in those days. This produced a total ship's complement of 938. The victualating staff attended to the needs of a maximum of 2165 passengers – 563 in first class, 464 in second class and 1138 in third class – giving the ship a civilian capacity of 3103 people.[6]

On the morning of 17 September 1907, *Mauretania* left the Tyne for the first time for preliminary trials in the North Sea, carrying officials and technicians from Swan Hunter, Wallsend Slipway and Engineering and

Cunard. *The Times* recorded that 'the enthusiasm was extraordinary; the entire population seemed to have turned out'. After several days of trials, the ship returned to the Wallsend yard for a month to have her stern stiffened against the excessive vibration initially produced by her speed. That issue resolved, the ship left Newcastle on the afternoon of 22 October for her official trials in the Firth of Clyde. 'All Tyneside seemed to take holiday on the occasion,' said *The Times*, 'for all Tynesiders are proud of the greatest ship which has ever been borne by the waters of the historic river, or by any other waters for that matter.' Swan Hunter invited about four hundred guests to make the passage around the north of Scotland from Newcastle to Liverpool in weather 'exceptionally fine for the time of year'.[7]

In October 1907, with *Lusitania* in service and *Mauretania* about to begin her sea trials, *The Times* noted that, though nominally sisters, the ships were built by different yards, with each builder given some latitude. This, the newspaper opined, 'may result in some slight differences in their respective performances at sea… Experience alone can decide which is actually the faster ship of the two.' The advantage belonged to *Mauretania*, whose distance trial began at 8am on Sunday, 3 November. *Lusitania* had averaged 25.4 knots on her forty-eight-hour trial. *Mauretania* improved upon that standard by more than half a knot. She covered the 304-mile course between Corsewall Light on the Firth of Clyde and Longships Light at Land's End twice in each direction in forty-seven hours and thirty-six minutes, for an average of 26.04 knots. *Mauretania*'s second southbound run, the third leg of the trial, averaged a blistering 27.36 knots.[8]

At the conclusion of her distance trial, the ship anchored close to Skelmorlie and at daybreak on Wednesday, 6 November, commenced her runs over the measured mile. *Mauretania* demonstrated remarkable consistency, averaging 26.03 knots in her speed tests on the Skelmorlie mile. Her trials satisfactorily concluded, Cunard accepted the ship, which docked at Liverpool on Thursday, 7 November, with nine days to prepare for her maiden voyage. In *Lusitania* and *Mauretania*, Cunard possessed the two largest and fastest ships in the world. *The Times* concluded that the steamship company had 'more than fulfilled [its] undertaking with the Government and the nation may be well content'.[9]

Once again the populace gathered; perhaps fifty thousand lined Liverpool's waterfront in a steady rain to watch *Mauretania* cast off just after 7.30pm on 16 November 1907. The 'immense crowd kept up a roar of cheers,' according to a reporter from *The Times* along for the voyage, 'and the good wishes were emphasized with a tumultuous discord of syrens and bells which followed us over the water until the home lights were fading into the mist'. The ship arrived at Queenstown at nine the next morning after a smooth passage. Two hours later, she departed for New York.[10]

Then November, not the best month to set speed records on the North Atlantic, had its say. A day out of Queenstown, pounding into heavy seas, *Mauretania*'s spare anchor stored on her forecastle worked loose 'and danced about the deck'. Captain John Prichard hove to for the two hours it took to secure the anchor, then resumed *Mauretania*'s trudge into the westerly gales. She arrived at New York on 22 November after a passage averaging a respectable 22.21 knots.[11]

Mauretania set the record for an eastbound passage on her first try, however. Clearing Sandy Hook on the afternoon of 30 November, she arrived at Queenstown, five time zones to the east, on the evening of 5 December in an hour and a half less than five days. She had averaged 23.69 knots and shaved twenty-one minutes from *Lusitania*'s record. Conditions, 'though not ideal, were favourable for December'. These included thirty hours of fog off the Grand Banks, which caused intermittent speed reductions, but also a day and a half of a 50-knot westerly gale, which pushed the ship to over 24 knots. Certainly *Mauretania* had not reached her potential, but *The Times* concluded that 'the Cunard Company and the public may rest satisfied with this early proof that the Mauretania is the fastest as well as the biggest liner afloat'.[12]

The westbound transatlantic record proved more elusive, however, *Lusitania* holding that honour until 1909. *Mauretania* finally exceeded *Lusitania*'s westbound standard on the twenty-sixth voyage of her career, which departed Liverpool on 25 September 1909. It was a year later, however, on her fortieth voyage, that *Mauretania* established her untouchable prewar records. She sailed from Liverpool on 10 September 1910 and made the passage from Daunt Rock, off Queenstown, to Ambrose Light in four days, ten hours and forty-one minutes at an average speed of 26.06 knots. On her return from

New York, which began on 21 September, she bettered her own eastbound mark with a crossing that averaged 25.89 knots. That December *Mauretania* posted a record round voyage of eleven days, twelve hours and twenty-three minutes, which included a layover at New York of only thirty-seven hours and twenty minutes.[13]

After the First World War and her demobilization voyages, Rostron and *Mauretania* returned to a changed civilian scene. Postwar passenger traffic patterns dictated different ports of call for Cunard's New York service. With American and Canadian immigration restrictions and Irish emigration effectively ended, the great liners stopped calling at Cobh, Republic of Ireland, the former Queenstown. The main traffic of the Twenties sailed in the opposite direction, with American tourists visiting the Continent in large numbers. That put Liverpool, three hundred miles north of Land's End on the Irish Sea, at a serious competitive disadvantage – out of position to serve the Continent and three times as far from London as was Southampton.[14]

If those circumstances had not been decisive, by the early twentieth century the largest liners had simply outgrown Liverpool. Its shifting sands, shallows and stiff tides made the Mersey one of the most challenging rivers in Britain to navigate. The shallows also meant that big ships could generally manoeuvre only close to high tide, limiting access to the port's landing stages. Cunard's great liners arriving in Liverpool during the prewar years usually unloaded quickly at the pier and then shifted to one of two large mooring buoys that the company had anchored in the relatively deep waters of the Sloyne, on the opposite side of the Mersey off Birkenhead. 'The ship at the buoy in the river,' McNeil explained, 'had to have all her coal, stores, cargo, [etc.], brought off to her; and tenders had to run to and fro for ship's people and workmen,' a time-consuming, laborious and expensive proposition.[15]

Thanks to its famous 'double tide', caused by the Isle of Wight diverting ebb tides from the English Channel into the Solent, Southampton Water enjoyed much longer periods of high water. This permitted the great liners better access and more flexible scheduling, which, combined with the port's proximity to London and the Continent, became the key factors in Southampton's emergence as Britain's preeminent passenger terminus. The White Star Line inaugurated the shift from Liverpool to Southampton in 1907, but Cunard, headquartered at Liverpool, continued to operate out

Rostron was a cadet aboard the school ship HMS *Conway* at Liverpool from February 1885 to December 1886. (Courtesy of The Conway Club.)

'Taught and trim as a yacht', the full-rigged *Cedric the Saxon* was Rostron's favourite sailing ship. He made three year-long voyages in her as an apprentice and one as chief mate. (Illustration by Jack Spurling in Basil Lubbock's *Sail: The Romance of the Clipper Ships*, 1936.)

Etruria, sister ship of Rostron's first Cunarder, *Umbria*. These vessels were nicknamed 'the Atlantic submarines' because of the wet ride they gave the deck watch. Rostron made numerous voyages in *Etruria* as both a junior and senior officer. (Author's collection.)

Chief Officer Rostron and his signature in 1906. He spent most of that year in *Etruria*. (Courtesy of the University of Liverpool Library, D42-PR2-2-109-9.)

The White Star liner *Titanic* casts off from Southampton on 10 April 1912, to begin her first and only voyage to New York. (Getty Images.)

Titanic survivors recover on *Carpathia*'s fore deck as she steams for New York. (US Library of Congress, LC-USZ62-56453.)

Part of the immense crowd that met *Carpathia* gathers in the rain on the street in front of Cunard's New York piers. The police officers were deployed at the pier's entrance to restrict access. (US Library of Congress, LC-DIG-ggbain-10347.)

White Star's chairman J. Bruce Ismay (hand to face) testifies at the Waldorf-Astoria Hotel in New York on 19 April 1912, as the first witness in the US Senate's enquiry into the *Titanic* disaster. Arthur Rostron would be the next witness. (US Library of Congress, LC-USZ62-68081.)

Rostron backs *Carpathia* into the Hudson River on the afternoon of 19 April, resuming her interrupted Mediterranean voyage. (US Library of Congress, LC-USZ62-84521.)

Rostron receives the loving cup awarded to him by a committee of *Titanic*'s survivors from Mrs. Margaret Brown on 29 May 1912. (US Library of Congress, LC-USZ62-47788.)

Rostron and some of his officers pose with the loving cup aboard *Carpathia*. In his memoirs, James Bisset identified them as Dr Frank McGee, Rostron, and Chief Officer Hankinson (seated left to right), Second Officer Bisset (framed by the porthole), and Purser E. F. G. Brown standing behind Third Officer Eric Rees (far right). Neither Chief Engineer Alexander Johnstone nor First Officer Horace Dean appears in this photograph. (US Library of Congress, LC-DIG-ggbain-10426.)

Two Captains of Titanic Disaster; Their Conduct and Their Rewards

CAPTAIN LORD, of the California, who went to lie down in his stateroom while signal rockets were being fired from the Titanic, sinking less than ten miles away:

CAPTAIN ROSTRON, of the Carpathia, whose vessel heard the distress call when 58 miles away, steamed through dangerous ice to the rescue and saved 703 souls:

Severely censured by Chairman Smith, of the Senate Investigating Committee, in his report.

"Failure of Captain Lord to arouse the wireless operator on his ship, who easily could have ascertained the name of the vessel in distress," says Senator Smith, "and reached her in time to avert loss of life, places a responsibility upon this officer which it will be difficult for him to escape."

Warmly praised in Senator Smith's report.

Receives the thanks of Congress, carrying with it the privilege of admission to the floor of the Senate and House for life. President Taft is authorized to have struck off and presented to Rostron a medal of honor containing $1,000 worth of gold.

The captain also receives the New York American's purse (now about $8,500), contributed by readers of The American.

In 'Two Captains of Titanic Disaster', the *New York American* of 29 May 1912, extols the hero of the tragedy. Five days later the newspaper presented Rostron with the large reward mentioned in the article.

Ethel and Arthur Rostron in New York on 25 February 1913. They travelled to Washington, DC, three days later to receive Rostron's Congressional Gold Medal. (US Library of Congress, LC-USZ62-105865.)

An illustration of Rostron's Congressional Gold Medal that appeared in *The New York Times* on 2 March 1913, the day after he received it from President William Howard Taft.

Accompanied by Ethel, Rostron receives the American Cross of Honor from James Bryce, Britain's ambassador to the United States, at the British Embassy in Washington, DC, on 1 March 1913. (US Library of Congress, LC-DIG-hec-02141.)

CUNARD LINE   R.M.S. "ANDANIA"   GROSS TONNAGE 14,000

Rostron made only one voyage as master of RMS *Andania*, but he commanded her sister ship *Alaunia* from November 1913 to September 1915. (Author's collection.)

HM Hospital Ship *Mauretania* made three voyages, all under Rostron's command, from October 1915 through January 1916.

Rostron sailed in RMS *Saxonia* on North Atlantic service as a senior watch officer in 1903 and 1904, and commanded her on the same routes during the war for most of 1916. (Author's collection.)

Rostron brings the doughboys home on 2 December 1918, aboard the dazzle-painted *Mauretania*, making her first appearance in New York Harbor since the Armistice. (US Library of Congress, LC-DIG-ggbain-27960.)

An enlarged portion of another photograph of *Mauretania*'s arrival shows
Rostron standing on the starboard bridge wing as his ship ties up. (Detail of
US Library of Congress, LC-DIG-ggbain-27963.)

R. M. S. "MAURETANIA".
LENGTH 788 Fr.   BREADTH 88 Fr.   TONNAGE 31,000.

RMS *Mauretania* in pre-war civilian service. (Author's collection.)

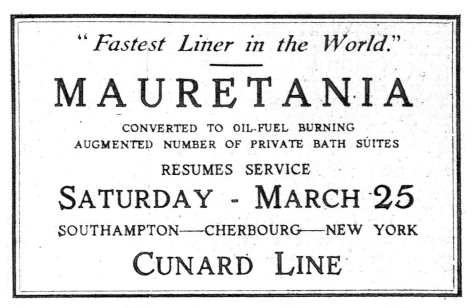

"Fastest Liner in the World."

MAURETANIA

CONVERTED TO OIL-FUEL BURNING
AUGMENTED NUMBER OF PRIVATE BATH SUITES

RESUMES SERVICE

SATURDAY - MARCH 25

SOUTHAMPTON——CHERBOURG——NEW YORK

CUNARD LINE

An announcement of *Mauretania's* return to service following repairs and alterations made after her shipboard fire of July 1921. (*The Times*, 17 March 1922.)

Captain Arthur Henry Rostron, CBE, RD, RNR, in 1926,
the year he was knighted. (Getty Images.)

S.15788.   CUNARD LINE R.M.S. "BERENGARIA" GROSS TONNAGE 52,700.

RMS *Berengaria*, the former HAPAG liner *Imperator*,
Rostron's final command. (Author's collection.)

Commodore Rostron and Prime Minister Ramsay MacDonald (left and right front)
aboard *Berengaria*. MacDonald became the first sitting prime minister to visit the United
States when Rostron's ship arrived at New York on 4 October 1929. (Getty Images.)

Staff Captain James Bisset bids farewell to his 'old friend, superior, and shipmate', Commodore Sir Arthur Rostron, on 5 November 1930, at the conclusion of Rostron's final voyage in command of RMS *Berengaria*. (Courtesy of the University of Liverpool Library, D42-PR2-2-7-35.)

Arthur and Ethel Rostron's grave in the Old Burial Ground, West End, Southampton. (Author's collection.)

of the Mersey and the Thames, experimenting before the war with landfalls at Fishguard, Wales, or Plymouth, England, to accelerate passengers' arrival at London by rail.[16]

With the war over, Cunard had to shift its New York passenger service to Southampton to remain competitive, whatever the feelings of Liverpool sailors such as Rostron and Bisset. The company's chairman, Sir Alfred Booth, announced the relocation of *Mauretania* and *Aquitania* in February 1919. This decision was permitted in part by the ouster of German lines from the port as a result of the First World War. Booth declared Cunard's intention to secure the previously German trade in the Southampton–Cherbourg–New York service and his company even acquired the former offices of Norddeutscher Lloyd for its Southampton headquarters. Fortnightly passenger service began that June, even as the line continued to repatriate North American soldiers. The change of ports quickly proved justified, with *The Times* reporting eighteen months later that Cunard's Southampton–New York express service 'has met with great success and Continental passengers have made full demands on the space in the *Aquitania* and *Mauretania*'. Those two ships were joined at the beginning of 1920 by the ex-German liner *Imperator*, which Cunard acquired in 1919 and renamed *Berengaria*. These vessels provided Cunard's three-ship service between Southampton and New York into the 1930s, with *Caronia* and *Carmania* operating in relief.[17]

Cunard's other immediate order of business after the war was to rebuild its ravaged fleet. By the Armistice only *Caronia*, *Carmania*, *Mauretania* and *Aquitania* remained of Cunard's prewar Atlantic liners. With more than half of the company's prewar tonnage sunk – twenty-two ships in all – Cunard took delivery of a dozen replacements in the five years after 1920. Five of these vessels, six-hundred-foot passenger steamers of about twenty thousand tons, mimicked *Caronia* and *Carmania*. The other seven were more in the mould of *Carpathia*, being five hundred-footers of about thirteen thousand tons. All twelve ships were twin-screw vessels but, a generation advanced from their prewar ancestors, were oil-fired and turbine-driven. Cunard set these ships to work from various British and Continental ports to North American destinations from the St Lawrence River to Chesapeake Bay. As the 1920s wore on, Cunard faced increased competition from other steamship lines, themselves slowly recovering from the First World War.[18]

The competition the Atlantic steamship companies reentered after the war was radically altered by significant immigration restrictions imposed by Canada and the United States. In 1921 the US Congress restricted annual immigration to three per cent of a nationality's total enumeration in the US Census of 1910. That law cost Cunard a thirty per cent reduction in its westbound, third-class traffic the following year. The Italian government further complicated matters by mandating carriage of Italian emigrants in Italian ships to protect its own merchant marine. In 1924, following pressure from Atlantic steamship companies and the British government, the US Congress changed the datum for the three per cent calculation to the census of 1890. Even that revision, which slightly favoured emigrants from the British Isles, still reduced annual transatlantic steerage traffic to about a third of what it had been in the last prewar year, 1913.[19]

In June 1924, Sir Ashley Sparkes, Cunard's resident director in the United States, admitted that US immigration restrictions had badly hurt the Atlantic passenger trade, but he believed that his company had largely offset the loss through operating efficiencies. Cunard tried to maximize its earnings by shortening its ships' turnarounds in the summer season, a process expedited by their conversion to burning oil fuel. In the spring of 1925 the company announced a 'speeding up programmme' for *Mauretania*. Under her new schedule, Rostron's ship sailed from New York on Wednesday evenings, arrived at Plymouth the following Tuesday morning to discharge urgent passengers and mails, made a call of about an hour at Cherbourg that midday to transfer passengers, baggage and mails to the Continent by tender and then sprinted back across the Channel once more to reach Southampton that evening – a relentless three ports of call in twelve hours.[20]

Eight months later, in November 1925, Cunard and White Star agreed to economize by offering alternate winter sailings. Until the following March, one or the other company offered one of its big three for a weekly passage, a system which kept one of each company's ships sailing to or fro and another preparing to sail. This offered the double advantage of reducing surplus capacity and of idling one of each company's ships for winter overhaul. Come spring, each resumed its regular three-ship service of weekly sailings from Southampton and New York.[21]

However, these efficiencies alone would not produce a profit. After losing most of their steerage trade, Atlantic liners had to find new customers. Lost immigrant traffic was partially replaced in the 1920s by tourists wishing to cross the Atlantic. To accommodate this new type of passenger, interested in economy as well as adventure, Atlantic steamship companies developed a new class known as tourist third. This offered passage at a third-class fare but provided additional amenities over steerage, such as cabin instead of dormitory accommodation. Cunard started by carrying Americans and Canadians, 'mostly professors and students', to Europe in tourist third. In 1925 the company began to run the service in the other direction for Britons wishing to visit the US or Canada on holiday. Cunard's westbound tourist-third cabin was 'designed to provide comfortable accommodation at a low cost and so bring the pleasures of an Atlantic crossing within the reach of holiday-makers and people who are not looking for luxury, but want to get a chance of seeing the New World'. The company suggested an outward passage via the St Lawrence to Quebec or Montreal, with a return via the St Lawrence or from Boston or New York. Those leaving from New York could return quickly on *Mauretania* or one of the company's other big ships.[22]

Cunard marketed tourist third as inexpensive and convenient and tried to allay any 'mistaken prejudice' against travelling third class. 'Today the third-class accommodation is far superior to the second-class of even 15 or 20 years ago,' claimed *The Times* in language that reads suspiciously like steamship company advertising copy. 'There are excellent bathrooms, beds composed of spring mattresses, spotless bed linen and warm blankets, large dining saloons in which six-course dinners are served and smoking rooms and lounges with comfortable carpets and furniture.' The writer extolled ships' libraries, orchestras, dances, shops and 'variety of popular deck games and sports'. In Rostron's opinion tourist class rated as the 'jolliest crowd on the whole ship' in a decade famous for its jolly crossings.[23]

Cruising increased as a source of steamship revenue in the 1920s. No longer just positioning voyages, Cunard cruised the Mediterranean from Southampton and tapped the American market with Caribbean cruises from New York or an occasional Mediterranean or even world cruise from that port. McNeil remembered of *Mauretania*'s later cruises that 'it was always pleasant to leave the steady grind of going to and from New York,' particularly since the cruises occurred in February or March, 'when the Atlantic is frequently in its least amiable mood'. In contrast, 'cruises with fine weather and happy passengers are always enjoyable'.[24]

Rostron commanded *Mauretania*'s first cruise, an ambitious undertaking. His ship arrived in New York on 2 February 1923, after a five-week overhaul in Southampton, and sailed for the Mediterranean five days later. Among her five hundred passengers sailed renowned Kansas newspaper editor William Allen White, *Titanic* survivor Emily Ryerson and an unfortunately named Professor William Boring.[25]

The cruise lasted sixty-nine days and covered 10,132 miles, with calls at Madeira and Cadiz in the Atlantic, then Gibraltar, Algiers, Naples, Monaco, Alexandria, Haifa, Constantinople and Athens in the Mediterranean and Aegean. The voyage to Constantinople included for Rostron a poignant passage of the Dardanelles not quite eight years after the Allies' futile campaign against the Gallipoli Peninsula. 'It was interesting to see the change,' he reflected. 'All was peace and the government of nature was once again supreme ... [still] one's thoughts went back to it all.' *Mauretania* called at Southampton in the first week of April, then simultaneously concluded her cruise and reentered transatlantic service when she crossed to New York a week later. *Mauretania* ultimately would make fifty-four cruises during her career, carrying aggregates of 31,517 passengers, 252,040 miles.[26]

Not inclined to miss a trick, Cunard even employed its big three as overgrown Channel steamers during Britain's summer holidays. *The Times* reported in September 1924 that the service between Southampton and Cherbourg, provided by *Mauretania,* *Aquitania* and *Berengaria*, 'has been largely used during the holiday season'. With no need of a cabin for the four-hour crossing, Britons visiting the Continent had access to each vessel's public rooms and 'plenty of opportunity to explore the ship'.[27]

Cunard also tried to attract passengers of all classes, particularly Americans, by repeatedly modernizing its ships. One of *Mauretania*'s refits of the latter 1920s listed among her 'considerable improvements' the reconditioning of one hundred staterooms. 'Hot and cold water has been introduced into every first-class state-room and also fans and electric radiators,' *The Times* reported. 'There is now a bed – not a bunk – in each stateroom.' Thanks to

Cunard's modernization of its older ships, its postwar building programme, its innovations and efficiencies and also to the general prosperity of the decade, the company remained financially sound throughout the 1920s.[28]

In May 1921 James Bisset rejoined *Mauretania* and the ranks of Rostron's officers, this time as senior first officer. He shared his captain's high opinion of the ship. 'She was a thoroughbred,' he wrote. 'Exactly what gave her that quality was difficult to define, but it was unmistakable in her. She was a personality.' Bisset made eleven voyages in *Mauretania* between May 1920 and July 1922 and regarded *Mauretania* as a happy or lucky ship. Events would prove that *Mauretania* was lucky to have Bisset.[29]

The world's fastest ocean liner arrived at Southampton, after her latest passage from New York and Cherbourg, on Friday, 22 July 1921. Rostron went home to Liverpool for a few days and most of the crew lay ashore as well. A skeleton force remained aboard, joined by a host of shore-based cleaners, to prepare the ship for her next departure, eight days hence. On the following Monday afternoon, 25 July, at about 2pm, one of the cleaners, using a combustible chemical to clean a carpet, started a fire in one of the first-class cabins on E deck.[30]

Bisset happened to be walking along the wharf returning to the ship to assume the afternoon duty when the alarm came. He raced aboard and encountered Cunard's Southampton marine superintendent, Captain Samuel McNeil, who confirmed the fire and informed Bisset that there was no pressure on *Mauretania*'s fire mains. Bisset passed word to the chief engineer, who hurried below to get the pumps working while Bisset headed for the scene of the fire. It took time to build water pressure, however, and only about thirty members of *Mauretania*'s crew were aboard to fight the blaze, which spread quickly. When Bisset arrived in the dining saloon he found its carpets and wooden panelling already on fire.

Without proper breathing equipment, he and the other sailors were soon driven away from the source of the fire, as dense smoke began erupting from *Mauretania*'s port side and superstructure. Southampton fire companies arrived on the pier, smashed out portholes on the port side and began pouring water into the ship, while two passing tugboats engaged the fire in a like manner on the starboard side. But these attempts to reach the seat of the fire from outside the hull proved ineffective and soon smoke and heat rising through the ventilation system and up the grand staircase began to damage the decks above. Gangs were stationed on those decks to cool hot spots, while other shipboard fire parties attacked the inferno on E deck.

After 6pm these teams were bringing the fire under control, but had poured tons of water into the ship to do so. The portside doors on D and E decks had been opened for use by the city's firefighters, but the starboard doors remained closed and the starboard scuppers were soon clogged with debris. *Mauretania* began listing to starboard, causing all of the water to pool up to six feet deep on starboard E deck with no outlet. The ship heeled fifteen degrees away from her pier, snapping mooring lines forward and anticipating the French liner *Normandie*'s terrible fate at New York twenty years later. *Mauretania* did not capsize, however, thanks to her engineers at the pumps and to Bisset and three crewmen, who spent half an hour taking turns with a wrench loosening the submerged nuts to open one of the E-deck gangway doors. Their success allowed the trapped water to drain into the harbour, righting the ship at 6.30pm. By 8pm the fire was subdued, but the damage extensive. The main first-class dining saloon on E deck had been destroyed, staterooms on D and E decks incinerated and the first-class lounge and library, next to the grand staircase on B deck, had suffered badly.[31]

In all of the excitement, nobody had remembered to contact the ship's master at his home in Liverpool. Rostron learned of the situation abruptly the next morning, when one of his sons awoke him with a newspaper bearing the headline: 'Mauretania Is on Fire.' Rostron reported to Cunard's Liverpool offices at once, where the company's general manager instructed him and the company's marine superintendent to inspect the ship and report. They reached *Mauretania* that afternoon and examined her accompanied by a host of other officials. In Rostron's opinion the damage, which included distortion of the deck in the first-class dining room, was 'extensive enough to make it impossible to go to sea'.[32]

Loath to lose her services in the high season, Cunard's managers considered boarding off *Mauretania*'s damaged sections and carrying on. Rostron and some of the company's other old salts dissuaded them from doing so, arguing that the seagoing public might lose confidence in the ship when confronted with such evidence of her injuries. That reasoning was perhaps a rationalization for their heartfelt belief as sailors that the great lady should never appear in public in déshabillé. The company made the best of the situation by ordering her back to Newcastle for modernization, rather than just to repair the damage.[33]

Mauretania had to wait until September for a berth to become available at the Wallsend works of Swan, Hunter & Wigham Richardson, at which point Rostron took her north to Newcastle. She stood up the Tyne on the tide at 11am on a fine Sunday with huge crowds gathered along the river to witness her only return to their city. *Mauretania* remained at Swan Hunter for six months undergoing 'extensive reconditioning … to bring the whole accommodation into line with modern practice'. The improvements included 'numerous additional private bathrooms', and 'a specially designed parquet floor for dancing in the lounge'. The most significant change, however, was the conversion of *Mauretania*'s boilers to burn fuel oil.[34]

Some thought had been given to building *Lusitania* and *Mauretania* as oil burners, but the technological limits of 1907 and the problem 'that oil fuel is mostly obtained from localities not under British control' discouraged that innovation initially. By the 1920s, however, although oil was still a foreign fuel and remained more expensive than coal, particularly in Europe, other advantages justified converting Atlantic liners to burn oil.[35]

Mauretania burned about five thousand tons of coal per crossing. Upon making port and after the ship's passengers and cargoes had been discharged, *Mauretania* was 'boomed off' twenty feet from her pier so that coal barges could be brought alongside port and starboard. Then the twenty coaling ports on each side of the ship were laboriously unbolted by hand and several days of loading, with its clouds of coal dust, commenced. As first officer, coaling *Mauretania* was Bisset's 'bugbear'. He observed: 'That was the greatest disadvantage of coal-burning passenger liners – they had to be coaled.'[36]

Oil fuelling eliminated the coal dust that complicated the ship's housekeeping and it turned refuelling the ship from a task of days into one of hours. That, by itself, offered significant savings through reduced layovers, permitting the ship to make more voyages every year. Further, hundreds of stokers and coal trimmers could be paid off permanently, reducing *Mauretania*'s original 393-man engineering force by more than half. Switching to oil also meant that Cunard was no longer vulnerable to supply problems caused by the coal strikes that beset Britain in the first part of the twentieth century.[37]

Aquitania underwent conversion to oil in 1920 and the results proved economical. Thus both *Mauretania* and *Berengaria* were converted on the Tyne the following year. Swan Hunter reconfigured *Mauretania*'s bunkers to accommodate 5350 tons of oil in thirty compartments previously used to carry 6000 tons of coal. Upon returning to service, she burned 750 tons of oil rather than 1000 tons of coal a day. Although fuel oil cost three times as much per ton as coal, the efficiencies gained produced a saving of about £5000 per round voyage.[38]

Oil fuel had other advantages that were not purely economic. Coal-fired furnaces had to be extinguished in rotation for daily cleaning, costing a ship horsepower; oil-fired furnaces operated continuously. Oil also burned more cleanly, at a higher temperature and more consistently than coal, and its delivery into a ship's boilers did not depend upon human strength. These characteristics naturally appealed to the captain and chief engineer of an ocean racer like *Mauretania*. Rostron stated before the conversion that 'with oil fuel it would be an easy task to maintain her old speed'. Nor were oil's superior performance properties lost on the company. As *Mauretania* prepared to depart for Newcastle, *The Times* quoted a source who predicted that the ship would produce 'a steady 27 knots' after her conversion. When the refurbished vessel arrived at Southampton in March 1922, the newspaper confided that 'it is understood that an effort will be made shortly to create new "records"'.[39]

And so it proved. *Mauretania* averaged 24 knots on her first oil-fired westbound passage at the end of that month, her fastest crossing since before the war, and Rostron said that he had no doubt that she would better her westbound record of September 1910 when conditions proved favourable. Although that mark would not fall while he commanded her, *Mauretania*, under Rostron, continued to improve upon her best postwar times throughout the year.[40]

Oil burning certainly improved *Mauretania*'s performance, but she had other engineering problems. Her seventeen-year-old power plant was repeatedly hobbled by breakdowns and needed significant overhaul. That came in the spring of 1924, but led to a series of adventures for both the ship and her master. In November 1923 Cunard announced *Mauretania*'s withdrawal from Atlantic service for five months to be 'completely overhauled and extensively improved'. The work, to be carried out at Southampton, would include re-blading her turbines and rehabilitating her machinery, as well as painting the ship throughout, enclosing a large part of the B deck promenade and making extensive improvements to her third-class accommodations.[41]

Unfortunately, those efforts went aground, in the end literally, due to a shipyard strike that left *Mauretania* with her turbine covers raised and delicate rotors exposed. With no end to the strike in sight and determined not to lose summer business, Cunard's management decided to have the engine repairs completed in Cherbourg, but that meant towing the powerless ship across the English Channel.

At 9am on 11 April 1924, five Dutch tugs began manoeuvring *Mauretania* down Southampton Water – a Friday towing if not quite a Friday sailing. Rostron 'left the method of towing to the towing experts. I took charge of the navigating.' The misadventures began almost immediately, with *Mauretania* touching bottom on Calshot Spit, where Southampton Water enters the Solent, although Rostron was later able to assure Cunard's chairman that 'the ship was and is quite all right'. He attributed the incident to 'a case of too many cooks – we had too many pilots and too many tugs – and – in my opinion – a too nervous pilot on board my ship'. After Rostron's ship reached the English Channel, the situation got even more exciting.[42]

Mauretania entered the Channel in calm conditions on Friday evening and had crossed to within sight of the French coast by the following morning, but by noon Saturday a moderate west-south-west gale and a flood tide began to complicate the job. The danger of rough weather was that it might loose the suspended fifteen-ton turbine covers to demolish the sensitive machinery below. To keep his ship as stable as possible, Rostron ordered the tugs to cease towing toward France and to turn west to keep *Mauretania* bow-on to the wind and sea and on as even a keel as possible. By 2pm, however, with the tugs forced to slow to 1.5 knots into the wind, the sea and a 5-knot tide were driving *Mauretania* astern, eastward, at 2 to 3 knots.

At the worst moment, *Mauretania* came within two miles of being driven ashore at Cape Barfleur on the north-east corner of the Cotentin Peninsula, fifteen miles east of Cherbourg. Relief came when the tide turned and the wind dropped and the tow began crawling westward again, but complicating the situation further another ship went aground at the same time and began to send distress signals. By law that required *Mauretania* to cease transmitting, preventing Rostron from sending the next of the progress reports he had been dispatching to Cunard every six hours. His 6pm Saturday report remained unsent for twelve and a half hours and the rumour was soon abroad that it was Rostron's ship on the rocks and sending distress signals, causing Cunard's headquarters to be besieged by relatives of those aboard *Mauretania*.[43]

She arrived safely at Cherbourg at 7pm on Sunday, 13 April, after a passage of fifty-eight hours. The odyssey concluded, Cunard's chairman, Sir Thomas Royden, sent Rostron a congratulatory telegram. Rostron responded with a hand-written note thanking Royden and admitting that 'we had rather a tough time but it was worth it to get her [in] safely after all'. *Mauretania* returned to Southampton six weeks later, on the evening of 22 May 1924, having tested her re-bladed turbines on her way across the Channel by steaming fourteen miles at top speed first with and then against the tide.[44]

One final improvement to *Mauretania*'s power train, the installation of a new set of propellers, remained. That opportunity came immediately, when she dropped a screw on her first westbound passage at the beginning of June 1924. She made one more round voyage on three screws before entering dry dock in July. Refits completed, 'with her four new turbines and four new propellers,' *Mauretania* raced westward on her next voyage. She arrived at New York on 13 August 1924, having made the passage at an average speed of 25.6 knots and having reduced the previous fastest time between Cherbourg and New York by more than four hours. Rostron credited her performance in part to her conversion to oil, telling a reporter that *Mauretania*'s rated horsepower was 72,000, but that her engineers had coaxed the ship to deliver 78,000 horsepower on that crossing.[45]

Mauretania departed New York for Cherbourg on 20 August with the eastbound record in view. 'We knew from the outset – the chief [engineer, Andrew Cockburn,] and I – that we were doing it,' Rostron later admitted. There was, however, 'no point in circulating the intention because anything might happen to interfere with our project,' meaning, principally, storm or fog. To Rostron's satisfaction, however, *Mauretania*'s eastward passage took place in 'fine weather, light breezes and a smooth sea'. Her first day's mileage set a record, as did the second. 'Passengers began to sit up and take notice,' he said, since the official daily mileage figure was public knowledge, it being used in the mileage betting pool held each day on Atlantic liners to benefit the seamen's charities. 'On the third day the run was higher than ever before.' Rostron was asked that evening at the captain's table whether *Mauretania* was out for the record. '"Oh no, just out to do our best, that's all," I replied. But they knew all right.'[46]

The fourth day of the run brought some apprehension in the form of a mist that reduced visibility somewhat, but *Mauretania* raced on. 'Excitement grew on board,' Rostron remembered. 'Naturally every member of the crew was interested, but their enthusiasm was nothing compared with that of the passengers. Every day when the run was posted there was a crowd intent as watchers of a horse race ... and I believe everyone was as pleased as the chief and I were when that bit of haze lifted.' Rostron believed that 'the progress of the ship was the chief entertainment that voyage, once it was obvious [we] were out for the record'.[47]

By the fifth day knowledge of the attempt was not even confined to the ship. The day before she reached Cherbourg, *The New York Times* noted that *Mauretania* had covered the first 1858 miles of her voyage at an average of 26.39 knots and that if that continued she would establish a new record passage between New York and Cherbourg 'by several hours'. The goal of a record crossing had never been a state secret, but in the best traditions of transatlantic racing 'Captain Rostron would not admit he was out to break the eastbound record of 5 days, 6 hours and 13 minutes, now held by the *Majestic*, on the present trip to Cherbourg'. Instead he told the newspaper 'we hope to do our best and if we "do it" we will talk about it afterward. We know our ship has it in her to do certain things and we will try to get them out of her, that's all.' He was also careful to reassure readers that 'safety and comfort are our main goal'.[48]

Those niceties aside, *Mauretania* arrived at Cherbourg on the evening of 26 August 1924, after a passage of five days, one hour and forty-nine minutes. She had averaged 26.25 knots for the crossing, with a best one-day average of 27.05 knots. She reduced *Majestic's* eastbound record between the two ports by more than four hours. *Mauretania* had set speed records between

Cherbourg and New York in both directions on one round voyage and had established the best eastbound average speed ever for an Atlantic crossing, adding these jewels to her crown as the speed queen of the Atlantic.[49]

Less than two years later Rostron would relinquish command of 'the most beautiful liner afloat', but before he did so they shared one last adventure. On 27 February 1926, the 2525-ton British freighter *Laleham* departed Santiago, Chile, for home. The 280-foot ship called for fuel at Newport News, Virginia and then sailed for Ipswich, England, on 25 March with a crew of thirty-seven aboard. Six days later she was four hundred miles south-east of Halifax in nasty weather and desperate trouble. When her captain dispatched his distress call on the afternoon of 31 March, *Laleham* was rolling onto her beam ends in heavy seas, with water gaining in her holds and bunkers and all of her lifeboats carried away. *Mauretania* was westbound for New York when the call arrived from *Laleham* at 3.20pm. This emergency found Rostron commanding not a fourteen-knot passenger-cargo liner, but the fastest merchantman in the world. He altered course toward the reported position, ordered Chief Engineer Cockburn to produce emergency power and signalled to *Laleham*: 'COMING YOUR ASSISTANCE. DISTANCE 180 MILES, SPEED 25.5 KNOTS.'[50]

For the next four hours, the great liner raced toward the stricken freighter. In a repetition of the events of fourteen years before, the ship's crew cleared lifeboats for launching, prepared food and arranged accommodations for the survivors. Unlike Rostron's previous run, however, *Mauretania*'s passengers were both awake and aware of the circumstances; they crowded her public rooms and kept abreast of the situation through wireless messages posted on the ship's bulletin board.

This time, however, a vessel closer to the scene arrived first. The British tanker *Shirvan* spotted *Laleham* at 5.30pm and, with night approaching, *Laleham*'s captain informed Rostron: 'We are abandoning ship to SS Shirvan, but please come ahead.' By 7pm *Shirvan* had begun the transfer, but Rostron held course and speed for *Laleham*. 'You can never tell what will happen,' he said, 'so I kept on.' With the situation apparently in hand, however, Rostron asked *Shirvan*'s Captain Goodrich to inform him when all of *Laleham*'s sailors were recovered so that *Mauretania* might proceed to New York. 'I did not want to seem to butt in on the rescue,' he said, 'and one man making a good job of it was enough.' When confirmation of the rescue came a few minutes later, Rostron congratulated Goodrich and set course for New York. But during her sprint for *Laleham*, *Mauretania*, Rostron's 'wonder ship of the age', then eighteen years old, had reached twenty-nine knots and held it for an hour – 'through heavy seas and in a strong gale'.[51]

CHAPTER 14

THE SOCIAL WHIRL

Captain Arthur Henry Rostron turned fifty in May 1919, the same month that *Mauretania* resumed her civilian service. His years working Cunard's Mediterranean and Canadian routes were over. And with the exception of a single round voyage to New York in February 1924 as a relief captain of *Tyrrhenia*, Rostron would not sail in any of Cunard's postwar-built ships. From the end of the First World War until his retirement from the sea twelve years later, Rostron commanded Cunard's three largest liners in the company's most prestigious service, between Southampton and New York. He sailed in *Mauretania* until July of 1926 and then served as master of *Berengaria* during his final years at sea. Rostron commanded the third ship in the New York service, *Aquitania*, on voyages in January and November 1927 in relief of Cunard's commodore, Sir James Charles.[1]

During the 1920s, Rostron was one of Cunard's senior captains, with an authority born of both his seniority and his successes. G. H. Slade, a junior assistant purser under Rostron aboard *Berengaria* at the end of the decade, remembered that junior deck officers and pursers 'regarded him with a considerable amount of awe, combined with a certain amount of – if not fear – certainly apprehension. When he hove in sight, most of the younger officers deemed it expedient to keep well to windward of him.'[2]

As before, however, Rostron's authority did not seem to Slade or others to emanate from his stature. 'In appearance he bore little resemblance to the seaman of popular imagination or fiction who had served his time in sail,' Slade recalled. 'He was a slim figure, not particularly tall, with a rosy complexion and white hair ... and [the] direct antithesis of his Chief Officer and later Staff Captain, a certain Bissett [*sic*]. This latter character, though of a most amiable

160

disposition, always looked as if he should have had a belaying pin in one hand and a fistful of tarry spunyarn in the other, in the company of all hands on deck, twenty-four hours a day; never so Rostron.' At Rostron's retirement in 1930, a *New York Times* reporter expressed similar sentiments, writing that, out of uniform, the captain 'would look just like the good Bishop or the dear old dean, but when he is wearing the insignia of his seagoing command there is no mistaking his life's role'.[3]

It appears that Rostron recognized, and even embraced, the theatrical aspects of his role as master of a great liner on the North Atlantic. Slade, in a somewhat irreverent recollection of his days as an over-awed junior purser, recalled Rostron's approach to that keystone social institution of ocean liners, the captain's table. Rostron, Slade observed, 'did not normally appear at the Captain's Table for the first twenty-four hours and had the art of making his entry in the "grand manner" on all occasions when he did take his meals at his table'. Once well at sea, Rostron would inform the chief steward of his intention to dine at the captain's table henceforth. 'Forewarned is forearmed of course and, thereafter, the Chief Steward proceeded to station two of his brightest "bell hops" outside the First Class Dining Room doors to receive him. One had the job of catching his cap, which [Rostron], in a somewhat lofty manner, used to discard from some distance away and no[n]ch[al]antly toss it, in a somewhat haphazard manner, for the lad to catch. Woe betide him if he muffed it and carpeted said headgear on the deck. The other dramatically swung open the Saloon doors and "Master under God" was then all set to break his fast.'[4]

Not all captains of Atlantic liners enjoyed their public role, but even in his early years Captain Rostron was a sociable host. Bisset remembered that during *Carpathia*'s positioning cruise of 1912 Rostron 'not only had no objection to our mixing with the passengers, but encouraged and urged us to be sociable. We joined in dancing, games, shipboard concerts and shore excursions.' In later years the animated and extroverted Rostron enjoyed hosting the prominent transatlantic travellers who dined at his table and later sometimes adjourned to his cabin. 'One forms [such] splendid friendships,' he observed. 'Something comes over people when they are at sea... It makes them really very nice to know. The sea broadens them as it broadens everyone. Small things go by the board, quite naturally. People turn to big things.'[5]

161

Rostron had the advantage of cultivating such friendships on his own terms, at his table or in his cabin, where he would sometimes host selected guests 'long after midnight'. Still, the often substantial egos of celebrity passengers needed to be matched on equal terms by the resolute character of a ship's captain in his element. In those days before private jets, the elites of Europe and North America had no choice but to patronize the Atlantic liners if they wished to pass between the continents. In the case of the Old World these passengers were often aristocrats or senior government officials and from the New World leading capitalists or celebrities in various fields. *Mauretania*'s first westbound crossing of August 1922, under Rostron's command, delivered to New York, along with 1457 other passengers, a Portuguese princess, two ambassadors bound for Washington, DC, the president of Standard Oil of New Jersey and the chief executive of the Boy Scouts of America. James Bisset wrote that for the ship's officers, 'it was always necessary to study the passenger-lists in advance carefully, so that we would know Who was Who and What was What during the five days that such precious human cargo was in our care'.[6]

Those precious humans were used to having things their own way and not shy about asking for them. In October 1923 one British knight cabled Cunard's chairman, Sir Thomas Royden – himself a British knight – 'ROYDEN CARE CUNARD LPOOL PROPOSE SAILING MAURETANIA SATURDAY HAVE TENTATIVELY RESERVED ACCOMMODATION WOULD GREATLY APPRECIATE YOUR IMPROVING SAME IF POSSIBLE.' Sir Thomas' secretary replied to say that the chairman 'has told our passenger people to do the very best possible for you in the matter of your accommodation in the "MAURETANIA"'.[7]

Sometimes Sir Thomas took a more active interest in the case, as when David Lloyd George crossed the Atlantic aboard *Mauretania* a year after resigning as Britain's prime minister. In the first week of October 1923 Rostron delivered the former prime minister to New York for a month-long speaking and sightseeing tour of the US and Canada. Accompanied by his wife and daughter on his first visit to the US, Lloyd George was met 'down the bay by a score of members of the Mayor's Special Committee to welcome distinguished foreigners,' and escorted to City Hall. Although *Mauretania*'s officers described it as a relatively smooth passage for that time of year, *The*

New York Times reported that 'Rostron appeared to have dodged his way across between the tail end of [a] hurricane and the commencement of the equinoctial storms'. Lloyd George inclined to the newspaper's version, describing his greeting by the American people as 'very much better than the reception I got from the Atlantic Ocean, which was rather mixed'.[8]

A week before *Mauretania* sailed from Southampton, Royden wrote to Lloyd George 'to express the great pleasure and gratification [it] gives us to have you as a passenger on our R.M.S. "MAURETANIA". I need hardly assure you that we shall spare no effort to make you and your party comfortable while on board and I trust that you will enjoy every minute of your trip to New York.' Salesman Royden continued, writing 'that it would give me personally particular pleasure if you were to decide to return Cunard – a Company which, as you know, is British throughout, both in ownership and personnel'. Royden's last sentiment, a jab at the White Star Line, proved unavailing. Declining to play favourites, Lloyd George and family sailed home on White Star's *Majestic* the following month.[9]

The Queen of Romania, her son and daughter, her entourage and their 229 pieces of luggage – including more than twenty boxes of American souvenirs – were mostly a problem for *Berengaria*'s purser and his staff. Nevertheless, it was Rostron who met her at the head of the gangway and escorted her to her suite and it was Rostron who was ultimately responsible for the comfort and safety of this Very Important Person on her crossing to Cherbourg in November 1926.[10]

Lesser figures than royalty also demanded Rostron's time and attention. Cunard's chairman often received letters from people seeking the 'mentioning [of] my name to the captain and purser,' among other favours. 'I have never crossed the ocean before and shall be utterly at sea in more senses than one,' wrote one such petitioner, the Reverend Robert Hyde, director of the Industrial Welfare Society in London, bound to America in October 1926. 'You need have no misgivings as to the ocean portion of your American adventure,' Royden replied the following day. 'I will see that while on board the "Berengaria" you receive every possible attention.' Royden dispatched a note to *Berengaria*'s chief steward and a letter of introduction to Rostron on Hyde's behalf. In another case, Royden wrote to Rostron to 'commend to your particular care' an aristocrat 'who is travelling with you and I should much appreciate anything you can do to make his trip a pleasant and comfortable one'. These were not idle words, coming from the chairman of the line and Rostron took such matters seriously. In 1925, Colonel Kenyon Joyce, the US military attaché in London, wrote to thank Royden 'after an exceedingly pleasant trip on the *Mauretania*,' a crossing 'enhanced by the most courteous treatment on the part of Captain Rostron, who, to my mind, is the highest type of Commander'.[11]

Plainly put, a liner captain's charisma was a financial asset to his company. Arthur Fowler, president of an American metals company, wrote to Cunard's chairman that 'personally, I consider [Rostron] the greatest skipper on the North Atlantic and one of the most charming of men. I always cross with him when I can and never fail to like him better each time.' This assessment, doubtless gratifying to Royden, was seconded by the junior purser, Slade, who described Rostron as 'very popular with the American travelling public of those days, who were very faithful to him. They used to take passage in whatever ship he commanded for their European tour.' Such repeat patronage was of great importance to Cunard, of course, and Rostron's ability to generate such loyalty made him that much more valuable to his company.[12]

Not every master mariner possessed Rostron's highly desirable combination of character, charm and correctness – the essential traits that separated the master of a great liner from his fellow captains. In fact, such men were relatively rare. One of Royden's assistants, A. C. F. Henderson, wrote a letter to his chief in 1928 discussing the need to discipline one of Cunard's passenger ship captains for two instances of what Henderson termed 'crass stupidity'. In one the captain in question made a remark about a female passenger to another passenger that compelled him to make a written apology and in the other he allowed a lady passenger continually in his cabin and to a late hour. Rather than discharge the captain from the company outright, Henderson recommended demoting him to chief officer with the understanding that he would never rise above that rank again. Continuing his letter, Henderson worried about the prospects of some of the line's other captains. Listing five masters of Cunard cargo ships, he lamented that 'none of these are really up to passenger ship standard'.[13]

Although Rostron enjoyed his socializing, it was certainly time-consuming. Harry Grattidge, commanding *Queen Mary*, once observed that 'the social revel', as he termed it, occupied 'six hours in twenty four'. And the master of an Atlantic passenger ship fulfilled several other social functions beyond his role as gracious host. 'We are a complete city in miniature when at sea,' Rostron observed. As benevolent dictator of said city, a captain's oversight and reach embraced all facets of his ship's operation. For a start, Rostron declared, 'the liner captain must be something of a hotel manager – of a tip-top hotel at that. He must understand food and cooking. Service is very important if passengers are to be satisfied and recommend his vessel above others. Competition is as keen in this respect as it is among first-class hotels on shore.' Beyond host and hotelier, Rostron interacted with his passengers in two other offices, representing religion and justice.[14]

The passenger-ship captain was also the vicar of his parish-on-sea, an agreeable role to the spiritually-minded Rostron. Although he sometimes delegated reading of the Sunday service to a subordinate or to a member of the Anglican or Episcopal clergy selected from among his passengers, Rostron did enjoy performing this duty himself. He found that 'people who attend feel something in that service they don't seem to get elsewhere. Apparently it does not reach them on shore.' Rostron thought his parishioners found renewed inspiration amidst the wonders of the deep. 'They come and try to tell me,' he said. 'I know what they mean.'[15]

Rostron occasionally saw passengers in less uplifting circumstances, after they strayed from the path of righteousness, in his role as chief magistrate. As captain, he was judge and jury without appeal, at least while his ship remained at sea. 'That is the awkward side of life aboard,' he found. 'It obtrudes very slightly, I'm glad to say. Most travelers are in a good mood.' Crime on passenger ships generally fell into three categories: the petty violence or vandalism associated with consuming too much alcohol; the activities of card sharps who preyed on wealthy passengers on transatlantic liners; and the attempts by some of those aboard to evade customs duties or restrictions.[16]

The 1920s were both the first decade of mass American tourism to Europe and the decade of American Prohibition. Yankees bound to Europe and not in harmony with the spirit of the Eighteenth Amendment could imbibe other spirits once their ship passed beyond the three-mile limit of US territorial waters. This was only true of European liners, however, since American-registered ships sailed dry. Rostron once commanded a dry ship on an early postwar voyage, although she did not start that way. *Mauretania* sailed eastward three weeks after Prohibition came into force and, *The Times* reported, arrived at Southampton on 13 February 1920, 'as "dry" as the most ardent prohibitionist could wish'. Her 1539 passengers, 'the great majority of whom were citizens of the United States,' emptied every bottle aboard 'long before the vessel reached port,' despite Cunard having laid in a larger supply of wine and liquor than normal in anticipation of the American thirst. By the 1920s, the era of closing the bar and turning out the lights in the public rooms of Atlantic liners at midnight was gone and the drinking and card games sometimes continued until dawn. As Rostron gently expressed it, 'more and more ship life inclines to start later in the morning and carry on later at night'. The all-night drinking sometimes ended in disputes damaging to passengers or the ship's furnishings. These skirmishes were usually brought to a close when Rostron imposed a suitable fine and a stern warning.[17]

Less amenable to a captain's admonishments to behave were the professional card players who made their livings on Atlantic liners by swindling affluent but innocent first-class passengers. Although steamship companies posted notices warning patrons about the sharps in their midst, these experts could usually still select a sucker from among the hundreds of potential victims held in close confinement on a five- or six-day crossing. A pattern developed, familiar to both the public room stewards and captains of Atlantic liners. Early in the voyage someone approached a likely individual needing a fourth for bridge. The subsequent days of the passage would be consumed by wagering on card games in convivial company, with the mark either winning or at least breaking even. But come the final act, usually on the last day of the voyage, the sharps would strike, dealing their victim a seemingly unbeatable hand upon which he would wager heavily, then relieving him of a sum of money that sometimes exceeded $10,000.[18]

If the loser believed he had been cheated, he would complain to one of the hotel staff and the matter might find its way to Rostron. With little evidence but the victim's recitation of the familiar story, Rostron's game when interviewing the gamblers was not bridge, but poker. To enhance his bluff, he went to the trouble to memorize a suspicious losing bridge hand that kept reoccurring, repeated it to the offending players and threatened dire consequences once ashore in an effort to convince them to refund their illegitimate take. Rostron was not averse to teaching the suckers a lesson, however, and to that end developed the habit of letting the sharps keep two thousand dollars of their winnings. Sometimes Rostron could adjust the matter without interviewing the perpetrators. In one case, he advised the victim to approach the gamblers in friendly innocence and ask to see the cheque that he had written to cover his losses on the pretext of having made some error when writing it. When a dull sharp unwittingly produced it, the victim snatched it from him and destroyed it, as Rostron had suggested. Rostron estimated that he recovered $53,000 for swindled passengers in one two-and-a-half-year interval during the 1920s.[19]

While he navigated the Atlantic's drunks and confidence men effectively, Rostron, or at least his ship, went aground rather sensationally on smuggling in 1928. *Berengaria* arrived in New York on the morning of 17 November. After she tied up, sixty customs agents swarmed aboard with flashlights and pry bars 'and spent the day rummaging the passenger cabins and crews' quarters'. Two agents even went through Rostron's bureau drawers and wardrobe. Rostron told an American friend who witnessed the search that this happened every time *Berengaria* arrived at New York. 'Apparently these are your customs,' he said, with a mixture of irritation and resignation, 'and I suppose we will have to abide by them.'[20]

One can only imagine Rostron's chagrin – and Cunard's – when the US Customs Service arrested *Berengaria*'s chief steward that afternoon for diamond smuggling. He was detained leaving the ship and a search of his quarters discovered two packages of diamonds in his bunk worth $50,000. The chief steward was the transatlantic link in a smuggling chain that included a New York City policeman assigned to Cunard's pier and a New York jeweller and his daughter. The arrests followed many months of investigation of a complex network that over the previous year had conveyed half a million dollars in diamonds from Amsterdam to Southampton and then smuggled them into New York. The following February, *Berengaria*'s former chief steward pleaded guilty to conspiracy to smuggle diamonds and testified against five other men eventually charged in the case.[21]

With the embarrassing exception of *Berengaria*'s chief steward, Rostron had the luxury of commanding the best sailors, engineers and hoteliers in the British merchant marine. But it was his job to get the most out of his crews and he did so. Rostron's commands consistently had reputations as happy ships. Chairman Royden wrote to Rostron in April 1930 that 'nobody believes more strongly than I do in the immense value of "atmosphere" and there is no doubt that your ship possesses this to a marked extent. I am continually hearing from your passengers how splendid is the "esprit de corps" and keenness of the ship's personnel and it has long been a matter of great pride to me that we have such a splendid set of men as those that sail under the Cunard flag.'[22]

Such an outcome demanded a master's constant attention to detail. 'Every voyage the captain inspects his entire ship, taking a section each day,' Rostron explained, 'and it's no use just looking in – he's got to know the work so that he can enquire intelligently about it. The conduct of the whole crew will reflect the capabilities of the captain.' James Bisset considered Rostron a strict disciplinarian, but Rostron saw ship's discipline as an essential tool of leadership. He wrote to Royden that 'we have wonderful material amongst our men, not only in this ship but throughout the fleet, if only we can get at them and lead them first so that they can lead their shipmates in turn. I'm fully convinced a happy and contented ship's company does not mean slackness but very much the reverse when discipline can be got by effective control and fair play.'[23]

To build a contented ship's company Rostron 'encouraged self-respect in every member of the personnel of the ships in which I have served, believing that it was for the good'. It also helped to leaven discipline with humanity. He explained that, in a music hall early in his career, he had heard a song called 'One Touch of Human Nature Makes the Whole World Kin'. Whatever the idea's merits as a song title, Rostron 'confess[ed] it appealed to me tremendously and throughout my long years in the service I have endeavoured to follow out the advice of the song'.[24]

Rostron's crews responded favourably to his leadership philosophy. Slade, the junior purser, remembered that Rostron 'had quite a following of "old ships" amongst Cunard crew members'. The respect was mutual; upon his retirement Rostron told a reporter 'that I could never have been more finely served than by the men I have commanded. They have been a splendid lot, a wonderful lot, and I am sorry to leave them.' The effects of this mutual esteem did not go unnoticed by outsiders. In September 1928, the American industrialist Arthur Fowler wrote to Royden of Rostron's *Berengaria*: 'You are to be complimented on the discipline and courtesy which pervade the ship. The "Esprit de corps" is admirable.' Royden replied with thanks, acknowledging that *Berengaria*'s sailors were 'very keen on their ship and terribly anxious to make her the best in the fleet'.[25]

Another obligation of the liner captain – paper shuffler – produced no such satisfactions. Slade remembered 'before entering port … a multitudinous mound of documents and papers requiring the Master's signature. It took anything from three-quarters of an hour to an hour of solid name signing on [Rostron's] part to accomplish this.' At least Slade and his supervisor contrived to relieve their captain of one onerous round of paperwork every voyage.[26]

Slade recalled that Americans headed to Europe *en masse* in the 1920s frequently toted a commercially produced souvenir travel diary. 'This particular horror of the stationer's art' had spaces for the ship captain's signature for the passages both across and back. Assigned to the purser's department in tourist-third class, Slade remembered that office being deluged with hundreds of these diaries on each transit, every one of which demanded the captain's signature. Slade, a devout practitioner of the junior officers' strategy of remaining well to windward of his captain, 'could just picture [Rostron's] face if one had had the temerity to ask him if he would sign this lot'.[27]

The pursers in tourist-third circumvented that nightmare by having a rubber stamp made of Rostron's bold, straightforward signature. Slade and his superior would then lock themselves in the office one evening near the end of the passage, his boss lightly applying the stamp and Slade tracing the signature. 'Eventually, with practice, we got so expert that we did not need the stamp and could forge the signature quite easily and with commendable speed.' Slade later declared this to be his first and only foray into crime, albeit in a good cause, 'and I should take a bet that [Captain] A. H. Rostron knew exactly what was going on'.[28]

All of his other obligations were additions to Rostron's primary role as captain of a transatlantic liner – sailor first, last and always. 'Despite the demands of society and business,' he wrote, 'the master's chief duty lies on the bridge.' As Bisset observed after many years as a master, command was no cure for a watch standing officer's sleep deprivation. 'The Captain may spend hours reclining on his settee,' Bisset found, 'but he never sleeps deeply, as he is on duty twenty-four hours a day… He dozes fitfully, but part of his mind is alert all the time. He hears the bells sounded at every half-hour and he is aware of the changes of the watch and of changes of weather and of any unusual sound or movement in the ship.' McNeil concurred, finding that 'it is rather remarkable how you get to sense any alteration in the ship's behaviour, brought about, for example, by a change of weather, speed or course. So far as I was concerned, any such change at night-time would wake me up.'[29]

Rostron demonstrated a captain's existence as the human sensory embodiment of his ship, constantly vigilant as to her well being, during an incident aboard *Mauretania*. While attending a four o'clock tea in the ship's upper foyer, Rostron suddenly felt the wind blow in through a starboard door. Knowing that the prevailing wind was from dead ahead when he came down to tea, he realized *Mauretania* had 'veered from her proper course'. He then felt the rhythm of the engines change and the ship begin to lose headway. Knowing that *Mauretania* was in no immediate danger, he decided to remain seated to avoid causing alarm. In a few minutes an officer arrived to inform him that the ship had dropped one of her propellers, whereupon the governor on the turbine on that shaft had automatically shut the engine down.[30]

Rostron accepted lost propellers, a surprisingly common occurrence, as part of the job, but other common hazards of the Atlantic were far more worrisome. 'Fog and ice' he declared 'the two bugbears of the North Atlantic!' Rostron had had as dramatic an encounter with ice as anyone in the history of that ocean in 1912 and he confronted the hazard regularly during his Canadian service in 1913 and 1914. Cunard's different routes to Canada and the St Lawrence River, depending upon the season, testified to the extent of the problem.[31]

The ice problem was often compounded by the fog problem – or perhaps it was the reverse. The worst fogs occurred off the Grand Banks of Newfoundland, agonizing in part because of their duration and intensity, but also because they could mask the presence of icebergs or fishing boats – either the unwieldy sailing schooners still working the trade or even the rowing boats from which individual dorymen fished. No matter where it happened, when fog closed in the captain took his station on a liner's bridge. As watches came and went, the captain often remained there for days and nights on end, getting what sleep he could in fitful naps taken in the fog chair installed on the bridge for his exclusive use. These ordeals occasionally produced sudden, life-saving decisions by a captain who had been 'staring out into nothingness for hours'. Rostron had one such near-miss encounter with an iceberg in fog in the Strait of Belle Isle and he averted a collision with a ship in a fog off the coast of Ireland. Bisset attributed an exhausted captain's ability to perceive danger before it became apparent to the regular bridge watch to 'the mental equipment of command, which gives a shipmaster a "sixth sense" – of full responsibility and sharpened alertness'.[32]

Captain McNeil crossed the Atlantic 'more than once … with not more than ten hours' sleep,' and declared stretches of fifty hours without sleep 'quite common'. Rostron wrote that his personal endurance record on a bridge came aboard *Saxonia* during the First World War. His ship left New York in thick fog at 6pm on Thursday, 9 August 1917, carrying 248 cabin-class and 2257 third-class passengers, doubtless soldiers, 581 sacks of mail and 261 bars of specie worth $215,934. She arrived at Halifax at 1pm the following Monday, 13 August, after making a completely fogbound three-and-a-half-day passage. Rostron spent the entire time on the bridge, only to be informed upon arriving at Halifax that a convoy was forming and asked when he could sail. He answered that he could depart in ninety minutes, most of which he used to take a bath, change uniforms and eat lunch. *Saxonia* returned to sea at 7pm and Rostron remained on the bridge for the rest of the Atlantic crossing because the convoy adopted zig-zag submarine evasion and 'I thought it was my job to see it through'. Thus, in Rostron's remembrance, the ninety-minute break in Halifax was the only time he left the bridge for eight days.[33]

The following year, the last of the war, Rostron expanded the fog watch into a full-time undertaking. Assigned to make fast Atlantic transits in the troopship *Mauretania*, he dispensed entirely with the notion of retiring to his cabin and simply lived on the bridge, snatching what rest he could on a cot set up behind a canvas screen. 'Many a night,' he slept there, 'ready for whatever might spring out of the enveloping darkness.'[34]

Rostron did not include storms among his North Atlantic bugbears, but in its surlier moods that ocean exhibits a ferocity approaching Cape Horn's. A huge wave once crashed completely over *Mauretania's* pilot house, seven decks above the waterline, smashing in several windows and lacerating the quartermaster with flying glass – this in the third week of June. Standing into a moderate westerly gale with heavy seas on 17 June 1925, Rostron went to the bridge at 11am and ordered the ship's speed reduced to 12 knots. 'I had just returned to my cabin again when I felt her dive and then heard a loud crash… I rushed up and saw the quartermaster with his face cut and bleeding and the buckets and gratings on the after part of the bridge floating about in the water that was washing about.' Rostron thereupon reduced speed again, to 10 knots, but that proved to be the only assault by a wave that day.[35]

Once winter descends, nasty becomes normal for North Atlantic winds and waves. One winter storm, during a voyage that Rostron described as one of the worst in his experience, almost obliterated the *Titanic* Hero before he could collect all of his medals. The night of 9 January 1913 found him commanding *Caronia* westbound, with hurricane-force winds inflicting considerable damage about her decks. Rostron was on the open bridge when lifeboat number 5, 'which weighs about two tons … was blown out of her chocks', and disappeared into the night with a shrieking sound. But not for long. He heard the noise, looked aft and saw the boat reappear on the crest of a huge wave headed directly for him. Rostron timed the wave's arrival, then ducked and got doused as the ninety-mile-per-hour wind flung the boat over him and shattered it on *Caronia*'s deck.[36]

Even *Berengaria*, one of the largest ships in the world, was not immune to the rough and tumble. Although two-and-a-half times the size of *Caronia*, *Berengaria* earned an unfortunate reputation in her earliest days as a tender ship inclined to excessive rolling. She lived up to it in storms during Rostron's years in command by inflicting bumps, bruises and even broken bones upon her passengers, despite his best efforts to reduce her rolling. A December blow in 1929, featuring some of the roughest weather Rostron could remember in all his years on the Atlantic, hurled hurricane-force winds and mountainous seas at the giant liner. Late in the afternoon the day after leaving Cherbourg an enormous wave crashed over *Berengaria*'s starboard bow, carried away two large forward ventilators, shattered eight windows on the upper promenade deck sixty feet above the waterline and 'bent in concave form' a half-inch-thick steel bulkhead. Two nights later another wave inflicted more damage on the ship's starboard quarter. During this maelstrom one elderly male passenger died of heart failure attributed to 'seasickness and nervousness', and five other passengers were injured. The crossing consumed nearly eight days at an average of less than sixteen and a half knots. Rostron held his ship at reduced speed for 102 hours and her worst day's run of 193 miles averaged barely eight knots. *The New York Times* recorded that 'Captain Rostron said the *Berengaria* rode over the waves well'.[37]

The hazards of the sea were bracketed by the hazards of entering and clearing port. White Star Commodore Sir Bertram Hayes once held that he had never had any adventures because the captain of a great liner could not afford to have adventures. Sometimes, however, circumstances conspired to create adventures for even the best of captains. Although Rostron was never shipwrecked, the challenges of mooring *Mauretania* in the Hudson River ensnared him a couple of times.[38]

On 24 November 1922, one of these adventures began near dawn at Ambrose Lightship, when the ship's engineers were able to confirm damage to *Mauretania's* starboard backing turbine which they had suspected since departing from Cherbourg. The ship anchored near the lightship for an hour and twenty minutes while Chief Engineer Cockburn and his staff immobilized the damaged turbine. That saved the equipment from further injury, but significantly increased the difficulty of landing *Mauretania* for her pilot and captain. With one of her two reversing turbines disabled, 'you can imagine how awkward it was to handle that large ship when we came to port with one propeller, giving her a sideways tendency which had to be corrected by the rudder' – a rudder rendered considerably less effective at the low speeds that docking required.[39]

To complicate the whole operation further, *Mauretania* stood up the harbour into a strong ebb tide and with a north-west gale howling across the Hudson. Two tugboats escorted *Mauretania* from Quarantine and Cunard's marine superintendent had another fourteen tugs waiting to wrestle her to her berth on the south, meaning downstream, side of Pier 54. Sixteen tugboats proved insufficient on this day, however.[40]

The most hazardous part of docking in the Hudson River came as a ship entered the slip. The required ninety-degree turn to starboard exposed her entire port side to the full force of any wind, tide and the river's current until she could reach the protective lee of the pier shed. Thus this phase of the operation was always conducted with as much dispatch as prudent, but that day the north-west wind caught *Mauretania's* exposed superstructure and, increasing the way on already, drove the big ship into the dock at the alarming speed of 6 knots. As the forward end of the ship entered the lee of Pier 54, the wind, tide and current began to force the after end downstream toward Pier 53. The tugboats shoving upstream on her stern and hauling downstream on her bow strained to arrest *Mauretania*'s charge into the slip, but 'the hawsers out fore and aft parted one after the other and the tugboats were [soon] helpless to stop the ship's way'.[41]

On *Mauretania*'s bridge, Rostron could not exert as much control as he would have liked to arrest this rapidly developing crisis. With his starboard astern turbine disabled, he had only half of his ship's normal backing power at his disposal and while reversing on the inner port propeller slowed the ship, it only increased the rate at which her stern fell off to starboard toward Pier 53. With *Mauretania*'s bow looming toward them, hundreds of onlookers retreated in haste to the sound of 'a good deal of grinding and a crash', as the ship came to rest 'with her nose at the head of the pier in a corner and her stern across the end of Pier 53'. She had mangled some drain pipes and other projections on the roof of the shed and demolished a painters' stage floating alongside the pier, at the cost of a few feet of her main deck railing. Fortunately 'a few hundred dollars will cover the damage'.[42]

Even in the best of circumstances, mooring or unmooring a large ocean liner in constricted waters was a daunting prospect. 'Those gathered on deck or pier to watch the operation little knew the mental strain undergone by the man on the bridge, the pivotal executive,' explained a *New York Times* reporter. Rostron told the reporter that he issued between two hundred and three hundred orders to the bridge and engine room in the half hour surrounding the docking or undocking of his ship. 'Captain Rostron said a man was so keyed up, engrossed to the point of being so oblivious to everything else, that woe betide thoughtless intruders who might try to introduce outside matters. "I could tear them apart!", he said.'[43]

Mauretania called at Queenstown, Fishguard and Liverpool before the war and at Plymouth, Cherbourg and Southampton in the 1920s. While only one landfall awaited Rostron on the western side of the Atlantic, it presented a sobering variety of challenges. 'Nowhere in Europe is there a river to compare with the East and North [Hudson] rivers off Manhattan Island,' wrote Captain McNeil, who declared that 'it is not exaggerating to describe [the Hudson] as the busiest water-thoroughfare in the whole world'. Traffic confronting an arriving or departing transatlantic liner in the Hudson included 'every type of large passenger steamer', as well as every variety of cargo ship, coaster, river craft and barge tow. All of these obstacles were compounded by numerous ferries crossing the river at right angles to arriving and departing traffic and garbage scows moving back and forth at all hours between Manhattan Island and their dumpsite off Sandy Hook.[44]

Those thick fogs of the western Atlantic also bedevilled New York Harbor, often delaying liners' landings and further compressing already-brief stopovers. In February 1928, *Berengaria* and her 1136 dissatisfied customers spent two days anchored off Staten Island in fog. The ship arrived on Tuesday afternoon, 7 February, but visibility of scarcely more than one hundred yards made it impossible for Rostron to bring the big ship into her berth. The fog finally relented enough to permit *Berengaria* to tie up at 10.30am Thursday morning, after being delayed more than forty hours.[45]

The landing relieved *Berengaria* of her anxious westbound passengers, but came only sixteen hours before her next scheduled departure at 2.30am the following morning. In that interval, the ship re-provisioned with 5000 tons of water, 6000 tons of fuel oil and all of the victuals required for a six-day passage. Forty thousand pieces of dirty laundry went ashore and were cleaned, returned and stowed before sailing. By 8pm the ship was ready to receive her eastbound passengers, but by 9.30pm was still hoisting cargo ashore and had not even begun to load mails. Five hours later *Berengaria* sailed as scheduled, with 12,000 bags of mail and 1200 tons of cargo aboard. Rostron credited this performance to 'organization and system', outstanding supervision, and 'willing hands'. 'The sea,' *Berengaria*'s master observed dryly, 'is no place for eight-hour-a-day men.'[46]

As Rostron's sailing schedule permitted, 'the social whirl', – as he described that facet of a liner captain's obligations – continued after his ship made fast. The Atlantic liners were character actors on the New York waterfront, regular visitors whose careers were followed with interest. In June of 1912 Cunard's *Carmania* made the top of the front page of *The New York Times* when she caught fire at her pier – in Liverpool. New York newspaper reporters traditionally greeted large liners entering the harbour, hoping to interview officials or celebrities, and the more prominent liner captains attained a degree of celebrity themselves. Reporters solicited their opinions on matters nautical and otherwise and Rostron's comments in the 1920s covered everything from the progress of the voyage just concluded, to remarks on the future of transatlantic travel, to comments on British politics and the international scene.[47]

'Men in charge of large ships are unofficial ambassadors of their countries,' Rostron explained. 'They are taken as the type of their countrymen. They have not only the opportunity but one might almost say the necessity for using what ambassadorial talents they may or may not possess, this wholly irrespective of the personal friendships that reward their work.' To that end and in the service of his company's ends, naturally, Rostron and his ship occasionally hosted functions while docked in New York. At one such gathering, *Mauretania* entertained 1500 delegates to an international police conference meeting in New York. On another occasion British and French delegates to an international advertising convention attended a farewell luncheon aboard *Mauretania* sponsored by the Association of Foreign Press Correspondents in the United States.[48]

Rostron took particular interest in the subject of European relations with the United States. In his remarks to the delegates at the foreign press luncheon, Rostron decried what he considered the 'pinpricks and petty jealousies' between the United States and Europe. The theme of Anglo-American understanding and cooperation appeared constantly in Rostron's writings, speeches and statements to the press through the last years of his career and in his retirement. He cautioned his fellow Britons against insularity and envy of the United States, 'plead[ing] for bigness in our relations with this young America'. In 1931 he would presciently declare 'a proper understanding' between Britain and the United States as 'the chief plank in the platform of world peace'.[49]

His interest in the United States and its international relations was understandable in a man who had been visiting the country regularly for thirty years. Rostron once estimated that he had spent 'fully four years' in the United States over the course of his career and described himself as 'almost as much at home in America as in England'. He had an avuncular affection for Americans, ascribing the excesses of their enthusiasm, such as Prohibition, to 'an idealism which seeks results too quickly'. Not that Rostron believed in the entire American experiment. 'It is absurd to quiz them about their speech,' he once gibed. 'For want of a national term it is called English.'[50]

Americans reciprocated Rostron's affection. They held him in high regard for the *Titanic* rescue, his war service and later his captaincy of Cunard's great liners. After decades of calling at New York in Cunard's service, Rostron counted hundreds of Americans among his friends and during the 1920s he made numerous calls ashore while in New York. He occasionally attended organized functions, sometimes as the guest of honour, and more frequently made social calls. He visited affluent American friends as an invited guest at their homes in the city or on their estates in the countryside. In June 1926, Mayor Jimmy Walker made New York City's esteem of Rostron official. At a luncheon aboard *Mauretania* during Rostron's next-to-last call at New York in that ship, Walker conferred upon him the Freedom of the City of New York 'for his splendid service to humanity and to the City of New York and the people of the United States over many years'.[51]

Rostron's standing with both Cunard and the Royal Naval Reserve imposed social obligations upon him while ashore in England in the 1920s. Thus Rostron's attendance upon His Majesty at the King's Levee at St James's Palace in March 1924 in his role as the merchant navy's aide de camp to the King, or his speech to the monthly Royal Naval Volunteer Reserve Club dinner at the Connaught Rooms near Covent Garden in London, in January 1930. And to these engagements he could add at least some society in Southampton. Rostron's daughter Margaret recalled the 'great rivalry' between Cunard and White Star at Southampton in the 1920s, but also remembered that 'it was all very friendly. It didn't stop my parents from mixing with White Star officers and personnel.'[52]

With all of Rostron's work and responsibility afloat, rank also had its privileges. He enjoyed the comforts of his cabin, a sanctum that was really a suite. There he hosted his late-night socials with celebrities and dignitaries. A reporter visiting *Mauretania* in 1924 noted that Rostron's cabin bookshelf contained two of that year's popular novels – Edna Ferber's *So Big*, which would win the Pulitzer Prize, and H. G. Wells' *The Dream* – and, unsurprisingly, a two-volume set about clipper ships, the gift of an admiral friend. The cabin had another amenity Rostron enjoyed through most of the decade, though one denied to him during his last two years at sea.[53]

Since 'Captain', Rostron's seagoing black cat aboard *Carpathia*, he had developed a fondness for white Persian cats, one of whom 'Abdul', occupied Rostron's cabin during voyages for many years. The elderly Abdul spent the 1920s sleeping on the captain's settee in the grand tradition of ships' cats, at least until the authorities decided to require the same standards of quarantine for cats that applied to dogs entering Great Britain. The new health regulation forced Abdul either to undergo six months of quarantine upon reentering the country or to retire from the sea. Thus *Berengaria* sailed into 1929 without Abdul, a circumstance not universally regretted according to *The New York Times*. 'Stewards of the ship were not sorry that Abdul had been left and judging from the way they spoke, the cat was not popular on board.'[54]

Whether the minor vexations of officialdom or the major hazards of the sea, Rostron took with an even strain all of the pressures of command in both war and peace, pressures that broke the health of some of his fellow captains. Two of Rostron's predecessors in *Berengaria* had been forced into premature retirement by exhaustion, but Sir Thomas Royden, who crossed the Atlantic several times with Rostron during the First World War, 'always used to marvel at his serenity of mind as well as his wonderful seamanship'.[55]

Once again, Rostron's faith sustained him. Before commencing any voyage he spent several moments kneeling in prayer in his cabin before turning to the business of a seaman. As he explained his serenity: 'I think that the closer to nature you live the more do you feel there is a Higher Command and that thought brings strength and comfort. If you have put yourself under Orders, as it were, then carry on, do your best and leave the issue. It takes away worry without in any way lessening the highest effort of which you are capable; indeed it encourages that effort, for the Commander expects your best.' Rostron had certainly delivered his best, something apparent to his employers, passengers and countrymen. High honours had come to him for the *Titanic* rescue and his service in the First World War. Even higher honours would distinguish the final five years of his career.[56]

CHAPTER 15

THE VERY BEST TYPE
OF SAILOR MAN

The year 1926 was the last that Rostron commanded *Mauretania*, the last that the Rostrons lived in Liverpool and the year that he received the greatest honour of his life. That January, Sir Thomas Royden hand-delivered a letter to 10 Downing Street urging Prime Minister Stanley Baldwin to nominate Rostron for a knighthood in the King's Birthday Honours list that July. Royden wrote that 'Captain Rostron occupies a position that is almost unique among the Captains of the Mercantile Marine,' and followed that observation with a recitation of the highlights of Rostron's career. These included the *Titanic* rescue in *Carpathia* 'after a hazardous journey at [the] highest speed the ship could attain and through ice flows,' as well as his distinguished war service and his appointment as aide de camp to the King in 1924.

Royden made another argument for knighting Rostron independent of his individual exploits: the 'recognition of the importance to the nation of its Mercantile Marine'. Royden believed that 'an occasional honour conferred by His Majesty the King on the men who have risen to the top of their profession emphasises in a very suitable way the high and responsible position that men like Captain Rostron occupy in our national life'. Royden thought that the morale of the merchant service had been 'greatly enhanced' by the knighthoods conferred upon Sir James Charles of Cunard and Sir Bertram Hayes of the White Star Line and concluded: 'I feel very strongly that it is in the national interest that the men of the Mercantile Marine should be proud of their profession and that, as a consequence, our ships should be manned by the right class of sailor man.'[1]

Prime Minister Baldwin concurred in Royden's assessment, as did King George V, and so the announcement appeared in *The London Gazette*:

Central Chancery of the Orders of Knighthood. St James's Palace, S.W.1, 3rd July, 1926. The KING has been graciously pleased on the occasion of His Majesty's Birthday, to give orders for the following promotions in and appointments to, the Most Excellent Order of the British Empire... To be [Knight Commander] of the Civil Division of the said Most Excellent Order:... Captain Arthur Henry Rostron, C.B.E., R.N.R., Captain of the 'Mauretania'.[2]

The Most Excellent Order of the British Empire has two divisions, Civil and Military, and five ranks: Knight Grand Cross, Knight Commander, Commander, Officer and Member. Rostron had been appointed a Commander of the Military Division at the close of the First World War, but Sir Arthur, as he was known henceforth, was appointed Knight Commander of the Civil Division in the same list as a permanent under-secretary for mines and a principal assistant secretary to the Board of Trade. Across the Atlantic, *The New York Times* found the 1926 Birthday Honours, which included forty-eight knighthoods, 'rather an uninteresting list', for whatever that was worth, but held Rostron's appointment to be 'one honor which will meet with the approval of the general public'.[3]

Fittingly, Rostron learned of his knighthood while at sea. The official letter from Prime Minister Baldwin notifying Rostron of the intended honour had arrived at his home in Crosby two weeks before on Saturday, 19 June – the same day *Mauretania* sailed from Southampton – where it lay unopened awaiting his return. *Mauretania* departed New York for home on 30 June and the official announcement reached her by wireless three days later. Rostron recalled that on the second day out fog set in, so he had spent much of his time on the bridge. The fog cleared at about 1.30am Saturday morning, 3 July, but Rostron had remained on the bridge. He was talking to the watch officer when a wireless operator approached with the morning's news and asked Rostron to step into the chart room. 'I supposed he had some special reason to want me to read the day's news in the middle of the night, so in I went... That was how I received the news that His Majesty had conferred on me the honour of knighthood.' Rostron wrote that he had 'been fortunate enough to receive many favours but none have given me greater pleasure than to have one from His Majesty'.[4]

In his congratulatory letter of 5 July to 'Sir Arthur Rostron', Royden wrote that he had 'seldom if ever seen an announcement in the newspapers that gave me greater pleasure than that of the honour which has been conferred upon you by His Majesty the King'. Royden continued, 'what makes the pleasure to me greater is the knowledge that never was an honour more thoroughly deserved, nor one that will receive such general approval'. Sir Thomas repeated to Sir Arthur the point he had made in his letter to Baldwin six months before: 'The Mercantile Marine has deserved well of its country and, in selecting you for this particular distinction, the King has honoured the Mercantile Service in a particularly appropriate way.' Rostron replied to Royden by telegram: 'Deeply appreciate your personal congratulations and proud the Cunard Company and *Mauretania* can share with me the honour.'[5]

By 1926 Rostron had spent seven years sailing *Mauretania* from Southampton but residing in Crosby, Merseyside. With his knighthood, Arthur and Ethel finally conceded the merit of Bisset's observation that 'a sailor's home can be only where his heart is and that is in his ship's home port'. They had 'Holmcroft' built on Chalk Hill Road in West End, an agricultural village located four miles north-east of Southampton. Their new home stood on about an acre of ground. Built on three levels and set into the side of a hill, it offered a view of the Hampshire countryside with Southampton's docks in the distance.[6]

Sir Arthur's change of residence ashore coincided with a change of billet afloat. Whatever Rostron's inclinations, it would hardly do for Cunard to assign one of its two knights and senior captains to *Mauretania*, the oldest and smallest of its big three. So in the same month that he was knighted, Rostron 'stood on the dock at Southampton and saw my old ship leave without me. It was a bit of a wrench; but the call came and had to be obeyed.' Although clearly no substitute for his favourite ship, Rostron described his new command, *Berengaria*, as a 'splendid vessel', and 'the most comfortable ship I have ever been in'. James Bisset rejoined his 'old friend, superior and shipmate' as *Berengaria*'s Chief Officer in June 1927 and sailed under Rostron for the final thirty-three voyages of Rostron's career. Bisset remembered the ship as a favourite of transatlantic passengers, 'a well built, well found "gigantic" steamer, with excellent seagoing qualities and comfortable accommodation. Her decorations and furnishings were of a somewhat heavy Teutonic style, but solid and good.'[7]

'Gigantic' was the right word for her. 'My first impression on joining,' wrote Rostron, 'was the hugeness of her; how small the Mauretania in comparison!' At the time that he commanded *Berengaria*, the 52,022-gross-ton liner was the third largest ship in the world, only a few thousand tons smaller than her larger and younger sisters – *Vaterland*, which sailed as *Leviathan* in the postwar years for the United States Lines and *Bismarck*, biggest of them all at 56,551 tons, which served White Star as *Majestic*. Cunard's *Aquitania*, at 45,647 tons, ran distinctly fourth in size. *Berengaria* dwarfed Rostron's previous largest command, the 31,937-ton *Mauretania*. His new ship was more than 120 feet longer and almost forty per cent larger, although she possessed little more than ninety per cent of the horsepower of the Atlantic speed queen.[8]

The three German giants finished their careers sailing under new names for British and American companies thanks to the Versailles Treaty that ended the First World War. The treaty stipulated that Germany accepted the responsibility of the Central Powers 'for causing all the loss and damage to which the Allied and Associated Governments and their nationals have been subjected as a consequence of the war'. Under the treaty, Germany recognized the victorious powers' right to 'the replacement, ton for ton ... and class for class, of all merchant ships and fishing boats lost or damaged owing to the war'. Since, as the victors acknowledged, Germany's existing tonnage did not approach what the winning countries had lost, Germany satisfied its obligation by ceding to the victors all ships in its merchant marine over 1600 gross tons, half of its tonnage of ships between 1000 and 1600 tons and a quarter of its tonnage of steam trawlers and fishing boats.[9]

Thus it was that Rostron assumed command of a ship launched by Kaiser Wilhelm as *Imperator* at Vulkan Werke, Hamburg, in May 1912. The maiden voyage of what was then the world's largest ship occurred in June of the following year, but after the 1913 season she was withdrawn from service for significant reconstruction due to her disturbing instability. Over the winter, Vulkan Werke reduced the height of her funnels, removed significant topside weight and poured 2000 tons of cement into her bottoms to reduce her rolling. *Imperator* spent the First World War laid up on the Elbe River at Cuxhaven. In April 1919 she sailed away from Germany forever as the US Navy Transport USS *Imperator* and spent the next four months repatriating American soldiers. At the end of 1919 she was assigned to Cunard, essentially as compensation for the lost *Lusitania*, and renamed *Berengaria*. She had served for four years as the biggest of Cunard's big three when Sir Arthur made his first crossing in her in August 1926. *Berengaria* would be the last of Rostron's twenty-seven merchant ships and seventeen commands.[10]

Two years into his service as master of *Berengaria*, Rostron reached the pinnacle of his profession, although his achievement would be shadowed by a tragedy. Sir James Charles, Cunard's commodore since 1921, was scheduled to retire in the summer of 1928 at Cunard's mandatory retirement age of sixty-three. Although four years older than Rostron, Charles also joined Cunard as a fourth officer in 1895. Knighted for his services in the First World War, he commanded *Aquitania* for a decade, making more than one hundred round voyages in her, before being reassigned to his final duty as relief captain for the big three liners at the beginning of 1928. Although sad to be leaving *Aquitania*, Sir James looked forward to his official retirement, after forty-six years at sea, on 2 August 1928, his sixty-third birthday.[11]

He never reached it. A few minutes after bringing *Aquitania* safely to anchorage at Cherbourg on his last homebound crossing, Sir James collapsed in his cabin. His staff captain commanded the ship on her crossing to Southampton, where the semi-conscious Charles was removed from *Aquitania* and died within the hour on 15 July. He had told passengers during his final crossing that he had not realized how hard it would be to leave his shipmates and in a farewell letter to the crew wrote that he felt he had become a part of *Aquitania*. Rostron, then in New York commanding *Berengaria*, was 'visibly affected' when informed of Sir James' death by a *New York Times* correspondent. He told the paper that it was 'with deepest regret and surprise' that he learned of the death of his 'old shipmate and friend'.[12]

Thus the commodore's flag passed to the 'Hero of [the] *Titanic* Disaster' in *Berengaria*. Commodore Sir Arthur Rostron sailed for the first time on 28 July 1928. The honour also brought with it a £100 annual bonus, making Rostron Cunard's highest paid master at £1600 per annum.[13]

Several more honours came Commodore Rostron's way in the two years and three months that remained of his life at sea. On the evening of 27 February 1929, in a ceremony held in *Berengaria*'s first-class lounge during a call at Cherbourg, Vice Admiral Besire, prefect of the port, awarded Rostron France's Légion d'honneur. At the same ceremony C. T. Quonian, president of the Cherbourg Chamber of Commerce, presented Rostron with the Chamber's silver medal for his services. 'A hero in war and a hero in peace,' Quonian declared, 'you have been well worthy of your country and of humanity.'[14]

Another high point of Rostron's years as commodore came seven months later, with the announcement that Ramsay MacDonald would make the first visit to the United States ever by a sitting British prime minister. The prime minister was to arrive in the US on 4 October, spend six days in Washington, DC, and then visit Philadelphia and New York City. From there he would travel to Niagara Falls and cross into Canada for a ten-day visit, before departing for home from Quebec on 25 October. Cunard arranged the first part of MacDonald's trip, a westbound passage aboard *Berengaria*, sailing from Southampton on 28 September under Commodore Rostron.[15]

MacDonald's specific purpose for visiting the United States was to seek agreement on naval disarmament issues prior to the London naval arms limitation conference of 1930. 'If all goes well,' he told reporters, 'the five-power conference will be held early in the new year.' Beyond the particulars of naval disarmament, MacDonald desired to achieve consensus between British and American leaders on how best to implement the Kellogg–Briand Pact of 1928 outlawing offensive war. The two countries, he believed, 'having the same objects, should proclaim them with a united voice'. He also wished to improve relations between the United Kingdom and United States generally, saying 'I hope to be able to do something to narrow the Atlantic.'[16]

MacDonald boarded *Berengaria* at 10.30pm the night of 27 September 'after an enthusiastic farewell from crowds at the pierhead and on the station platforms along the route from London'. Thousands saw the prime minister and his party off at Waterloo Station. The travelling party of nine accompanying the prime minister included Ishbel MacDonald, his daughter and official hostess at 10 Downing Street, two representatives from the foreign office, Britain's postmaster general, two aides, two secretaries and a Scotland Yard detective. A retinue of seventeen British and American journalists joined the official party for the crossing. Although sailing day 'dawned bright', a bank of fog settled over the harbour just before *Berengaria's* scheduled 7.30am departure, delaying her voyage. The fog evaporated two hours later and within minutes Rostron had his ship underway, seen off by 'hundreds on the end of the dock as the great liner pulled out into mid-stream'.[17]

The prime minister was a person of considerable interest to his fellow first-class passengers as well as to the press during the voyage. The passengers, mostly Americans returning home at the end of the summer season, kept a respectful distance. The press reported approvingly that the prime minister and his daughter rose early and took exercise about the deck, did not suffer from the seasickness that afflicted some of his staff and mixed with their fellow passengers. *The New York Times'* correspondent reported of 1 October: 'Aside from the usual long walks on deck, Mr. MacDonald's day is taken up by reading, having tea with the captain and posing for his portrait... The Premier has taken all his meals in the public dining room, using the imperial suite which he is occupying merely for sleeping and working.' MacDonald used *Berengaria's* wireless to stay in contact with London and Washington, DC, but also tried to relax some before his visit to North America.[18]

Relaxation caused the prime minister and his daughter to miss the Sunday Church of England service that Rostron conducted on *Berengaria's* first full day at sea. Rostron informed MacDonald that he would hold the service at 10.15am, as usual. MacDonald planned to attend, but fell asleep in his chair at nine after his morning exercise. Ishbel decided not to awaken him, knowing that he wanted to rest, and he awoke after Rostron had finished. The prime minister and commodore did interact on the rest of the voyage. Rostron hosted MacDonald and various guests at afternoon teas in his cabin and the two of them attended a luncheon with the journalists in the ship's chapel. This space had been converted into a newsroom for the voyage and MacDonald used it to hold informal briefings with the press.[19]

As *Berengaria* approached North America, preparations began afloat and ashore for the prime minister's arrival in the United States. On 2 October Rostron reduced the liner's speed so as to bring her to anchor at quarantine early on Friday morning, 4 October. On the same day, the correspondent for *The New York Times* informed his paper of 'great excitement aboard tonight with the report that two United States cruisers were coming to escort the Berengaria tomorrow'. Light cruisers *Memphis* and *Trenton* had been dispatched from Hampton Roads, Virginia, that afternoon to rendezvous with *Berengaria* in the vicinity of the Nantucket Lightship. In London, *The Times* reported that Commodore Rostron responded to the American honour by ordering *Berengaria* to dress ship.[20]

Prime Minister MacDonald spent his last day at sea as those aboard ship universally do, preparing for landfall. Much more was involved in the prime minister's arrival than that of one of *Berengaria's* less illustrious passengers. He spent his final day at sea 'completely occupied with scores of wireless messages, the dictation of important memoranda and the writing of a formal statement which he is expected to issue when the liner reaches quarantine'. To complete the day, *Memphis* and *Trenton* hove in view at 8.45pm, as *Berengaria* steamed past Nantucket, 'and at once took up positions abaft and abeam'. MacDonald observed their arrival, as did many of his fellow passengers, 'who hurried to the decks when word was passed that they were visible'.[21]

Memphis and *Trenton* escorted *Berengaria* from Nantucket Light to the mouth of Ambrose Channel, where they rendered a final salute before retiring to the south. 'The Berengaria presented an impressive spectacle as she approached New York,' reported *The Times*, 'first with her cruiser escort and afterwards as she was accompanied by a dozen aeroplanes' dispatched from Long Island's Mitchell Field. *Berengaria* passed into the harbour and dropped anchor at quarantine at 7.03am on 4 October 1929. After a slight delay, the municipal passenger vessel *Macom*, which would carry the prime minister from quarantine to landfall at the Battery, arrived alongside *Berengaria*. The ship's rails 'were lined with passengers, who cheered as the municipal welcome began with prolonged blasts of [*Macom's*] siren'. After *Macom* tied up, a welcoming committee boarded *Berengaria*, greeted MacDonald and accompanied him back to the harbour craft.[22]

Wearing a ribbon of MacDonald tartan embellished by a sprig of white heather supplied by *Berengaria's* florist, the prime minister crossed from the liner to *Macom* at 9.25pm. He departed New York's Penn Station for Washington, DC, two hours and eight minutes later. In the interval 'the harbour roared its welcome … [and] Broadway paid its tribute of cheering throngs and swirling ticker tape'. *Macom* stood back to the Battery to cheers from *Berengaria's* passengers and the strains of 'God Save the King' from the city's police band aboard an accompanying municipal vessel. Farther up the harbour came the thunder of a nineteen-gun salute from Governor's Island and a display of fountain-salutes from two of the city's fireboats.[23]

MacDonald and his party landed at the Battery at 10am, to be greeted by US Secretary of State Henry Stimson and Sir Esme Howard, Great Britain's ambassador to the United States. After the ticker tape parade up Broadway, Mayor Jimmy Walker welcomed the prime minister at City Hall and granted to MacDonald the same Freedom of the City he had awarded to Rostron three years before. At the conclusion of that ceremony, the prime minister and his party left for Pennsylvania Station to board the train for Washington.[24]

MacDonald's visit to the United States went well. On 6 October, two days after he reached the US capital, a White House official announced that Great Britain would extend formal invitations to the United States, Japan, France and Italy to attend the naval disarmament conference at London in January 1930. The following day, MacDonald addressed the US Senate on the subjects of Anglo-American relations, naval disarmament and applying the Kellogg–Briand Pact. The Anglo-American commitment to the pact was reaffirmed two days later, on 9 October, in a joint statement issued by Prime Minister MacDonald and President Herbert Hoover. MacDonald departed Washington, DC, the next day and visited Philadelphia, New York City and Buffalo before crossing into Canada at Niagara Falls on 15 October. The prime minister and his party spent ten days in Canada making official calls and vacationing, before departing from Quebec for Liverpool on 25 October aboard Canadian Pacific's new twenty-thousand-ton, twin-screw steamer *Duchess of York*.[25]

Rostron's association with this diplomacy had ended when MacDonald stepped across to *Macom*, leaving the commodore to tend to the more prosaic problems of berthing his ship and preparing her for her return voyage five days later. By the time *Berengaria* returned to England from delivering Prime Minister MacDonald to the United States, Commodore Sir Arthur Rostron, aged sixty, had only thirteen months remaining of his life at sea. Cunard had previously retired its masters at the age of sixty-three, but several of the company's captains had been forced to retire in the 1920s due to ill health brought on by overwork and the death of Sir James Charles on his last voyage at the age of sixty-two jolted Cunard's management.[26]

Even before Charles' death in July 1928, Cunard had taken steps to reduce the stress endured by the captains of its three big ships, appointing Charles himself to serve as relief captain from January 1928 until his retirement. Four captains for three ships meant that each commanded for three round voyages then took leave during the fourth. Rostron supported this policy; in November 1928 Chairman Royden wrote to Cunard's commodore that he was 'very pleased indeed to learn that the arrangements we have made to lessen the strain of continuous command of the express ships meet with the approval both of yourself and the other captains concerned'.[27]

Another problem Cunard faced was that the great number of men in its service over sixty blocked the promotion of many of their long-serving subordinates. In September 1928, one of Royden's assistants wrote to him about the company's 'many real first class Chief Officers who are well worth promotion but have been stuck through no fault of their own'. This sentiment was expressed publicly the following June by Cunard's deputy chairman, Sir Percy Bates. Bates believed that since so many men over sixty were blocking promotion of their juniors, the only choice was to lower retirement to that age, a solution that would bring Cunard's practice into agreement with that of several other Atlantic lines, including White Star.[28]

Cunard's directors made the new retirement policy official in the last week of October 1930, after canvassing sea and shore staff, each of which approved. Rostron was in New York aboard *Berengaria* when the company announced the decision. *The New York Times* reported that once the ship returned to Southampton, she would be withdrawn from service for her winter refit. The paper speculated that Rostron would leave *Berengaria* then, 'and make a final voyage early in the new year in command of his old ship, the Mauretania, to say goodbye to his friends in the United States'.[29]

In fact, *Berengaria*'s final eastbound passage of 1930 would be Rostron's last crossing in command. Although his decision to retire had been made for him by the rules change, Cunard had not revealed the date of his last voyage. Samuel McNeil, commanding *Mauretania* at the time, thought that withholding the exact date of their last voyage from captains was a good idea, otherwise, 'the nearer it approached, the more nervous and strung-up they became'. Rostron concurred. He applied for official retirement at his sixty-second birthday in May 1931, but 'months before that time came round I was given leave, a gracious concession. So the last time I brought the *Berengaria* to dock, I never knew but I should be taking her across again. I think now it was a kindly act on the part of the directors. There is a certain sense of the ominous about a last voyage. We remember how my predecessor as Commodore, Sir James Charles, knew he was making his last passage. It was in every sense of the word his last voyage.'[30]

And so, on the afternoon of 5 November 1930, after manoeuvring *Berengaria* into her Southampton dock with the aid of the pilot, Commodore Rostron, aged sixty-one years and five months, ordered 'finished with engines' for the last time. He gave a final interview to the press and bade farewell to his officers that afternoon, including his staff captain and long-time shipmate, James Bisset. In a ceremony held aboard, Bisset 'had the privilege of presenting him, on behalf of the crew, with an illuminated address'. *The New York Times* told readers that 'the great sailor, perhaps the best known and surely one of the most popular figures in the Atlantic service ... will live quietly at his country home near his regular port of call, dividing his time between his children and his flowers'.[31]

Following the death of Sir James Charles, the company assigned as captains Rostron in *Berengaria*, E. G. Diggle in *Aquitania*, Samuel McNeil in *Mauretania* and William Prothero, *Carpathia*'s last master, in 'relief for big ships'. The company readjusted its senior captains again at Sir Arthur's retirement. Edgar Britten, himself destined to become a knight and commodore later in the decade, assumed command of *Berengaria*. Diggle remained in *Aquitania* and hoisted the commodore's flag succeeding Rostron. Diggle's tenure as commodore was brief; also past sixty, he retired in August 1931, not three months after Rostron and Prothero had in May. All of these retirements created opportunities to promote a few of their deserving subordinates, one of whom was James Bisset, appointed a captain in Cunard's service in May of 1931.[32]

Rostron retired at the beginning of a new era. The Great Depression precipitated by the stock market crash of the year before would reconfigure the Atlantic's commercial seascape once more. Cunard's ageing and expensive express fleet would have to be modernized to increase efficiency and to compete with the big, fast ships being built by German, Italian and French companies. On 1 December 1930, within a month of Rostron's final voyage, Cunard signed the contract for delivery of *Queen Mary* and construction began a month after that. With service speeds exceeding 30 knots, *Queen Mary* and her half-sister *Queen Elizabeth* would replace three ships to maintain Cunard's weekly New York service after the Second World War.[33]

Rostron had left his impress on a previous age. Southampton's daily newspaper declared Cunard's retiring commodore 'one of the most distinguished men the British Mercantile Marine has ever produced,' while *Lloyd's List and Shipping Gazette* noted that Rostron had 'probably gained more honours than any other captain in the British merchant navy'. But Sir Thomas Royden probably praised Rostron in the way he would have most appreciated. In a letter to Sir Ronald Waterhouse, Prime Minister Baldwin's private secretary, Royden wrote: 'I don't know whether you have ever encountered [Rostron] in your journeyings about the surface of the globe, but, if you have not, I can assure you that he is the very best type of sailor man.'[34]

CHAPTER 16

HOME FROM THE SEA

H ome from the sea but not yet officially retired, Sir Arthur spent the first
half of 1931 writing his memoir. He divided it into seventeen chapters,
three of which recounted his early years in sail, in steam and in command
before 1912. The *Titanic* tragedy received its own chapter, followed by four
chapters on Rostron's experiences during the First World War. These consisted
of two chapters on Mediterranean operations, particularly at Gallipoli and
two chapters about his days aboard *Mauretania* as a hospital ship and as a
troop transport. Rostron recalled his postwar years as master of two of the
North Atlantic's most significant liners in three chapters, two of which he
devoted to the social side of the transatlantic trade and one to *Mauretania's*
peacetime adventures under his command. He spent an entire chapter
discussing the Americans, whom he characterized for his British readers as
well-intentioned if somewhat rambunctious younger brothers. Rostron ended
his memoir with a chapter entitled 'Then and Now', which compared life at
sea during his early years with conditions at his retirement, one on leadership
and another titled 'Go to Sea, My Lads' that appealed to Britain's youth to
consider careers in seafaring. He concluded with some speculations about the
giant new Cunarder then rising beside the Clyde.

Published that autumn of 1931 by Macmillian, *Home from the Sea* is
an enjoyable voyage for the armchair mariner, but rougher sailing for the
maritime historian. Rostron's memoir is his memories, which, like everyone
else's, were fallible. His imprecise memory, unaided by research, led him to
make some factual errors, such as placing *Mauretania's* fire in 1925. The book
is devoid of the names of his associates, personal or professional. He dedicated
Home from the Sea 'to all my old shipmates', but mentioned by name only one,

232 pages in, a purser – and him in connection with a bridge foursome. Even *Carpathia*'s Harold Cottam, whom Rostron specially credited in the book's dedication and whose name he could have recovered easily, appears only as 'the wireless operator'. The work also contains very few dates, the first being the year of his marriage, 1899, but even Minnie never appears by name. Perhaps Rostron's tack was to mention none in order to avoid offending some. All that said, *The New York Times Book Review* endorsed *Home from the Sea*, describing it as a 'lively', sometimes 'hard-bitten' story, 'written with dignity and good taste, interesting both because of his adventurous, capable, significant life and because of the sincerity, the warm-heartedness, the zest of memory with which it is written'.[1]

After retiring officially from seafaring in May 1931, one of the first things Rostron did was undertake a sea voyage. This one combined a little business, some pleasure and a final farewell. On 10 July Sir Arthur and Lady Rostron arrived in New York as passengers aboard *Berengaria* for a five-day visit. The Rostrons stayed at Ar-Y-Bryn at Tuxedo Park as guests of the New York socialites Louis and Augusta Ogden, Rostron loyalists since their truncated voyage to the Mediterranean nineteen Aprils before. Mr Ogden had used his new camera to take pictures of some of *Titanic*'s lifeboats arriving alongside *Carpathia*. These, *The New York Times* announced shortly after the Rostrons' visit, would be used to illustrate Sir Arthur's book. Rostron also reprised his role as informal ambassador between the US and Britain, telling the newspaper that 'I feel that now [that] I have retired as a shipmaster there is no better service I can give to my own countrymen than to attempt to make them see and understand the real America as I do.' This would be Rostron's last visit to the United States, however. When *Berengaria* returned to sea the following Wednesday, 15 July, it would be Rostron's last glimpse of a harbour he had visited scores of times over thirty-six years. Landed at Southampton, Arthur Rostron apparently never went to sea again.[2]

Instead, as Rostron had predicted, he devoted his retirement to 'his children and his flowers'. Perhaps surprisingly, he tended his flowers in Southampton. Only five years in residence at Holmecroft in West End, the Rostrons nevertheless decided to retire there rather than to return to their native Lancashire. Proximity to their children and grandchildren and to the centre of Cunard's passenger operations made that decision a reasonable one.[3]

By the time Rostron became commodore in 1928, at the age of fifty-nine, all of his children except Margaret had reached adulthood. The oldest, Harry Maxwell Rostron, married Catherine May Brooks in February 1927 and Arthur and Ethel's first grandchild, Arthur John Rostron, known as John, was born on 11 July 1928. Catherine delivered Sir Arthur's second grandson, David, on 13 November 1930, eight days after the commodore's last voyage. The Rostrons' second son, Robert, married Marjorie Bignall, a union which produced Sandy and Peter. In 1935 Arnold Rostron, Arthur and Ethel's third son, married Elizabeth Ward, bringing Rosemary and Jervis to the family. The following year, Margaret Rostron wed John Howman, a marriage that produced Mike, Jill, Jacqueline and Roger.[4]

Sir Arthur hired a permanent gardener to maintain his large, well-kept garden. John Rostron, who lived in nearby Swaythling to the age of fifteen and often visited his grandparents, said that while his parents and grandparents conversed, he and David amused themselves in the garden, talked with the gardener, or played with some steam engine models that Sir Arthur kept in the garden shed. John recalled that Sir Arthur liked to get out in the garden, which included a chestnut tree, and enjoyed building bonfires in the autumn, both to clear the garden and to roast chestnuts. He remembered his grandfather as 'a quietly-spoken man' and his grandmother as a pleasant woman who organized the household and managed the servants. Of their marriage John recalled that 'there was great courtesy and they were happy'.[5]

The Rostrons' affluent circumstances were not shared by Sir Arthur's former employer. By the time the Rostrons sailed home from the United States in July 1931, the Great Depression had struck with full force, annihilating the profit from the Atlantic passenger business. *The Times* reported that shipping companies on the North Atlantic lost ten million pounds in revenue in 1931 compared to 1930. In April 1931, Cunard announced that it would increase its schedule of short cruises to employ its big ships during their five-day layovers in New York. The company offered a total of seventeen cruises to the Caribbean that year, with ships heading south the day after their Friday arrivals in New York and returning the day before their eastbound crossings the following Wednesday. In the following years, Cunard filled the time of its big three liners in Europe with similar short cruises to Gibraltar and Madeira. *The Times* reported that 'short trips of this nature have proved popular in America and it is hoped that they will be equally successful in Europe'.[6]

Hand in hand with more work in season came less work out of season. In August 1931, the month after the Rostrons returned home, Cunard and White Star announced an agreement to both reduce off-season sailings and lengthen the off season. The companies agreed to begin alternate sailings on 1 October, rather than at the end of November as they had previously, with the limited schedule maintained through the following March. By 1933 the companies were reduced to announcing a combined winter service intended to maintain what *The Times* called 'a more or less regular schedule by fast liners'.[7]

The ugly truth apparent by then was that two British transatlantic passenger steamship companies was one more than the Great Depression could sustain. Cunard had entered the decade in reasonably good financial condition, having spent the 1920s rebuilding its fleet and expanding its markets while reducing its operating costs and debt. By December 1931, however, Cunard's financial situation had become precarious enough that the company's board decided to suspend construction of its great liner laid down at Clydebank twelve months before.[8]

If Cunard Steamship Company was wallowing by the end of 1931, the Oceanic Steam Navigation Company was foundering, unable to make the interest payments on its debt. White Star's financial troubles started in 1925, when its American holding company, International Mercantile Marine, began to sell off that cartel's foreign assets. Cunard unsuccessfully negotiated to purchase White Star over the next six years, but resisted a merger with that company. Cunard's directors eventually agreed to a merger because of their need for government subsidy of their company's shipbuilding.[9]

The three-sided arrangement that emerged from extended negotiation in 1933 satisfied Cunard's need for capital, White Star's need to be rescued from insolvency and the British government's desire to consolidate the two companies and to provide work for thousands of Clydebank's unemployed. The agreement, which took effect on 1 January 1934, created Cunard-White Star, Limited. The British government agreed to support the new company with £9.5 million in low-interest loans. These provided one and a half million pounds for operating capital, three million pounds to complete Hull 534 at

Clydebank and five million pounds for the construction of a second such ship later in the decade. The new company acquired the North Atlantic fleets of fifteen Cunard and ten White Star ships, the contract with John Brown and Company and the unfinished Hull 534. In exchange for transferring their assets to the new company, Cunard would receive sixty-two per cent of its shares and White Star thirty-eight per cent, with the exclusively British board of the merged company to consist of six members from Cunard and four from White Star. With these arrangements completed, work resumed that spring at John Brown on Hull 534, launched and christened *Queen Mary* on 26 September 1934.[10]

Sir Arthur, meanwhile, was addressing depression relief for British maritime industries from the opposite end. He once described Britain's ships as 'the barometer of our prosperity', but the Great Depression had idled more than the nation's ships. Throughout much of the 1930s Rostron served as a regular member of the general council of King George's Fund for Sailors. This aid society, founded in 1917, was charged with the impossible task of sailors' relief during the Great Depression. It granted tens of thousands of pounds to other aid societies throughout the Empire during the 1930s, trying to sustain thousands of unemployed merchant sailors and their families. In the same year as the Cunard-White Star merger, 1934, King George's Fund distributed £51,000 among nearly one hundred seafarers' benevolent institutions engaged in relief.[11]

Rostron involved himself in several other civic associations and activities during his retirement. A Southampton newspaper described him as 'a keen worker for the British Legion, in which he [has] held various offices'. The Legion, founded in 1921, became the principal British veterans' organization conducting memorial observances associated with the First World War. On 25 April 1934, at the Cenotaph in London's Whitehall, Rostron, representing the Merchant Navy of the United Kingdom, laid one of more than a dozen wreaths presented by various services in a ceremony commemorating the anniversary of the Gallipoli invasion.[12]

Rostron occasionally participated in other public functions, such as attending the Founders' Day celebration at the Nautical College at Pangbourne in 1933. He sometimes gave speeches, as when he addressed the annual meeting of the Society for the Propagation of the Gospel in Foreign Parts at Albert

Hall in Manchester on 2 December 1935. With the Bishop of Manchester presiding, Rostron spoke on a favourite subject: 'The Sailor and Religion.' He told his audience that for the thinking sailor, regularly confronted with both the terrors and glories of nature, religion was fundamental. Rostron called the brotherhood of the sea the finest on the planet and wondered why humanity could not achieve a similar brotherhood on land throughout the world.[13]

The following year Rostron made a public appearance of an entirely different sort, lending his name to an advertising campaign for the Fifty Shilling Tailors, a national chain of clothing stores. The series, which ran from July through November 1936 in *The Times*, featured profiles of eleven 'men of character … whose activities and interests were representative of many sections of public life and opinion,' who endorsed the company's suits in exchange for donations to the charity of their choice.[14]

The retired commodore remained in contact with the sea through active membership in the Southampton Master Mariners' Club, founded in 1928 by a group of former square-rigger sailors. Rostron served the organization as 'Staff Captain' and 'Captain' – vice-president and president – in 1935 and 1936, respectively and the 'clubroom bears evidence of his goodwill, for he presented pictures, books and nautical instruments which are of the greatest interest to all connected with the sea and ships'. By the mid-1930s, however, the muster of ships that Rostron had sailed in was dwindling, thanks to the Great Depression and the Cunard-White Star merger that rendered many of them surplus.[15]

The most poignant moment during Rostron's retirement occurred in July 1935, when *Mauretania* steamed to the breakers. Putting sentiment aside, as managers must, withdrawing *Mauretania* from service was not a difficult decision. Of Cunard's big three liners of the 1920s, she was the oldest, smallest and most expensive to operate. Once she lost the cachet of 'Fastest Liner in the World' to Norddeutscher Lloyd's *Bremen* in the summer of 1929, these ruthless economic realities began to assert themselves.[16]

Mauretania survived the early years of the Depression by unconvincingly donning the white livery of a cruise ship and working the Caribbean and Mediterranean circuits. Cunard used her legendary speed to cover long stretches of ocean on short schedules, but with her high fuel consumption, lack of air conditioning and shortage of the *en suite* bathrooms that cruising Americans desired, she was ill-fitted to the trade. She made her last Caribbean cruises in the summer of 1934 and bade her final farewell to New York on 26 September 1934 – the day *Queen Mary* was launched. *Mauretania* tied up at Southampton for the last time five days later, making her final Atlantic crossing at an average speed of almost precisely 24.5 knots, faithful to the Admiralty's requirements to the last.[17]

Mauretania idled at Southampton throughout the winter and into the following spring while rumours swirled about her fate. At the beginning of April 1935, word came: Cunard had sold *Mauretania* to Metal Industries, Ltd., Glasgow, for dismantling at Rosyth.[18]

In *Mauretania*'s case, however, sentiment could not be dismissed completely. Cunard's dowager queen was no ordinary ship; she was 'by far the best-known and best-loved ship in her day' in James Bisset's opinion. A day after announcing her sale to Metal Industries, *The Times* published what amounted to an obituary for 'A Great Liner'. After reviewing her construction, speed records and war service, *The Times* declared *Mauretania* 'a fine sea vessel and extremely popular with passengers'. *The New York Times* produced a similar eulogy two weeks later, particularly extolling *Mauretania*'s war service.[19]

Nevertheless, her end had come after twenty-seven years, three million miles, a million and a quarter passengers carried across the Atlantic, another quarter million taken on cruises and over three hundred visits to New York. First came the sale of her fittings and furnishings, held at Southampton for ten days starting on 14 May. The auction of everything from *Mauretania*'s lifeboats to her lettering yielded about £15,000. On the evening of 1 July 1935, flying a pennant commemorating the Blue Riband she had held for twenty years, *Mauretania* departed Southampton for Rosyth, across the Firth of Forth from Edinburgh.[20]

Among those gathered on the quay to bid farewell were Southampton's mayor, a brass band from the Southern Railway and Cunard's retired commodore, Sir Arthur Henry Rostron. Rostron did not join the crew of sixty – many with long service aboard *Mauretania* – and a like number of invited guests on the final voyage of his beloved former command, now rust streaked, her interiors gutted and her masts pruned to funnel height to clear the Forth Bridge. The *Southampton Daily Echo* noted that Rostron 'declined all invitations to go aboard during the day', and said: '"No, I couldn't bear to see her interior as it is to-day; I prefer to remember her as she was in all her glory."' The newspaper concluded that everyone who knew Sir Arthur and his love of ships and the sea 'will agree that his decision was a wise one'.[21]

So he remained ashore – 'a slight, silent figure who watched the scene from the balcony of a quayside shed' – one among the thousands gathered 'along the whole stretch of Southampton Water,' reported *The Times*, at 'every point from which a good view could be obtained of her'. They watched *Mauretania* stand away from her pier under her own power at dusk to the strains of 'The Last Post' from the ship's bugler and Auld Lang Syne from the railway band on the pier. She sailed away south to the Channel accompanied by airplanes and escorted by small craft as ships in the harbour boomed their whistle tributes. The *Echo* declared it 'a wonderful goodbye'.[22]

On her northbound passage – watched by people all along the coast and saluted by vessels of all kinds – *Mauretania* paused off the mouth of the Tyne on the morning of 3 July. There she received the Lord Mayor of Newcastle and the mayor of South Shields, who boarded from a tugboat, and exchanged farewells with the town that created her. The following morning she reached Rosyth and tied up for the last time, greeted by saluting ships and by a piper on the pier playing the Scottish funereal lament 'Flowers of the Forest'. Yet, of all of the honours rendered to her, perhaps *Mauretania*'s best and most affectionate eulogy was Rostron's: 'She gave of her best, served the Cunard Company well, was an honour and credit to her builders, to her owners and to Britain, was loved by all who ever served in her and admired by all who crossed in her.'[23]

Ten months after the deposed empress sailed to her destruction, the new monarch, *Queen Mary*, joined the Cunard-White Star fleet. Cunard first considered replacing *Mauretania* with a new speed queen in 1926. At the end of 1928 the company organized a committee to consider the design of the new vessel and in the autumn of 1929 Cunard determined to build one large, fast ship to replace *Mauretania* and to compete with the new giants of rival European steamship companies. Once the British government assured Cunard that it would assume whatever risks for the new vessel that private insurers would not cover, the company authorized construction. On

1 December 1930, twenty-six days after Commodore Rostron's last voyage, Cunard signed the contract for the new ship with John Brown and Company, Clydebank.[24]

Cunard's Southampton marine superintendent escorted Sir Arthur, Lady Rostron and their adult daughter Margaret about *Queen Mary* before her maiden voyage in May 1936. The eighty-thousand-ton liner destined to recover the Blue Riband for Britain – a ship half again as large as *Berengaria* and more than two-and-a-half times the size of *Mauretania* – mocked Rostron's prediction of a dozen years before 'that the day of the "big boat" has reached its zenith for a long time'. Cunard's purpose in building ships of such scale and speed was both to reclaim the record and to reduce the number of ships necessary to maintain a weekly transatlantic service from three to two. A decade of depression and war would pass before Cunard-White Star could put that two-ship service into effect, but meanwhile, with a surplus of ships thanks to the merger, the company could retire some of its elderly vessels.[25]

The next to go of Cunard's big three of the 1920s was Rostron's last ship, *Berengaria*. Although slightly larger than *Aquitania*, *Berengaria* began to suffer electrical fires in 1936. Two fires in March 1938 made it apparent that the ship could not return to sea without an extensive electrical overhaul uneconomical in a twenty-five-year-old ship. *Berengaria* therefore lay idle at Southampton until she steamed to the breakers that December.[26]

Aquitania, which Rostron commanded on two voyages, was the youngest and longest surviving of the big three. She entered service in the spring of 1914 as a somewhat mismatched running mate for *Lusitania* and *Mauretania*. Although she provided the third ship necessary to maintain the weekly sailings of the company's New York service, *Aquitania* resembled White Star's Olympic-class ships in size and speed rather than her own company's pair of ocean racers. In ordinary circumstances, *Aquitania* would have been replaced by *Queen Elizabeth*, Cunard-White Star's second great liner launched in the 1930s. But by the time that ship was ready for service in the summer of 1940, the United Kingdom was once again at war. After a long and successful career, the new crisis granted *Aquitania* a decade's reprieve. She earned thereby the distinction, unique among the great liners, of serving through both World Wars and demobilizations before finally sailing for the boneyard in 1950.[27]

Four months before the Second World War began, Sir Arthur Rostron turned seventy. Younger men than he would fight the new war's battles, among them his own sons. Rostron's eldest son, Harry, was in a 'reserved occupation' as an engineer, first at Pirelli engineering works at Eastleigh and later at Liverpool. When not thus employed, he served as a lieutenant in the Home Guard. Sir Arthur's two younger sons both served overseas. Thirty-one-year-old Arnold Rostron joined the Royal Army Ordnance Corps as a lieutenant in February 1939, was assigned to the 43rd (Wessex) Division and served for many months in North Africa. Robert Rostron, then thirty-seven, joined the South Lancashire Regiment as a second lieutenant in June 1940. He served as part of a military mission to the Soviet Union after that country entered the war in 1941. Sir Arthur's son-in-law, Margaret's husband John Howman, was a civilian test pilot at Bristol during the war.[28]

The war at sea fell to Rostron's sons of a different sort: the merchant mariners who had sailed under him as junior officers and since achieved commands of their own. James Bisset, like Rostron a generation before, spent the last years of a world war commanding great liners racing across the Atlantic carrying men and materials to Europe. For his war service in *Queen Mary* and *Queen Elizabeth*, Bisset, too, would be knighted and would retire as Cunard's commodore.[29]

More typical, however, was the price paid by others. Harry Grattidge, one of Rostron's junior officers in the 1920s and Cunard's commodore in the 1950s, had the misfortune to be chief officer of Cunard's *Lancastria* during the British evacuation from France in 1940. Grossly overloaded with escaping military personnel and civilians when attacked by the Luftwaffe off St Nazaire on 17 June, *Lancastria* sank with a significantly greater loss of life than *Titanic*. Grattidge survived, but arrived in London stinking of his lost ship's oil and seared by his experience. Even so, he fared better than Eric Rees, Rostron's third officer on *Carpathia*. Thirty years to the week after the *Titanic* rescue, Rees, commodore of convoy PQ-14, disappeared into the Barents Sea, obliterated when a German submarine torpedoed his explosives-laden ship on the notorious Murmansk run.[30]

That Sir Arthur was not involved personally in this war did not prevent it from visiting the Rostron residence dramatically in the summer of 1940. After the collapse of British and French resistance on the Continent that June, the German military turned its attention to defeating the United Kingdom. Preparatory to invading Britain, the Luftwaffe began attacking southern England, both to disable its industries and to destroy the Royal Air Force. The first bombs fell on Southampton on 19 June 1940 and raids continued with increasing intensity throughout that summer on the area's factories, port facilities and railroad network. While the agricultural village of West End was not an obvious target, its location seconds by air from the shipyards and Spitfire works at Southampton and the large rail yard and airfield at Eastleigh sometimes brought the town into the Luftwaffe's crosshairs.[31]

It was during one of these summer raids that a Luftwaffe pilot strafed Holmcroft. The bullets struck the south side of the house, several flying into the dining room while the family was there. On their next visit, grandsons John and David found another bullet inside a water butt just outside the dining room. John said that the attack 'caused a little damage but no casualties fortunately'. Concerned for their safety after the strafing, however, Arthur and Ethel began to sleep every night in a bomb shelter built in the garden, a precaution that ultimately proved unnecessary since the house was never attacked again during the years the Rostrons lived there.[32]

It was also a precaution that may have proved fatal. John Rostron believed that his grandfather probably became sick from sleeping in the shelter in the autumn of 1940. However his final illness came about, Sir Arthur Henry Rostron died at age seventy-one on Monday, 4 November 1940 – one day short of ten years after completing his final voyage in command. He died not in West End or Southampton, but in Cottage Hospital at Chippenham. The Rostrons had travelled to Calne, near Bristol where John Howman was stationed, to visit their daughter Margaret and their grandchildren. The *Southampton Daily Echo* reported that before the Rostrons could return to West End, Sir Arthur contracted gastric influenza and 'pneumonia supervened, with fatal results'. The newspaper continued that Rostron's death 'will occasion deep regret among a very wide circle of friends and particularly among the shipping community'.[33]

In its notice of Rostron's passing, *The Times* described the late commodore as 'at least as well known in the United States as in the United Kingdom'. Rostron's obituaries in the American press supported that assertion. On Tuesday, 5 November, an announcement of his death by the Associated Press appeared on the first page of newspapers as varied as the *Portsmouth Herald* of New Hampshire and the *Ogden Standard Examiner* of Utah. Such front-page recognition was an impressive testimonial in itself, since it occurred on the same day as the US presidential election of 1940.[34]

Sir Arthur's funeral service was held in West End's Parish Church of St James, followed by burial at the West End Cemetery, on Thursday, 7 November 1940. The vicar, the Reverend R. H. Babington, conducted the service, assisted by the Reverend W. A. H. Barnes, chaplain of the Missions to Seamen, Southampton and of the Southampton Master Mariners' Club, two of Rostron's interests. Another of Rostron's associations, the West End and Bitterne branch of the British Legion, posted a guard of honour at both the church and the cemetery and Rostron's casket was draped with the Union Jack and adorned with his dress sword.[35]

Among the seventy-five mourners listed as attending were fifteen members of Rostron's family, excluding his son Arthur, posted overseas. The mayors of both Southampton and Eastleigh attended, as did thirteen officials or sailors from Cunard-White Star, four representatives from the Master Mariners' Club, sixteen people from various divisions of civil government or maritime interests, seven representing industrial or civic groups and the eighteen members of the guard of honour. Thirty-five floral tributes were presented by family members, private individuals, Cunard-White Star, the Southampton Master Mariners' Club, The Missions to Seamen, Southampton, the shipbuilders John L. Thornycroft and Co., the Minerva Lodge of Freemasons, the British Legion, the Old Boltonians' Association, the Northern Counties of England Association and the West End Tennis Club.[36]

Ethel Minnie Rostron survived her husband by only thirty-two months. After he died, she left their home on Chalk Hill Road and moved in with her eldest son Harry and daughter-in-law Catherine two miles away at Swaythling. Ethel died on 7 July 1943, at age sixty-nine, and was buried in the West End Cemetery beside her husband of forty-one years. After her death, the Rostrons' eldest child, Harry, embarked upon a homecoming of sorts that same year when he assumed management of the Liverpool Overhead Railway Company. He restored a railroad badly damaged by the Liverpool Blitz, ran the line until it ceased operating in 1956 and then formed the engineering company that dismantled it. A number of Arthur and Ethel's descendants settled in Devon or Cornwall, including their longest-surviving child, Margaret, who died at Truro, Cornwall, in 2005, sixty-five years after her father's death.[37]

Across those years Arthur Rostron retained his fame thanks to resurgent interest in the *Titanic* disaster following the publication of Walter Lord's *A Night to Remember* in 1955. As the fascination with *Titanic* has blossomed into innumerable books, programmes and societies, *Carpathia*'s captain has returned to her bridge in various venues and raced again to the rescue.

The captain has also assumed his place ashore. At Sharples on 6 February 1999, the Bolton and District Civic Trust unveiled a plaque identifying the childhood residence on Blackburn Road of the man who 'went to the rescue of the survivors of the R.M.S. Titanic in the early hours of Monday 15th April, 1912'. The West End Local History Society's museum features a small dual memorial to Rostron and James Jukes, a local man lost with *Titanic*. The British Titanic Society assisted in creating the memorial, unveiled by Margaret Howman, then eighty-four, on 17 April 1999, with *Titanic* survivor Millvina Dean in attendance. The following year the West End Parish Council and the Royal Naval Reserve granted funds to rehabilitate the Rostrons' sixty-year-old tombstone. Arthur and Ethel's headstone, 'completely refurbished and … looking as good as new,' now gleams, somewhat incongruously, in West End's Old Burial Ground. A decade later, in 2011, the Eastleigh Borough Council, at the suggestion of the West End Local History Society, named a new street in the Chalk Hill section of West End 'Rostron Close'.[38]

On Sunday morning, 15 April 2012, the centenary of *Carpathia*'s race to the rescue, more than 120 people gathered in the Old Burial Ground to honour her late captain. The mayor of Eastleigh and the chairman of the West End Local History Society presided at the ceremony. The vicar of St James' Church conducted a short service and representatives from the Rostron family, Cunard, the City of Southampton, the Southampton Master Mariners' Club, the Conway Club and the British Titanic Society placed floral tributes on Sir Arthur and Lady Rostron's grave. That afternoon, many of the same individuals met at Holmcroft and Rosemary Pettet, Arnold Rostron's daughter and Sir Arthur's granddaughter, unveiled a heritage plaque commemorating the Rostrons' years in the house.[39]

The honours of his lifetime and the remembrances of generations since befit Arthur Rostron and his achievements. He was not a great historical figure, perhaps, but Rostron knew what he wished to be and to do and to achieve from his youngest days and he carried it off about as well as anyone could. Most of his personal life is obscured, first by privacy and now by time, but everywhere his seafaring life can be sounded, from the decks of HMS *Conway* to his obituaries written fifty-four years later, he is universally esteemed an excellent and devoted sailor.[40]

He was not, however, typical of the master mariners of his era. Commodore Harry Grattidge characterized the Atlantic captain of his junior years, Rostron's era, as 'that strange mixture of great seamanship, ruthless conservatism, blasphemy and strange inarticulate warmth'. Except upon the first count, Rostron hardly matches Grattidge's profile at all. Considering Grattidge's points in reverse, Rostron's warmth was neither strange nor inarticulate. He both enjoyed and was skilled at the social side of his duties. 'A fine seaman,' *The Times* observed, 'Rostron also found time to be a genial host in the great liners he commanded.'[41]

He was also devout. Bisset wrote that during Rostron's formative years in sail and on China Station 'he had seen life in the rough and the raw, afloat and ashore, but his religious faith remained, as his source of inner strength'. Rostron himself believed that his faith and his success were intertwined. He looked back from retirement with a mixture of pride and reverence at the 'millions of miles of sea I have traversed and thousands of people I have carried – with never a life lost through the ship's cause. That thought brings justification of a simple faith that goes with the sailor, a faith which long ago formed the basis of my philosophy in life – there is a Providence which shapes our ends.'[42]

As to Rostron's conservatism, if such it was, he was certainly an establishment figure, understandable in a man who rose from obscurity to knighthood within the established order. What would move him to fundamentally criticize the workings of a system in which he had succeeded so handsomely? It is thus unsurprising, for example, to find Rostron's signature on a petition to the House of Commons against eliminating the traditional 'tiller rules' for helm orders in oceangoing vessels, as proposed in the Merchant Shipping Bill of 1931. The old ways that had served him so well should continue to serve his successors.[43]

Rostron came to represent and reflect the established order, exuding the competence, the confidence and occasionally the chauvinism of the Empire at its apex. He expressed little faith in the capability or honesty of Mediterranean peoples,[44] and was similarly unsympathetic, at least later in life, when it came to class issues. He remembered vividly the hard life of his days in sail – 'the seaman was just the fool to be sent to do the dirty work, take all the risks and chances. And, of course, the officers and master took the responsibility as well' – to which he ascribed the rise and success of the seamen's unions. Once ensconced in the captain's cabin, however, he may have become less sensitive to the sailor's discontents. Thus his characterization of 'a spirit of good will prevailing' among the sailors on the ships he commanded as responsible for labour harmony, as well as his dismissal of Britain's 1925 seamen's strike as 'obviously engineered by Bolshevik propaganda'.[45]

Rostron developed in his early years and maintained throughout his life a sharp moral vision that shaped his understanding of the world. He did not proselytize his world view, but he held himself to it, navigating by his stars most capably and with great success. 'He was an idealist,' wrote James Bisset, but others perhaps more inclined to take the world as it came, such as Bisset himself, achieved similar results.[46]

Of Rostron's great seamanship there was no question then or since. Southampton's weekly newspaper entitled his obituary: 'Death of [a] Brilliant Sailor.' That celebrated test of a sailor, the *Titanic* rescue, was 'a piece of work well and courageously done' in Lawrence Beesley's opinion. It required of *Carpathia*'s crew 'the utmost vigilance in every department both before and after the rescue and a capacity for organization that must sometimes have been taxed to the breaking point'. That they carried it off so well, wrote Beesley in the year of the disaster, 'stands to the everlasting credit of the Cunard Line and those of its servants who were in charge of the *Carpathia*. Captain Rostron's part in all this is a great one.' Of the days following the rescue, *Titanic* survivor and widow Mahala Douglas said simply: 'The history of our wonderful treatment on the *Carpathia* is known to the world. It has been underestimated.'[47]

Sixty years later, Rostron's fellow HMS *Conway* alumnus, G. H. Slade, thought that, if anything, Rostron did not receive enough credit for the rescue. Rostron faced the defining crisis of his career, wrote Slade, 'absolutely single-handed at a comparatively early age, without any kind of qualified staff to advise him'. Slade believed that Rostron's 'shrewd personal individualistic planning, without modern aids [to navigation or reconnaissance] ... enabled him to [organize the rescue] on the spot, literally as he sailed along, in the comparative space of a very few hours'. Slade, too, lauded Rostron's behaviour during *Carpathia*'s return to New York, observing that 'throughout the aftermath when pressures must have been well nigh unbearable, he never for a moment lost either his head or his heart and maintained a shrewd unruffled calm notwithstanding'.[48]

Commodore Sir James Bisset, a brilliant sailor himself, observed Rostron on that night of nights and across all but the first sixteen months of his twenty-three years in command. Bisset rose from third officer to staff captain while serving in Rostron's first, last and two most historically significant commands. He described his 'old friend and mentor' as compiling 'a record of service at sea that few have equalled or excelled. I ... served with him in four ships – the *Brescia*, the *Carpathia*, the *Mauretania* and the *Berengaria* – and never saw him make any serious mistake of judgment or seamanship.' Bisset wrote that 'at all times I had the greatest respect for him as a seaman, a disciplinarian and as a man who could make a decision quickly – and stick to it... He was not a typical shipmaster, either in appearance or in his inner piety; yet in any nautical crisis or routine work he was excellent in his profession: one of the greatest merchant sea-captains of his time.'[49]

'A busy life and a good one,' was Sir Arthur's assessment. 'If I could go back I should want to do just what I have done;' a most satisfying outcome for the boy from Bolton who never had any ambition other than to go to sea.[50]

APPENDIX:

MATTERS *TITANIC*

T he story of the *Titanic* rescue has been told and retold through the
years. Even so, certain elements of *Carpathia*'s night to remember
remain unclear. I shall speculate below about some of the mysteries associated
with Rostron, *Carpathia* and the *Titanic* rescue in the order in which they
occurred.

CARPATHIA'S DASH: SPEED AND DISTANCE

In *Carpathia*'s legend, she steamed directly toward the *Titanic*'s distress position
on Rostron's 'North 52 West,' arrived at daybreak, recovered the survivors and
headed for New York – simple as that. However, the discovery of the position
of *Titanic*'s wreck on the floor of the Atlantic seventy-three years later indicates
a more complex combination of circumstances. First, *Carpathia* never reached
Titanic's wireless distress position, 41.46N, 50.14W – nor did *Titanic*. The
Canadian Pacific passenger steamer *Mount Temple* arrived at *Titanic*'s reported
position from the west at daybreak, to be greeted by pack ice floating on an
otherwise empty sea. By the time she stopped *Mount Temple* was actually
east of the distress position; Captain James Moore's dawn sun fix put *Mount
Temple* at 50 degrees 9.5 minutes West.[1]

Moore estimated that *Carpathia*, which he could see conducting the
rescue on the opposite side of the ice field, was 'at least eight miles' further
east. When US Senator Theodore Burton confronted *Titanic*'s fourth officer,
Joseph Boxhall, with Moore's testimony – 'The Captain of the *Mount Temple*
maintains that the course as conveyed by the distress signal was wrong; that
the *Titanic* was actually eight miles distant from the place indicated. What do
you say as to that?' – Boxhall answered: 'I do not know what to say. I know

our position, because I worked the position out and I know that it is correct. One of the first things that Capt[ain] Rostron said after I met him was, "What a splendid position that was you gave us."'[2]

Location of the wreck in 1985 proved Moore right and Boxhall and Rostron wrong. Such significant errors in establishing a ship's position were possible because of the dead reckoning navigation used in 1912. Ships' actual positions were established accurately by sextant observations several times a day, especially at dawn and dusk, but were estimated at all other times. These were educated estimates, but estimates all the same. Boxhall, when ordered by Captain Smith to establish *Titanic*'s position for the distress call, worked up his figures from observations Lightoller had taken at dusk, more than four hours before. He added what he thought were *Titanic*'s course and speed since Lightoller's fix to establish the distress position, but overestimated the liner's speed and could not account for the effects of ocean currents on her course. His dead-reckoned position (41.46N, 50.14W) thus located *Titanic* about thirteen and a half miles west-north-west of where Robert Ballard's expedition discovered the wreck in 1985 (41.43N, 49.56W).[3]

Thus *Carpathia*, racing toward Boxhall's dead-reckoned position, should have passed well to the west of *Titanic*'s lifeboats, at least if Rostron's own dead reckoning were accurate. The evidence indicates that *Carpathia* recovered *Titanic*'s boats significantly to the east and slightly to the south of *Titanic*'s reported distress position, but somewhat south-west of the actual site of the sinking. *Carpathia* arrived at Boxhall's boat at 4am, about a mile south of a cluster of flotsam, and spent almost four hours moving slowly northward recovering boats. 'It was only when we got to the last boat that we got close up to the wreckage,' Rostron told the Board of Trade's enquiry. 'It would be about a quarter to eight when we got there.'[4]

This debris field, however, was a modest one, consisting of 'a few deck chairs and pieces of cork from lifebelts and a few lifebelts knocking about and things of that description, all very small stuff … [and] very little indeed,' remembered Rostron, 'no more flotsam that one can often find washed onto a seashore by the tide' – and only one body. That last grim bit of evidence alone indicates that *Carpathia* never reached the main debris field at all. Senator Smith, comprehending this, said to Boxhall, 'there must have been hundreds of bodies in the water about the *Titanic*'. Boxhall, who had stood on *Carpathia*'s bridge as she slowly searched the area, responded: 'No one ever saw any, at all.' The cable ship *Mackay Bennett*, dispatched from Halifax two days after the disaster to recover bodies, would amply verify Senator Smith's dismal conjecture. Stanley Lord, master of *Californian*, the second ship on the scene, gave the position of this wreckage when *Californian* left it late that morning as 41.33N, 50.1W. Even allowing for inaccuracy in this position fix or what would by then have been about eight hours of drift, it at least suggests a recovery of *Titanic*'s boats south-west of the site of her sinking and south-east of her wireless distress position.[5]

Carpathia never reached the site of the sinking because, as the discovery of the wreck revealed, she was not heading for it. An interesting fact about *Carpathia*'s first sighting of one of the green flares shown by Fourth Officer Boxhall in *Titanic*'s lifeboat number 2 is that it appeared half a point, about five degrees, off *Carpathia*'s port bow, meaning slightly to the west of the ship's line of advance. Rostron, who had been steering for *Titanic*'s distress position as reported by wireless, thereupon steered for the flares. In the absence of any wind that night, currents may have set *Titanic*'s boat into *Carpathia*'s line of advance. Perhaps lifeboats pulling for the ship visible to the north-west unwittingly rowed into her path. Or perhaps mutual errors in dead reckoning made in the excitement by Boxhall and Rostron nullified themselves. Whatever the cause, the effect was the same and, for a rare time that night, fortune favoured *Titanic*'s survivors. Rostron followed the flares directly to Boxhall's boat. With no way of knowing the actual location of *Titanic*'s sinking, or the effects of drift and the night's activities on her boats, Rostron told the Senate's investigation 'that the position given me by the *Titanic* was absolutely correct'.[6]

These circumstances also help explain another point which has been a matter of some controversy: *Carpathia*'s speed to the rescue site and the distance that she travelled. Rostron told the Board of Trade's enquiry in June 1912 that 'we worked up to about seventeen and a half that night,' but he retreated to 'about seventeen knots' in an article published in *Scribner's Monthly* magazine in March 1913. To cover the fifty-eight miles Rostron calculated as *Carpathia*'s distance from *Titanic* in the three and a half hours between 12.35 and 4.05, would require an average speed of 16.57 knots. The time taken to speed up and slow down at each end of the run, however, would have to have been compensated by a top speed of 17 knots or better at some point in the run. Some authors have accepted such a speed as possible, while others do not believe that *Carpathia* had it in her, even under emergency power.[7]

Rostron stopped *Carpathia*'s run at Boxhall's boat and, come daylight, found himself about a mile from the small debris field, with *Titanic*'s boats spread out before him over an area of four or five miles. So *Carpathia* stopped south of the debris field, which was south of the place where *Titanic* lowered her boats into the water and then sank, which was south of *Titanic*'s wireless distress position that was the basis for Rostron's calculation of fifty-eight miles. If, in reality, the distance from where *Carpathia* turned to go to the rescue to where she stopped were, say, fifty-five miles instead of fifty-eight, the run would have required an average speed of 15.71 knots and a top speed of 16 knots or a little more. That was certainly within the bounds of possibility for a ship 'built to steam from 14 to 15 knots' in normal circumstances.[8]

SEEING BOXHALL'S FLARES

Rostron repeated consistently in his various accounts of the rescue that it was at 2.40am that he first sighted one of the green flares ignited by Boxhall in lifeboat number 2. Rostron gave this time in his testimony before both the US and British enquiries, in a report he made to his company and issued to the press before he left New York on 19 April, in another account composed at sea dated 27 April, in his *Scribner's Monthly* article in 1913 and in his memoir in 1931.[9]

That time is difficult to reconcile with other facts of that night, however. At 2.40am *Carpathia* would still have been about twenty-two miles from the disaster site, putting Boxhall's boat below the horizon. Further, it is unclear whether Boxhall was firing rockets aloft or simply holding flares above his head at a maximum height of about ten feet above the water. Boxhall described himself as 'showing green lights in the boat', which he described as 'pyrotechnic lights' which made 'a very brilliant light'. James Johnson, a steward rowing in Boxhall's boat, testified that 'the officer must have burned about eight or nine' flares. Johnson's choice of verb is interesting: 'burned', not 'shot' or 'fired' or 'launched'. Johnson described these devices as both 'flashlights' and 'Roman candles'. Quartermaster George Rowe testified to steering Collapsible C toward 'a boat that was carrying a green light'. And if these flares were thrown aloft, why didn't the watch on *Californian*, which saw both *Carpathia* and *Titanic*'s launched rockets, also see them?[10]

However, two occupants of Boxhall's boat used language suggesting thrown pyrotechnics. Able Seaman Frank Osman said Boxhall 'found a bunch of rockets... Having them in the boat, the officer fired some off.' Mahala Douglas, a first-class passenger whom Boxhall recruited to steer the boat ('and she assisted me greatly in doing that'), used words even more explicit, saying Boxhall 'put in the emergency boat a tin box of green lights, like rockets. These he commenced to send off at intervals.'[11]

Rostron's statements about the flares were also ambiguous. He told the Senate committee that when he sighted the first flare he 'took it for granted that it was the *Titanic* itself ... as I knew we were a long way off and it seemed so high'. He used almost the same words when testifying at the Board of Trade's enquiry two months later, saying, 'naturally, knowing I must be at least twenty miles away, I thought it was the ship herself still'. Of course, neither statement was true – even if the time was 2.40am, *Titanic* had sunk twenty minutes before – and once upon the scene of the rescue, both Rostron's perspective and his statements changed. A few minutes after he stopped engines 'I saw the boat's light again. This was the first time I knew really it was a boat and not the ship herself... Of course, I could not see the boat itself, but only the light when he showed the flare.' Rostron added an important detail in his article for *Scribner's Monthly*. Arriving on the scene 'we had seen the green flare light low down not long before and so knew it must be a boat'. So the green flares were 'high' when presumed to be coming from a ship at 2.40am and 'low down' when coming from a boat at 4am.[12]

Bisset's memoir, published forty-seven years later and perhaps drawing on Rostron's statements, agrees with Rostron's times and observations: high in the air at 2.40am, low on the water at 4am. Bisset's explanation for the early flares was 'a pyrotechnic rocket, flaring at 500 feet above sea-level to appear to us to be on the horizon from our distance of twenty-five miles away'. But Boxhall's 'tin box of green lights' which Osman believed 'was put in the boat by mistake for a box of biscuits' seems incapable of producing at least eight or nine such powerful pyrotechnics, never mind the problems involved with launching them out of a lifeboat.[13]

So how did *Carpathia*'s watch, however 'keyed up', spot flares low on the water from more than twenty miles away? The answer is that they probably did not and that Rostron simply did not remember the time correctly. David Gittins, an ocean navigator and student of the *Titanic* disaster, postulates a credible theory that when gathering his thoughts before his initial testimony Rostron confused 2.40am in the morning with two hours and forty minutes into *Carpathia*'s run, which began just after 12.35am. Rostron can be forgiven for such an error. Asked for the time of *Carpathia*'s departure from New York eight days before, on 11 April, Rostron told the senators: 'I cannot give you the exact time now, because, as a matter of fact, I have not looked at a single date or time of any kind. I have not had the time to do so.' If Gittins' theory about Rostron's confusion is correct, that would put the sighting of the first green flare at about 3.15am, at a much more reasonable distance of about twelve miles. That time would also better conform to the testimony of Mahala Douglas, who said that Rostron 'stated he saw our green lights 10 miles away and, of course, steered directly to us, so we were the first boat to arrive at the *Carpathia*'.[14]

STANLEY LORD, HERBERT STONE AND THE *CALIFORNIAN*

I should know better than to stick my hand into the controversies surrounding Captain Stanley Lord and the *Californian*, but will do so to make a few points about Rostron and Lord, whom, as we have seen, the enquiries, press and public came to consider displaying the polar opposites of conduct during the tragedy.

The story of the Leland liner *Californian* is an essential part of *Titanic* lore. Captain Lord stopped his ship for the night at 10.20pm on Sunday, 14 April, on the eastern edge of the ice field toward which *Titanic* was then steaming at full speed. *Californian* was a third or fewer miles from *Titanic*'s signalled distress position than *Carpathia*, but the exact distance remains both controversial and unknowable, given the dead-reckoning navigation of 1912. Lord testified to both the American and British enquiries that his position was 42.5N, 50.7W – 19.5 miles north and slightly east of *Titanic*'s wireless distress position. However, both of those tribunals found *Californian's* actual distance from the sinking *Titanic* to be much closer, 'not more than eight to ten miles,' in Lord Mersey's opinion.[15]

After 11pm that night, *Californian's* watch officer, Third Officer Charles Groves, saw a ship to the south steam into the area from the east and stop at about 11.40pm. At ten minutes after midnight, Groves handed over the watch to Second Officer Herbert Stone, who was assisted by the ship's officer apprentice, James Gibson.[16]

At about 12.45am, *Titanic* began to launch explosive white distress rockets, trying to attract the attention of a ship about five miles away. Stone, who had been watching a ship he estimated to be about five miles distant bearing south-south-east, testified: 'I saw one white flash in the sky, immediately above this other steamer. I did not know what it was; I thought it might be a shooting star.' Stone then 'brought the ship under observation with the binoculars' and saw four more rockets fired at three- to four-minute intervals. At that point, about 12.55am, the apprentice, Gibson, joined Stone on the bridge. Together, they watched three more rockets explode over the ship to the south, the last at about 1.40am. They then watched the vessel disappear at 2.20am, steaming away to the south-west, Stone believed.[17]

Captain Lord had retired to the chartroom at quarter past twelve and several times during his watch Stone informed Lord of the situation. At 1.10am he called down the voice tube to report the rockets fired by the ship to the south. At 2am he sent Gibson down to the chartroom to tell Lord that the ship had fired eight rockets and was disappearing to the south-west. At about 2.40am Stone called down on the voice tube again to report that the ship had disappeared twenty minutes before. Lord asked several times about the colour of the rockets and instructed Stone to contact the ship with *Californian's* Morse lamp, which Stone attempted unsuccessfully, but Lord never left the chart room to come to the bridge himself to assess the situation. He would later testify that he did not remember the details of Stone's voice-tube reports and had slept through Gibson's visit.[18]

At about 3.30am, at the end of their watch, Stone and Gibson saw three more rockets fired, this time low on the horizon far to the south, followed by the arrival of another ship on the scene just after 4am. Stone did not report these latest developments to Lord. He did, however, describe the events of his watch to his relief, Chief Officer George Stewart, who eventually roused *Californian*'s wireless operator who learned of the disaster. Lord, as we have seen, was censured by both the Senate and Board of Trade enquiries for *Californian*'s inaction and his culpability had been fiercely debated since.[19]

In the opinion of his defenders, most ardently articulated by Peter Padfield in *The Titanic and the Californian*, Lord was the victim of disaster enquiries headed by a fool – Senator Smith, a self-important man 'not overburdened with intelligence' – and two knaves – Lord Mersey and Sir Rufus Isaacs – compelled by hysteria or interest to frame Lord as a scapegoat regardless of substantial evidence to the contrary. Padfield never explained why or how American senators, British barristers and maritime experts on both sides of the Atlantic conspired to carry off this injustice. Instead, he focused on inconsistencies in testimony at the enquiries in an attempt to raise reasonable doubt about *Californian*'s proximity to and involvement in the events of that night and thus about Lord's responsibility.[20]

A favourite theory of Lord's defenders, including Padfield, is that a mystery ship lay between *Californian* and *Titanic* sowing confusion and thus justifying *Californian*'s inaction. Padfield wrote that 'the most likely theory about the rockets is that they *were Titanic*'s rockets seen by a strange coincidence over the deck lights, but below the masthead lights, of the other ship which lay to the South [*sic*] of the *Californian*'. Two points, however, invalidate that reasoning. First, the theory omits contradictory testimony from both Gibson and Stone. Gibson stated that while he had the ship visible to the south under observation through binoculars he saw one of the rockets come off her deck. Stone also testified that he saw one of the rockets come from that ship. Second, for all of the complaints about the lubberly-ness of the Senate enquiry, its report disarmed the mystery-ship defense in a sentence: 'There is no evidence that any rockets were fired by any vessel between the *Titanic* and the *Californian*, although every eye on the *Titanic* was searching the horizon for possible assistance.' If the ship Stone and Gibson saw to the south firing rockets was some other ship than *Titanic*, then why did no one on *Titanic* see a ship to the north firing rockets?[21]

And if that were not evidence enough, it is Rostron's arrival in *Carpathia* that fixes Lord and *Californian's* general position, both at sea and in history. *Carpathia's* intrusion means that to make the mystery-ship theory work requires not one mystery ship, but three: the ship seen from *Californian* firing rockets that was not *Titanic*; the one seen from *Titanic* not firing rockets that was not *Californian*; and the one seen from *Californian* racing up from the south-east firing rockets after 3.30am that was not *Carpathia*. One mystery ship on exactly the line of bearing between *Titanic* and *Californian* is possible, if improbable. The spectacle of *Titanic*, *Californian* and two mystery ships – one firing white rockets like *Titanic* – later joined by another rocket-firing mystery ship arriving on the scene from the same direction and at the same time as *Carpathia* – and these two sets of seemingly identical events occurring simultaneously within a few miles of each other – burdens plausibility beyond what it can bear.[22]

Rostron personally entered the *Californian* controversy briefly thanks to an affidavit concerning the rescue that he gave at New York at the behest of the Leland Line's counsel on 4 June 1912. In it he said in part: 'At 5 o'clock it was light enough to see all round the horizon. We then saw two steamships to the northwards, perhaps seven or eight miles distant. Neither of them was the *Californian*. One of them was a four-masted steamer with one funnel [which describes *Californian*, *Mount Temple* and a host of other ships, including *Carpathia*] and the other a two-masted steamer with one funnel… The first time that I saw the *Californian* was at about 8 o'clock on the morning of 15th April. She was then about five to six miles distant, bearing W.S.W. true and steaming toward the *Carpathia*.' Lord's defenders have taken this statement as evidence that *Californian* was not in proximity to the disaster, as both enquiries found.[23]

When Lord wrote to Rostron that summer asking for further exoneration, however, Rostron could not supply it, writing 'I cannot give you any detailed description of the two steamers seen by me. All I know – one, a four-masted steamer dodging about, I suppose amongst the ice to [the north]; the other, two masts and one funnel coming from [west] to [east] straight on his [*sic*] course. I did not see colour of funnels or notice anything which might distinguish either. You can imagine I was quite busy enough.' Rostron later told a shipmate that he had been mistaken in his affidavit about not identifying *Californian* to the north when others aboard *Carpathia* had, saying 'I had so much to do, I wasn't thinking of the *Californian* and didn't recognize her.'[24]

All of that said, the idea offered in the reports of the American and especially the British enquiry that had *Californian*'s officers interpreted what they were seeing correctly and acted promptly 'she might have saved many if not all of the lives that were lost' bears scrutiny. If *Californian*'s officers 'were all on the *qui vive*' that night, getting her underway for *Titanic* by 1.15am, as a sympathetic examiner postulated for Lord at the British enquiry, could she, he asked, have reached *Titanic* before 3am, forty minutes after the sinking? 'No, most certainly not,' answered Lord. 'I would have made every effort to go down to her,' Lord said, but continued, 'I do not think we would have got there before the *Carpathia* did, if we would have got there as soon.' This is a reasonable assessment from someone who would have had to feel his way through a known ice field in darkness. At best, *Californian* could have arrived at the scene of the sinking at about the time of the sinking. More than a thousand desperate swimmers would have overwhelmed her lifesaving capacity. Still, if *Californian* could have saved even one of those who died, her inaction, as the Senate report states, 'is most reprehensible and places upon the commander of the *Californian* a grave responsibility.'[25]

As the world's reigning heaviest sleeper, I have some sympathy for Captain Lord slumbering through the crisis on his chartroom settee. My long-suffering wife could tell you of extended conversations she has had with me of which I retain no memory upon awakening hours later. Since everything that occurs on his ship is the captain's responsibility, Lord took the fall, but Padfield made the fair point that 'if a captain cannot trust his senior officers he must lead an impossible life'. Lord was certainly undone by his feckless second officer, Herbert Stone.[26]

Stone watched two different sets of pyrotechnics launched over much of his mid-watch, but, even with his own ship stopped in an ice field, these displays did not disquiet Stone sufficiently to move him to act decisively. Instead, he spent that watch observing a ship firing rockets and discussing the situation with the apprentice Gibson, at one point remarking notoriously 'that a ship is not going to fire rockets at sea for nothing'. In such circumstances, it was not Stone's duty to speculate with the apprentice or pass reports via voice tube to the chart room; it was his duty to rouse his captain, even if that meant planting a shoe on his settee, as in the graceless manner in which Dean and Cottam alerted Rostron.[27]

Neither Second Officer Herbert Stone nor Captain Stanley Lord assumed the initiative, however. 'If it had been a distress signal, the officer on watch would have told me,' Lord told the Board of Trade's enquiry on 14 May 1912. Later the same day, Stone testified that 'if there had been any grounds for supposing the ship would have been in distress the Captain would have expressed it to me'. So *Californian* remained inert.[28]

Speculations abound about Stone, Lord and their relationship. Was Stone simply a tragically weak and indecisive individual come the crisis? Was Lord a tyrant who had crushed the authority and initiative out of Stone? Whatever the reason, Stone saw the rockets but did not react effectively. A pathetic three-sided exchange occurred at the British enquiry between Stone and an increasingly vexed Lord Mersey and Thomas Scanlan, representing the National Sailors' and Firemen's Union.[29]

Scanlan: I suppose before you sat for [your first mate's] examination, you read something about signals?

Stone: I learned them.

Scanlan: Do you mean to tell his Lordship that you did not know that the throwing up of 'rockets or shells, throwing stars of any colour or description, fired one at a time at short intervals,' is the proper method for signalling distress at night?

Stone: Yes, that is the way it is always done as far as I know.

Scanlan: And you knew that perfectly well on the night of the 14th of April?

Stone: Yes.

Mersey: And is not that exactly what was happening?

Scanlan: You have heard my Lord put that question. That was what was happening?

Stone: Yes.

Mersey: The very thing was happening that you knew indicated distress?

Stone: If that steamer had stayed on the same bearing after showing these rockets –

Mersey: No, do not give a long answer of that kind. Is it not the fact that the very thing was happening which you had been taught indicated distress?

Stone: Yes.

Scanlan: You knew it meant distress?

Stone: I knew that rockets shown at short intervals, one at a time, meant distress signals, yes.

Scanlan: Do not speak generally. On that very night when you saw those rockets being sent up you knew, did you not, that those rockets were signals of distress?

Stone: No.

CARPATHIA'S COMMUNICATIONS

The idea that Cottam and Bride conspired to withhold news so as to be able to sell their exclusive stories for profit has lived beyond the Senate enquiry and newspaper stories of the day. In their book *Titanic: Signals of Disaster*, John Booth and Sean Coughlan wrote that Harold Cottam and Harold Bride, bombarded by messages from newspapers offering cash for their stories, 'and apparently confident that authority could be shrugged off when inconvenient ... had a considerable incentive for not rushing information ashore,' and 'must have known that they had an opportunity to turn their apparent misfortune to their own advantage'. In his book *Titanic Legacy: Disaster as Media Event and Myth*, Paul Heyer wrote that Cottam and Bride 'worked tirelessly and, as it turned out, conspiratorially' to withhold news;

partly, wrote Heyer, out of loyalty to the Marconi Company and partly for the chance to profit personally.[30]

Besides the missed message sent to *Carpathia* on behalf of President Taft, Senator Smith and subsequent writers have focused on a telegram Bruce Ismay sent to inform the world of the disaster: 'DEEPLY REGRET ADVISE YOU TITANIC SANK THIS MORNING, AFTER COLLISION WITH ICEBERG, RESULTING SERIOUS LOSS LIFE. FURTHER PARTICULARS LATER,' it read. This message was handed to Cottam on Monday, 15 April, but not received in New York until Wednesday morning, 17 April, leading to speculation about the delay. The news-blackout conspiracy was confirmed, for some, by another telegram, this one addressed to Cottam and Bride aboard *Carpathia* and sent by the Marconi Company's chief engineer, Frederick Sammis, reading: 'ARRANGED FOR YOUR EXCLUSIVE STORY FOR DOLLARS IN FOUR FIGURES. MR. MARCONI AGREEING. SAY NOTHING UNTIL YOU SEE ME.'[31]

The Senate committee's report did not go so far as to accuse *Carpathia*'s wireless operators directly of conspiracy. Rather it implied such, then gently chastised the Marconi Company:

> The committee does not believe that the wireless operator on the
> *Carpathia* showed proper vigilance in handling the important work
> confided to his care after the accident. Information concerning an
> accident at sea had been used by a wireless operator prior to this
> accident [Jack Binns in *Republic* in 1909] for his own advantage.
> That such procedure had been permitted by the Marconi Co. may
> have had its effect on this occasion. The disposition of officials
> of the Marconi Co. to permit this practice and the fact of that
> company's representatives making the arrangements for the sale of
> the experiences of the operators of the *Titanic* and the *Carpathia*
> subjects the participants to criticism and the practice should be
> prohibited.[32]

Though embarrassing to both the Marconi Company and its author when published, the message Sammis sent has no bearing on any conspiracy of Cottam and Bride's to suppress news in the days before *Carpathia* reached

New York. It was transmitted by Seagate Marconi station on Thursday evening at 8.30pm, which was after *Carpathia* had entered the Hudson River.

Summoned to testify about the communications chaos, Sammis and Marconi did their best to educate the senators about the realities of wireless operations at sea and the limits that governed their operators. Marconi several times characterized his operators in ways usually ignored by the conspiracy-minded. Marconi pointed out that Cottam and Bride were young, relatively inexperienced men of limited scope, ruled by the dictates of their captain, with little ability or opportunity to compose stories for newspapers. Asked by Senator Duncan Fletcher if they could answer enquiries, Marconi answered: 'Well, of course, the inquiries ought to be properly addressed to the captain. The wireless operator is only a subordinate official, whose business it is to operate the wireless. He is not usually a man who can give very accurate information concerning matters relating to a ship.' When Senator Francis Newlands asked if it would have been possible for one of *Carpathia*'s operators to send a long account of the disaster, Marconi replied that 'it would have been very difficult to send a long account. Some short account might have been sent,' and several were, as we have seen, 'but you must remember these operators who have been before this committee are men of not very much experience in general matters, but rely very much upon the captain instructing them'.[33]

And those instructions were law. Asked if the captain could give orders about sending messages, Marconi implicitly endorsed Rostron's actions, telling Fletcher that 'there is a special clause in our agreements with [the shipping companies] that [it] shall be fixed so that in case of emergency or danger the captain is absolute chief and head and ruler of everything concerning the wireless and all commercial rules which hold in ordinary times are suspended at the discretion of the captain'.[34]

Even in ordinary times, Marconi told the committee, 'there is a rule in these [wireless] companies that operators must not act as reporters. They must accept messages from everyone in the order in which they are presented and they are bound to transmit them. But it is not encouraged that they should send stories of their own; at least, they would be dismissed if they did it.' Marconi added that 'on an occasion like this it would have been a good thing if some report had been sent. But this was a matter that depended on the discretion of the operator and he used his discretion in such a way that he did not send any.'[35]

With his testimony, Sammis acquainted the senators with the rules of traffic priority that subordinated press messages to the service traffic and private messages that overwhelmed *Carpathia*'s operators on the return to New York. During a somewhat combative exchange, Smith asked Sammis if their desire to sell their stories had anything to do with Cottam and Bride's 'failure' to get news ashore quickly. 'Absolutely nothing whatever,' replied Sammis. 'I should say that the boys obeyed their rules, the rules of conscience and the rules of the international telegraph convention, which they were forced to do. They followed them blindly. I believe I should have done the same in their place.'[36]

Booth and Coughlan suggested three possible explanations for the lack of news from *Carpathia*. One was that the Marconi company and *The New York Times* worked in concert to withhold the story and provide the newspaper with exclusives in exchange for its compensation of Marconi employees. This idea, discounted by the authors, runs counter to Marconi's efforts to acquire news from *Carpathia* himself and to have the *New York American*'s Jack Binns put aboard the rescue vessel. A second possibility was that Cottam and Bride, deluged with newspaper offers of cash for their stories, 'decided independently to protect their own valuable story and chose to accept the deal [later] arranged by their employers'. The other possibility, according to Booth and Coughlan, was 'that the operators chose to devote their depleted energies to sending survivors' messages and that enquiries, whether from families, newspapers, or heads of state, were considered of little or no importance. This presumes that the two young operators felt sufficiently secure in their judgment to act without reference to their captain or their company and simply acted in the way that seemed most appropriate in such confused circumstances.' Heyer concurs with this notion, writing that 'responsibility for what was sent from the *Carpathia* and whether messages received were acted upon or not, was in the hands of Cottam and Bride'.[37]

This idea that Cottam and Bride controlled the circumstances of their work is exactly the opposite of what occurred, of course. Rostron stated repeatedly and explicitly in his testimony and in his comments to the press that he had ordered his wireless operators to send service traffic, then the lists of survivors and then the survivors' personal messages, in that priority. Cottam said that Rostron told him: 'Do not deal with anything otherwise than official traffic and passengers' messages.' Cottam and Bride could not have misinterpreted such an order, which was not negotiable. In fairness to the operators, it should also be noted that *The New York Times* paid Cottam and especially Bride for accounts of their personal experiences, stories that were unaffected by whether or not general information about the wreck had preceded them ashore.[38]

One can sense Rostron reaching his limit with *Carpathia*'s communications imbroglio by May. On 4 May, Senator Smith dispatched a telegram to Rostron aboard *Carpathia*. 'I DESIRE CABLE FROM YOU,' it read, containing the contents of Ismay's 15 April message and indicating when it was sent and to what ship or shore station. 'ALSO WHETHER OPERATOR WAS PREVENTED BY YOU FROM SENDING THIS MESSAGE OR ANY OTHER CONCERNING ACCIDENT.' Rostron replied – two weeks later – 'I DID NOT FORBID RELAYING [ISMAY'S] MESSAGE TO ANY SHIP. ON CONTRARY, PARTICULARLY MENTIONED DOING ALL POSSIBLE TO GET OFFICIAL MESSAGES, NAMES OF SURVIVORS, THEN SURVIVORS' MESSAGES AWAY BY MOST CONVENIENT MEANS... ONLY MESSAGES I PREVENTED SENDING WERE FURTHER PRESS MESSAGES.' Rostron pointed out to Smith that Ismay's message was 'almost identical to mine'; in fact, Rostron's messages to the steamship companies and the Associated Press, among the first things Cottam dispatched, contained considerably more detail about the disaster than Ismay's, eliminating any rationale for withholding Ismay's message to maintain a news blackout. Rostron ended his reply to Smith's desires with one of his own: 'I DESIRE FULL INVESTIGATION MY ACTIONS.' Given both Rostron's forthrightness and his new stature as *Titanic* Hero, that investigation was not forthcoming and there the matter ended.[39]

To the press Rostron was even more forthright. The *New York American* quoted him telling reporters who met his ship at Gibraltar: 'There has been a lot said in the American press about the silence of the *Carpathia* when she was bringing to New York the *Titanic*'s survivors. The truth is, I found it necessary to establish a censorship on the messages sent. I instructed the operator that he must send nothing but private messages and the names of survivors, the latter first. Showing that these orders were followed out, we had 205 private messages still unsent when we reached New York. The suggestion that I withheld news to make money out of it is a wicked lie.'[40]

Table 1: Rostron's ships (as derived from 'Lloyd's Captains' Register', 18567, v. 69, *Home from the Sea*, vessel crew lists, etc.). Data from *Lloyd's Register of British and Foreign Shipping*, 1889–90; 1893–4; 1895–6, v. 1 and v. 2; 1910–11, v. 1; 1915–16, v. 2; 1924–5, v. 2; 1925–6, v. 2:

Ship (official no.)	Year	Builder	Built	Reg. ton.	LBP*	Beam	Hull	Engine(s)	Propulsion
Cedric the Saxon (74467)	1875	J. Reid & Co.	Port Glasgow	1705	259	40	iron		fully rigged
Red Gauntlet (48809)	1864	R. Steele	Greenock	1087	204	33	iron		barque
Camphill (96333)	1889	C. J. Bigger	Londonderry	1240	226	36	steel		barque
River Avon (87631)	1882	H. McIntyre & Co.	Paisley	1069	235	32	iron	compound	single screw
Umbria (91159)	1884	J. Elder & Co.	Glasgow	8128	501	57	steel	compound	screw barque
Aurania (87839)	1883	J. & G. Thomson	Glasgow	7269	470	57	steel	compound	screw barque
Etruria (91187)	1884	J. Elder & Co.	Glasgow	8120	501	57	steel	compound	screw barque
Ultonia (109478)	1898	C. S. Swan & Hunter, Ltd.	Newcastle	10,402	500	57	steel	triple expn.	twin screw
Servia (84172)	1881	J. & G. Thomson	Glasgow	7392	515	52	steel	compound	screw barque
Cherbourg (71694)	1874	J. & G. Thomson	Glasgow	1614	251	32	iron	compound	screw brigntne
Saxonia (110648)	1900	John Brown & Co., Ltd.	Glasgow	14,297	580	64	steel	quad. expn.	twin screw
Campania (102086)	1893	Fairfield Co., Ltd.	Glasgow	12,950	601	65	steel	triple expn.	twin screw
Pannonia (118080)	1903	John Brown & Co., Ltd.	Glasgow	9851	486	59	steel	triple expn.	twin screw
Ivernia (110643)	1900	C. S. Swan & Hunter, Ltd.	Newcastle	14,278	582	64	steel	quad. expn.	twin screw
Brescia (118021)	1903	J. L. Thompson & Sons	Sunderland	3235	330	45	steel	triple expn.	single screw
Veria (110564)	1899	Armstrong Whitworth & Co.	Newcastle	3229	330	45	steel	triple expn.	single screw
Pavia (106853)	1897	Workman, Clark & Co.	Belfast	2945	332	45	steel	triple expn.	single screw
Carpathia (118014)	1903	C. S. Swan & Hunter, Ltd.	Newcastle	13,603	540	64	steel	quad. expn.	twin screw

Ship (official no.)	Year	Builder	Built	Reg. ton.	LBP*	Beam	Hull	Engine(s)	Propulsion
Caronia (120826)	1905	John Brown & Co., Ltd.	Glasgow	19,687	650	72	steel	quad. expn.	twin screw
Carmania (120901)	1905	John Brown & Co., Ltd.	Glasgow	19,524	650	72	steel	turbine	triple screw
Lusitania (124082)	1907	John Brown & Co., Ltd.	Glasgow	31,550	762	87	steel	turbine	quad. screw
Alaunia (135513)	1913	Scotts' Ship Bld. & Eng. Co.	Greenock	13,405	520	64	steel	quad. expn.	twin screw
Mauretania (124093)	1907	Swan, Hunter & W. R. Ltd.	Newcastle	31,938	762	88	steel	turbine	quad. screw
Andania (135481)	1913	Scotts' Ship Bld. & Eng. Co.	Greenock	13,405	520	64	steel	quad. expn.	twin screw
Tyrrhenia (145943)	1922	W. Beardmore & Co., Ltd.	Glasgow	16,243	552	70	steel	turbine	twin screw
Berengaria (144301)	1912	Vulcan Werke	Hamburg	52,226	883	98	steel	turbine	quad. screw
Aquitania (135583)	1914	John Brown & Co., Ltd.	Glasgow	45,647	868	97	steel	turbine	quad. screw

*Since Lloyd's was interested in capacity rather than appearance, *Lloyd's Register* did not use length overall (stem to stern), but rather 'length between perpendiculars' (essentially stem to sternpost). Since that measurement excluded the counter sterns suspended aft of the sternpost on most of these ships, they were generally slightly longer than the lengths indicated here. *Mauretania*, for example, measured 790 feet overall but only 762 feet between perpendiculars. For consistency, I have used Lloyd's figures throughout these tables.

Table 2: Rostron's commands (as derived from 'Lloyd's Captains' Register,' 18567, v. 69, *Home from the Sea*, etc.):

Ship	Official no.	Reg. tonnage	LBP	Beam	Dates in command (mo./yr.)	
					from	to
Brescia	118021	3235	330	45	Aug 1907	Dec 1909
Veria	110564	3229	330	45	Dec 1909	May 1910
Saxonia	110648	14,297	580	64	July 1910	July 1910
Pavia	106853	2945	332	45	July 1910	Oct 1910
Pannonia	118080	9851	486	59	Jan 1911	Dec 1911
Carpathia	118014	13,603	540	64	Feb 1912	Dec 1912
Caronia	120826	19,687	650	72	Jan 1913	Jan 1913
Campania	102086	12,950	601	65	Jan 1913	Feb 1913
Carmania	120901	19,524	650	72	Mar 1913	Apr 1913
Campania	102086	12,950	601	65	Apr 1913	Oct 1913
Lusitania	124082	31,550	762	87	Oct 1913	Nov 1913
Alaunia	135513	13,405	520	64	Nov 1913	Sep 1915
Mauretania	124093	31,938	762	88	Oct 1915	Feb 1916
Ivernia	110643	14,278	582	64	Apr 1916	Dec 1916
Andania	135481	13,405	520	64	Mar 1917	Apr 1917
Saxonia	110648	14,297	580	64	June 1917	Jan 1918
Carmania	120901	19,524	650	72	Jan 1918	Mar 1918
Mauretania	124093	31,938	762	88	Mar 1918	Nov 1923
Tyrrhenia	145943	16,243	552	70	Jan 1924	Feb 1924
Mauretania	124093	31,938	762	88	May 1924	July 1926
Berengaria	144301	52,226	883	98	July 1926	Jan 1927
Aquitania	135583	45,647	868	97	Jan 1927	Feb 1927
Berengaria	144301	52,226	883	98	Mar 1927	Oct 1927
Aquitania	135583	45,647	868	97	Nov 1927	Nov 1927
Berengaria	144301	52,226	883	98	Nov 1927	Nov 1930

GLOSSARY OF TERMS

able seaman (AB): A merchant sailor rated more proficient than an ordinary seaman.

abaft: To the rear of.

abeam: Bearing 90 degrees from the fore-and-aft axis of a ship. More generally, indicates the areas to 45 degrees of either side of dead abeam.

abreast: Beside of.

aft: Toward the stern of the ship.

after guard: A reference to the officers of a sailing ship, who were quartered aft, under the poop deck.

aloft: In reference to the masts and rigging of a ship, or into the air as with a rocket.

amidships: Toward the middle of the ship from either fore and aft or side to side.

barque: A three-masted sailing ship with the two forward (fore and main) masts square rigged and the after (mizzen) mast fore-and-aft rigged.

beam: The maximum width of a ship.

beam ends: A ship rolling, heeling or listing close to 90 degrees is said to be 'on her beam ends', a dire situation.

belaying pin: A wooden rod used to secure lines, often to the ship's rail. Also occasionally used to win arguments.

bend on: To attach one thing to another with rope, such as a sail to a yard.

binnacle: The supporting structure adjacent to the helm that houses a magnetic compass.

boatswain: A merchant or naval rating whose duties concern deck and boat seamanship.

bow: The forward end of a ship. Also port and starboard bows, indicating the areas to 45 degrees of either side of dead ahead.

broach to: To be thrown broadside to a heavy sea.

bulkhead: Vertical partition walls within a ship, usually from side to side, used both to strengthen the ship and to isolate and contain flooding.

carry away: To part or to break loose, often to be washed overboard.

compass deviation: Error in the readings from a magnetic compass caused by magnetic elements in a ship. Deviation was counteracted by adjusting metal spheres

on the binnacle. The other factor creating magnetic compass error, *variation*, is caused by the difference between magnetic and geographic north, which varies with the location of the ship and must simply be included in calculations when navigating.

compass point: The division of the 360-degrees of the compass card into thirty-two points, making each point equivalent to 11.25 degrees. Sailing ships were generally steered by points and steamships by degrees, though points were retained in steamers to indicate direction, as with Boxhall's flares sighted a half a point off *Carpathia*'s port bow.

davits: Small cranes used in pairs that are suspended outboard to lower or raise a ship's boats.

dead reckoning: System of navigation that involves estimating a ship's present position through cumulative calculations from her last known, or 'fixed', position determined by sextant or visual observation. It is imprecise because it accounts only poorly for the effects of winds and currents. The term supposedly derived from the abbreviation 'de'd' for 'deduced' reckoning.

donkeyman: A sailor paid extra to operate the ship's donkey engine, a small steam winch used to move cargo while in port and named for the draft animal previously so employed.

ensign: A national flag flown by a vessel. The United Kingdom's ensign featured fields of three different colors: *white* for Royal Navy ships, *blue* for merchant ships with a captain and sufficient percentage of officers and ratings being naval reservists, and *red* for other merchant ships.

falls: The system of tackle used to lower or raise a ship's boats.

fore: Towards the bow or the forward part of the ship.

forecastle: A short raised deck at the forward end of a ship, under which the ordinary and able seamen had their quarters. The term thus refers to the deck, the living space, and, by extension, to the un-rated seamen themselves.

frames: The vertical wooden or steel ribs that extend from the keel perpendicularly to the main deck to produce the shape of the hull and to which the outer planks or plating are attached. *Carpathia*'s frames were six inches wide, with the standard two-foot interval between. Frames are numbered consecutively working forward with the sternpost, the vertical framing member from which the rudder hangs, being frame 0.

freeboard: The vertical distance from the waterline to the main deck. In sailing ships freeboard was minimal to provide maximum room to carry sails and to keep the ship's center of gravity as low as possible. As Rostron discovered, this left the main deck awash in any but fair weather.

frigate: A smaller full-rigged warship with one or two gun decks used for scouting, communicating, or raiding. Able to outrun what could out-hit her and out-hit what could outrun her.

full-rigged (or fully rigged) ship: A sailing ship with at least three masts, all square-rigged, as was *Cedric the Saxon* (see illustration).

furl: To gather together and secure, as with a sail.

gam: A friendly meeting and exchange between sailing ships at sea. More generally, a pleasant conversation.

heel: The leaning of a ship to port or starboard due to a temporary external force, such as wind in the sails or a sharp turn at high speed.

hove to: Past tense of 'heave to', to bring a ship to a halt, generally with the bow into the wind, to lower boats, effect repairs or ride out rough weather.

inboard: Towards the center of a ship.

keel: The central, fore-and-aft, wooden or metal spine at the bottom of a ship, to which the frames are affixed.

knot: A measure of speed equal to one nautical mile per hour. The term derived from the practice of measuring speed in sail by throwing a log over the stern attached to the ship by a line with knots tied in it at intervals. The number of knots that paid out over a given time indicated the speed. Knot is also the general term for the variety of bends and hitches used to secure lines to each other or to objects and more precisely referred to as bends or hitches.

lee: In the opposite direction of the wind, thus the downwind side of a ship. The opposite of windward. When recovering a boat, a ship will shelter it by maneuvering upwind of the boat to create a calm lee.

let go: Command given to drop the anchor by releasing the cable to run free.

lie to: To stop a ship without anchoring or mooring her.

line: The proper term for a rope used about the ship for various purposes. With only rare exceptions (e.g. footrope), 'rope' only refers to the cordage delivered to a ship from a manufacturer.

list: The leaning of a ship to port or starboard due to an internal condition such as flooding or an unbalanced distribution of cargo.

lubberly: An un-seamanlike person (lubber) or condition.

midshipman: An apprentice naval officer, so named from being quartered in a house amidships under sail.

nautical mile: A distance equivalent to one minute of the earth's 360-degree arc at the equator, approximately 6,080 feet or 1.15 the length of a statute mile of 5,280 feet.

ordinary seaman: The lowest ranking member of a ship's company. With sufficient sea time and knowledge an ordinary becomes an able seaman.

outboard: Away from the center of a ship.

pitch: The vertical rise and fall of a ship along her fore-and-aft axis, which the author always found much more bilious than rolling.

port: The left side of a ship looking forward or, more generally, to the left.

quarter: The port and starboard quarters are the areas to 45 degrees of either side of dead astern.

rail: The wooden or metal barricade at the outboard edges of the deck of a ship.

rating: A sailor possessing particular skills, such as a boatswain, carpenter or sailmaker, for which he received higher wages and better quarters (amidships in sail).

reciprocating steam engine: A steam engine that produced power using the expansion of steam in a cylinder to drive a piston in a reciprocating motion. A compound engine employed the steam more efficiently by using additional cylinders, each of which had to be larger than the previous one to compensate for the loss of steam pressure. Quadruple-expansion engines achieved the practical limit of this technology, with *Carpathia*'s featuring cylinders with diameters of 26, 37, 53 and 76 inches.

rigging: The lines, wires and associated hardware used to support topside structures and perform their work. Rigging generally subdivides into *standing*, which provides fixed support for structures (e.g. masts), and *running*, which the crew adjusts to do work (e.g. hoisting sails).

RMS: Royal Mail Ship; a designation given to ships contracted to carry mail for the British government.

roll: The motion of a ship from vertical to port and starboard perpendicular to her fore-and-aft axis.

Royal Naval Reserve: Established by the Naval Reserve Act of 1859 to provide naval training to a pool of merchant officers and ratings used to expand the Royal Navy in times of war.

screw: The common name for a ship's propeller, which proved significantly more efficient and hardy than the paddlewheels that drove early steamers.

scuppers: Exit ports through the railing along her decks that permit a ship to shed water more efficiently.

service traffic: Wireless messages, generally sent in the captain's name, that concerned the operation or provisioning of his ship.

square rigged: A sail arrangement in which most of the sails are suspended from yards carried roughly perpendicularly to the fore-and-aft axis of the masts. This arrangement maximizes power at the expense of the maneuverability of fore-and-aft sail rigs.

steerage: The least-desirable passenger accommodations in the ship, including those in the vicinity of the steering gear, occupied by immigrant passengers charged the lowest rate for their passage. The term also came to mean the passengers themselves, as in 'steerage trade'.

stem: The solitary vertical framing member attached to the keel at the very bow of the ship and to which the outer planks or plating are attached.

stern: The after end of a ship.

tarry spunyarn: Light-weight cordage consisting of loosely wound rope yarns and used to bend on sails, among other things.

tender: As a noun, a smaller vessel used to deliver passengers, mail and cargo from shore to a larger vessel at a mooring buoy or at anchor. As an adjective, said of a ship with a high center of gravity prone to excessive rolling and heeling and slow to return to the vertical.

trim: A ship in proper balance, especially fore and aft. Trim is maintained by balancing the fluids in various tanks and ensuring that cargo is evenly distributed. Trimming was the most important duty of coal trimmers after seeing that their firemen were adequately supplied.

turbine steam engine: A rotary engine containing of a series of blades against which steam expands, generating a very rapid, smooth and powerful spinning motion. Loss of steam pressure is compensated by continuously increasing the diameter of the blades to gain leverage.

watch and watch: System of alternating four-hour watches served by the two watch sections (generally designated port and starboard) into which a ship's company was usually divided. While this system maximizes the available hands, it minimizes the available sleep.

watch below, the: Especially in a sailing ship, sailors nominally off duty but subject to immediate call at any hour to work sails or address other urgent situations.

weather eye: To keep one's eye on meteorological developments to the weather or windward side of a ship, from whence the trouble usually comes. More generally, to be alert to danger, 'keep your weather eye open'.

windward: In the direction of the wind, thus the upwind side of a ship (also called the weather side). The opposite of lee.

well deck: A portion of the main deck surrounded fore and aft by raised decks (such as the forecastle or poop) or superstructure. The well decks were home to the cargo hatches and doubled as the immigrants' cluttered deck space while at sea.

yard: A long timber centered on a mast and used to carry square sails.

NOTES

PREFACE

[1] This account derives from front-page stories in *The New York Times* of 1, 2 and 3 December, 1918 and from photographs in the digital image collection of the US Library of Congress.

CHAPTER 1

[1] 'Certified Copy of an Entry of Birth' for Arthur Henry Rostron, reproduced in *Bolton Evening News*, 22 Jan 1999, via clippings book B11.28, Bolton Heritage Centre (hereafter BHC); 'Marriage of James Rostron and Nancy Lever,' 19 June 1867, Marriage Register, 1848–79, page 106, entry 211, at Lancashire On-Line Parish Clerk Project (www.lanc-opc.org.uk), accessed 25 June 2011; Census data for James Rostron and Family, 'Census Returns of England and Wales,' 1871, 1881, National Archives, Kew, London (hereafter NAK); Arthur John Rostron ('John', grandson), letter to the author, 21 Oct 2011, included a copy of the 'Family Register' from inside the Rostron family bible in his possession.

[2] *Axon's Commercial and General Directory of Bolton… 1881* (Little Bolton: Henry Axon, 1881), i, iii.

[3] 'Marriage of James Rostron and Nancy Lever,' 19 June 1867; Baptism of Arthur Henry Rostron, 19 June 1869, Baptisms Register, 1867–81, page 34, entry 268, Lancashire On-Line Parish Clerk Project, accessed 29 June 2011; Census data for James Rostron and Family, 'Census Returns of England and Wales,' 1871, 1881, 1901, 1911 and for Fredric Rostron, 1911, NAK; Bolton Church Institute School War Memorial, 'Names, 1914–1918, George Rostron,' (www.bolton-church-institute.org.uk), accessed 24 Oct 2012 (cites the *Bolton Journal and Guardian*, 12 Apr 1918); *Axon's Commercial and General Directory of Bolton*, iii; *Slater's Royal National Commercial Directory of Lancashire and the Manufacturing District around Manchester* (Manchester: Isaac Slater: 1882), 103, contains an entry: 'Murton, George and Co. (yarn and counterpane), Sharples Bleach Works, near Bolton.' See the card catalog, Bolton Heritage Centre, for a reference to James Rostron with Murton's bleachers.

[4] Arthur Henry Rostron, *Home from the Sea* (London: Macmillan, 1931), 6.

[5] Rostron, *Home from the Sea*, 6, 7; 'Copy of a brief account of Capt. Rostron's career, written by his daughter, Mrs. M. E. Howman of Bristol,' DX 949 (R) 1988 258, Merseyside Maritime Museum Archive, Liverpool (hereafter MMM); 'Mauretania's Master Tells of His Sea,' *New York Times*, 24 Aug 1924; 'Footnotes on a Week's Headliners,' *New York Times* 16 Nov 1930.

[6] 'Distinguished Old Boys,' Old Boys' Association, Bolton School, www.boltonschool.org (accessed 17 July 2013); *Axon's Commercial and General Directory of Bolton… Second Edition, 1885* (Bolton: Henry Axon, 1885), v; *Post Office Bolton Directory for 1876–1877* (Bolton: Tillotson & Son: 1876), 260, 316; John Aldred, *A Brief History of Canon Slade School, 1855–2005* (Bolton: McGrath Regional Publications Ltd., 2005), 20, 24; '*Bolton Journal and Guardian* Pictorial Bolton Series, No.XLIV,' 10 Jan 1885, (booklet containing article) B373 CHU, BHC.

[7] *Post Office Bolton Directory for 1876–1877*, 260, 316; '*Bolton Journal and Guardian* Pictorial Bolton Series, No.XLIV,' 10 Jan 1885.

8   'Sir Arthur Rostron Sails as Commodore,' *New York Times*, 29 July 1928; *Post Office Bolton Directory for 1876–1877*, 260, 316; *Axon's Commercial and General Directory of Bolton… 1885*, 164.

9   R. A. 'Bob' Evans, *Mersey Mariners* (Merseyside: Countyvise Limited, 1997), 217–18, 226; HMS Conway, 1859–1974, 'The Third HMS Conway – HMS *Nile*, 1826–1876,' www. hmsconway.org/history_third (accessed 15 July 2013).

10 Evans, *Mersey Mariners*, 219; 'HMS *Conway* Registers of Cadets,' Batch 2, Reel 6, no. 70, D/CON/13/8, 1884–7, MMM.

11 Mercantile Marine Service Association, Liverpool, 'School Ship "Conway". Annual Reports, 1884 to 1894,' 'Report of the Proceedings at the Distribution of Prizes, on Thursday, July 22, 1886, by His Worship the Mayor of Liverpool (Sir David Radcliffe),' 14, Batch 1, Reel 1, D/CON/1/2–3, 1864–94, MMM; 'HMS Conway 1859–1974: Britain's premier Merchant Navy school ship,' 'Slop Chest,' www.hmsconway.org; Evans, *Mersey Mariners*, 220.

12 HMS *Conway* Registers of Cadets, Batch 2 Reel 6, D/CON/13/8, 1884–7, MMM; Mercantile Marine Service Association, Liverpool, 'School Ship "Conway", Annual Reports, 1884 to 1894, Report of the Proceedings at the Distribution of Prizes, on Wednesday, July 22nd, 1885…,' 8–10, 30–1, HMS *Conway*: Annual Reports, D/CON/1/2–3, 1864–94 , Batch 1, Reel 1 MMM.

13 HMS *Conway*, 'Distribution of Prizes…1885,' 30–1.

14 Rostron, *Home from the Sea*, 7. The assertion that Rostron made head boy was repeated by his daughter Margaret in: M. E. Howman, 'Copy of brief account of Capt. Rostron's career, written by his daughter'; HMS *Conway*, 'Report on the Distribution of Prizes… 1886,' ('Details of Scholastic Examination. Midsummer, 1886. Senior Class.') 74, MMM.

15 HMS *Conway*, 'Report on the Distribution of Prizes… 1886,' 8–12, 21.

16 HMS *Conway*, 'Report on the Distribution of Prizes… 1886,' 8–12, 21, 22, 25, 26, 27.

17 'Register of Cadets,' no. 70; Arthur H. Rostron, Royal Naval Reserve Service Record, ADM 340/120 12C, 1, NAK; Rostron, *Home from the Sea*, 236. Conway also issued ordinary certificates, as in the case of the next cadet in the register, who was deemed to have demonstrated fair conduct and good ability. He also landed an apprenticeship on a merchant ship. Cadets also occasionally left or were asked to leave before graduating.

CHAPTER 2

1   'Ordinary Apprentice's Indenture,' between Arthur Rostron and Williamson, Milligan and Co., 24 Feb 1887, reprinted in *Titanic Commutator* II, no. 24 (win. 1979): 31.

2   'List of Owners of Ships Recorded in the Register Book, 1st July, 1889,' *Lloyd's Register of British and Foreign Shipping* (London: Lloyd's, 1888–9), 98; 'Commodore of Cunard,'[Southampton] *Southern Daily Echo*, 5 Nov 1930.

3   *Cedric the Saxon*, 74467, *Lloyd's Register of British and Foreign Shipping*, 1886–7.

4   William P. Haines, 'Lloyd's Captains' Register,' MS18567, 34, (1880–7), London Metropolitan Archives (hereafter LMA); 'Agreement and Account of Crew,' *Cedric the Saxon* (vessel no. 74467), 28 Feb 1887, voyage of 28 Feb 1887 to 15 Jan 1888, Hull to Liverpool, 1–4, 6, 10, Maritime History Archive, Memorial University, St John's, Newfoundland (hereafter MHA).

5   *Shipping and Mercantile Gazette and Lloyd's List* (hereafter *Lloyd's List*), 3 Mar 1887, 3 (*Lloyd's List* is normally cited by column, rather than page; I have therefore cited by column here and hereafter); Rostron, *Home from the Sea*, 7, 9, 13; 'Mauretania's Master Tells of His Sea', *New York Times*, 24 Aug 1924.

6   Rostron, *Home from the Sea*, 6, 9.

7   Capt. S[amuel]. G. S. McNeil, *In Great Waters: Memoirs of a Master Mariner* (New York: Harcourt, Brace and Co., 1932), 22, 309; Harry Grattidge, *Captain of the Queens: The Autobiography of Captain Harry Grattidge, Former Commodore of the Cunard Line* (New York: E. P. Dutton and Co., 1956), 41. In one respect Rostron considered himself fortunate, writing that 'my early experiences [though gruelling] were by no means exceptional. Other boys in bad ships lived through horrors that fortunately were not our lot. The ships I served in were as good as any afloat and had splendid officers who found no especial joy in "taking it out" of a lad.' (Rostron, *Home from the Sea*, 237.)

8   Rostron, *Home from the Sea*, 220–1.

9   Rostron, *Home from the Sea*, 221; 'Agreement and Account of Crew,' *Cedric the Saxon*, 28 Feb 1887, 10–11. The agreement, which contains an account of the incident, gives the position of Wilkinson's loss as 56.45S, 71.37W.

10 *Lloyd's List*, 16 Aug 1887, 21; Rostron, *Home from the Sea*, 10–12.

11 'Agreement and Account of Crew,' *Cedric the Saxon*, 28 Feb 1887, 2–4, 10; Rostron, *Home from the Sea*, 13; *Lloyd's List*, 30 July 1887, 11; 31 Aug 1887, 21; 5 Sep 1887, 23; 1 Oct 1887, 11; 6 Jan 1888, 11; 16 Jan 1888, 5.

12 'Agreement and Account of Crew,' *Cedric the Saxon*, 27 Feb 1888, voyage of 29 Feb 1888 to 23 Feb 1889, 1, BT99/1614, NAK; *Lloyd's List*, 1 Mar 1888, 4; 26 Apr 1888, 19; 24 May 1889, 13; 23 Feb 1889, 6.

13 James Veysey, 'Lloyd's Captains' Register,' 18567, no. 56, LMA; 'Agreement and Account of Crew,' 27 Feb 1888, 1–5, 10.

14 'Agreement and Account of Crew,' 27 Feb 1888, 2–5.

15 'Agreement and Account of Crew,' 27 Feb 1888, 2–5; *Lloyd's List*, 6 Sep 1888, 12; 7 Sep 1888, 10; Alfred Thompson Pope, 'Lloyd's Captains' Register,' 18569, v. 031, LMA; 'Agreement and Account of Crew,' 27 Feb 1888, 1–6; *Lloyd's List*, 26 Oct 1888, 22; 14 Feb 1889, 4; 21 Feb 1889, 6; 23 Feb 1889, 6. Williamson and Milligan's confidence in the young Pope was certainly vindicated by his career. Toward the end of more than forty years in sail and steam, Pope won Lloyd's Medal for Meritorious Service for his actions against an enemy submarine in September 1917 and was appointed a Companion of the Distinguished Service Order five months later 'in recognition of zeal and devotion to duty shown in carrying on the trade of the country during the war'. (Pope, 'Lloyd's Captains' Register', 18569, v. 031.)

16 'Agreement and Account of Crew,' *Cedric the Saxon*, 14 Mar 1889, voyage of 16 Mar 1889 to 12 July 1890, Liverpool to Barry, 1, 2, 11–12, 15, MHA; Rostron, *Home from the Sea*, 13–14; *Lloyd's List*, 18 Mar 1889, 7; 21 June 1889, 16; 23 Aug 1889, 14; 25 Oct 1889, 13; 21 Mar 1890, 14; 4 June 1890, 4; 6 June 1890, 25; 17 June 1890, 12; 11 July 1890, 11; 12 July 1890, 4.

17 Undated letter from 'Williamson Milligan Co.' reprinted in *Titanic Commutator* II, no. 24 (win. 1979): 32; Rostron, *Home from the Sea*, 18; 'Agreement and Account of Crew,' *Red Gauntlet*, 10 Oct 1890, voyage of 10 Oct 1890 to 19 Aug 1891, Barry to Rouen, 2–3, MHA.

18 Redgauntlet (vessel no. 48809), *Lloyd's Register of British and Foreign Shipping*, 1889–90; 'Agreement and Account of Crew,' *Red Gauntlet*, 10 Oct 1890, 1–2, 11; *Lloyd's List*, 11 Aug 1890, 6; 16 Aug 1890, 22; 25 Sep 1890, 3; 16 Oct 1890, 3; 12 Jan 1891, 13; 22 Apr 1891, 14; 12 Aug 1891, 3; 15 Aug 1891, 10; 22 Aug 1891, 23; 9 Sep 1891, 9; 15 Sep 1891, 4; 'Agreement and Account of Crew,' *Red Gauntlet*, 7 Sep 1891, voyage of 10 Sep 1891 to 14 Sep 1891, Rouen to Liverpool, 1, MHA. Her name appears as 'Redgauntlet' in *Lloyd's Register*

to distinguish her from 'Red Gauntlet,' a 75-foot wooden schooner registered in Guernsey. Rostron (*Home from the Sea*, 18) also called her 'Redgauntlet.'

19 Rostron, *Home from the Sea*, 18; *Lloyd's List*, 31 Oct 1891, 4; 17 Dec 1891, 20; 25 Jan 1892, 14; 12 Mar 1892, 25.

20 Rostron, *Home from the Sea*, 19–20. 'Sir Arthur Rostron to Retire from Sea,' *New York Times*, 1 Nov 1930.

21 *Lloyd's List*, 30 June 1892, 14; 14 July 1892, 15; 3 Sep 1892, 14; 6 Sep 1892, 14; 28 Oct 1892, 13; 27 Feb 1893, 3; 24 Mar 1893, 2; 2 Apr 1893, 1. Sailing ships often returned to Europe from Australia and even China by the longer but downwind passage via Cape Horn, rather than beating to windward back around the Cape of Good Hope. It seems likely that Rostron's ships did this, and thus circumnavigated the earth, after calling at Port Pirie on his last voyage as an apprentice in *Cedric the Saxon* and his first as second officer in *Red Gauntlet*. In his memoir written forty years later, however, Rostron declared his second voyage in *Red Gauntlet* to be 'my first voyage round the world'. (James Bisset, *Sail Ho! My Early Years at Sea* (New York: Criterion Books, 1958), 100, 264; Rostron, *Home from the Sea*, 22.)

22 *Camphill* (vessel no. 96333), *Lloyd's Register of British and Foreign Shipping*, 1892–3. *Lloyd's List*, 3 Apr 1893, 23; 27 Apr 1893, 9; 21 July 1893, 9. Rostron, *Home from the Sea*, 23; 'Agreement and Account of Crew,' *Camphill*, 17 July 1893, voyage of 19 July 1893 to 9 May 1894, Antwerp to Liverpool, 1, MHA.

23 'James Butters,' Lloyd's Captains' Register, 18567, v. 044, LMA; Rostron, *Home from the Sea*, 23; 'Agreement and Account of Crew,' *Camphill*, 17 July 1893, 2–3.

24 'Agreement and Account of Crew,' *Camphill*, 17 July 1893, 2–5, 10; Rostron, *Home from the Sea*, 23; *Lloyd's List*, 25 Oct 1893, 25.

25 'Agreement and Account of Crew,' *Camphill*, 17 July 1893, 2–5 (seven of the crew, including half of the Scandinavians, left the ship at Valparaiso by mutual consent, to be replaced by four Britons, two Irishmen, an American and a Latvian); Charles H. Lightoller, *Titanic and Other Ships* (London: I. Nicholson and Watson, Ltd., 1935), 109; *Lloyd's List*, 10 Jan 1894, 11; 16 Feb 1894, 12; 6 Mar 1894, 13; 30 Apr 1894, 5; 7 May 1894, 25; 9 May 1894, 4. Probably this was Butters' last voyage; at the very least he did not return to command at sea for several years. ('James Butters,' Lloyd's Captains' Register, 18567, v. 044, LMA.)

26 Rostron, *Home from the Sea*, 26. The articles that the crew signed for one of Rostron's voyages in sail included the hand-written admonishment that 'any member of the crew using insulting, offensive, or abusive language to the master or any of the officers will be fined 5 [shillings] for each offense.' 'Agreement and Account of Crew,' *Cedric the Saxon*, 24 June 1895, voyage of 5 July 1895 to 29 Apr 1896, 1, MHA. Rostron (*Home from the Sea*, 35) noted that sailors were not above taking swings at apprentices when aloft if upset about something. To counter 'one had to hold on to a becket on the yard or else the jack-stay with one hand using the other for pugilistic purposes. One is standing on a foot rope at such times with the deck seventy feet below.'

27 McNeil, *In Great Waters*, 77, 80; *Rostron, Home from the Sea*, 31–2.

28 Rostron, *Home from the Sea*, 16, 22.

29 The US Immigration and Naturalization Service, for reasons known but to the INS, recorded the age, height and weight of the masters of ships arriving at New York. A number of these records survive in the US National Archives from among Rostron's many visits to the port. The results of this guessing game list him as anywhere from 5' 6.5" to 5' 10" and weighing from 154 to 175 pounds. Most of the estimates were around 5' 8" and 160 pounds, however, hence the use of those figures. See: Immigration and Naturalization

Service, 'Passenger and Crew Lists of Vessels Arriving at New York,' microfilm rolls: T715 3956, p. 80; 2018, 122; 2536, 42; 2554, 147; 2563, 270; 2635, 233; 2682, 111; and 3448, 37, US National Archives, Washington, DC; '$10,000 in Gold for Rostron,' *New York American*, 2 June 1912; Lt. Cmdr. G. H. Slade, 'A Distinguished Old Conway (Commodore Sir Arthur H. Rostron, R.D. – A Memory, 1929),' *The Cadet* (Sep 1973): 242 (copy in file DX 949 (R), MMM); James Bisset, *Tramps and Ladies: My Early Years in Steamers* (London: Angus and Robertson, 1959), 229–30. Rostron's favourite exclamation, judging from his memoir, was 'Jove!'

[30] Lightoller, *Titanic and Other Ships*, 15; Rostron, *Home from the Sea*, 29. Lightoller (*Titanic and Other Ships*, 18) also wrote: 'Hard, bitter hard, though ship life often was, yet we were glad to see the Golden Gates, with all they stood for, fading away and finally disappearing below the horizon. At least the sea was clean.' Lightoller was not the only Cape Horner with a poor opinion of San Francisco. Samuel McNeil (*In Great Waters*, 83) called it 'especially dangerous for sailors,' noting that 'the dockland, away on the outskirts of the town, was lonely, lawless and a hunting-ground for the scum of the city, who would commit any act of violence for the sake of ten dollars' worth of plunder.'

[31] Rostron, *Home from the Sea*, 14–15.

[32] Psalm 107.23–24 *King James Version*; Rostron, *Home from the Sea*, 137, 233; 'Mauretania's Master Tells of his Sea,' *New York Times*, 24 Aug 1924.

[33] Bisset, *Tramps and Ladies*, 230 ('his beliefs were his own and he did not discuss them aboard ship'); 'Sir Arthur H. Rostron,' *Bolton Evening News*, 25 Jan 1992. Rostron's remarks are from a speech he gave at the town hall in Bolton in 1928 to open a nautical exhibition and fair in aid of the Seamen's Missions. The *Bolton Evening News* recorded that Rostron's condemnation of sailors toting prayer books and bibles was greeted with 'applause and calls of "hear, hear"'.

[34] 'Mauretania's Master Tells of his Sea,' *New York Times*, 24 Aug 1924. Rostron, *Home from the Sea*, 8, 33, 220, 225.

[35] *River Avon* (vessel no. 87631), *Lloyd's Register of British and Foreign Shipping*, 1893–4; Rostron, *Home from the Sea*, 27.

[36] *Lloyd's List*, 12 Sep 1894, 20; 20 Sep 1894, 9; 4 Oct 1894, 8; 5 Oct 1894, 3; 12 Oct 1894, 4; 23 Oct 1894, 15; 2 Nov 1894, 12; 3 Nov 1894, 9; 9 Nov 1894, 6. Had Rostron remained with River Avon to year's end, he would have had another story to tell. *Lloyd's List* (24 Dec 1894, 17) reported on Christmas Eve: 'The steamer *River Avon*, from Aguilas, with esparto grass, arrived in the Mersey on Saturday morning [the 22nd] with a great wedge-shaped hole in her bows.' *River Avon* disappeared from *Lloyd's Register of British and Foreign Shipping* in both name and official number the following year, doubtless scrapped.

[37] Rostron, RNR Service Record, 1.

CHAPTER 3

[1] Rostron, *Home from the Sea*, 28, 212, 213. Rostron never abandoned his admiration for sail. Five years after he retired, the *Manchester Guardian* ('The Sailor and Religion; Sir A. Rostron's View,' 3 Dec 1935) reported: 'Sir Arthur said he first went to sea in the days of the sailing ships and sailors had to be sailors then. He regretted the passing of the sailing ships. Today we had not got two large sailing ships sailing under the British flag, to our great shame.'

[2] Rostron, *Home from the Sea*, 27, 215–16.

³ Rostron, *Home from the Sea* , 214–15; Cunard Steamship Co., 'Register of Officers,' case 257, 'Arthur Henry Rostron,' D42/GM16/2, Cunard Collection, Special Collections and Archives, Sydney Jones Library, Liverpool University (hereafter SJL).

⁴ Rostron, *Home from the Sea*, 30; 'Commodore of Cunard,' *Southern Daily Echo*, 5 Nov 1930; 'Cunard Line,' *New York Times*, 29 Jan 1895; 'Mauretania's Master Tells of his Sea,' *New York Times*, 24 Aug 1924; 'Cunard Line – Royal Mail Steamers' (advertisement), *The Times* (London), 29 Jan 1895.

⁵ *Umbria*, *Lloyd's Register*, 1889–90; Francis E. Hyde, *Cunard and the North Atlantic, 1840–1973: A History of Shipping and Financial Management* (London: Macmillan Press Ltd., 1975), 33; Neil McCart, *Atlantic Liners of the Cunard Line: From 1884 to the Present Day* (Wellingborough, Northamptonshire, Eng.: Patrick Stephens, 1990), 14–15. Rostron's appointment to *Umbria* does not appear in his listing in Lloyd's Captains' Register, which gives his first voyage with a master's certificate as *Cedric the Saxon*'s voyage of July 1895. The articles for that voyage, however, list his previous ship as *Umbria* and Rostron's memoir and various newspaper accounts of him (e.g. 'Sir Arthur Rostron Sails as Commodore,' *New York Times*, 29 July 1928) confirm *Umbria* as his first Cunard ship.

⁶ Gerald Aylmer, *RMS Mauretania: The Ship and her Record* (London: Marshall, 1934; reprint with additional text: Stroud, Gloucestershire, UK: Tempus Publishing, Ltd., 2000), 8; Hyde, *Cunard and the North Atlantic*, 3, 5.

⁷ Aylmer, *RMS Mauretania*, 8; Hyde, *Cunard and the North Atlantic*, 5–8.

⁸ Aylmer, *RMS Mauretania*, 8; Hyde, *Cunard and the North Atlantic*, 9, 11, 12, 14; Stephen Fox, *Transatlantic: Samuel Cunard, Isambard Brunel and the Great Atlantic Steamships* (New York: Perennial, 2004), 31, 57.

⁹ Aylmer, *RMS Mauretania*, 8; Hyde, *Cunard and the North Atlantic*, 15, 16, 24.

¹⁰ Hyde, *Cunard and the North Atlantic*, 54, 326–31.

¹¹ Hyde, *Cunard and the North Atlantic*, 27–30, 33–4, 73, 93; John Malcolm Brinnin, *The Sway of the Grand Saloon: A Social History of the North Atlantic* (New York: Delacorte Press, 1971), 141–50, 165–98.

¹² Hyde, *Cunard and the North Atlantic*, 328–9; McCart, *Atlantic Liners of the Cunard Line*, 12; Aylmer, *RMS Mauretania*, 8–9. See also: Brinnin, *Sway of the Grand Saloon*, 276–7, 281–2, 286–8, 305–6, 345.

¹³ Rostron, *Home from the Sea*, 31; 'David Rees,' Lloyd's Captains' Register, 18567, v. 54, LMA; 'Agreement and Account of Crew,' *Cedric the Saxon*, 24 June 1895, voyage of 5 July 1895 to 28 Apr 1896, Antwerp to London, 1, 4–5, MHA.

¹⁴ 'Agreement and Account of Crew,' *Cedric the Saxon*, 24 June 1895, 1, 3, 4–7; 'David Rees,' Lloyd's Captains' Register, LMA; *Lloyd's List*, 6 July 1895, 26; 12 Nov 1895, 17; 13 Jan 1896, 15; 28 Apr 1896, 28.

¹⁵ 'Account of Crew and Other Particulars of a Foreign Going Ship,' *Cedric the Saxon*, 18 June 1896, voyage of 4 July 1896 to missing, London to foreign, MHA; *Cedric the Saxon*, case no. 2611, 'Lloyd's Missing Vessels Book, 1897–1900,' Guildhall Library, London (hereafter GLL), 24; *Lloyd's List*, 3 July 1896, 19; 4 July 1896, 1; 22 Sep 1896, 12; 2 Oct 1896, 21.

¹⁶ *Lloyd's List*, 12 May 1897, 14; *Cedric the Saxon*, 'Lloyd's Missing Vessels Book,' 24; Rostron, *Home from the Sea*, 4, 83.

¹⁷ 'The United States,' *The Times* 30 July 1895; 'The United States,' *The Times*, 31 July 1895; *Aurania* (official no. 87839), *Lloyd's Register*, 1889–90.

[18] Rostron, *Home from the Sea*, 36.

[19] Rostron, *Home from the Sea*, 30–1. *Titanic*'s senior survivor Charles Lightoller (*Titanic and Other Ships*, 204) agreed that 'everything was devoted to making a passage, with the result that the ship was driven smashing through everything and anything in the way of weather, pretty well regardless of damage done'. Each man, in his memoir, questioned the wisdom of maintaining speed into heavy seas at all hazards, but it was common practice during their days as junior officers in the years around 1900. Bisset (*Tramps and Ladies*, 194) remembered that *Umbria*, and her sister *Etruria*, were jokingly referred to as the Atlantic submarines. 'When hard driven, as she usually was, she often shipped purlers over the bow.' Rostron (*Home from the Sea*, 48) also said of *Campania*: 'we used to call her a semi-submersible.'

[20] McNeil, *In Great Waters*, 104; Lightoller, *Titanic and Other Ships*, 206. McNeil (*In Great Waters*, 229–30) noted that even on the mighty *Mauretania*, on her westbound record run of August 1929, 'shipping heavy sprays over the bridge … our rig, up there, was sea-boots and oil-skins'.

[21] Bisset, *Tramps and Ladies*, 195; McNeil, *In Great Waters*, 107. *Titanic*'s fifth officer, Harold Lowe, who remembered neither the collision nor being first told about it afterward, famously testified: 'You must remember that we do not have any too much sleep and therefore when we sleep we die.' (US Senate, 'Titanic' *Disaster Hearings before a Subcommittee of the Committee on Commerce United States Senate Sixty-Second Congress Second Session* (Washington, DC. USGPO, 1912), 388. (Hereafter: *Senate* Titanic *Hearings*.)

[22] Rostron, *Home from the Sea*, 237, 239; McNeil, *In Great Waters*, 119; Lightoller, Titanic *and Other Ships*, 206.

[23] Rostron, RNR Service Record, 2; James Bisset, *Commodore: War, Peace and Big Ships* (London: Angus and Robertson, 1961), 60.

[24] Cunard SS Co. Ltd., 'Report Book Officers, &c' case 227, Arthur Henry Rostron, DX/ 949 (R), 1988. 252, MMM; Cunard, 'Register of Officers,' case 247, 'William B. Cresser.'

[25] Rostron, RNR Service Record, 2; Rostron, *Home from the Sea*, 147; Ethel Minnie Stothert, Baptism, St James Free Church of England, Atherton, Lancashire, 13 Nov 1873, Lancashire Online Parish Clerk Project (accessed 15 Sep 2011). For the Stothert Family, see also Baptisms for James Stothert, 1 June 1864; Priscilla, 13 Sep 1865; William, 1 Apr 1868; Richard, 6 Apr 1870; and Herbert, 10 May 1876, Lancashire Online Parish Clerk Project.

[26] Arthur Henry Rostron and Ethel Minnie Stothert, Marriage, St John the Baptist, Atherton, Lancashire, 14 Sep 1899, Lancashire Online Parish Clerk Project (accessed 25 June 2011); John Rostron, letter to the author, 21 Oct 2011; '$10,000 in Gold for Rostron,' *New York American*, 2 June 1912.

[27] *Gore's Directory of Liverpool and its Environs* (London: Kelly's Directories, Ltd., 1901, 1904, 1905, 1907, 1908), page 1369 in 1901, 1442 in 1904, 1463 in 1905, 1474 in 1907 and 1475 in 1908. The prefaces to these directories are dated in December of the year prior to issue, meaning, presumably, that the data was also compiled by then. 'Arthur Rostron,' Census Returns of England and Wales, 1901, NAK. The Rostrons of 1901 were sufficiently prosperous to employ a nineteen-year-old maid named Evelyn Ashton. General Index, Births Registered in England and Wales, in the Months of Jan–Mar 1901 (microfiche 4464), p. 469 Harry Maxwell; Jan–Mar 1903 (mf 4521), 478 Robert James; Oct–Dec 1907 (mf 4658), 449 Arnold Richard; and Jan–Mar 1915 (mf 5033), 383 Margaret E[thel]., Crosby Public Library (hereafter CPL); Bolton Church Institute, 'Family of George Rostron,' (www.bolton-church-institute-org.uk/ trees/rostron-g.pdf); '$10,000 in Gold for Rostron,' *New York American*, 2 June 1912; John Rostron, letter to the author, 21 Oct 2011. The Rostron family register included in John Rostron's correspondence lists Robert as born in 1902 and Arnold in 1905. The other sources indicated, however, all show their births occurring in the years 1903 and 1907, respectively.

The *New York American* article of 1912 has Rostron giving the ages of his sons as eleven and a half, nine and a half and five and a half, but said that the youngest son was born on the day he assumed command of the cargo steamer *Brescia*, which was 30 August 1907. (Rostron, *Home from the Sea*, 49; Arthur Rostron, 'Lloyd's Captains' Register,' 18569, v. 33.) The Rostron household was not enumerated in the 1911 national census.

28   J. H. Plumb, et al., *The English Heritage* (St Louis, MO: Forum Press, 1980), 330–1.

29   'Modern British Ports. Southampton,' *The Times*, 20 June 1911.

30   P. Ransome-Wallis, *North Atlantic Panorama, 1900–1976* (Shepperton, Middlesex, Eng.: Ian Allen Ltd., 1977), 14; Rostron, *Home from the Sea*, 44; 'Return of Invalids from the Front,' *The Times*, 24 May 1900; 'Embarcation of Troops,' *The Times*, 8 June 1900; 'Return of Invalids,' *The Times*, 27 July 1900; '$10,000 in Gold for Rostron,' *New York American*, 2 June 1912. The form recording the award of Rostron's Sea Transport Medal with South Africa clasp, for his service as first officer aboard *Aurania*, contains the notation: 'Presd by H. M. the King 4 11 03 [4 Nov 1903].' ('Sea Transport Medal,' South African War, 1899–1902, 'List of Officers Eligible for the Sea Transport Medal. Cunard Co.,' 75, ADM 171/52, NAK.)

31   *Cherbourg* (official no. 71694), *Lloyd's Register*, 1889–90; Arthur Rostron, Lloyd's Captains' Register, 18569, v. 33. In the spring of 1901 a British census canvasser listed Rostron as '1st Off. Cunard SS Co.' ('Census Returns of England and Wales,' 1901, NAK.) Rostron is listed as chief officer of *Cherbourg* for his evaluation of 30 June 1901 on his 'Report Book Officers' sheet. (Cunard, 'Report Book Officers,' case 227.)

32   Rostron, 'Lloyd's Captains' Register,' 18569, v. 33; Cunard, 'Report Book Officers,' case 227. It was while serving in *Campania* on the April voyage that Rostron claimed to have seen a sea monster while on watch approaching Queenstown. Whatever the zoological merits of his observation, Rostron held to it, repeating his story to various newspapers and at length in his memoir twenty-four years later (*Home from the Sea*, 45–7). It did not hurt him; he made his next revenue voyage as a captain. John P. Eaton and Charles A. Haas (*Titanic: Triumph and Tragedy* (2nd ed. New York: W. W. Norton and Co., 1994), 176) give an unattributed date for this encounter of 26 April 1907. In his memoir Rostron wrote that the sighting occurred on a Friday evening off Galley Head about thirty-five nautical miles west of Queenstown. *The Times* of Friday, 26 April ('Mail News… Inward'), said that *Campania*'s mails 'are to be expected for delivery early tomorrow'.

CHAPTER 4

1   Hyde, *Cunard and the North Atlantic*, 98–9.

2   McCart, *Atlantic Liners of the Cunard Line*, 22, 24, 25; Aylmer, *RMS* Mauretania, 10.

3   John Maxtone-Graham, *The Only Way to Cross*, (1972; reprint: NY: Barnes and Noble Books, 1997), 11; Hyde, *Cunard and the North Atlantic*, 137–8.

4   Hyde, *Cunard and the North Atlantic*, 110, 112–13, 137–8, 139, 147–8.

5   Hyde, *Cunard and the North Atlantic*, 109, 110, 141, 145–6, 147, 157–8.

6   'From the Tyne to the Mersey in the Mauretania,' *The Times*, 25 Oct 1907; Hyde, *Cunard and the North Atlantic*, 146; Aylmer, *RMS* Mauretania, 11; McCart, *Atlantic Liners of the Cunard Line*, 55, 61.

7   Maxtone-Graham, *Only Way to Cross*, 15, 18; Ken Smith, *Turbinia: The Story of Charles Parsons and his Ocean Greyhound* (Newcastle, Eng.: Tyne Bridge Publishing, 2009), 50.

8   Maxtone-Graham, *Only Way to Cross*, 18, 20; Smith, *Turbinia*, 23, 48.

9   McCart, *Atlantic Liners of the Cunard Line*, 46, 47–8, 54, 56; Maxtone-Graham, *Only Way to Cross*, 21; 'The Cunard Steamship Company,' *The Times*, 6 Sep 1907.

10 McCart, *Atlantic Liners of the Cunard Line*, 56, 63; 'Launch of the Lusitania,' *The Times*, 8 June 1906.

11 Rostron, *Home from the Sea*, 48, 49; 'The Cunard Liner Lusitania,' *The Times*, 28 June 1907.

12 'The New Cunarder Lusitania,' *The Times*, 30 July 1907; 'Institution of Naval Architects,' *The Times*, 10 Apr 1908.

13 'The Lusitania. Results of the Official Trials,' *The Times*, 3 Aug 1907; 'Institution of Naval Architects,' *The Times*, 10 Apr 1908.

14 'The Lusitania's First Voyage,' *The Times*, 9 Sep 1907; McCart, *Atlantic Liners of the Cunard Line*, 62.

15 'The Lusitania's Voyage,' *The Times*, 14 Sep 1907; 'The Lusitania's Record Voyage,' *The Times*, 12 Oct 1907.

16 Arthur Rostron, 'Lloyd's Captains' Register,' 18569, v. 33; *Lloyd's List*, 'Brescia,' 2 Sep 1907, 8; Rostron, *Home from the Sea*, 49.

17 *Brescia* (official no. 118021), *Lloyd's Register*, 1910–11, v. 1; Bisset, *Tramps and Ladies*, 229, 230, 238.

18 Hyde, *Cunard and the North Atlantic*, 16–17, 20–1, 22, 54.

19 Hyde, *Cunard and the North Atlantic*, 330–1; Bisset, *Tramps and Ladies*, 227, 230–1.

20 Bisset, *Tramps and Ladies*, 232, 234–5, 243.

21 *Brescia*, Cunard Steamship Co., 'Ships' Movement Book,' v. 3 (17 Mar 1906 through 15 Feb 1908), D42/GM1/3, Cunard Collection, SJL; *Lloyd's List*, 2 Sep 1907, 8; 3 Sep 1907, 35; 6 Sep 1907, 4; 12 Sep 1907, 11; 13 Sep 1907, 12; 18 Sep 1907, 29; 20 Sep 1907, 13; 23 Sep 1907, 19; 24 Sep 1907, 34; 28 Sep 1907, 13; 2 Oct 1907, 12; 5 Oct 1907, 13; 7 Oct 1907, 18. In his memoir (*Home from the Sea*, 50), Rostron claimed that he tore the bilge keels from *Brescia* clearing the entrance of Swansea dock, 'hardly an auspicious start as master'. Neither Cunard's nor Lloyd's records make any mention of such an incident, however.

22 *Brescia*, Cunard 'Ships' Movement Book,' 3; *Lloyd's List*, 8 Oct 1907, 17; 12 Oct 1907, 14; 19 Oct 1907, 14; 31 Oct 1907, 14; 5 Nov 1907, 15; 11 Nov 1907, 18; 18 Nov 1907, 8.

23 'Mauretania Goes 30.5 Miles an Hour,' *New York Times*, 22 Sep 1907.

24 'The New White Star Liners,' *The Times*, 1 Sep 1908; Eaton and Haas, Titanic: *Triumph and Tragedy*, 126–35.

25 'The New White Star Liners,' *The Times*, 22 Nov 1909; 'Launch of the Olympic,' *The Times*, 21 Oct 1910; 'Shipbuilding,' *The Times*, 13 Jan 1911; 'The Maiden Voyage of the Olympic,' *The Times*, 15 June 1911; 'The Maiden Voyage of the Olympic,' *The Times*, 22 June 1911.

26 'Launch of the Titanic,' *The Times*, 1 June 1911 ; 'The Floating Islands,' *The Times*, 23 Dec 1910.

27 Arthur Henry Rostron, 'Lloyd's Captains' Register,' 18567, v. 85, (1904–11) LMA.

28 Rostron, 'Lloyd's Captains' Register,' 18567, v. 85; *Pannonia* (official no. 118080), *Lloyd's Register*, 1910–11, v.1; 'Cunard The Fastest Steamers in the World' (advertisement), *New York American*, 27 Apr 1912; Bisset, *Tramps and Ladies*, 229–30; 'The Brave Captain Rostron Should be Fitly Rewarded,' *New York American*, 28 April 1912.

29 Rostron, RNR Service Record, 2; *Gore's Directory of Liverpool and its Environs...* 1911, 1481; Cunard, 'Register of Officers,' case 257, Arthur Henry Rostron.

30 Rostron assumed command of *Carpathia* on 18 Jan 1912 (*Senate Titanic Hearings*, 18) and was promoted to commander in the Royal Naval Reserve the following day, 19 Jan 1912 (Rostron, RNR Service Record, 1); 'Deaths,' *Bolton Evening News*, 15 Nov 1911; 'Transcriptions of the Memorial Inscriptions in the "New Ground" Part of the Church Yard of Christ Church, Walmsley, Bolton.' (Bolton and District Family History Society, 1999), 97 ('Rostron, J. 797, grave owner'), BHC; John Rostron, letter of 21 Oct 2011.

CHAPTER 5

1 Ken Smith, *Tyne to* Titanic*: The Story of Rescue Ship* Carpathia (Newcastle upon Tyne: Newcastle Libraries and Information Service, 1998), 5; McCart, *Atlantic Liners of the Cunard Line*, 42–3.

2 Hyde, *Cunard and the North Atlantic*, 58, 60, 77, 94, 98–9.

3 Hyde, *Cunard and the North Atlantic*, 111; McCart, *Atlantic Liners of the Cunard Line*, 35–6, 38; Bisset, *Tramps and Ladies*, 178; Rostron, *Home from the Sea*, 44.

4 'The Cunard Steamer Carpathia,' *The Times*, 27 Apr 1903; 'New Cunard Liner Carpathia,' *New York Times*, 4 May 1903; Hyde, *Cunard and the North Atlantic*, 76.

5 Article from *The Marine Engineer*, 1 Sep 1902, reprinted in: *Titanic Commutator* II, no. 22 (sum. 1979): 24–5; 'Cunard Carpathia Capacity Plan' (blueprint), March 1913, B/CUN/8/1903.1/1/2, MMM; Smith, *Tyne to* Titanic, 8; Brian J. Ticehurst, *The* Titanic*'s Rescuers: Captain Arthur Henry Rostron, the Crew of the* Carpathia *and the* Carpathia (Southampton: B&J Printers, 2001), 2. If needed for trooping, Carpathia could carry 3000 soldiers.

6 'Carpathia Capacity Plan,' 1913; Reprint from *The Marine Engineer*, 1 Sep 1902.

7 'Big New Liner Due Today,' *New York Times*, 7 June 1903; Reprint from *The Marine Engineer*, 1 Sep 1902; 'The Cunard Steamer Carpathia,' *The Times*, 27 Apr 1903. The *New York Times* article noted that *Carpathia*'s engines had twenty-six-, thirty-seven-, fifty-three- and seventy-six-inch cylinders with a fifty-four-inch stroke and that *Carpathia* soothed those aboard with an air conditioning of sorts delivered 'by means of thermotanks, which contain fans driven by electric motors, which pass the air through coils and thus give a complete change of atmosphere in each compartment on the average of once in every five minutes. The fans can be used either to exhaust hot air or to force cool, fresh air into the various sections.'

8 'Cunard Line – Royal Mail Steamers' (advertisement), *The Times*, 2 May and 20 May 1903; Smith, *Tyne to* Titanic, 13–4; Bisset, *Tramps and Ladies*, 168, 178, 260; 'The Cunard Steamship Company,' *The Times*, 6 Sep 1907; 'Cunard the Fastest Steamers in the World' (advertisement), *New York Times*, 11 Apr 1912.

9 Bisset, *Tramps and Ladies*, 179, 181.

10 Bisset, *Tramps and Ladies*, 178, 179; 'Immigration Records all Beaten this Week,' *New York Times*, 17 Apr 1906.

11 Bisset, *Tramps and Ladies*, 178, 179, 181, 183, 189, 265; Rostron, *Home from the Sea*, 45.

12 Bisset, *Tramps and Ladies*, 181; Rostron, *Home from the Sea*, 45.

13 Bisset, *Tramps and Ladies*, 188, 189, 191.

14 'Mothers in Sorrow Leave Ellis Island,' *New York Times*, 20 Nov 1910; 'Two Liners Held Up,' *New York Times*, 7 June 1911.

[15] 'Hastens to Marry his Mother's Choice,' *New York Times*, 13 May 1910; Rostron, *Home from the Sea*, 241.

[16] 'The Stork Pays a Mid-Ocean Visit,' *New York Times*, 22 Nov 1907.

[17] 'Cunard Line Royal Mail Steamers' (advertisement), *The Times*, 16 Sep 1905; Ticehurst, *Titanic's Rescuers*, 2; Smith, *Tyne to* Titanic, 14; Bisset, *Tramps and Ladies*, 262, 265.

[18] 'Cunard Line Royal Mail Steamers' (advertisement), *The Times*, 16 Sep 1905; 'The Cunard Steamship Company,' *The Times*, 6 Sep 1907; 'Cunard Winter Cruise,' *The Times*, 12 Jan 1910; 'Pleasure Cruises in Ocean Liners,' *The Times*, 5 Feb 1910.

[19] 'Big New Liner Due Today,' *New York Times*, 7 June 1903; Grattidge, *Captain of the Queens*, 65; Bisset, *Tramps and Ladies*, 261; 'Cunard the Fastest Steamers in the World' (advertisement), *New York Times*, 8 Apr 1912; Testimony of Arthur Rostron, *Senate* Titanic *Hearings*, 18.

[20] *Ivernia* (official no. 110643), *Saxonia* (official no. 110648), *Lloyd's Register*, 1910–11, v. 1; McCart, *Atlantic Liners of the Cunard Line*, 33, 38.

[21] *Carpathia*, Cunard 'Ships' Movement Book,' no. 6 (24 Dec 1911 to 22 Nov 1913), D42/GM1/6, Cunard Collection, SJL.

[22] *Carpathia*, Cunard 'Ships' Movement Book,' 6.

[23] *Carpathia*, Cunard 'Ships' Movement Book,' 6; Bisset, *Tramps and Ladies*, 189.

[24] *Carpathia*, Cunard 'Ships' Movement Book,' 6; Bisset, *Tramps and Ladies*, 190; Ticehurst, *Titanic's Rescuers*, 27; McCart, *Atlantic Liners of the Cunard Line*, 43.

[25] 'The Titanic,' *The Times*, 11 Oct 1911; 'The Largest Vessel Afloat,' *The Times*, 11 Apr 1912; 'The Titanic,' *The Times*, 12 Apr 1912.

[26] Rostron, *Senate* Titanic *Hearings*, 19; 'Cunard the Fastest Steamers in the World' (advertisement), *New York Times*, 8 Apr 1912; Cunard, 'Ships' Movement Book,' 6; Bisset, *Tramps and Ladies*, 182; 'Mail and Shipping Intelligence,' *The Times*, 13 April 1912. Bisset (*Tramps and Ladies*, 268) put *Carpathia*'s complement for the voyage as 120 first-class, 50 second-class, 565 third-class and about 300 crew, making a total of 1035 people aboard a ship certified to carry 2100.

CHAPTER 6

[1] Testimony of Frederick Fleet (seaman, *Titanic*), *Senate* Titanic *Hearings*, 317.

[2] Wreck Commissioners' Court. Scottish Hall, Buckingham Gate, 'Proceedings before the Right Hon. Lord Mersey, Wreck Commissioner of the United Kingdom… on a Formal Investigation Ordered by the Board of Trade into the Loss of the SS "Titanic",' Titanic Inquiry Project (www.titanicinquiry.org), Testimony of Joseph Boxhall, question 15610 (hereafter: 'British Titanic Enquiry').

[3] Bisset, *Tramps and Ladies*, 276.

[4] 'Carpathia Capacity Plan,' 1913; 'Titanic's "C.Q.D." Caught by a Lucky Fluke,' *New York Times*, 19 Apr 1912.

[5] 'Titanic's "C.Q.D." Caught by a Lucky Fluke,' *New York Times*, 19 April 1912. Rostron, 'British Titanic Enquiry,' 25389.

[6] Rostron, 'British Titanic Enquiry,' 25388. Arthur H. Rostron, 'The Rescue of the "Titanic" Survivors,' *Scribner's Monthly* 53 (Mar 1913): 354; Rostron, *Senate* Titanic *Hearings*, 19.

7 'Titanic's "C.Q.D." Caught by a Lucky Fluke,' *New York Times*, 19 April 1912; Rostron, *Senate* Titanic *Hearings*, 20. The chief engineer's name appears as 'Johnstone' in *The Times* ('The Titanic Disaster. Carpathia's Officers' Rewards,' 5 July 1912 and 'Liverpool Awards to Carpathia's Crew,' 16 Dec 1912), but a number of later sources spell it 'Johnston'.

8 'Captain's Official Reports,' *New York Times*, 20 Apr 12. Both *Carpathia*'s maximum speed and the distance that she covered that night are disputed. Please see '*Carpathia*'s Dash: Speed and Distance' in the appendix.

9 Rostron, *Home from the Sea*, 50.

10 Rostron, 'Rescue of the "Titanic" Survivors,' 354; Rostron, *Senate* Titanic *Hearings*, 20.

11 Rostron, 'Rescue of the "Titanic" Survivors,' 355; Testimony of Herbert Haddock (master, *Olympic*), *Senate* Titanic *Hearings*, 1127; Rostron, *Senate* Titanic *Hearings*, 20–1.

12 Bisset, *Tramps and Ladies*, 279–80. Rostron, 'British Titanic Enquiry,' 25413.

13 Rostron, *Home from the Sea*, 54; Rostron, *Senate* Titanic *Hearings*, 27.

14 'Made Women Leave Against Their Will,' *New York Times*, 19 Apr 1912.

15 Rostron, 'Rescue of the "Titanic" Survivors,' 356. Rostron, *Senate* Titanic *Hearings*, 21; 'British Titanic Enquiry,' 'Findings of the Court, Question 18, Submitted – Wireless messages in connection with "Titanic" sent the evening of April 14–15 1912,' 'British Titanic Enquiry,' Titanic Enquiry Project (these times are approximate, as slight variations exist in the times indicated among the three vessels); Rostron, 'British Titanic Enquiry,' 25394; Testimony of James Moore (master, *Mount Temple*), *Senate* Titanic *Hearings*, 777. After the last message he heard from *Titanic* at 1.45am, Cottam continued to listen for sparks from *Titanic*'s emergency set, but 'when I didn't hear it I was sure that he had gone down'. ('Titanic's "C.Q.D." Caught by a Lucky Fluke,' *New York Times*, 19 Apr 1912.)

16 Affidavit of Mahala Douglas, *Senate* Titanic *Hearings*, 1101; Lightoller, *Titanic and Other Ships*, 248; Testimony of James Johnson (steward, *Titanic*), 'British Titanic Enquiry,' 3546.

17 Rostron, 'Rescue of the "Titanic" Survivors,' 356; Rostron, *Senate* Titanic *Hearings*, 21; 'Captain's Official Reports,' *New York Times*, 20 Apr 1912; Rostron, 'British Titanic Enquiry,' 25394. Rostron said he sighted this flare, which he identified at the British enquiry as 'the White Star Company's night signal,' a point to port in his *Scribner's Monthly* magazine article of 1913, from which the quote is derived and in his memoirs of 1931. In his senate testimony and company report of April 1912, days after the event, however, he said it was half a point to port, so that estimate is used here. Rostron's time of 2.40am as the time of *Carpathia*'s first sighting of one of Boxhall's green flares is dubious and the location of that flare off *Carpathia*'s port bow is curious. For further discussion of these issues, please see '*Carpathia*'s Dash' and 'Seeing Boxhall's Flares' in the appendix.

18 Bisset, *Tramps and Ladies*, 283; Rostron, 'British Titanic Enquiry,' 25420–5; Rostron, *Home from the Sea*, 60.

19 Rostron, 'British Titanic Enquiry,' 25401; Rostron, 'Rescue of the "Titanic" Survivors,' 357; Bisset, *Tramps and Ladies*, 283.

20 Rostron, 'Rescue of the "Titanic" Survivors,' 357; Rostron, 'British Titanic Enquiry,' 25401; Lawrence Beesley, *The Loss of the SS Titanic: Its Story and Its Lessons* (1912; reprint: Boston: Houghton Mifflin, 2000) 91–3.

21 Rostron, 'British Titanic Enquiry,' 25401, 04, 06, 67, 69, 71, 73; Bisset, *Tramps and Ladies*, 285–6. Boxhall also tried to signal *Carpathia* by waving his hat in front of a lamp he held aloft. (Johnson, 'British Titanic Enquiry,' 3547.)

22 Beesley, *Loss of the SS* Titanic, 91–3; 'Mary C. Wellman Dies at 80,' *New York Times*, 26 Nov 1975, 32.

23 Rostron, 'Rescue of the "Titanic" Survivors, 357–8; Testimony of various witnesses, *Senate* Titanic *Hearings*, 242–3, 277, 326, 451, 520, 598, 615, 827.

24 Rostron, 'British Titanic Enquiry,' 25491; Rostron, 'Rescue of the "Titanic" Survivors,' 360; Testimony of George Hogg (seaman, *Titanic*), *Senate* Titanic *Hearings*, 579; Rostron, 'British Titanic Enquiry,' 25499; 'Boats in Detail,' *Senate* Titanic *Hearings*, 1159–63.

25 Beesley, *Loss of the SS* Titanic, 98. Rostron, *Senate* Titanic *Hearings*, 21. After boat 7 arrived alongside, Hogg 'assisted in putting a bowline around all the ladies, to haul them up aboard'. (Hogg, *Senate* Titanic *Hearings*, 579.) A passenger aboard *Carpathia* said that ropes were tied around waists of survivors to help them climb ladders, while 'little children and babies were hoisted on to our deck in bags'. ('On Board the Carpathia,' *The Times*, 20 Apr 1912.)

26 Rostron, *Home from the Sea*, 69. Beesley, *Loss of the SS* Titanic, 137–8. Bisset, *Tramps and Ladies*, 287. Rostron, Beesley and Bisset made their observations on deck, however. Below, survivor Gladys Cherry described the women coming aboard as 'some unconscious, some hysterical and all more or less collapsed'. (Gladys Cherry, letter to mother written aboard *Carpathia*, 17 Apr 1912, DX/1522/1, MMM.) An unidentified *Carpathia* steward remembered even more emotional scenes: 'While we were pulling in the boat-loads the women were quiet enough, but when it seemed sure that we should not find any more people alive then Bedlam came. I hope never to go through it again. The way those women "took on" for the folk they had lost was awful. We could not do anything to quieten [*sic*] them until they cried themselves out.' ('The Deathless Story of the Titanic: Complete Narrative with Many Illustrations,' issued by *Lloyd's Weekly News*, n.d. (c. 1912), 22, DX 949 R 1988 258, MMM.)

27 Statement of Mrs Lucian P. [Eloise Hughes] Smith (passenger, *Titanic*), *Senate* Titanic *Hearings*, 1150; Testimony of Arthur Peuchen (passenger, *Titanic*), *Senate* Titanic *Hearings*, 349; Affidavit of Mrs E. B. [Emily] Ryerson (passenger, *Titanic*), *Senate* Titanic *Hearings*, 1108.

28 Mrs Paul [Emma] Schabert, letter written 18 Apr 1912 aboard *Carpathia*, reprinted in *Titanic Commutator* II, no. 22 (Sum 1979): 4; Rostron, 'British Titanic Enquiry,' 25496–8, 25508; 'Captain's Official Reports,' *New York Times*, 20 Apr 12; Rostron, *Senate* Titanic *Hearings*, 30. Rostron ('British Titanic Enquiry,' 25501) sent a junior officer to the top of the wheelhouse to count icebergs, the officer counted twenty-five of 150 to 200 feet in height, 'and stopped counting the smaller ones; there were dozens and dozens all over the place'. Rostron said that two or three miles from the position of the wreckage lay 'a huge ice-field extending as far as we could see, northwest to southeast'. Rostron ('British Titanic Enquiry,' 25527) also testified that 'when daylight broke and we were picking up the passengers from the first boat, I was looking round and 200 yards on my port quarter I saw a lump of ice twenty feet long and ten feet high, which we had not seen at all'.

29 Lightoller, Titanic *and Other Ships*, 253–4; 'Captain's Official Reports,' *New York Times*, 20 Apr 1912.

30 Archibald Gracie, *The Truth about the* Titanic (NY: M. Kennerley, 1913), 111; 'Captain's Official Reports,' *New York Times*, 20 Apr 1912; Rostron, *Senate* Titanic *Hearings*, 24.

31 Testimony of Stanley Lord (master, *Californian*), *Senate* Titanic *Hearings*, 715–7; Testimony of Cyril Evans (wireless operator, *Californian*), *Senate* Titanic *Hearings*, 734, 735–6; Testimony of Cyril Evans, 'British Titanic Enquiry,' 8991–7, 9026.

32 Evans, *Senate* Titanic *Hearings*, 736–7; Evans, 'British Titanic Enquiry,' 8927, 8935, 9056–85, 9165–6; Lord, 'British Titanic Enquiry,' 7005, 7259, 7260, 7264, 7388, 7401;

Lord, *Senate* Titanic *Hearings*, 718. Evans identified the vessel informing him of the disaster as *Frankfurt* at the American enquiry and *Mount Temple* at the British enquiry. Lord testified that *Californian* arrived at the scene of the rescue at 8.30am. In both his senate testimony and his official report to Cunard (*Senate* Titanic *Hearings*, 22; 'Captain's Official Reports,' *New York Times*, 20 Apr 12) Rostron said that *Californian* arrived alongside *Carpathia* at 8am, as did Bisset decades later (*Tramps and Ladies*, 291).

33 Rostron, *Senate* Titanic *Hearings*, 22–3. By about 7.45am, *Carpathia* had worked her way far enough north to encounter some of *Titanic*'s debris (Rostron, 'British Titanic Enquiry,' 25496–8). The nature of the debris field, however, suggests that *Carpathia* never reached the site of the sinking itself. Please see '*Carpathia*'s Dash' in the appendix.

34 Rostron, *Home from the Sea*, 63; 'Submitted Wireless Messages,' 'British Titanic Inquiry,' Titanic Enquiry Project.

35 'Captain's Official Reports,' *New York Times*, 20 Apr 1912; Rostron, *Senate* Titanic *Hearings*, 29.

36 Rostron, 'Rescue of the "Titanic" Survivors,' 359; US Senate, 'Titanic' *Disaster Report of the Committee on Commerce United States Senate* (Washington, DC: USGPO, 1912), 15.

37 Rostron, *Senate* Titanic *Hearings*, 32; US Senate, 'Titanic' *Disaster Report*, 17; 'Log as Made by Wireless Operator Moore on SS Olympic,' *Senate* Titanic *Hearings*, 1138; 'Titanic Sinks Four Hours After Hitting Iceberg,' *New York Times*, 16 Apr 1912.

CHAPTER 7

1 'New Liner Titanic Hits an Iceberg,' *New York Times*, 15 Apr 1912.

2 'The News In New York,' 'Titanic Disaster,' 'The Titanic is Sunk,' 'Rescue of the Passengers,' *The Times*, 16 Apr 1912.

3 'International Mercantile Marine Lines' (advertisement), *New York Times*, 11 Apr 1912.

4 Herbert Haddock (master, *Olympic*), testifying and quoting excerpts from *Olympic*'s wireless log, Titanic *Senate Hearings*, 1128–30; 'Log as Made by Wireless Operator Moore on SS "Olympic",' *Senate* Titanic *Hearings*, 1137–9.

5 'Log as Made by Wireless Operator Moore on SS "Olympic",' *Senate* Titanic *Hearings*, 1139.

6 'Log as Made by Wireless Operator Moore on SS "Olympic",' *Senate* Titanic *Hearings*, 1139–40. Moore's 8.45pm New York time, would have been about 10pm apparent ship's time. However Rostron (*Senate* Titanic *Hearings*, 33; 'Rescue of the "Titanic" Survivors,' 362) put the time of losing contact with *Olympic* much later, at 1am or thereafter Tuesday.

7 'Titanic Sinks Four Hours After Hitting Iceberg,' *New York Times*, 16 Apr 1912; 'Olympic Reports but 675 Souls Saved,' *New York American*, 16 Apr 1912; 'Sorrow Mingles with Joy, for Invariably Where a Mother Was Saved a Father Was Lost,' *New York American*, 17 Apr 1912.

8 'Titanic Sinks, 1500 Die,' *Boston Daily Globe*, 16 Apr 1912; 'Titanic Sinks Four Hours After Hitting Iceberg,' *New York Times*, 16 Apr 12.

9 '1200 to 1500 Dead,' *New York American*, 16 Apr 1912; 'Titanic Rent in Twain,' *New York American*, 17 Apr 1912; 'Story of the Disaster… An Iceberg Struck,' *The Times*, 16 Apr 1912.

10 'No Rescues by Other Ships,' *New York Times*, 17 Apr 1912; 'Globe Man Finds Only 705 Saved,' *Boston Daily Globe*, 18 Apr 1912; 'Death List Now Fixed at 1,535,' *New York American*, 17 Apr 1912; 'Carpathia off Sable Island,' *Boston Daily Globe*, 17 Apr 12; 'To Break Seal of Silence,' *Boston Daily Globe* (Evening Edition), 17 Apr 1912; 'Titanic Disaster,' *The Times*, 16 Apr 1912; 'Only 400 Titanic Survivors Named by Carpathia,' *New York Times*,

17 Apr 1912; 'Hopes and Fears in New York,' *The Times*, 17 Apr 1912; 'Details Still Lacking,' *The Times*, 17 Apr 1912.

11 'Times Bulletins Sent Far and Wide,' *New York Times*, 17 Apr 1912; 'Only 400 Titanic Survivors Named by Carpathia,' *New York Times*, 17 Apr 1912; 'Carpathia off Sable Island,' *Boston Daily Globe*, 17 Apr 1912.

12 'Sumner Chafes at Delay,' *New York Times*, 17 Apr 1912.

13 'International Mercantile Marine Lines' (advertisement), *New York Times*, 11 Apr 1912; Ransome-Wallis, *North Atlantic Panorama*, 40; John Booth and Sean Coughlan, Titanic: *Signals of Disaster* (Westbury, Wiltshire, UK: White Star Publications, 1993), 65, 68; Testimony of Harold Cottam, *Senate* Titanic *Hearings*, 110.

14 'Names of 326 Saved Have Been Received,' *New York American*, 17 Apr 1912; 'Carpathia off Sable Island,' *Boston Daily Globe*, 17 Apr 1912; 'Four Days of Terrible Suspense Breed Wild Rumors,' *New York Times*, 28 Apr 1912. Of the survivors' names from *Carpathia*: 'Many names were mis-spelled, many duplicated and in many cases only the first or the last words in the name were received. ('No Rescues by Virginian or Parisian,' *The Times*, 17 Apr 1912.)

15 'Only 400 Titanic Survivors Named by Carpathia,' *New York Times*, 17 Apr 1912; 'Many Reasons for the Delay in Getting Messages from Carpathia,' *Boston Daily Globe* (Evening Edition), 17 Apr 1912; 'Carpathia off Sable Island,' *Boston Daily Globe*, 17 Apr 1912; 'Cunard Line's Messages,' *New York Times*, 18 Apr 1912.

16 'Scout Cruisers Rush to Scene of Wreck,' *New York Times*, 17 Apr 1912; 'Congress Resolution,' *The Times*, 17 Apr 1912; 'To Break Seal of Silence,' *Boston Daily Globe* (Evening Edition), 17 Apr 1912.

17 'Carpathia has the 705 Saved,' *Boston Daily Globe* (Evening Edition), 17 Apr 1912; 'Carpathia Here Tonight with Titanic's Survivors,' *New York Times*, 18 Apr 1912; 'Deaf to Enquiries for Wreck Details,' *Boston Daily Globe* (Evening Edition), 18 Apr 1912.

18 Rostron, 'Rescue of the "Titanic" Survivors,' 363; 'No New Names Added,' *Boston Daily Globe* (Evening Edition), 17 Apr 1912; 'Carpathia Here Tonight with Titanic's Survivors,' *New York Times*, 18 Apr 1912; 'The Passenger Lists. Anxious Enquiries in London,' *The Times*, 18 Apr 1912.

19 'The Carpathia's Company. Number of the Survivors on Board,' *The Times*, 18 Apr 1912; 'Weary Day at Boston Office,' *Boston Daily Globe*, 17 Apr 1912.

20 'Awaiting the Carpathia,' *The Times*, 19 Apr 1912; 'Astor and Widener Gone,' *Boston Daily Globe* (Evening Edition), 18 Apr 1912; '78 Women in Cabin Fail of Rescue – Many Men Saved,' *New York American*, 18 Apr 1912; 'Astor and Widener Gone,' *Boston Daily Globe* (Evening Edition), 18 Apr 1912; 'Cunard Line's Messages,' *New York Times*, 18 Apr 1912.

21 'N.Y. American Tug in Touch with the Survivors Today,' *New York American*, 18 Apr 1912; Marconi, *Senate* Titanic *Hearings*, 850; 'Marconi Company Asked "American" in "Name of Humanity" To Put Its Man on Board Carpathia,' *New York American*, 23 Apr 1912; 'New York American's Special Tug Kept in Contact with Carpathia,' *New York American*, 19 Apr 1912.

22 'Waiting for Carpathia,' *Boston Daily Globe*, 19 Apr 1912; 'Globe Man Finds Only 705 Saved,' *Boston Daily Globe*, 18 Apr 1912.

23 '78 Women in Cabin Fail of Rescue,' *New York American*, 18 Apr 1912; 'Survivors in Awful Condition,' *Boston Daily Globe* (Evening Edition), 18 Apr 1912; 'Deaf to Enquiries for Wreck Details,' *Boston Daily Globe* (Evening Edition), 18 Apr 1912.

24 Booth and Coughlan, Titanic: *Signals of Disaster*, 71, 92; Marconi, *Senate* Titanic *Hearings*, 846.

[25] 'Awaiting the Carpathia,' *The Times*, 19 Apr 1912; 'Carpathia Here Tonight with Titanic's Survivors,' *New York Times*, 18 Apr 1912. The next day *The New York Times* published a message dispatched from USS *Salem* at 8am on 18 April, which, the paper said, demonstrated that *Carpathia* had 'persistently declined to answer any message of enquiry, although sometimes acknowledging calls'. The article went on to say that 'officials of the Navy Department are suspending judgment upon the conduct of officers of the *Carpathia*, who have treated with scant courtesy requests for information transmitted through the scout cruisers *Salem* and *Chester* by Government officials including the President of the United States. Whether responsibility rests with the Captain of the Cunarder or President Ismay of the White Star Line, who is reported as a survivor of the Titanic aboard the *Carpathia*, is a matter of conjecture.' ('Ignored by the Carpathia,' *New York Times*, 19 Apr 1912.)

CHAPTER 8

[1] Nick Barratt, *Lost Voices from the* Titanic: *The Definitive Oral History* (New York: Palgrave Macmillan, 2010), 158 (letter by Laura Mabel Francatelli).

[2] Gracie, *Truth about the Titanic*, 112.

[3] Beesley, *Loss of the SS Titanic*, 138; 'No Rush for Boats,' *Boston Daily Globe*, 19 Apr 1912.

[4] 'The Lost Liner,' *The Times*, 19 Apr 1912; 'Made Women Leave Against Their Will,' *New York Times*, 18 Apr 1912; 'Rostron Lunches with Mrs. Astor,' *New York American*, 1 June 1912.

[5] Beesley, *Loss of the SS Titanic*, 139, 143; Bisset, *Tramps and Ladies*, 291, 295, 296; Rostron, *Home from the Sea*, 71.

[6] 'Log as Made by Wireless Operator Moore on SS "Olympic",' *Senate Titanic Hearings*, 1137–8; Rostron, *Home from the Sea*, 71–2.

[7] Rostron, *Senate Titanic Hearings*, 25, 28; Barratt, *Lost Voices*, 150 (account of his life by Karl Behr); Beesley, *Loss of the SS Titanic*, 145–6; 'Made Women Leave against Their Will,' *New York Times*, 19 Apr 1912; Rostron, 'British Titanic Enquiry,' 25565. Behr, in a reminiscence about his life written later in life, remembered this meeting as having occurred in the saloon 'after lunch on the first day,' which suggests Monday, 'to select a committee to assist in caring for the rescued'. Lawrence Beesley, in an account written six weeks after the disaster, states that 'a roll-call of the rescued was held in the *Carpathia*'s saloon on the Monday,' and that 'on Tuesday the survivors met in the saloon and formed a committee among themselves to collect subscriptions for a general fund' to assist the steerage passengers and to recognize Rostron and his crew, with any money remaining going to *Titanic*'s crew. (Beesley, *Loss of the SS Titanic*, 140, 145.)

[8] Beesley, *Loss of the SS Titanic*, 91, 149–50; Barratt, *Lost Voices*, 150–1 (account by Karl H. Behr); *Carpathia*, Cunard 'Ships' Movement Book,' 6.

[9] 'Carpathia Should Arrive with the Survivors Late Tonight,' *New York Times*, 18 Apr 1912; Mildred Brown, letter to mother written aboard *Carpathia*, 17 Apr 1912, D/BRW/2, MMM.

[10] Gladys Cherry, letter to her mother written aboard *Carpathia*, 17 Apr 1912, DX/1522/1; Gladys Cherry, letter to mother written aboard *Carpathia*, 18 Apr 1912, DX/1522/2, MMM.

[11] Beesley, *Loss of the SS Titanic*, 147, 149. Beesley (149) said that his press statement 'ended up in the possession of an AP reporter and served its intended effect'.

[12] Schabert, letter of 18 Apr 1912; 4; Cherry, letter to mother, 18 Apr 1912.

13   'Carpathia Should Arrive With the Survivors Late To-night,' New York Times, 18 Apr 1912; 'News of Titanic Horror Held up for Eight Hours,' *New York American*, 18 Apr 1912; 'Deaf to Enquiries for Details,' *Boston Daily Globe*, 18 Apr 1912. For more details on the issues associated with *Carpathia*'s wireless communications following the rescue please see '*Carpathia*'s Communications' in the appendix.

14   'Lloyd's Not Victimized,' *New York Times*, 19 Apr 1912; Rostron, *Senate Titanic Hearings*, 32–3; Haddock, *Senate Titanic Hearings*, 1129, 1130.

15   Cottam, *Senate Titanic Hearings*, 108–9, 124–6; Beesley, *Loss of the SS Titanic*, 140; Testimony of Harold Bride (wireless operator, *Titanic*), *Senate Titanic Hearings*, 896; 'Thrilling Story by Titanic's Surviving Wireless Man,' *New York Times*, 19 Apr 1912. Some confusion exists as to when, exactly, Bride arrived to assist Cottam. Bride told the senate enquiry that he relieved Cottam Tuesday night, Cottam (*Senate Titanic Hearings*, 126) testified that Bride was brought up to relieve him on Wednesday 'about 5 o'clock in the afternoon'. Bride's version is sustained by a telegram sent over his initials at 5.25am Wednesday morning (Booth and Coughlan, *Titanic: Signals of Disaster*, 66). Before Bride arrived Tuesday night or Wednesday morning, Cottam had been on duty continuously for at least sixty hours.

16   Cottam, *Senate Titanic Hearings*, 96, 110, 924; Rostron, *Senate Titanic Hearings*, 34; 'The Carpathia's Progress,' *The Times*, 18 Apr 1912; 'Carpathia not Expected until Thursday Night with Survivors,' *New York Times*, 17 Apr 1912; 'Carpathia off Sable Island,' *Boston Daily Globe*, 17 Apr 1912.

17   Evans, *Senate Titanic Hearings*, 736. Rostron's receipt of *Olympic*'s message late Monday afternoon asking for information surprised him. He had assumed that his morning messages had gone through, but when he summoned Cottam for an explanation, the operator explained that he had not been able to forward them because, until *Olympic* came within range, he had not been able to raise a steamer with equipment powerful enough to transmit them ashore. ('Titanic Survivors Honor Capt. Rostron,' *New York Times*, 30 May 1912.) Cottam had informed White Star's *Baltic* of the situation that morning, but she was heading east across the Atlantic out of contact with land and declined to forward the information to other ships not of the White Star line. (Testimony of Gilbert Balfour (wireless inspector, *Baltic*), *Senate Titanic Hearings*, 1059–60.)

18   Balfour, *Senate Titanic Hearings*, 1057–8; Testimony of James Henry Moore (master, *Mount Temple*), including extracts from the wireless operator's log, SS *Mount Temple*, *Senate Titanic Hearings*, 782; Balfour, including extracts of P. V. [Proces-Verbal] book, Marconi office, steamship *Baltic*, *Senate Titanic Hearings*, 1057–8, 1063; *Mount Temple* P.V., *Senate Titanic Hearings*, 929.

19   'Log as Made by Wireless Operator Moore on SS Olympic,' *Senate Titanic Hearings*, 1137.

20   '10 Liners at Hook Cripple Wireless,' *New York American*, 16 Apr 1912.

21   Cottam, *Senate Titanic Hearings*, 503–4. Sources refer to the town at the mouth of New York harbor as 'Sea Gate,' the Marconi station as 'Seagate'.

22   'Carpathia Here Tonight with Titanic's Survivors,' *New York Times*, 18 Apr 1912.

23   'The Loss of the Titanic,' *The Times*, 17 Apr 1912; 'Many Stations Interfering,' *Boston Daily Globe* (Evening Edition), 18 Apr 1912. See also: '58 Men in First Cabin, 24 in Second were Saved,' *New York American*, 17 Apr 1912; 'Carpathia Should Arrive with the Survivors Late Tonight,' *New York Times*, 18 Apr 1912; 'Amateurs Interfere,' *Boston Daily Globe* (Evening Edition), 16 Apr 1912; and 'Foolish Messages Blocked Wireless,' *New York American*, 20 Apr 1912.

24 'Thrilling Story by Titanic's Surviving Wireless Man,' *New York Times*, 19 Apr 1912; Harold Bride, letter to Marconi Co., *Senate Titanic Hearings*, 1054; 'Carpathia Should Arrive with the Survivors Late Tonight,' *New York Times*, 18 Apr 1912.

25 Booth and Coughlan, *Titanic: Signals of Disaster*, 88; Testimony of Frederick Sammis (chief engineer, Marconi Wireless Telegraph Co.), *Senate Titanic Hearings*, 877; 'Carpathia Should Arrive with the Survivors Late Tonight,' *New York Times*, 18 Apr 1912.

26 'Carpathia Here Tonight with Titanic's Survivors,' *New York Times*, 18 Apr 1912; 'Astor and Widener Gone,' *Boston Daily Globe* (Evening Edition), 18 Apr 1912. A copy of the wireless silence order appears in: Testimony of Guglielmo Marconi, *Senate Titanic Hearings*, 851.

27 'Carpathia Not Expected Until Thursday Night with Survivors… Two Messages from the Carpathia,' *New York Times*, 17 Apr 1912; 'Cunard Line's Messages,' *New York Times*, 18 Apr 1912.

28 Booth and Coughlan, *Titanic: Signals of Disaster*, 72; Cottam, *Senate Titanic Hearings*, 925; Ernest Moore, *Senate Titanic Hearings*, 1131; Bride to Marconi Co., *Senate Titanic Hearings*, 1054; 'Plead with Sable Island,' *New York Times*, 17 Apr 1912; Cottam, *Senate Titanic Hearings*, 504.

29 Paul Heyer, *Titanic Legacy: Disaster as Media Event and Myth* (Westport, CT: Praeger Pub., 1995), 65; Ernest Moore, *Senate Titanic Hearings*, 1133, 1137.

30 Ernest Moore, *Senate Titanic Hearings*, 1137; Booth and Coughlan, Titanic: *Signals of Disaster*, 119–21.

31 Booth and Coughlan, Titanic: *Signals of Disaster*, 71, 120–1.

32 Marconi, *Senate Titanic Hearings*, 854; Cottam, *Senate Titanic Hearings*, 924; Bride, *Senate Titanic Hearings*, 1054; 'Capt. Rostron Explains Wireless Censorship,' *New York American*, 6 May 1912; 'Marconi Pays Visit to the Rescue Ship,' *New York Times*, 19 Apr 1912.

33 Bride, *Senate Titanic Hearings*, 1054; 'Marconi Pays Visit to the Rescue Ship,' *New York Times*, 19 Apr 1912. For more please see '*Carpathia*'s Communications' in the appendix.

34 'Carpathia Should Arrive with the Survivors Late Tonight,' *New York Times*, 18 Apr 1912.

35 Cottam, *Senate Titanic Hearings*, 923; Testimony of C. E. Henry Stengel (passenger, *Titanic*), *Senate Titanic Hearings*, 976.

36 Sammis, *Senate Titanic Hearings*, 866. For more please see '*Carpathia*'s Communications' in the appendix.

37 Cottam, *Senate Titanic Hearings*, 122; 'Log as Made by Wireless Operator Moore on SS "Olympic",' *Senate Titanic Hearings*, 1137–8.

38 'Carpathia Should Arrive with the Survivors Late Tonight,' *New York Times*, 18 Apr 1912; 'Taft Asks About Butt and Artist F. D. Millet,' *New York American*, 18 Apr 1912; 'Deaf to Enquiries for Details,' and 'Carpathia Refuses to Give Facts to President Taft,' *Boston Daily Globe*, 18 Apr 1912; 'Taft Message Is Refused by the Carpathia,' *New York American*, 18 Apr 1912. Both *The Times* and the *Globe* printed the signal as: 'The President of the United States is very anxious to know if Major Butt, Mr. Millet and Mr. Moore are safe. Please inform me at once so that I can transmit to him.'

39 'Offense to Taft Denied,' *New York American*, 18 Apr 1912; 'Taft's Brother in White Star Crowd,' *New York Times*, 18 Apr 1912; Cottam, *Senate Titanic Hearings*, 499; Rostron, *Senate Titanic Hearings*, 32; 'Capt. Rostrum's [*sic*] Story,' *New York American*, 19 Apr 1912.

40   'The Loss of the Titanic,' *The Times*, 17 Apr 12; 'Rescue Ship Arrives – Thousands Gather at the Pier,' *New York Times*, 19 Apr 1912; Bisset, *Tramps and Ladies*, 307.

41   'Marconi Co. Asked "American" in "Name of Humanity" to Put its Man on Board Carpathia,' *New York American*, 23 Apr 1912; 'Awaiting the Carpathia,' *The Times*, 19 Apr 1912.

42   Barratt, *Lost Voices*, 151; Bisset, *Tramps and Ladies*, 307, 308.

43   'Eager-Eyed Crowds Besiege White Star Offices All Day,' *New York American*, 17 Apr 1912; 'Rescue Ship Arrives – Thousands Gather at the Pier,' *New York Times*, 19 Apr 1912; 'Awaiting the Carpathia,' *The Times*, 19 Apr 1912.

44   'Stock Exchange Sends $20,000 to the Pier,' *New York American*, 18 Apr 1912; Gladys Cherry, letter to her mother, 19 Apr 1912, DX/1522/2, MMM; Beesley, *Loss of the SS Titanic*, 152.

45   'Rescue Ship Arrives – Thousands Gather at the Pier,' *New York Times*, 19 Apr 1912; Bisset, *Tramps and Ladies*, 309.

46   'Carpathia Cheered as She Sails Again,' *New York Times*, 20 Apr 1912; 'Carpathia to be Held until Friday; Reporters Barred,' *New York American*, 18 Apr 1912; 'Carpathia, Mourning Ship, Arrives – Silent Thousands at Pier,' *New York American*, 18 Apr 1912; 'Rescue Ship Arrives – Thousands Gather at the Pier,' *New York Times*, 19 Apr 1912.

47   'Rescue Ship Arrives – Thousands Gather at the Pier,' *New York Times*, 19 Apr 1912; '10,000 in Silent Jam at Pier as Carpathia Arrives with Titanic's Sad Remnant,' *New York American*, 19 Apr 1912.

48   'Carpathia Brings the Rescued Survivors Here,' *New York Times*, 28 Apr 1912; 'Rescue Ship Arrives – Thousands Gather at the Pier,' *New York Times*, 19 Apr 1912; *Carpathia*, Cunard 'Ships' Movement Book', 6; Bisset, *Tramps and Ladies*, 311; 'The Lost Liner,' *The Times*, 19 Apr 1912; 'Carpathia Cheered as She Sails Again,' *New York Times*, 20 Apr 1912.

49   'Carpathia, Mourning Ship, Arrives – Silent Thousands at Pier,' *New York American*, 18 Apr 1912; 'Carpathia Brings the Rescued Survivors Here,' *New York Times*, 28 Apr 1912; 'Rescue Ship Arrives – Thousands Gather at the Pier,' *New York Times*, 19 Apr 1912; Cherry, letter to mother, 19 Apr 1912; 'The Lost Liner,' *The Times*, 19 Apr 1912.

50   Bisset, *Tramps and Ladies*, 311; Beesley, *Loss of the SS Titanic*, 153.

51   Story of *New York World* reporter Carlos F. Hurd in *Titanic Commutator* II, no. 24 (Win. 1979): 23–4; 'Carlos F. Hurd, 73, St Louis Reporter,' *New York Times*, 9 June 1950. Hurd's *World* byline also appeared in *The Boston Globe* (Carlos F. Hurd, 'Loss of Titanic,' *Boston Daily Globe* (Evening Edition), 19 Apr 1912).

52, 53   Bisset, *Tramps and Ladies*, 309–10; 310–1.

54, 55   '"My Hands Were Tied," Says Carpathia's Captain as to News Suppression,' *New York American*, 19 Apr 1912.

56   'Captain's Official Reports,' *New York Times*, 20 Apr 1912; Rostron, *Home from the Sea*, 74.

CHAPTER 9

1   Rostron, 'Rescue of the "Titanic" Survivors,' 364; Bisset, *Tramps and Ladies*, 311.

2   'To Call Bruce Ismay in Congress Enquiry,' *New York Times*, 18 Apr 1912. The *Titanic* disaster struck in high circles in the United States government. Down with the ship went Major Archibald Butt, President William Howard Taft's friend and military advisor, who was returning from a visit to the Vatican as the president's envoy. Benjamin Guggenheim,

one of the millionaires claimed by the disaster, was the brother of US Senator Simon Guggenheim of Colorado, while Congressman James Anthony Hughes of West Virginia lost his new son-in-law Lucian Smith in the sinking. ('Bitter on Titanic,' *Washington Post*, 29 May 1912.)

3 'Senators Hasten Here for Enquiry,' *New York Times*, 19 Apr 1912. Charles Lightoller also had hoped to depart New York for England promptly to avoid 'the inquisition that would otherwise be awaiting us. Our luck was distinctly out. We were served with Warrants, immediately on arrival.' (Lightoller, *Titanic and Other Ships*, 254–5.)

4 'Senators Hasten Here for Enquiry,' *New York Times*, 19 Apr 1912; 'Rescue Ship Arrives – Thousands Gather at the Pier,' *New York Times*, 19 Apr 1912.

5 Lightoller, *Titanic and Other Ships*, 225, 255.

6 US Senate, *Titanic Disaster Report*, 1.

7 'Ismay's Escape Causes Comment in London,' *New York American*, 18 Apr 1912; 'Mention of Ismay Angers Widener,' *New York American*, 18 Apr 1912; 'Many Needlessly Died on Titanic,' *New York Times*, 20 Apr 1912; 'Ismay Knew Icebergs Near,' *Boston Daily Globe*, 20 Apr 1912.

8 'Many Needlessly Died on Titanic,' *New York Times*, 20 Apr 1912. During Rostron's testimony (*Senate Titanic Hearings*, 27), Smith asked him about posting lookouts at night. Rostron gave as his 'ordinary complement of a night lookout, two men. We keep one in the crow's nest and one in the eyes – that is, right forward,' a precaution *Titanic*'s Captain Smith notoriously neglected.

9 Rostron, *Senate Titanic Hearings*, 32–3.

10 Rostron, *Senate Titanic Hearings*, 33.

11 Rostron, *Senate Titanic Hearings*, 28, 35.

12 Rostron, *Senate Titanic Hearings*, 35, 37; Ticehurst, *Titanic's Rescuers*, 26.

13 'The Titanic Enquiry,' *The Times*, 20 Jun 1912; Rostron, RNR Service Record ('Employment'), 1; 'Senate Enquiry. The Ship Reported Ahead of the Titanic,' *The Times*, 24 Apr 1912.

14 'Parliament and the Titanic,' *The Times*, 23 Apr 1912; 'Obituary – Lord Mersey,' *The Times*, 4 Sep 1929; Eaton and Haas, *Titanic: Triumph and Tragedy*, 260. Bigham only held the presidency of the Probate, Divorce and Admiralty Division for a year before he retired and was created Baron Mersey in March 1910. After the *Titanic* enquiry, Mersey would remain involved in maritime matters, most notably presiding over the International Conference on Safety of Life at Sea in 1913 and the enquiries into the sinkings of *Empress of Ireland* in 1914 and *Lusitania* in 1915.

15 Wreck Commissioners' Court, 'Proceedings before the Right Hon. Lord Mersey… into the Loss of the SS "Titanic"'; Eaton and Haas, *Triumph and Tragedy*, 260.

16 Leslie Reade, *The Ship That Stood Still: The Californian and her Mysterious Role in the Titanic Disaster* (New York: W. W. Norton, 1993), 235; Lightoller, *Titanic and Other Ships*, 257.

17 Rostron, 'British Titanic Enquiry, 25372–3; 'The Titanic Enquiry,' *The Times*, 22 June 1912. *The New York Times* ('England Thanks Rostron,' 22 June 1912) characterized Rostron as 'loudly cheered' upon receiving these congratulations.

18 Rostron, 'British Titanic Enquiry,' 25353–574. The two questions about the return to New York are 25564 and 25565.

19 Rostron, 'British Titanic Enquiry,' 25540–3; 'The Titanic Enquiry,' *The Times*, 22 Jun 1912; Rostron, RNR Service Record ('Employment'), 1.

20 'Titanic Verdict Is Negligence,' *New York Times*, 29 May 1912; William Alden Smith, Speech to the US Senate, 28 May 1912, Titanic Inquiry Project. Among those listening to Smith's speech from the floor were Senator Simon Guggenheim, brother of *Titanic* victim Benjamin Guggenheim and from the gallery *Titanic* survivor and widow Eloise Smith. ('Bitter on Titanic,' *Washington Post*, 29 May 1912.)

21 US Senate, *Titanic Disaster Report*, 15.

22 Booth and Coughlan, *Titanic: Signals of Disaster*, 146, 151; Haddock *Senate Titanic Hearings*, 1134.

23 Senate Committee on Commerce, *Titanic Disaster Report*, 18.

24 'Bitter on Titanic,' *Washington Post*, 29 May 1912; 'Capt. Arthur Henry Rostron,' US House of Representatives, 62nd Congress, 2nd Session, Report No. 830, United States Congressional Serial Set No. 6132; 'Titanic Hero in Congress,' *Washington Post*, 10 Dec 1912; 'Senators Greet Rostron,' *New York Times*, 10 Dec 1912.

25 'Wreck Commissioner's Enquiry, Report on the Loss of the "Titanic" (SS)... Report of the Court... Rescue by the SS Carpathia,' Titanic Inquiry Project.

CHAPTER 10

1 'Rayner Puts Blame upon Bruce Ismay,' *New York Times*, 20 Apr 1912; 'Senator Rayner Insists Senate Fix the Blame,' *New York American*, 20 Apr 1912; '"Go Faster!" Said Ismay Amid Ice,' *New York American*, 20 Apr 1912; '"Wait, Whip in Hand, for Ismay to Return," Says Bottomley,' *New York American*, 26 Apr 1912; 'Britons Grill Ismay,' *Washington Post*, 5 June 1912; Testimony of J. Bruce Ismay, 'British Titanic Enquiry,' 18866–7. For the most notorious example of Ismay being hanged before the trial, see the editorial cartoon 'Laurels of Infamy for J. Brute Ismay,' *New York American*, 20 Apr 1912.

2 'The Scapegoat,' *Saint Louis Post Dispatch*, 22 Apr 1912. Walter Lord, *The Night Lives On: The Untold Stories and Secrets Behind the Sinking of the 'Unsinkable' Ship – Titanic!* (New York: Avon Books, 1986), 178–81.

3 For an account of Lightoller's life, see: Patrick Stenson, *The Odyssey of C. H. Lightoller* (New York: W. W. Norton, 1984).

4 US Senate, *Titanic Disaster Report*, 11, 12; 'Circumstances in Connection with the SS *Californian*,' *British Wreck Commissioner's Enquiry Report*, Titanic Inquiry Project; Peter Padfield, *The Titanic and the Californian* (New York: The John Day Company, 1965) 17, 177–8, 268–9, 278–9; Testimony of Herbert Stone, 'British Titanic Enquiry,' 8028. For more on the controversy surrounding Captain Stanley Lord, Second Officer Herbert Stone and the *Californian* please see 'Stanley Lord, Herbert Stone and the *Californian*' in the appendix.

5 'Marconi Cheered for Wireless Feats,' *New York Times*, 18 Apr 1912; 'Great Ovation for Marconi,' *Boston Daily Globe* (Evening Edition), 18 Apr 1912. See also: 'Marconi Urges Need of Strong Wireless,' *New York Times*, 19 Apr 1912.

6 'Titanic Hero in Congress,' *Washington Post*, 10 Dec 1912; 'Loving Cup to Rostron from Titanic's Rescued,' *New York American*, 20 Apr 1912; 'Carpathia Cheered as She Sails Again,' *New York Times*, 20 Apr 1912. The better-known presentation of a second loving cup by Mrs Margaret Tobin Brown would occur when *Carpathia* returned to New York at the end of the following month. With insufficient time to send her laundry ashore for cleaning, *Carpathia* swapped laundry with *Saxonia*, moored across the pier.

7 'Rostron Lunches with Mrs. Astor,' *New York American*, 1 June 1912; *Carpathia*, Cunard 'Ships' Movement Book,' 6; Bisset, *Tramps and Ladies*, 313.

8   *Carpathia*, Cunard 'Ships' Movement Book,' 6; Bisset, *Tramps and Ladies*, 313–14.

9   'Crowds to Thank Rostron,' *New York American*, 29 May 1912.

10   'Titanic Survivors Honor Capt. Rostron,' *New York Times*, 30 May 1912; Bisset, *Tramps and Ladies*, 239.

11   'Survivors of Titanic Lavish Gifts upon the Carpathia's Captain,' *New York American*, 30 May 1912; '$2,500 to Rostron by Mrs. Widener,' *New York American*, 30 Apr 1912; 'Titanic Survivors Honor Capt. Rostron,' *New York Times*, 30 May 1912.

12   'Survivors of Titanic Lavish Gifts upon the Carpathia's Captain,' *New York American*, 30 May 1912; 'Titanic Survivors Honor Capt. Rostron,' *New York Times*, 30 May 1912. *The New York Times* reported that *Carpathia*'s chief and second engineers, first-class doctor, purser and chief steward all received gold medals like Rostron's, while the ship's other officers received silver medals and the crew was awarded bronze medals. Bisset, however, said he received a gold medal, a claim bourn out by the '14kt' stenciled on the back of the one that appears in a photograph in his memoirs (*Tramps and Ladies*, 239).

13   'Mrs. Astor Gives Luncheon Today to Capt. Rostron,' *New York American*, 31 May 1912; 'Audience Cheers Rostron,' *New York Times*, 31 May 1912.

14   'Mrs. Astor Gives Luncheon Today to Capt. Rostron,' *New York American*, 31 May 1912; 'Mrs. J. B. Thayer Gives a Dinner for Rostron,' *New York American*, 1 June 1912; '$10,000 in Gold for Rostron,' *New York American*, 2 June 1912; 'Capt. Rostron at Concert,' *New York Times*, 3 June 1912.

15   '$10,000 to Capt. Rostron,' *New York Times*, 4 June 1912; 'The Brave Captain Rostron Should Be Fitly Rewarded,' *New York American*, 28 Apr 1912. For Rostron's convenience, the money was converted to £2,052, 8s, in a draft on the London County and Westminster Bank.

16   '$2,500 to Rostron by Mrs. Widener,' *New York American*, 30 Apr 1912.

17   '$2,500 to Rostron by Mrs. Widener,' *New York American*, 30 Apr 1912; '$10,000 to Capt. Rostron,' *New York Times*, 4 June 1912; 'For a Purse for Captain Rostron,' *New York American*, 28 Apr 1912; 'New York American's Rostron Purse Fund,' *New York American*, 6 May 1912; '$10,000 in Gold for Rostron,' *New York American*, 2 June 1912; 'Captain Rostron Gets $10,000 Purse,' *New York American*, 4 June 1912. Six years later, *The New York Times* ('Carpathia Sunk; 5 of Crew Killed,' 20 July 1918) reported that Rostron ultimately 'received about $25,000 [i.e. £5,000] from Americans as a token of appreciation for his work.' The *Liverpool Echo* ('Hero of Titanic Disaster Death Of Famous Cunard Captain,' 5 Nov 1940) reported that company rules had prohibited Rostron from accepting his £2,000 cash gift in 1912, but that the money was invested for him and he received it at his retirement in 1931, by which time, said the paper, it had increased in value to £20,000.

18   'Captain Rostron Gets $10,000 Purse,' *New York American*, 4 June 1912.

19   'Captain Rostron Gets $10,000 Purse,' *New York American*, 4 June 1912; '$10,000 in Gold for Rostron,' *New York American*, 2 June 1912. In his 2 June interview, the *American* reported Rostron as saying that his eldest son, then eleven, 'was exhibiting a talent for the profession of mechanical engineer,' and that the reward would give Rostron 'enough money to educate him in that profession'. The article continued with Rostron's diplomatic suggestion that Columbia University's engineering school in New York might be the place for such an education. Whatever the veracity of that exchange, Rostron's eldest boy did become an engineer.

20   'Girls Give Rostron Mascot,' *New York American*, 5 June 1912; *Carpathia*, Cunard 'Ships' Movement Book,' 6. That same sailing day, Rostron also sat for an affidavit submitted to the British enquiry concerning *Californian*'s presence at the scene of the disaster.

For more discussion of this, please see 'Stanley Lord, Herbert Stone and the *Californian*' in the appendix.

21 'Senators Greet Rostron,' *New York Times*, 10 Dec 1912; 'Titanic Hero in Congress,' *Washington Post*, 10 Dec 1912; 'Commodore of Cunard,' *Southern Daily Echo*, 5 Nov 1930; 'Sir Arthur Rostron Sails as Commodore,' *New York Times*, 29 July 1928; Ticehurst, *Titanic's Rescuers*, 9.

22 Rostron, *Home from the Sea*, 77; 'Congress Thanks Rostron,' *New York Times*, 2 July 1912; 'Approves Rostron Thanks,' *Washington Post*, 11 July 1912.

23 'News and Notes of the Art World,' *New York Times*, 2 Mar 1913; 'Rostron Gets Medal To-day,' *New York Times*, 1 Mar 1913; 'Rostron Here for Medal,' *Washington Post*, 1 Mar 1913; Copy of advertisement for Medallic Art Company, Danbury, CT, (Ephemera envelope) DX/949R, MMM, 1988, 258, MMM *The New York Times* ('News and Notes') said the medal was struck by Henry Weil of New York.

24 *Carmania*, 'Passenger and Crew Lists of Vessels Arriving at New York, New York,' 24 Feb 1913, microfilm T715 2018 (Records of the Immigration and Naturalization Service, p. 122), US National Archives, Washington DC, 'Rostron Here for Medal,' *Washington Post*, 1 Mar 1913; 'Rostron Gets His Medal,' *Washington Post*, 2 Mar 1913; 'Capt. Rostron Gets Medal,' *New York Times*, 2 Mar 1913.

25 'Rostron Here for Medal,' *Washington Post*, 1 Mar 1913; 'Rostron Gets His Medal,' *Washington Post*, 2 Mar 1913; 'Capt. Rostron Gets Medal,' *New York Times*, 2 Mar 1913; Ticehurst, *Titanic's Rescuers*, 9; 'American Cross of Honor,' *New York Times*, 13 Aug 1907.

26 Rostron, *Home from the Sea*, 78; 'Shipping and Mails,' *New York Times*, 2 Mar 1913; 'Awards to British Seamen by Foreign Governments,' #96, BT261/8, NAK; Ticehurst, *Titanic's Rescuers*, 10.

27 'The Titanic Rescue. Carpathia's Captain Honoured,' and 'The Carpathia's Captain,' *Liverpool Echo*, 26 June 1912. The society, established in 1839, awarded its first gold medal for a rescue at sea the following year. (Sydney Jeffery, *The Liverpool Shipwreck and Humane Society, 1839–1939* (Liverpool: Daily Post Printers, n.d. [1939?]), 8, 35.)

28 'The Titanic Rescue. Carpathia's Captain Honoured,' *Liverpool Echo*, 26 June 1912. Eight days after decorating Rostron, the Society presented its silver medal and certificate of thanks to *Carpathia*'s Chief Officer Thomas Hankinson, Chief Engineer Alexander Johnstone, Purser Ernest Brown, Chief Steward Evan Hughes, her wireless operator, Harold Cottam and the ship's doctors, Frank McGee, Arpad Leuyel and V. Risicati. ('The Titanic Disaster. Carpathia's Officers' Rewards,' *The Times*, 5 July 1912; Jeffery, *Liverpool Shipwreck and Humane Society*, 66–7.) At another ceremony in December Chief Engineer Johnstone received 'a substantial cheque,' a silver tea and coffee set and a punch bowl. *Carpathia*'s other engineering officers received gold watches 'with suitable inscriptions and monograms,' and a check for forty-eight pounds was presented to the sailors' and firemen's union to be distributed among the forty-eight firemen, trimmers and greasers involved in the rescue. ('Liverpool Awards to Carpathia Crew,' *The Times*, 16 Dec 1912.)

29 'Cunard Company and the Titanic,' *The Times*, 11 June 1912; 'Reward Carpathia's Crew,' *New York Times*, 11 June 1912. Bisset (*Tramps and Ladies*, 314) remembered the crew's award as two months' pay. If so, perhaps Cunard matched White Star's tribute. Cash also came to the crew from survivors and other donors. The *Liverpool Echo* ('Carpathia Captain's Cup,' 20 June 1912) mentioning Rostron's cash award of £2000 – the *American*'s $10,000 – noted that 'the officers and crew of the liner were also handsomely rewarded'. In America they were even celebrated in song. In June 1912, A. W. Perry and Sons Music Company of Sedalia, Missouri, published the 'Carpathia Grand March' for piano, composed by one E. Moore and 'dedicated to the brave officers and crew of the rescue-ship Carpathia'. The song lacks lyrics,

alas. ('Carpathia Grand March' (sheet music), *Titanic Commutator* Vol. II, Issue 24 (Win. 1979): 25–6; 'Catalog of Copyright Entries,' Musical Compositions, Library of Congress Copyright Office, 1912, entry 11447, 14 June 1912, p. 676.)

30 Jim Gawler, *Lloyd's Medals, 1836–1989: A History of Medals Awarded by the Corporation of Lloyd's* (Toronto: Hart Publishing, 1989), 19; 'Rewards Given by His Majesty's Government,' 1910–32, BT261/6, NAK; 'The Commons… The Carpathia and the Titanic,' *The Times*, 18 June 1912.

31 Ticehurst, *Titanic's Rescuers*, 8; 'France Honors Rostron,' *New York Times*, 28 Feb 1929. For some examples of Rostron cited as Titanic hero years later see: 'Marine Heroes Honored,' *New York Times*, 2 Nov 1926; 'Sir Arthur Rostron Sails as Commodore,' *New York Times*, 29 July 1928; 'Footnotes on a Week's Headliners,' *New York Times*, 16 Nov 1930.

32 'Capt. Rostrum's [*sic*] Story,' *New York American*, 19 Apr 1912; '$10,000 in Gold for Rostron,' *New York American*, 2 June 1912.

33 '$10,000 in Gold for Rostron,' *New York American*, 2 June 1912; 'Capt. Rostron Guest of Mrs. J. J. Astor,' *New York Times*, 1 June 1912; Rostron, *Home from the Sea*, 188–9.

34 '$10,000 in Gold for Rostron,' *New York American*, 2 June 1912; 'Titanic Survivors Honor Capt. Rostron,' *New York Times*, 30 May 1912; 'Ismay Knew Icebergs Near,' *Boston Daily Globe*, 20 Apr 1912; 'Carpathia Sails Again,' *Washington Post*, 20 Apr 1912.

35 'Captain Rostron Gets $10,000 Purse,' *New York American*, 4 June 1912; 'Audience Cheers Rostron,' *New York Times*, 31 May 1912.

36 Rostron, *Home from the Sea*, dedication page. Beesley (*Loss of the SS* Titanic, 133) described Rostron's as 'a modesty that is conspicuous in its nobility,' and we have the *New York American*'s effusions noted in the text, but others less rapturous made the same point. He impressed his grandson John Rostron as 'quietly-spoken' and granddaughter Rosemary Rostron Pettet as 'a humble man'. (Arthur John Rostron, interview with the author at the National Museum of Scotland, Edinburgh, 18 July 2011; Ray Turner, 'West End's First Blue Plaque Unveiled,' *Eastleigh News*, 15 Apr 2012.)

37 Rostron, 'Captains' Register,' 18569, 033; 'Death of Famous Captain,' *Southern Daily Echo*, 5 Nov 1940. Ironically, Rostron was assigned to relieve *Lusitania*'s regular master, James W. T. Charles, so that Charles could serve as a member of the Royal Commission on Life Saving Apparatus at Sea, meeting to address the problems manifested by the *Titanic* disaster. ('Gen. Booth Arrives; Will Visit the West,' *New York Times*, 1 Nov 1913.)

38 'The Olympic to Leave Liverpool,' *New York Times*, 18 Aug 1914; 'Atlantic Travelers,' *New York Times*, 3 Sep 1914; '5,000 from America to Submarine Zone,' *New York Times*, 11 May 1915; 'Three Munition Ships Sail,' *New York Times*, 24 Feb 1917; *Carpathia*, Cunard 'Ships' Movement Book,' nos. 7 (23 Nov 1913 through 26 Jan 1915), 8 (27 Jan 1915 through 10 June 1916), 9 (11 June 1916 through 17 Nov 1917) and 11 (18 Nov 1917 through 26 Apr 1919), D42/GM1/7,8,9,11, Cunard Collection, SJL.

39 'Carpathia Sunk; 5 of Crew Killed,' *New York Times*, 20 July 1918; 'Carpathia Cut in Half,' *New York Times*, 21 July 1918; 'Tells of Carpathia Sinking,' *New York Times*, 7 Aug 1918; 'The Carpathia Torpedoed,' *The Times*, 20 July 1918.

CHAPTER 11

1 Rostron, RNR Service Record, 1; Bisset, *Commodore*, 3, 4, 24; Sir Archibald Hurd, *A Merchant Fleet at War* (London: Cassell and Company, Ltd., 1920), 12.

2   Rostron, RNR Service Record, 1, 2. Samuel McNeil (*In Great Waters*, 103) underwent exactly the same course of study. At age 26, after two years as a sub-lieutenant, RNR, he took the gunnery and torpedo courses, followed by a year's deployment, the whole programme lasting eighteen to twenty months.

3   Rostron, RNR Service Record, 2; *Conway's All the World's Fighting Ships, 1860–1905* (London: Conway Maritime Press, Ltd., 1979), 65, 66.

4   *Conway's… Fighting Ships*, 66.

5   *Conway's… Fighting Ships*, 76–7; Rostron, *Home from the Sea*, 37–8; Rostron, RNR Service Record, 2; Rostron, 'Lloyd's Captains' Registers', 18569, 33. In *Home from the Sea* (36), Rostron indicates that his ship on China Station was HMS *Iphigenia*, an Apollo-class cruiser like *Pique*. Perhaps, writing more than thirty years later, Rostron confused the latter with the former and remembered *Iphigenia* from some later deployment. His service record lists China service in *Grafton* and never shows duty in *Iphigenia*.

6   Rostron, RNR Service Record, 2.

7   Rostron, RNR Service Record, 1, 2, 3; 'Birthday Honours… RNR Officers' Decoration,' *The Times*, 9 Nov 1909. Rostron may have been recalled to service during the Russo–Japanese War of 1904–5. His service record does not indicate this, but the story was repeated often enough in newspapers in later years to give it some credence. If so, that service occurred in the second half of 1904 and almost certainly did not involve a return to the Far East. (Rostron, RNR Service Record, 2; Rostron, Lloyd's Captains' Registers, 18567, v. 69.) For mention of Rostron's alleged service with the Royal Navy during the Russo–Japanese War, see: 'Sir Arthur Rostron to Retire from Sea,' *New York Times*, 1 Nov 1930; 'Captain Rostron, Titanic Rescuer,' *New York Times*, 6 Nov 1940. The *New York American* ('$10,000 in Gold for Rostron,' 2 June 1912) had this service taking place aboard HMS *Grafton*, which suggests that the paper confused the Russo–Japanese War of 1904–5 with the Spanish–American War of 1898 and Rostron's coincidental 1897–8 deployment to the Far East and that other papers then repeated that error.

8   The Royal Navy certainly took the view that Rostron was exclusively a merchant sailor during the First World War. The government form listing his medals won as a merchant seaman contains the handwritten notation 'Oak Leaf issued by Admly [Admiralty] in error; applicant had no Naval Service but [and?] Oak Leaf not to be issued by this Deptmt.' ('Medal card of Rostron, Arthur Henry', British World War I Medals issued to merchant seamen, BT351/1, image 1243; reference 122103, NAK.)

9   Rostron, 'Lloyd's Captains' Register', 18569, 33; 'Fear Wilson Abroad Zimmerman Thinks', *New York Times*, 27 Jan 1913; 'Gen. Booth Arrives; Will Visit the West,' *New York Times*, 1 Nov 1913.

10 Hyde, *Cunard and the North Atlantic*, 136, 165, 166; McCart, *Atlantic Liners of the Cunard Line*, 86–7. Cunard also purchased the Anchor Line, one if its North Atlantic competitors with routes to India, in 1912 and acquired the Commonwealth and Dominion Line, a cargo service to Australia and New Zealand, in 1916.

11 Bisset, *Commodore*, 216.

12 Bisset, *Commodore*, 214, 224–5.

13 Hyde, *Cunard and the North Atlantic*, 132; McCart, *Atlantic Liners of the Cunard Line*, 93, 94; *Lloyd's Register of British and Foreign Shipping, 1915–6*, v. 2. The third ship of the programme, *Aurania*, built by Swan Hunter at Newcastle, was not completed until 1916. She was lost while trooping two years later and never sailed in revenue service. ('New Liner for the Cunard,' *The Times*, 19 Dec 1913; Ransome–Wallis, *North Atlantic Panorama*, 47.)

[14] Cunard 'Register of Officers,' Case 257, Arthur Henry Rostron; Rostron, RNR Service Record, 2.

[15] *Alaunia*, Cunard 'Ships' Movement Book,' 6 and 7.

[16] *Alaunia*, Cunard 'Ships' Movement Book,' 7. The March voyage featured an unusual four-day layover at Portland, Maine, on the return trip because *Alaunia* 'in leaving the harbour, touched the ground but did not stop'. In the same announcement *Lloyd's List* (18 Mar 1914, 21) reported that the ship 'has been surveyed and found undamaged'.

[17] *Lloyd's List*, 27 May 1914, 21; 1 Jun 1914, 32; *Alaunia*, Cunard 'Ships' Movement Book,' 7; Ransome–Wallis, *North Atlantic Panorama*, 29. McNeil (*In Great Waters*, 146) described the Canadian service as 'not monotonous, by any means; most other routes can be… but this particular one gives you more to think about. There is often plenty of fog and not a little ice. Still, no matter what you get, there is always that wonderful river, the St Lawrence and with it, in summer or autumn, views that compensate you for all your previous trials.'

[18] *Alaunia*, Cunard 'Ships' Movement Book,' 7; 'Dodging Cruisers, Liners Reach Port,' *New York Times*, 18 Aug 1914; Rostron, *Home from the Sea*, 80–2.

[19] Rostron, *Home from the Sea*, 82; Hyde, *Cunard and the North Atlantic*, 160; *Alaunia*, Cunard 'Ships' Movement Book,' 7.

[20] *Alaunia*, 'Ships' Movement Book', 7; Rostron, *Home from the Sea*, 83–5; 'Lloyd's Weekly Index Confidential Index to the Movements of Allied Vessels,' (microfilm) Reels 245 and 246, GLL.

[21] John Keegan, *The First World War* (New York: Vintage, 2000), 237.

[22] Keegan, *First World War*, 236, 37; Bisset, *Commodore*, 46.

[23] Keegan, *First World War*, 238–40.

[24] Victor Rudenno, *Gallipoli: Attack from the Sea* (New Haven, CT: Yale University Press, 2008), 47; Keegan, *First World War*, 237, 240.

[25] Rostron, *Home from the Sea*, 86; Fred W. Odhams, letter from Alexandria, Egypt, to his mother and sister, 7 Apr 1915, Documents: Odhams, F. W., 93/25/1, IWM; *Alaunia*, Cunard 'Ships' Movement Book,' 7.

[26] Odhams, letter, 7 April 1915; *Alaunia*, Cunard 'Ships' Movement Book,' 7.

[27] Keegan, *First World War*, 235, 242; Rostron, *Home from the Sea*, 79, 86–9.

[28] Keegan, *First World War*, 241–2, 245.

[29] Bisset, *Commodore*, 63; Michael Hickey, *Gallipoli* (London: John Murray, 1995), 142–3; Nigel Steel and Peter Hart, *Defeat at Gallipoli* (London: Papermac, 1995), 353.

[30] Rostron, *Home from the Sea*, 94–5, 116–17. Rostron was not alone in this suspicion, either during the war or after. See: Sir Archibald Hurd, *The Merchant Navy, vol. 3: History of the First World War* (London: John Murray, 1929), 299. And even if not directly attacked, hospital ships were still vulnerable to the hazards of war. The White Star line lost *Britannic*, the third of its Olympic class, to a mine in the Aegean on 18 November 1916, without her ever seeing revenue service (Brinnin, *Sway of the Grand Saloon*, 385).

[31] Rostron, *Home from the Sea*, 94–5, 96; *Alaunia*, Cunard 'Ships' Movement Book,' 7 and 8.

[32] Keegan, *First World War*, 248; Sgt. H. Elliot, RAMC, diary (10 July 1915 to 12 Mar 1916), entries for 10, 14, 17 July, Documents: Elliot, H., 99/62/1, IWM.

[33] Elliot, diary, 20, 22–24 July 1915.

34 Elliot, diary, 25 and 29 July, 8–12 Aug, 22 Oct and 1 Dec 1915.

35 Rostron, *Home from the Sea*, 98; Keegan, *First World War*, 248.

36 *Alaunia*, Cunard 'Ships' Movement Book,' 8; Rostron, 'Lloyd's Captains' Register,' 18569, 33.

CHAPTER 12

1 *Mauretania*, Cunard 'Ships' Movement Book,' 7.

2 Aylmer, *RMS Mauretania*, 56.

3 Hickey, *Gallipoli*, 212; Bisset, *Commodore*, 52, 54, 57.

4 *Mauretania*, Cunard 'Ships' Movement Book' 7; Bisset, *Commodore*, 55, 57, 61, 75, 77; Hickey, *Gallipoli*, 243; *Mauretania*, Cunard 'Ships' Movement Book,' 8; Aylmer, *RMS Mauretania*, 56. Even with *Mauretania*'s operations confined to the Mediterranean, Bisset (*Commodore*, 53–5, 75–7) documented the constant logistical struggle to provide enough coal to keep her moving.

5 *Mauretania*, Cunard 'Ships' Movement Book' 8; 'Mauretania's War Log Is Now Told,' *New York Evening Post*, 2 Jan 1919; Bisset, *Commodore*, 78; Rostron, *Home from the Sea*, 115.

6 Bisset, *Commodore*, 78, 80; 'War Log of the Mauretania,' *New York Evening Post*, 2 Jan 1919.

7 Rostron, *Home from the Sea*, 114; 'War Log of the Mauretania,' *New York Evening Post*, 2 Jan 1919.

8 McNeil, *In Great Waters*, 163–4.

9 Steel and Hart, *Defeat at Gallipoli*, 353; Bisset, *Commodore*, 52, 53, 79.

10 'War Log of the Mauretania,' *New York Evening Post*, 2 Jan 1919; Bisset, *Commodore*, 52, 65.

11 Bisset, *Commodore*, 65–6. As if that weren't enough excitement for one evening, within twelve hours, *Mauretania*, running blacked out at top speed, had a sideswipe collision with the blacked out British freighter *Cardiff Hall*. The freighter's bow struck *Mauretania* on her starboard side at her fourth funnel, holing a coal bunker and forcing her to put in at Malta for patch repairs before resuming her voyage home. (Bisset, *Commodore*, 69, 71, 72.)

12 Rostron, *Home from the Sea*, 98, 119.

13 *Mauretania*, Cunard 'Ships' Movement Book,' 8; 'Lloyd's Weekly Confidential Index,' Reel 248; Bisset, *Commodore*, 80–1.

14 Bisset, *Commodore*, 81–2; *Mauretania*, Cunard 'Ships' Movement Book,' 8; 'Lloyd's Weekly Confidential Index,' Reel 248.

15 *Mauretania*, Cunard 'Ships' Movement Book,' 8; 'Use of Hospital Ships,' *The Times*, 6 Dec 1915; Hurd, *Merchant Navy, v. 3*, 299; Bisset, *Commodore*, 82–3.

16 Bisset, *Commodore*, 80, 81; Hurd, *Merchant Navy, v. 3*, 299. This statement, circulated by the Allies, was the first official announcement of *Mauretania*'s service as a hospital ship. ('Use of Hospital Ships,' *The Times*, 6 Dec 1915.)

17 *Mauretania*, Cunard 'Ships' Movement Book', 8; Bisset, *Commodore*, 83. I have used the meticulous memoirist Bisset's figures (*Commodore* 80, 81, 83) for casualties transported on *Mauretania*, which total 6307 for her three hospital voyages. Aylmer (*RMS Mauretania*, 56) says *Mauretania* brought back 6298 from Mudros, but carried 8655 wounded and medical staff during the war. However, these three voyages were the vessel's only service as a hospital ship. Seven weeks after the end of the war, Rostron estimated that *Mauretania* transported 'about

9,000' casualties as a hospital ship. ('War Log of the Mauretania,' *New York Evening Post*, 2 Jan 1919.)

[18] *Mauretania*, Cunard 'Ships' Movement Book', 8; Bisset, *Commodore*, 84; Rostron, 'Lloyd's Captains' Register,' 18569, 33.

[19] Elliot, diary, 20 Dec 1915; Keegan, *First World War*, 248, 249; Steel and Hart, *Defeat at Gallipoli*, 416.

[20] Keegan, *First World War*, 248; Robert O'Neill, 'For Want of Critics... The Tragedy of Gallipoli,' 65–81, in: Sir Martin Gilbert (intro.), *The Straits of War: Gallipoli Remembered* (Phoenix Mill, Gloucestershire, UK: Sutton Publishing Co., 2000), 70; Prince Philip, Duke of Edinburgh, 'Ends and Means,' 24–36, in Gilbert, *Straits of War*, 36; Rudenno, *Gallipoli: Attack from the Sea*, 271.

[21] Leonard Thornton, 'Echoes of Gallipoli,' 109–21, in Gilbert, *Straits of War*, 116.

[22] Rostron, *Home from the Sea*, 86, 87; Rudenno, *Gallipoli*, 66.

[23] Rostron, *Home from the Sea*, 102, 103; McNeil, *In Great Waters*, 168.

[24] Rostron, *Home from the Sea*, 100–3. On idling in the Naval Transport offices 'pending the convenience of some official[, s]ome of us adopted the method of saying: "If So-and-So is engaged, I shall be at – . Please send and inform me when he is at liberty."'

[25] McNeil, *In Great Waters*, 152.

[26] Steel and Hart, *Defeat at Gallipoli*, 301; Bisset, *Commodore*, 61, 63.

[27] Keegan, *First World War*, 250, 253–5.

[28] McCart, *Atlantic Liners of the Cunard Line*, 37; Rostron, *Home from the Sea*, 120, 123; *Ivernia*, Cunard 'Ships' Movement Book,' 8 and 9; Rostron, *Home from the Sea*, 120.

[29] Rostron, *Home from the Sea*, 104, 121.

[30] *Ivernia*, Cunard 'Ships' Movement Book,' 9; 'Lloyd's Weekly Confidential Index,' Reel 248, issues 20–27 Aug 1916 to 17–23 Dec 1916; 'Lusitania's Captain Quits,' *New York Times*, 11 Nov 1919; McCart, *Atlantic Liners of the Cunard Line*, 36; 'Capt. Turner Saved in New Torpedoing,' *New York Times*, 12 Jan 1917.

[31] Alymer, *RMS Mauretania*, 56; 'Mauretania on Fire,' *The Times*, 26 July 1921; *Mauretania*, Cunard 'Ships' Movement Book,' 9.

[32] Rostron, *Home from the Sea*, 124–5.

[33] Rostron, *Home from the Sea*, 125–7; *Mauretania*, Cunard 'Ships' Movement Book,' 9.

[34] Rostron, *Home from the Sea*, 127; *Andania*, Cunard 'Ships' Movement Book,' 9 and 11; 'Artillery Moved Germans,' *New York Times*, 26 Mar 1917.

[35] McCart, *Atlantic Liners of the Cunard Line*, 36–7; *Saxonia*, Cunard 'Ships' Movement Book,' 9 and 11; Rostron, 'Lloyd's Captains' Registers,' 18569, 33.

[36] *Saxonia*, Cunard 'Ships' Movement Book,' 11; Rostron, *Home from the Sea*, 127; 'The Halifax Explosion,' CBC Canada, www.cbc.ca/halifaxexplosion (accessed 27 Oct 2012).

[37] *Carmania*, Cunard 'Ships' Movement Book,' 11.

[38] 'Mauretania's War Log,' *New York Evening Post*, 2 Jan 1919.

[39] 'Mauretania's War Log,' *New York Evening Post*, 2 Jan 1919; 'Commodore of Cunard,' *Southern Daily Echo*, 5 Nov 1930. The Admiralty introduced dazzle painting in 1917 and over

2,700 British merchant ships were thus camouflaged by October 1918. (Exhibit 'First World War,' viewed 15 July 2011, IWM.)

40 Rostron, RNR Service Record, 1; Rostron, *Home from the Sea*, 101.

41 'Mauretania's War Log,' *New York Evening Post*, 2 Jan 1919. *Mauretania's* seven wartime voyages of 1918 from Liverpool to New York and return occurred from 11 Mar to 1 Apr; 10 Apr to 6 May; 14 May to 11 June; 15 June to 7 July; 17 July to ?; 17 Aug to ?; and 30 Oct to 17 Nov 1918. ('Lloyd's Weekly Confidential Index,' Reel 250 (6 Jan to 23 Nov 1918).) Aylmer (*RMS Mauretania*, 56) gives the total of soldiers transported on the seven voyages as 33,610.

42 Sir Thomas Royden, letter to Sir Ronald Waterhouse, 2 Feb 1926, Royden Correspondence File, D42/C2/121, Cunard Collection, SJL; 'Mauretania's War Log,' *New York Evening Post*, 2 Jan 1919. Rostron also may have avoided engaging the submarine because he lacked faith in *Mauretania's* weapons. He noted that they were elderly and that the forward guns tended to immerse themselves in any sort of a sea at the speeds *Mauretania* maintained. (Rostron, *Home from the Sea*, 133.)

43 Rostron, *Home from the Sea*, 142; 'Lloyd's Weekly Confidential Index,' Reel 250 (issues of 6–12 Jan 1918 to 17–23 Nov 1918); *Mauretania*, Cunard 'Ships' Movement Book,' 11; '3,707 Troops Here on Mauretania,' *New York Times*, 31 Dec 1918; Aylmer, *RMS Mauretania*, 56; Rostron, RNR Service Record, 1.

44 Bisset, *Commodore*, 107; 'Liners in the War,' *The Times*, 25 Sep 1934; Hyde, *Cunard and the North Atlantic*, 163, 169.

45 Rostron, *Home from the Sea*, 107; 'Sea Transport Medal,' [South African War, 1899–1902], 75, ADM 171/52, NAK; 'Medal card of Rostron, Arthur Henry,' BT351/1, image 1243; reference 122103, NAK; Cdr. A. H. Rostron, RNR, 'Medals and Clasps Issued,' 29, ADM 171/63, NAK; John W. Mussell (ed.), *The Medal Yearbook, 2011* (Honiton, Devon: Token Publishing, Ltd., 2011), 170–1; Sarah Paterson (comp.), *Tracing Your Family History, Army* (London: Imperial War Museum, 2006), 25.

46 Rostron, RNR Service Record, 2; Supplement to the *London Gazette*, 31 May 1916, 5416–7.

47 *London Gazette*, 1 Jan 1919, 111, 116; Rostron, RNR Service Record, 6; 'Made King's Aid [*sic*],' *Oakland [CA] Tribune*, 19 Mar 1924. Rostron petitioned for retirement at the rank of commodore, but did not get his wish. Later he also petitioned the Admiralty for permission to wear on his naval uniform several decorations he had received from other countries over the years. The Admiralty authorized him to wear his Congressional Gold Medal and his Légion d'honneur, both awarded by foreign governments, but not his American Cross of Honor, a private award. (Rostron, RNR Service Record, 2, 8.)

48 The Imperial War Museum's exhibit 'Survival at Sea: Stories of the Merchant Navy in the Second World War' (viewed 15 July 2011) gives the total killed in the British merchant and fishing fleets during the First World War as 14,721; Bisset (*Commodore*, 71) offers figures of sixteen thousand men killed in the British merchant service and 3400 seagoing British ships sunk; Hyde, *Cunard and the North Atlantic*, 170.

49 Rostron, *Home from the Sea*, 199; 'Lloyd's War Losses: The First World War: Casualties to Shipping through Enemy Causes, 1914–1918. A Facsimile Reprint of the Original Held at the Guildhall Library, City of London' (London: Lloyd's of London Press, Ltd., 1990), 12, 31, 63, 82, 187, 225; Hurd, *Merchant Fleet at War*, 40, 42, 43, 54, 111–12, 118. Another of Rostron's former Cunard commands, *Campania*, which had been converted into the seaplane carrier HMS *Campania*, sank six days before the Armistice after dragging anchor in the Firth of Forth and colliding with two other warships.

[50] Rostron, *Home from the Sea*, 83.

[51] John Rostron, interview, 18 July 2011; John Rostron, letter to the author, 21 Oct 2011; 'Medal Card of Rostron George Cheshire Regiment 36988 Private Machine Gun Corps Second Lieutenant,' WO 372/17, NAK; Commonwealth War Graves Commission, 'Index No. M. R. 20, Arras Memorial, Part XIX,' 1099; 'Transcriptions of the Memorial Inscriptions… Christ Church, Walmsley, Bolton,' 97; Bolton Church Institute School War Memorial, 'Names, 1914–1918, George Rostron.'

[52] Keegan, *First World War*, 406–7, 408, 410–12.

CHAPTER 13

[1] Rostron, *Home from the Sea*, 1.

[2] Rostron, 'Lloyd's Captains' Register,' 18569, 33; Rostron, RNR Service Record, 1; Humfrey Jordan, *Mauretania: Landfalls and Departures of Twenty–Five Years* (London: Hodder and Stoughton, 1936), 320.

[3] 'Mauretania Goes 30.5 Miles an Hour,' *New York Times*, 22 Sep 1907; Aylmer, *RMS Mauretania*, 26–7; Jordan, *Mauretania*, 318; 'From the Tyne to the Mersey in the Mauretania,' *The Times*, 25 Oct 1907.

[4] 'The Trials of the Mauretania,' *The Times*, 8 Nov 1907; Aylmer, *RMS Mauretania*, 17.

[5] Aylmer, *RMS Mauretania*, 17–18; 'The Cunard Express Liners Lusitania and Mauretania' (1907; reprint, *Ocean Liners of the Past, No. 2. in a series of reprints from 'The Shipbuilder,'* Greenwich, CT: New York Graphic Society, Ltd., 1970), plates 5 and 6 (*Mauretania* deck plan); Jordan, *Mauretania*, 318–19; 'From the Tyne to the Mersey in the Mauretania,' *The Times*, 25 Oct 1907.

[6] Jordan, *Mauretania*, 319; *The Cunard Turbine-Driven Quadruple-Screw Atlantic Liner 'Mauretania'* (1907; reprint: Wellingborough, Eng.: Patrick Stephens Ltd., 1987), 3.

[7] 'The Mauretania's Trials,' *The Times*, 18 Sep 1907; 'The Mauretania's Trials,' *The Times*, 19 Sep 1907; 'From the Tyne to the Mersey in the Mauretania,' *The Times*, 25 Oct 1907; John Maxtone-Graham, *Only Way to Cross*, 38–9.

[8] Aylmer, *RMS Mauretania*, 29; 'The Atlantic Passage,' *The Times*, 17 Oct 1907; 'The Trials of the Mauretania,' *The Times*, 8 Nov 1907.

[9] 'The Trials of the Mauretania,' *The Times*, 8 Nov 1907; 'Special Articles. The Mauretania,' *The Times*, 13 Nov 1907; Aylmer, *RMS Mauretania*, 29.

[10] 'The Maiden Voyage of the Mauretania,' *The Times*, 18 Nov 1907; 'West and East in the Mauretania,' *The Times*, 9 Dec 1907.

[11] 'The Voyage of the Mauretania,' *The Times*, 22 Nov 1907; 'The Voyage of the Mauretania,' *The Times*, 23 Nov 1907; 'West and East in the Mauretania,' *The Times*, 9 Dec 1907; Jordan, *Mauretania*, 320.

[12] 'The Mauretania,' *The Times*, 6 Dec 1907. *The Times*' reporter aboard *Mauretania* was not uncritical of the new ship. He informed readers that when making 25 knots the vibration made it 'not very easy to read and distinctly difficult to write anywhere except on the lower decks or in the cabins'. He found the ship 'extremely steady in quiet weather' but reported that three days of gales on the return passage 'confirm[ed] the impression that the Mauretania rolls more heavily than was anticipated'. He also reported that a passenger that he interviewed with

experience of forty crossings expressed surprise 'at the deep plunging of so vast a ship'. ('West and East in the Mauretania,' *The Times*, 9 Dec 1907.)

[13] Jordan, *Mauretania*, 307–8; 'Mauretania Again Ready,' *The Times*, 7 Feb 1927. Jordan lists this fastest eastbound average speed of 25.89 knots as being set in July 1909, but *The Times* has it as occurring in 'the same month' as the westbound record speed and time of September 1910.

[14] Maxtone-Graham, *Only Way to Cross*, 163, 169–70.

[15] McNeil, *In Great Waters*, 214, 215.

[16] 'Special Article. Modern British Ports. Southampton,' *The Times*, 20 June 1911; 'Southampton's Sea Trade,' *The Times*, 10 Sep 1921; McNeil, *In Great Waters*, 214–16; Hyde, *Cunard and the North Atlantic*, 109. Cunard's Canadian service did call at Southampton before the war.

[17] Bisset *Commodore*, 55; 'Two Cunarders for Southampton,' *The Times* 22 Feb, 1919; 'Cunard and Southampton,' *The Times*, 1 May 1919; 'Southampton to US New Fortnightly Cunard Service Today,' *The Times*, 14 June 1919; 'Cunard Line's Growing Fleet,' *The Times*, 4 Jan 1921; 'Cunard and Plymouth Call,' *The Times*, 31 Dec 1919; 'More Voyages for the Mauretania,' *The Times*, 10 June 1920; 'North Atlantic Plans,' *The Times*, 19 Jan 1920. McNeil (*In Great Waters*, 218) believed that *Mauretania* was able to hold her own among Cunard's big three and against the company's competitors, most of them significantly newer and larger ships, due to 'her speed and regularity and to the preference of a large number of regular travelers for crossing the Atlantic in a ship and not in a vast, floating hotel'. At the end of her career, Alymer (*RMS Mauretania*, 15) compared *Mauretania*'s appearance favourably to 'so many modern ships [with] the appearance of a block of tenement dwellings that had somehow slid off the land'. If only McNeil and Alymer could have seen the 21st century.

[18] Hyde, *Cunard and the North Atlantic*, 170, 173–5; Bisset, *Commodore*, 208.

[19] Bisset, *Commodore*, 153; Hyde, *Cunard and the North Atlantic*, 171–3.

[20] 'Mauretania Here after Stormy Trip,' *New York Times*, 7 June 1924; 'Mauretania to Call at Plymouth,' *The Times*, 11 Sep 1924; 'Mauretania's Fast Trip,' *The Times*, 29 Oct 1924; 'Cunard Express Service,' *The Times*, 4 Apr 1925; Bisset, *Commodore*, 129. *Aquitania* and *Berengaria* continued to call only at Cherbourg and Southampton. McNeil (*In Great Waters*, 224, 235) remembered *Mauretania*'s landfalls as occurring between 5 and 6 in the morning at Plymouth, some time between 12 and 12.45 at Cherbourg and between 5 and 6 in the evening at Southampton. 'Calling at three ports in one day is always rather tiring,' he observed.

[21] 'Atlantic Winter Sailings,' *The Times*, 28 Nov 1925.

[22] Bisset, *Commodore*, 153; Hyde, *Cunard and the North Atlantic*, 173, 179; Capt. E. G. Diggle, *The Romance of a Modern Liner* (London: Sampson Low, Marston & Co., Ltd., 1930), 10; 'Cheap Atlantic Travel. Cunard and White Star Tours,' *The Times*, 7 Jan 1925.

[23] 'Cheap Atlantic Travel,' *The Times*, 7 Jan 1925; Rostron, *Home from the Sea*, 151.

[24] McNeil, *In Great Waters*, 240.

[25] Jordan, *Mauretania*, 316–17; 'Mauretania Docks with 1,090 Voyagers,' *New York Times*, 3 Feb 1923; '500 to Sail Today on 66-Day Cruise,' *New York Times*, 7 Feb 1923.

[26] '500 to Sail Today on 66-Day Cruise,' *New York Times*, 7 Feb 1923; Jordan, *Mauretania*, 310, 316, 317; Rostron, *Home from the Sea*, 120.

[27] 'Cross-Channel Liner Trips,' *The Times*, 11 Sep 1924.

28 'Mauretania Ready Again,' *The Times*, 7 Feb 1927; Hyde, *Cunard and the North Atlantic*, 205.

29 Bisset, *Commodore*, 56, 57, 126.

30 'Mauretania on Fire,' *The Times*, 26 July 1921; McNeil, *In Great Waters*, 219; Bisset, *Commodore*, 136–7; Rostron, *Home from the Sea*, 205.

31 Bisset, *Commodore*, 136–40; 'Mauretania on Fire,' *The Times*, 26 July 1921; 'Mauretania Afire at Southampton; Interior is Ruined,' *New York Times*, 26 July 1921; McNeil, *In Great Waters*, 219–20. McNeil, in overall command of the firefighting in Rostron's absence, remembered *Mauretania*'s potential capsize somewhat differently and less dramatically than did Bisset, in command at the scene of the fire. 'I was expecting the ship to heel over at some period on account of the weight of water that was accumulating on "E" deck,' McNeil wrote in his memoirs, published eleven years later. Therefore he took the precaution of dispatching twenty men in two boats to close the ship's coaling ports and 'to have the doors in the ship's side ready to open; and as soon as she listed, the First Officer [Bisset], standing in over 4 feet of water, pulled the one remaining bolt'. McNeil remained aboard overnight with twenty men on watch. 'We were out several times, with hoses and chemical extinguishers.'

32 Bisset, *Commodore*, 140–1; Rostron, *Home from the Sea*, 204–5.

33 Rostron, *Home from the Sea*, 205.

34 Bisset, *Commodore*, 142; 'Cunard Oil-Fuel Plans,' *The Times*, 3 Sep 1921, 8; 'Mauretania's Return,' *The Times*, 14 Mar 1922.

35 'From the Tyne to the Mersey in the Mauretania,' *The Times*, 25 Oct 1907. In the late Twenties Cunard tried to offset the price disadvantage of European oil by increasing the bunker capacity of its liners to allow them to buy more oil more cheaply in the United States. (Hyde, *Cunard and the North Atlantic*, 182.)

36 Bisset, *Commodore*, 128.

37 Hyde, *Cunard and the North Atlantic*, 181; Jordan, *Mauretania*, 318–19; Diggle, *Romance of a Modern Liner*, 55. Jordan lists *Mauretania*'s original engineering complement as 36 engineers, 204 firemen, 120 trimmers and 33 greasers. All of the trimmers and most of the firemen were redundant after the conversion. Diggle put the converted *Aquitania*'s engineering force at 'but little more than one-third what it was in the days of coal-firing'.

38 Aylmer, *RMS Mauretania*, 56; *Cunard Express Liners Lusitania and Mauretania*, 100; 'Mauretania Here as an Oil Burner,' *New York Times*, 1 Apr 1922.

39 Diggle, *Romance of a Modern Liner*, 54; Rostron, *Home from the Sea*, 205; 'Mauretania Afire at Southampton; Interior is Ruined,' *New York Times*, 26 July 1921; 'Cunard Oil-Fuel Plans,' *The Times*, 3 Sep 1921; 'Mauretania's Return,' *The Times*, 14 Mar 1922. Diggle calculated that with 28 of *Aquitania*'s 168 furnaces cleaned in every watch, so that all were cleaned daily, it cost the ship approximately eight thousand horsepower every four hours.

40 'Mauretania Here as an Oil Burner,' *New York Times*, 1 Apr 1922; 'Mauretania Makes New Speed Record,' *New York Times*, 12 Aug 1922; 'Mauretania Makes Fastest Run since War, Taking 5 Days 7 Hours and 33 Minutes,' *New York Times*, 4 Nov 1922.

41 'Overhaul of the Mauretania,' *The Times*, 6 Nov 1923. In September 1922 *Mauretania* arrived at New York with her port low-pressure turbine disabled; not three months later, she entered the harbour with her starboard backing turbine inoperable. ('Mauretania Docks with Turbine Dead,' *New York Times*, 3 Sep 1922; 'Mauretania, Lamed, Crashes into Pier,' *New York Times*, 25 Nov 1922.)

42 Rostron, *Home from the Sea*, 39–40; Rostron, hand-written note on *Mauretania* letterhead to Thomas Royden, dated Cherbourg, 14 Apr 1924, Royden Correspondence File, D42/C2/121, Cunard Collection, SJL.

43 Rostron, *Home from the Sea*, 39–42; 'Mauretania Safe. Arrival at Cherbourg,' *The Times*, 14 Apr 1924.

44 'Mauretania Safe,' *The Times*, 14 Apr 1924; 'The Mauretania,' *The Times*, 23 May 1924; Rostron, note to Royden, 14 Apr 1924.

45 'Mauretania Here After Stormy Trip,' *New York Times*, 7 June 1924; 'Curran Back, Says Consuls Are Ready,' *New York Times*, 28 June 1924; 'Mauretania Making Good Time,' *New York Times*, 13 Aug 1924; 'Mauretania's Master Tells of His Sea,' *New York Times*, 24 Aug 1924; Jordan, *Mauretania*, 318. Aylmer, *RMS Mauretania*, 56.

46 Rostron, *Home from the Sea*, 197–8. Chief Engineer Andrew Cockburn, O.B.E., joined Cunard's seagoing engineering staff as a second engineer aboard *Lucania* in 1893. He survived the sinkings of *Lusitania* and *Aurania* during the First World War, to be appointed chief engineer of *Mauretania* in September 1919. He would serve aboard her even longer than Rostron, retiring from his post at the end of 1932. (Aylmer, *RMS Mauretania*, 81; Jordan, *Mauretania*, 321.)

47 Rostron, *Home from the Sea*, 198.

48 'Mauretania's Master Tells of His Sea,' *New York Times*, 24 Aug 1924; 'Fast Clip by Mauretania,' *New York Times*, 24 Aug 1924.

49 Aylmer, *RMS Mauretania*, 56; Rostron, *Home from the Sea*, 199; 'Sir Arthur Rostron Sails as Commodore,' *New York Times*, 29 July 1928; Jordan, *Mauretania*, 311. Jordan lists these figures as four days and nineteen hours, but at an average speed of 26.16 knots, still significantly better than her previous best eastbound average of 25.89 knots.

50 'Crew of 28 Saved from Sinking Ship by British Tanker,' *Washington Post*, 1 Apr 1926; '28 Saved at Sea while Mauretania Sped to the Rescue,' *New York Times*, 1 Apr 1926; 'Rescue Story Told in Mauretania Log,' *New York Times*, 3 Apr 1926; Rostron, *Home from the Sea*, 203.

51 'Rescue Story Told in Mauretania Log,' *New York Times*, 3 Apr 1926; 'The Mauretania,' *New York Times*, 18 Apr 1935.

CHAPTER 14

1 Rostron, 'Lloyd's Captains' Register,' 18569, 33; *Tyrrhenia*, from Liverpool, 5 Feb 1924, 'Passenger and Crew Lists of Vessels Arriving at New York, New York,' microfilm roll T715,3448, p. 37, USI.N.S., US National Archives, Washington, DC; Ransome-Wallis, *North Atlantic Panorama*, 70–1.

2 Slade, 'Distinguished Old Conway,' 242.

3 Slade, 'Distinguished Old Conway,' 242; 'Footnotes on a Week's Headliners,' *New York Times*, 16 Nov 1930. Slade, perhaps not completely convinced of Rostron's virtues, also declared that 'he looked something like a Mephistophelean Cherub'.

4 Slade, 'Distinguished Old Conway,' 243.

5 Bisset, *Tramps and Ladies*, 262; 'Mauretania's Master Tells of His Sea,' *New York Times*, 24 Aug 1924. In contrast to Rostron's character, Bisset (*Tramps and Ladies*, 202) found Cunard's commodore William Turner 'taciturn and austere, [and] inclined to be shy of sociable contacts with passengers… He usually had lunch in his cabin.'

6   Rostron, *Home from the Sea*, 145–6; 'Mauretania Makes New Speed Record,' *New York Times*, 12 Aug 1922; Bisset, *Commodore*, 128. Rostron devoted two chapters of his memoir to the social side of an Atlantic liner, including his dealings with the celebrity passengers of his day. In those chapters he engages in considerable name-dropping of 'figures of world-renown in varying spheres,' an indulgence completely uncharacteristic of the rest of the book.

7   Telegram to Sir Thomas Royden, n.d. and letter from H. J. Flewitt in reply, 18 Oct 1923, Royden Correspondence File, D42/C2/264/8, part 1, SJL.

8   'Formal Greeting to Lloyd George,' *New York Times*, 6 Oct 1923; 'Mauretania Darts between 2 Storms,' *New York Times*, 6 Oct 1923.

9   Sir Thomas Royden, letter to Mr Lloyd George, 24 Sep 1923, Royden Correspondence File, D42/C2/264/8 part 1, SJL; 'Lloyd George Sails, Sorry to Leave Us,' *New York Times*, 4 Nov 1923.

10 'The Queen of Rumania,' *The Times*, 25 Nov 1926; 'Queen Marie Bids Farewell to the United States,' *Davenport* [Iowa] *Democrat and Leader*, 24 Nov 1926.

11 Robert R. Hyde, letter to Sir Thomas Royden, 11 Oct 1926, D42/C2/264/8 part 2; Sir Thomas Royden, letter to Sir Arthur Rostron, 12 Oct 1926, D42/C2/264/8, part 2; Sir Thomas Royden, letter to Sir Arthur Rostron, 23 Mar 1927, D42/C2/264/8, part 3; Col. Kenyon A. Joyce, letter to Sir Thomas Royden, 1 Dec 1925, D42/C2/264/8, part 2; Royden Correspondence File, Cunard Collection, SJL.

12 Arthur A. Fowler, letter to Sir Thomas Royden, 11 Jan 1927, Royden Correspondence File, D42/C2/121, SJL; Slade, 'Distinguished Old Conway,' 242.

13 A. C. F. Henderson, letter to Sir Thomas Royden, 3 Sep 1928, Royden Correspondence File, D42/C2/264/8 part 3, Cunard Collection, SJL. Rostron's assessment of the essential traits (*Home from the Sea*, 244): 'the captain must be very patient and polite – and firm.'

14 Grattidge, *Captain of the Queens*, 224; Rostron, *Home from the Sea*, 150, 238.

15 Grattidge, *Captain of the Queens*, 102; 'Mauretania's Master Tells of His Sea,' *New York Times*, 24 Aug 1924.

16 Rostron, *Home from the Sea*, 156.

17 'Cunard Liner Arrives "Dry",' *The Times*, 14 Feb 1920; Rostron, *Home from the Sea*, 151, 155–6.

18 Maxtone-Graham, *Only Way to Cross*, 205–10; 'Gamblers on Liner Exposed by Victim,' *New York Times*, 14 May 1927; Rostron, *Home from the Sea*, 154.

19 Rostron, *Home from the Sea*, 152–5. The game was old-fashioned, non-auction bridge. The sucker's hand was in hearts, with the victim getting the ace, king, queen, jack, nine and one other. The sharps sprung the trap by ensuring that the remaining seven hearts ended up in one opponent's hand.

20 'Berengaria Brings Gold Coast Chief,' *New York Times*, 18 Nov 1928.

21 'Alleged Diamond Smuggling,' *The Times*, 20 Nov 1928; 'A Liner Sensation. Alleged Diamond Smuggling,' *Southern Daily Echo*, 19 Nov 1928; 'The Alleged Diamond Smuggling,' *Southern Daily Echo*, 20 Nov 1928; 'Alleged Diamond Smuggling. Ballyn Pleads Guilty,' *Southern Daily Echo*, 19 Feb 1929.

22 Bisset, *Tramps and Ladies*, 261; 'Mauretania on Fire,' *The Times*, 26 July 1921; Sir Thomas Royden, letter to Sir Arthur Rostron, 8 Apr 1930, Royden Correspondence File, D42/C2/121, SJL. Reporting on her fire, *The Times* noted that 'the Mauretania has long been

under the command of Captain A. H. Rostron. She has the reputation of being a very happy ship…'

23 Rostron, *Home from the Sea*, 240; Bisset, *Commodore*, 79; Sir Arthur Rostron, letter to Sir Thomas Royden, 7 Apr 1930, Royden Correspondence File, D42/C2/121, SJL. Rostron (*Home from the Sea*, 242) admitted of his inspections that 'perhaps I made a bit of a fetish out of them'.

24 Rostron, *Home from the Sea*, 240; Bisset, *Commodore*, 229; Rostron to Royden, 7 Apr 1930; 'Commodore of Cunard,' *Southern Daily Echo*, 5 Nov 1930.

25 Slade, 'Distinguished Old Conway,' 242–3; 'Commodore of Cunard,' *Southern Daily Echo*, 5 Nov 1930; Arthur A. Fowler, letter to Sir Thomas Royden, 12 Sep 1928, D42/C2/121; Sir Thomas Royden, letter to Arthur A. Fowler, 19 Oct 1928, D42/C2/121, Royden Correspondence File, Cunard Collection, SJL.

26 Slade, 'Distinguished Old Conway,' 243.

27 Slade, 'Distinguished Old Conway,' 243.

28 Slade, 'Distinguished Old Conway,' 243.

29 Rostron, *Home from the Sea*, 255; Bisset, *Tramps and Ladies*, 196; McNeil, *In Great Waters*, 258.

30 Rostron, *Home from the Sea*, 206.

31 Rostron, *Home from the Sea*, 140, 206; Bisset, *Commodore*, 214, 216, 224–5. In August 1898, on his first voyage for Cunard since returning from China, *Aurania* lost her only propeller a hundred miles west of Fastnet Rock, Ireland, eastbound in calm seas and light airs. She drifted helplessly for two days before 'a small tramp hove in sight and we were ignominiously towed into Queenstown by a vessel one-fifth our size'. (Rostron, *Home from the Sea*, 39.)

32 Lightoller, *Titanic and Other Ships*, 208; Bisset, *Tramps and Ladies*, 197; Rostron, *Home from the Sea*, 138–9; Bisset, *Commodore*, 218.

33 McNeil, *In Great Waters*, 247; *Saxonia*, Cunard 'Ships' Movement Book,' 9; Rostron, *Home from the Sea*, 110–11.

34 Rostron, *Home from the Sea*, 179.

35 'Mauretania Rips Pier while Docking,' *New York Times*, 20 June 1925. From the beginning, *Mauretania* developed a reputation as prone to plunge into heavy seas – on her maiden voyage, she 'pitched with a vigor which finally disproved the prophecies of those who thought that her size would keep her steady' ('West and East in the Mauretania,' *The Times*, 9 Dec 1907) – but McNeil (*In Great Waters*, 227) thought that she behaved 'wonderfully well' in bad weather, writing that she would 'make 14 knots in a high head sea, with a more or less dry forecastle-head'.

36 'Cedric Brings Aid to Helpless Ship,' *New York Times*, 14 Jan 1913; 'Mauretania's Master Tells of His Sea,' *New York Times*, 24 Aug 1924; 'Capt. Rostron in Peril,' *Washington Post*, 14 Jan 1913.

37 'Many on Berengaria Hurt in Hard Storm,' *New York Times*, 15 Jan 1927; 'Two Liners Arrive Battered by Gales,' *New York Times*, 13 Dec 1929; 'Berengaria in a Gale,' *The Times*, 17 Jan 1927.

38 'Tales of Mystery and Adventure,' *Charleston* [SC] *Daily Mail*, 25 Dec 1932.

39 'Mauretania, Lamed, Crashes into Pier,' *New York Times*, 25 Nov 1922; Rostron, *Home from the Sea*, 207.

40 'Dine Capt. Rostron on the Mauretania,' *New York Times*, 4 Apr 1922; 'Mauretania, Lamed, Crashes into Pier,' *New York Times*, 25 Nov 1922.

[41] 'Mauretania, Lamed, Crashes into Pier,' *New York Times*, 25 Nov 1922.

[42] 'Mauretania, Lamed, Crashes into Pier,' *New York Times*, 25 Nov 1922. Two and a half years later, in June of 1925, when *Mauretania* clipped a roof girder with her port bridge wing attempting another landing on the south side of Pier 54, causing slight damage to both, Rostron declared it 'my unlucky side of the pier. I am always all right when I go to the north side.' ('Mauretania Rips Pier while Docking,' *New York Times*, 20 June 1925.)

[43] 'Mauretania's Master Tells of His Sea,' *New York Times*, 24 Aug 1924.

[44] 'The Year of the Liner,' *The Times*, 13 Jan 1911; 'Mauretania to Call at Plymouth,' *The Times*, 11 Sep 1924; McNeil, *In Great Waters*, 244–5. Not that the Hudson presented the only hazards to navigation. Eastbound voyages ended after passing the notorious Bramble Bank, the sandbar creating 'that "S" course which is the entrance to Southampton Harbour'. (Rostron, *Home from the Sea*, 257.)

[45] 'Lloyd George's Son Here for a Visit,' *New York Times*, 28 Jan 1920; 'Dense Fog in Harbor Paralyzes Shipping,' *New York Times*, 14 Dec 1927; '1,136 on Berengaria Fogbound 40 Hours,' *New York Times*, 9 Feb 1928; Rostron, *Home from the Sea*, 239.

[46] Rostron, *Home from the Sea*, 239.

[47] 'Fire on Carmania Wrecks Interior,' *New York Times*, 3 June 1912; 'Mauretania's Master Tells of His Sea,' *New York Times*, 24 Aug 1924; 'Says British Tax Issue Dims Parley Fervor,' *New York Times*, 29 Mar 1930. *Mauretania* received similar page-one coverage of her fire. ('Mauretania Afire at Southampton,' *New York Times*, 26 July 1921.)

[48] 'Dinner on Mauretania,' *New York Times*, 6 May 1923; 'Mauretania's Master Tells of His Sea,' *New York Times*, 24 Aug 1924; 'Journalists Hosts to Advertising Men,' *New York Times*, 29 June 1926.

[49] 'Journalists Hosts to Advertising Men,' *New York Times*, 29 June 1926; 'R.N.V.R. Club Dinner,' *The Times*, 20 Jan 1930; Rostron, *Home from the Sea*, 181, 182–3.

[50] 'Rostron Arrives for Five-Day Visit,' *New York Times*, 11 July 1931; Rostron, *Home from the Sea*, 181, 183, 194.

[51] Rostron, *Home from the Sea*, 180; 'Marine Heroes Honored,' *New York Times*, 2 Nov 1926; 'Notes of Social Activities in New York and Elsewhere,' *New York Times*, 20 June 1929; 'Notes of Social Activities in New York and Elsewhere,' *New York Times*, 21 June 1929; 'H. H. Rogers Sails; Barely Catches Liner,' *New York Times*, 10 June 1926.

[52] 'The King's Levee. St James's Palace Ceremony,' *The Times*, 12 Mar 1924; 'R.N.V.R. Club Dinner,' *The Times*, 20 Jan 1930; Hyslop, *Titanic Voices*, 291.

[53] 'Mauretania's Master Tells of His Sea,' *New York Times*, 24 Aug 1924.

[54] 'Britain to Isolate All Imported Cats,' *New York Times*, 26 Dec 1928; 'Rostron's Cat Left Here,' *New York Times*, 6 Jan 1929; 'Footnotes on a Week's Headliners,' *New York Times*, 16 Nov 1930.

[55] 'Sir James Charles Dies on Last Trip,' *New York Times*, 16 July 1928; Sir Thomas Royden, letter to Arthur A. Fowler, 28 Dec 1926, Royden Correspondence File, D42/C2/121, SJL.

[56] 'Obituary Captain Sir Arthur Rostron,' *Lloyd's List and Shipping Gazette*, 6 Nov 1940; Rostron, *Home from the Sea*, 138.

CHAPTER 15

[1] Sir Thomas Royden, letter to the Rt. Hon. Stanley Baldwin, M.P., n. d., Royden Correspondence File, D42/C2/121, SJL.

[2] Supplement to *The London Gazette* of 2 July 1926, published 3 July 1926, 4409–10.

[3] 'Birthday Honours,' *Lloyd's List*, 3 July 1926; 'Mauretania's Captain is Honored by King,' *New York Times*, 3 July 1926.

[4] Jordan, *Mauretania*, 311; Rostron, *Home from the Sea*, 208–10.

[5] Sir Thomas Royden, letter to Sir Arthur Rostron, 5 July 1926, Royden Correspondence File, D42/C2/121; Sir Arthur Rostron, telegram to Sir Thomas Royden, n.d. but office stamped 'Liverpool 5 JUL 26', Royden Correspondence File, D42/C2/121, SJL. Rostron left no account of his investiture ceremony, alas.

[6] Rostron, RNR Service Record, 6; Bisset, *Commodore*, 152; Ray Turner, 'West End's First Blue Plaque Unveiled,' *Eastleigh News*, 15 Apr 2012; 'Hero of the Hour,' *Westender: Newsletter of the West End Local History Society* 8, no. 5 (May–June 2012): 1; *Kelly's Directory of Southampton and Neighbourhood* (London: Kelly's Directories); 36th ed. (1928–9), 757; 45th ed. (1937–8), 993, 998; Letter to Titanic Historical Society Secretary Ed Kamuda from Arthur John Rostron, *Titanic Commutator* II, no. 22 (sum 1979): 40.

[7] Rostron, *Home from the Sea*, 208, 211; Bisset, *Commodore*, 204, 206. Harry Grattidge, who sailed in her as first officer in the 1930s, classified *Berengaria* as 'one of the few ships for which I have had little affection'. Grattidge, a more sensitive soul than either Rostron or Bisset to judge from their memoirs, found *Berengaria* to be 'a ship of gloomy panelled majesty, hard to handle, clumsy and Teutonic, a creation of industry without pretentions to beauty'. Grattidge's opinion of the vessel was not improved by *Berengaria*'s deteriorating wiring, which started the numerous electrical fires that caused Cunard to withdraw her from service and consign her to the breakers in 1938. (Grattidge, *Captain of the Queens*, 127; McCart, *Atlantic Liners of the Cunard Line*, 119–20.)

[8] Rostron, *Home from the Sea*, 211; Ransome-Wallis, *North Atlantic Panorama*, 44, 49, 52, 53; Hyde, *Cunard and the North Atlantic*, 331, 335.

[9] Part VIII, Articles 231, 232 and Annex III, 1.1, *Treaty of Versailles*, signed 28 June 1919 (text available at firstworldwar.com).

[10] McCart, *Atlantic Liners of the Cunard Line*, 110–17; Maxtone-Graham, *Only Way to Cross*, 105, 106, 110. 'Admiral Billard Back,' *New York Times*, 7 Aug 1926. For Rostron's ships and commands, please see tables 1 and 2.

[11] 'Obituary. Sir James Charles,' *The Times*, 16 July 1928; 'The Aquitania Refitted,' *The Times*, 6 Jan 1927; 'Sir James Charles Dies on Last Trip,' *New York Times*, 16 July 1928.

[12] 'Sir J. Charles. Sudden Death on Last Trip,' *The Times*, 16 July 1928; 'New Commodore of the Cunard Fleet,' *The Times*, 28 July 1928; 'Sir James Charles Dies on Last Trip,' *New York Times*, 16 July 1928. Sir James Charles would not be the last Cunard captain to die in peacetime command. On the morning of 28 October 1936, Sir Edgar Britten suffered a stroke in his cabin aboard *Queen Mary* two hours before she was due to sail for New York. He died ashore that afternoon, aged 62. ('Death of Sir Edgar Britten,' *The Times*, 29 Oct 1936.)

[13] 'Sir Arthur Rostron Sails as Commodore,' *New York Times*, 29 July 1928; A. C. F. Henderson, letter to Thomas Royden, 3 Sep 1928. Rostron earned £1500 in base salary for commanding *Berengaria*, plus the bonus. Captain E. G. Diggle made £1500 commanding *Aquitania*, Samuel McNeil made £1250 as captain of *Mauretania* and William Prothero earned £1250 as the relief master. Next came a tier of masters earning £1000 per annum on Cunard's smaller passenger ships and then another rank below that earning in the range of £650 to £850.

14   'France Honors Rostron,' *New York Times*, 28 Feb 1929; 'Telegrams in Brief,' *The Times*, 28 Feb 1929; Rostron, RNR Service Record, 6. Both Rostron (*Home from the Sea*, 210) and *The Times* ('Sir Arthur Rostron,' 6 Nov 1940) said he 'was a Chevalier de la Legion d'honneur'.

15   'MacDonald to Stay 3 Days with Hoover,' *New York Times*, 25 Sep 1929; Ramsay MacDonald, telegram to Sir Thomas Royden, received Liverpool, 28 Sep 1929, Royden Correspondence File, D42/C2/121, SJL.

16   'MacDonald Departs for Visit to Hoover,' *New York Times*, 28 Sep 1929; 'MacDonald to Sail Tomorrow to Weld Anglo-Saxon Amity,' *New York Times*, 27 Sep 1929.

17   'MacDonald Departs for Visit to Hoover,' *New York Times*, 28 Sep 1929; 'MacDonald Misses Religious Service at Sea,' *New York Times*, 30 Sep 1929; 'MacDonald at Sea After Delay by Fog; Enjoying the Trip,' *New York Times*, 29 Sep 1929.

18   'Premier Proves a Good Sailor,' *Kingsport* [TN] *Times*, 2 Oct 1929; 'MacDonald Pleased by Wide Approval,' *New York Times*, 2 Oct 1929; 'MacDonald at Sea After Delay by Fog,' *New York Times*, 29 Sep 1929; 'MacDonald Misses Religious Service at Sea,' *New York Times*, 30 Sep 1929; 'Premier Gets Word Dominions Back Him,' *New York Times*, 1 Oct 1929.

19   'MacDonald Misses Religious Service at Sea,' *New York Times*, 30 Sep 1929; 'MacDonald, Daughter Hike for Miles; Miss Services on Ship,' *Nevada State Journal* (Reno), 30 Sep 1929; 'MacDonald Pleased by Wide Approval,' *New York Times*, 2 Oct 1929; 'Premier Proves a Good Sailor,' *Kingsport Times*, 2 Oct 1929; 'Premier Gets Word Dominions Back Him,' *New York Times*, 1 Oct 1929.

20   'MacDonald Hopeful Aims Will Be Won,' *New York Times*, 3 Oct 1929; 'Liner Slows Down for M'Donald Fete,' *Washington Post*, 3 Oct 1929; 'Mr. MacDonald in US,' *The Times*, 5 Oct 1929.

21   'MacDonald to Be Greeted by City Today,' *New York Times*, 4 Oct 1929.

22   'Mr. MacDonald in US,' *The Times*, 5 Oct 1929; 'MacDonald Greets Hoover at Capital after a Warm Welcome in New York,' *New York Times*, 5 Oct 1929.

23   'MacDonald Greets Hoover at Capital… Gets Freedom of City,' *New York Times*, 5 Oct 1929; 'Mr. MacDonald in US,' *The Times*, 5 Oct 1929.

24   'MacDonald Greets Hoover at Capital,' *New York Times*, 5 Oct 1929; 'Mr. MacDonald in US,' *The Times*, 5 Oct 1929.

25   'Hoover Announces Naval Parley Jan 20 After Talk with M'Donald in Camp,' *New York Times*, 7 Oct 1929; 'M'Donald Tells Senate Wars are Over if Kellogg Pact Is Made Effective,' *New York Times*, 8 Oct 1929; 'Hoover and MacDonald Join in Saying War between Us Is Now "Unthinkable",' *New York Times*, 10 Oct 29; 'MacDonald Hailed by Toronto Throng,' *New York Times*, 16 Oct 1929; 'MacDonald Starts Home from Quebec,' *New York Times*, 26 Oct 1929.

26   'Shipping and Mails… Outgoing Passenger and Mail Steamships,' *New York Times*, 5 Oct 1929; 'Cunard to Reduce Age Limit to 60,' *New York Times*, 6 June 1929; 'Cunard Line Cuts Its Age Limit to 60,' *New York Times*, 26 Oct 1930.

27   Sir Thomas Royden, letter to Sir Arthur Rostron, 8 Nov 1928 (in reply to Rostron's of 7 Nov), Royden Correspondence File, D42/C2/121, SJL. *The New York Times* ('Captain Prothero Is Retired at 60,' 26 May 1931) attributed Cunard's creation of the relieving captain to the death of Sir James, but that contradicts the paper's own reporting on the commodore's death ('Sir James Charles Dies on Last Trip,' 16 July 1928), which noted his appointment as relief captain in January 1928.

28   'Cunard to Reduce Age Limit to 60,' *New York Times*, 6 June 1929; Henderson to Royden, 3 Sep 1928.

29 'Cunard Line Cuts Its Age Limit to 60,' *New York Times*, 26 Oct 1930. Within a few years of Rostron's retirement, the merged Cunard-White Star Line reversed course on retirement age, with Britten serving as commodore at age sixty-two in 1936. Commodore James Bisset retired in January 1947, aged 63 years, 6 months. ('Death of Sir Edgar Britten,' *The Times*, 29 Oct 1936; Bisset, *Commodore*, 464.)

30 McNeil, *In Great Waters*, 320; Rostron, *Home from the Sea*, 259. Rostron's daughter, Margaret, wrote that after Charles' death 'my father said he hoped he would never know when his last voyage was to be'. (M. E. Howman, 'Copy of Brief Account of Capt. Rostron's Career.')

31 'Commodore of Cunard,' *Southern Daily Echo*, 5 Nov 1930; Bisset, *Commodore*, 212; 'Garden Lures Skipper of the Berengaria, Sir Henry Rostron [*sic*], After 45 Years at Sea,' *New York Times*, 9 Nov 1930.

32 Henderson, letter to Royden, 3 Sep 1928; 'Cunard Employes [*sic*] to Honor Rostron,' *New York Times*, 3 Nov 1930; 'To Command Berengaria,' *New York Times*, 23 Dec 1930; 'Captain Prothero Is Retired at 60,' *New York Times*, 26 May 1931; 'Diggle Ends Sea Service,' *New York Times*, 6 Aug 1931; 'New Commander for the Berengaria,' *The Times*, 23 Dec 1930; 'New Commodore of Cunard Fleet,' *The Times*, 18 June 1931; 'Commodore of Cunard Fleet Retiring. Captain Diggle's Last Voyage,' *The Times*, 6 Aug 1931; Bisset, *Commodore*, 209.

33 'New Cunard Liner,' *The Times*, 14 Mar 1930; 'New Cunard Liner,' *The Times*, 9 Apr 1931; McCart, *Atlantic Liners of the Cunard Line*, 169.

34 'Commodore of Cunard,' *Southern Daily Echo*, 5 Nov 1930; 'Captain Sir A. Rostron,' *Lloyd's List and Shipping Gazette*, 2 June 1931; Royden, letter to Waterhouse, 2 Feb 1926.

CHAPTER 16

1 Rostron, *Home from the Sea*, 43, 204, 232; 'A Cunard Commodore,' *New York Times Book Review*, 8 Nov 1931. Rostron dedicated the copy of *Home from the Sea* that he gave to Minnie: 'With love and my life long appreciation to my own darling wife for the help & encouragement she has always given me and all my very best wishes. From her husband & Chum. A. H. R.' The inscription, in Rostron's hand, is reproduced on the inside front cover of: *Sir Arthur Rostron, The Loss of the Titanic* [John Booth, comp.] (Melksham, Eng.: Norton Press Printing, 1991).

2 'Rostron Due Today as Ship Passenger,' *New York Times*, 10 July 1931; 'Rostron Arrives for Five-Day Visit,' *New York Times*, 11 July 1931; 'Notes of Social Activities in New York and Elsewhere,' *New York Times*, 10 July 1931; 'Book Notes,' New York Times, 22 July 1931. Rostron's ledger in 'Lloyd's Captains' Register' (18569, 33), an incomplete account, lists 196 voyages to the US in ships serving New York.

3 'Garden Lures Skipper of the Berengaria,' *New York Times*, 9 Nov 1930.

4 John Rostron, letter to the author, 21 Oct 2011.

5 John Rostron, interview, 18 July 2011.

6 'Decline in Transatlantic Traffic,' *The Times*, 22 Dec 1931; 'Cunard Cruises from New York,' *The Times*, 18 Apr 1931; 'Atlantic Liners for Cruises,' *The Times*, 9 Jan 1932; 'Mauretania's Whitsun Cruise,' *The Times*, 22 Dec 1931.

7 'Fewer Atlantic Sailings,' *The Times*, 22 Aug 1931; 'Reduction of Atlantic Sailings,' *The Times*, 13 Oct 1933.

8 Hyde, *Cunard and the North Atlantic*, 189, 206; McCart, *Atlantic Liners of the Cunard Line*, 169.

9   Hyde, *Cunard and the North Atlantic*, 191–5; McCart, *Atlantic Liners of the Cunard Line*, 170.

10 Hyde, *Cunard and the North Atlantic*, 215–16; McCart, *Atlantic Liners of the Cunard Line*, 170; 'Cunard–White Star, Ltd.,' *The Times*, 9 Feb 1934.

11 Rostron, *Home from the Sea*, 235; 'A Helping Hand to Sailors,' *The Times*, 9 Dec 1932; 'King George's Fund for Sailors,' *The Times*, 19 Oct 1932; 'King George's Fund for Sailors,' *The Times*, 28 June 1933; 'Relief of Sailors in Distress,' *The Times*, 28 June 1934; 'Charities for Sailors,' *The Times*, 2 July 1936; 'Calls on Marine Charities,' *The Times*, 27 Feb 1935.

12 'Death of Brilliant Sailor,' *Hampshire Advertiser and Southampton Times*, 9 Nov 1940; 'Gallipoli and Anzac Day,' *The Times*, 21 Apr 1934.

13 'Pangbourne Nautical College,' *The Times*, 3 June 1933; 'Ecclesiastical News,' *The Times*, 9 Nov 1935; 'Fleet Commodore to Address Meeting,' *Manchester Guardian*, 2 Dec 1935; 'The Sailor and Religion. Sir A. Rostron's View,' *Manchester Guardian*, 3 Dec 1935.

14 'Rational Tailoring An Investigation,' *The Times*, 22 July 1936. The campaign, which ran from July to the end of November 1936, consisted of eleven advertisements, each, after the introductory one, containing a profile of one of the individuals, who was quoted as endorsing the company's products. All of the profiles were eventually featured except Rostron's. Although Rostron's endorsement of the Fifty Shilling Tailors was apparently not carried through, he may have had prior experience as a celebrity pitchman. The automotive section of the 9 September 1928 issue of the *Columbus Dispatch* of Ohio carried a photograph of Sir Arthur and Lady Rostron standing before an automobile. The caption to the photograph read in part: 'Sir Arthur, who is well known and popular in "Atlantic circles," and has a fine World war [*sic*] record, enjoys his brief respites from his sea duties in his Willys-Knight Six.'

15 The Cachalots: The Southampton Master Mariners, 'Past Captains and Officers' (www. cachalots.org.uk); 'Death of Famous Sea Captain,' *Southern Daily Echo*, 5 Nov 1940.

16 Hyde, *Cunard and the North Atlantic*, 183–4; 'The Mauretania. Her Own Record Beaten,' *The Times*, 22 Aug 1929.

17 'Cunard Cruises,' *The Times*, 11 Nov 1931; 'Mauretania's Whitsun Cruise,' *The Times*, 22 Dec 1931; '"Club" Cruises in the Mauretania,' *The Times*, 4 Mar 1933; Jordan, *Mauretania*, 315. *The Times* ('Whitsun Cruises of the Mauretania,' 19 May 1933) mentioned *Mauretania*'s spring 1933 sailings, first from Southampton to Casablanca and return, then almost immediately to Madeira and back, a schedule which involved over five thousand miles of steaming in just over ten days. The newspaper noted that 'only the vessel's reserve of speed will enable the programme to be completed'. McNeil (*In Great Waters*, 240–1), commanding *Mauretania* in 1931, noted the same thing about her American cruises. Rather than have the ship lay over six days at her New York pier 'eating her head off' between crossings, Cunard used her speed to whisk New Yorkers on four-day cruises to Nassau, departing on Friday evenings. 'Very many Americans, on account of the prevailing depression, did not care to go away for such a period as a voyage to Europe would entail, but they did not mind an absence of a few days; hence the popularity of these short trips.'

18 'Mauretania Bought for Scrap,' *The Times*, 3 Apr 1935.

19 Bisset, *Commodore*, 268; 'Mauretania Bought for Scrap,' *The Times*, 3 Apr 1935; 'A Great Liner,' *The Times*, 4 Apr 1935; 'The Mauretania,' *New York Times*, 18 Apr 1935.

20 Bisset, *Commodore*, 268; Jordan, *Mauretania*, 307–15; 'Sale of Mauretania Fittings,' *The Times*, 24 May 1935; McCart, *Atlantic Liners of the Cunard Line*, 84; 'Mauretania's Last Voyage,' *Southern Daily Echo*, 2 July 1935.

21 'Last Voyage of the Mauretania,' *The Times*, 2 July 1935; 'Mauretania's Last Voyage,' *Southern Daily Echo*, 2 July 1935; 'Southampton Sees Last of Mauretania,' *Southern Daily Echo*, 2 July 1935; McCart, *Atlantic Liners of the Cunard Line*, 84.

22 'Mauretania's Last Voyage,' *Southern Daily Echo*, 2 July 1935; 'Southampton Sees Last of Mauretania,' *Southern Daily Echo*, 2 July 1935; 'Last Voyage of the Mauretania,' *The Times*, 2 July 1935.

23 McCart, *Atlantic Liners of the Cunard Line*, 85; 'The Beginning of the End of the Mauretania,' *Hampshire Advertiser and Southampton Times*, 6 July 1935; Maxtone-Graham, *Only Way to Cross*, 347; 'The Mauretania,' *New York Times*, 18 Apr 1935.

24 McCart, *Atlantic Liners of the Cunard Line*, 170; Ransome-Wallis, *North Atlantic Panorama*, 119; Hyde, *Cunard and the North Atlantic*, 203, 204.

25 M. E. Howman, 'Copy of a Brief Account of Captain Rostron's Career'; 'Mauretania's Master Tells of His Sea,' *New York Times*, 24 Aug 1924.

26 McCart, *Atlantic Liners of the Cunard Line*, 119–20.

27 Rostron, 'Lloyd's Captains' Register,' 18569, 33; 'W. Furtwaengler, Conductor, Here,' *New York Times*, 3 Feb 1927; 'Mrs. Belmont Back After Year Abroad,' *New York Times*, 12 Nov 1927; Ransome-Wallis, *North Atlantic Panorama*, 53–4; McCart, *Atlantic Liners of the Cunard Line*, 105.

28 John Rostron, letter to author, 21 Oct 2011; *London Gazette*, 10 Feb 1939, 950; Supplement to the *London Gazette*, 19 July 1940, 4420.

29 Bisset, *Commodore*, 464. Bisset retired in January 1947 after forty-eight years at sea.

30 Grattidge, *Captain of the Queens*, 150–9, 161; 'The U-boat Wars, 1939–45' (www.uboat.net); Robert Carse, *A Cold Corner of Hell: The Story of the Murmansk Convoys, 1941–1945* (Garden City, NY: Doubleday, 1969), 40–1. *Lancastria* was the former *Tyrrhenia*, which Rostron commanded for one voyage at the beginning of 1924.

31 Troy Brody, *The Southampton Blitz* (1977; reprint, Southampton: Itchen Printers, Ltd., 1978), 8; Roy Andrews, museum volunteer, interviewed by the author at the West End Local History Museum and Heritage Centre, 2 July 2011; John Rostron, letter to the author, 21 Oct 2011.

32 John Rostron, interview, 18 July 2011; Letter to Titanic Historical Society Secretary Ed Kamuda from Arthur John Rostron, *Titanic Commutator* II, no. 22 (sum 1979): 40. In the interview John speculated that Sir Arthur 'probably wasn't so quiet spoken at the time of the machine gunning of the house'.

33 John Rostron, interview, 18 July 2011; 'Death of Famous Sea Captain,' *Southern Daily Echo*, 5 Nov 1940. John Rostron (letter to the author, 21 Oct 2011) wrote that 'air-raid shelters were rapidly being constructed in garden[s], parks, school playing fields, around factories, etc., during the so-called 'phoney war' [in] 1939... to early 1940... So, my grandparents were able to immediately occupy an air-raid shelter in the garden near the house, as I remember, after the machine-gunning. This was obviously a one-off attack I think and seemingly no necessity [existed] for them to sleep [in or] occupy the shelter unless the air-raid warning siren sounded... To spend each night in the shelter probably caused AHR to develop [the] pneumonia from which he died.'

34 'Sir Arthur Rostron,' *The Times*, 6 Nov 1940; 'Commodore Dies,' *Portsmouth* [NH] *Herald*, 5 Nov 1940; 'Commodore Is Ill,' *Ogden* [UT] *Standard Examiner*, 5 Nov 1940;

35 'Funeral of Sir Arthur Rostron,' *Southern Daily Echo*, 8 Nov 1940.

36 'Death of Brilliant Sailor,' *Hampshire Advertiser and Southampton Times*, 9 Nov 1940; 'Funeral of Sir Arthur Rostron,' *Southern Daily Echo*, 8 Nov 1940.

37 John Rostron, interview, 18 July 2011; 'Photos Hidden for 50 Years in an Attic Bring the Dockers' Umbrella Back to Life; Last Manager Harry Rostron's Archives Found in Son's Loft,' (Liverpool) *Daily Post*, 12 Jan 2002; Family Tree of George Rostron, Bolton Church Institute (www.bolton-church-institute.org.uk).

38 'No Mistake Over Captain's House,' *Bolton News*, 4 Feb 1999; Rostron historical plaque at the West End Local History Museum and Heritage Centre; Andrews, interview, 2 July 2011; 'Sir Arthur Rostron's Grave Gets a Clean-up,' *Westender: Newsletter of the West End Local History Society* 2, no. 10 (Feb–Apr 2001): 1; 'Street Named After Carpathia's Captain Arthur H. Rostron,' BBC News (online), 25 Nov 2011; Eastleigh Borough Council, 'Naming of Streets in Hedge End and West End,' 13 Sep 2010 (www.eastleigh.gov.uk/meetings/documents/s18792/Report.pdf).

39 'Hero of the Hour,' *Westender: Newsletter of the West End Local Historical Society* 8, no. 5 (May–June 2012): 3, 6.

40 'Obituary. Captain Sir Arthur Rostron,' *Lloyd's List and Shipping Gazette*, 6 Nov 1940.

41 Grattidge, *Captain of the Queens*, 103; 'Sir Arthur Rostron,' *The Times*, 6 Nov 1940.

42 Bisset, *Tramps and Ladies*, 230; Rostron, *Home from the Sea*, 3–4.

43 'Proposed Change in Helm Orders,' *The Times*, 23 June 1931. Under the 'tiller rules' the helmsmen turned the wheel and the ship moved in the opposite direction from the command given, as with a tiller. After the new rule came into force on 1 Jan 1933, the helmsman spun the wheel in the same direction as the command, thereby turning the ship in that direction. Bisset (*Commodore*, 224) wrote that 'despite the forebodings of the nautical conservatives, the change of steering-orders was effected without any serious mishaps,' although he recalled that to prevent chaos officers and pilots gave the order as 'wheel to port' for many months.

44 Rostron, *Home from the Sea*, 246–8; 'So This Is Old England – Or So the English Say,' *New York Times Magazine*, 20 Feb 1938. This is a polite way to acknowledge Rostron's occasional use of ethnic epithets in *Home from the Sea* (128, 248). While such slurs are unacceptable in our era and were crass in his own, that sort of language was a part of his maritime environment, which was simultaneously cosmopolitan and severe.

45 Rostron, *Home from the Sea*, 251, 230–1. About Bolshevism Sir Arthur did not equivocate. In his 1931 memoir he worried about another world war, but not with Germany. 'Not when there is the shadow of Russia lengthening across the globe. Russia is civilisation's enemy and I for one hate to see this country have any dealings with her.' (Rostron, *Home from the Sea*, 105.)

46 Bisset, *Commodore*, 79.

47 Beesley, *Loss of SS Titanic*, 133–4; Mahala Douglas, *Senate Titanic Hearings*, 1102.

48 Slade, 'Distinguished Old Conway,' 244.

49 Bisset, *Commodore*, 212; Bisset, *Tramps and Ladies*, 226, 227, 229–30.

50 Rostron, *Home from the Sea*, 6, 255, 256.

APPENDIX

1 James Moore, *Senate Titanic Hearings*, 764–5, 766–7, 777–8.

2 James Moore, *Senate Titanic Hearings*, 777–8; Boxhall, *Senate Titanic Hearings*, 931.

[3]   Boxhall, *Senate Titanic Hearings*, 932; Robert Ballard, *The Discovery of the Titanic: Exploring the Greatest of All Lost Ships* (Toronto: Madison Press Books, 1987), 199.

[4]   Rostron, 'British Titanic Enquiry,' 25499.

[5]   Rostron, 'British Titanic Enquiry,' 25496; Rostron, *Home from the Sea*, 63; Boxhall, *Senate Titanic Hearings*, 254; Testimony of Stanley Lord (master, *Californian*), 'British Titanic Enquiry,' 7039. *Californian*, which relieved *Carpathia* at the debris field and searched the area saw no bodies and little wreckage. (Lord, 'British Titanic Enquiry,' 7029–38.)

[6]   Rostron, *Senate Titanic Hearings*, 26.

[7]   Rostron, 'British Titanic Enquiry,' 25390; Rostron, 'Rescue of the "Titanic" Survivors,' 356. Among those in favour of 17 knots: Reade, *Ship that Stood Still*, 89; opposed: Smith, *Tyne to Titanic*, 19; Dave Gittins, 'Carpathia: Legends and Reality' (www.titanicebook.com).

[8]   Bisset, *Tramps and Ladies*, 287: Rostron, 'British Titanic Enquiry,' 25491; 'The Cunard Steamer Carpathia,' *The Times*, 27 Apr 1903.

[9]   Rostron, *Titanic Senate Hearings*, 21; Rostron, 'British Titanic Enquiry,' 25394; 'Captain's Official Reports,' *New York Times*, 20 Apr 1912; Copy of hand-written account of *Titanic* rescue by Rostron, dated *Carpathia* 'At Sea April 27th 1912,' 1988, 258 [ephemera envelope] DX/949R, MMM; Rostron, 'Rescue of the "Titanic" Survivors,' 356; Rostron, *Home from the Sea*, 59.

[10] Boxhall, 'British Titanic Enquiry,' 15349; Boxhall, *Senate Titanic Hearings*, 244, 248; Johnson, 'British Titanic Enquiry,' 3546, 3536, 3537; Testimony of George Rowe (quartermaster, *Titanic*), *Senate Titanic Hearings*, 519.

[11] Testimony of Frank Osman (able seaman, *Titanic*), *Senate Titanic Hearings*, 538; Boxhall, *Senate Titanic Hearings*, 243, 244; Douglas, *Senate Titanic Hearings*, 1101.

[12] Rostron, Senate Titanic Hearings, 21; Rostron, 'British Titanic Enquiry,' 25394, 25404, 25473; Rostron, 'Rescue of the "Titanic" Survivors,' 357.

[13] Bisset, *Tramps and Ladies*, 282, 284; Douglas, *Senate Titanic Hearings*, 1101; Osman, *Senate Titanic Hearings*, 538.

[14] Gittins, '*Carpathia: Legends and Reality*'; Rostron, *Senate Titanic Hearings*, 19; Douglas, *Senate Titanic Hearings*, 1101.

[15] Lord, 'British Titanic Enquiry,' 6701–2, 6704; Lord, *Senate Titanic Hearings*, 716; 'Wreck Commissioner's Enquiry, Report on the Loss of the "Titanic" (SS)… The Circumstances in Connection with the SS Californian,' Titanic Inquiry Project.

[16] Lord, 'British Titanic Enquiry,' 6717, 6764; Testimony of Charles Groves (third officer, *Californian*), 'British Titanic Enquiry,' 8217–20; Testimony of Herbert Stone (second officer, *Californian*), 'British Titanic Enquiry,' 7808.

[17] Testimony of George Rowe (quartermaster, *Titanic*), 'British Titanic Enquiry,' 17684; Boxhall, *Senate Titanic Hearings*, 236, 910; Stone, 'British Titanic Enquiry,' 7819–20, 7832, 7838, 7842–3, 7890–1, 7935, 7971–6; Testimony of James Gibson (officer apprentice, *Californian*), 'British Titanic Enquiry,' 7466, 7483.

[18] Lord, 'British Titanic Enquiry,' 6783, 6857–61, 6886–94, 6897–6900, 6902, 6930–3, 6945–53, 7077, 7275–95, 7300–12; Stone, 'British Titanic Enquiry,' 7829–30, 7874, 7878, 7934, 7949, 7971–6, 7999; Gibson, 'British Titanic Enquiry,' 7552–72.

[19] Stone, 'British Titanic Enquiry,' 8008–13, 8016–7; Gibson, 'British Titanic Enquiry,' 7579–80, 7586–90, 7596.

20   Peter Padfield, *The Titanic and the Californian* (New York: John Day Company, 1965), 17–19, 116, 160, 165, 177–8, 251, 267–9. In any such proceeding there are always inconsistencies in testimony, of course, as in the more benign example of Boxhall's flares discussed above.

21   Padfield, *Titanic and the Californian*, 274 (emphasis original); Gibson, 'British Titanic Enquiry,' 7495; 'Stone, British Titanic Enquiry,' 7923–7; US Senate, *Titanic Disaster Report*, 11.

22   Gibson, 'British Titanic Enquiry,' 7579–80, 7586–90, 7596; Stone, 'British Titanic Enquiry,' 8008–13, 8016–7.

23   Rostron, 'British Titanic Enquiry,' 25550–1.

24   Reade, *Ship that Stood Still*, 274, 305–9.

25   US Senate, *Titanic Disaster Report*, 11; 'Circumstances in Connection with the SS *Californian*,' *British Wreck Commissioner's Enquiry Report*, Titanic Enquiry Project; Lord, 'British Titanic Enquiry,' 7406, 7408–9.

26   Padfield, *Titanic and the Californian*, 176.

27   Gibson, 'British Titanic Enquiry,' 7529; Stone, 'British Titanic Enquiry,' 7983–5. Padfield attempted to discredit Gibson's testimony by characterizing him as the apprentice and not especially smart, but at twenty years of age and with three and a half years at sea, Gibson was neither a child nor a novice. (Padfield, *Titanic and the Californian*, 175, 205–6; Gibson, 'British Titanic Enquiry,' 7413, 7795.)

28   Lord, 'British Titanic Enquiry,' 6934; Stone, 'British Titanic Enquiry,' 7994.

29   Charles Groves, 'The Middle Watch' (reprinted in: Barratt, *Lost Voices from the Titanic*, 240–7), 241; Daniel Allen Butler; *The Other Side of the Night: The Carpathia, the Californian and the Night the Titanic Was Lost* (Philadelphia: Casemate, 2009), 49–50, 188; Stone, 'British Titanic Enquiry,' 8027–34. Butler (*The Other Side of the Night*, 199–206, 220) goes so far as to declare Lord a sociopath, a judgement which seems an overreach without supporting psychiatric evidence.

30   Booth and Coughlan, *Titanic: Signals of Disaster*, 147–8, 151; Heyer, *Titanic Legacy*, 46–7.

31   US Senate, *Titanic Disaster Report*, 17; Sammis, *Senate Titanic Hearings*, 861.

32   US Senate, *Titanic Disaster Report*, 18.

33   Marconi, *Senate Titanic Hearings*, 492, 488.

34   Marconi, *Senate Titanic Hearings*, 489.

35   Marconi, *Senate Titanic Hearings*, 477. And again, Cottam did send several messages about the disaster, including Rostron's official messages and his own 122-word informal summary of the situation, dispatched to *Olympic* upon first contact at 2pm, New York Time, Monday: 'I received distress signals from Titanic at 11.20 [sic] and we proceeded right to the spot mentioned. On arrival at daybreak we saw field ice 25 miles, apparently solid and a quantity of wreckage and a number of boats full of people. We raised about 670 souls. The Titanic has sunk. She went down in about two hours. Captain and all engineers lost. Our captain sent order that there was no need for Baltic to come any farther. So with that she returned on her course to Liverpool. Are you going to resume your course on that information? We have two or three officers aboard and the second Marconi operator, who had been creeping his way through water 30 [degrees] sometime [sic]. Mr. Ismay aboard.' ('Log as Made By Wireless Operator Moore on SS "Olympic",' *Senate Titanic Hearings*, 1137.)

36   Sammis, *Senate Titanic Hearings*, 866, 870.

37 Booth and Coughlan, *Titanic: Signals of Disaster*, 151; Heyer, *Titanic Legacy*, 46. Heyer also discusses the business relationship between the Marconi Company and *The New York Times* (48).

38 Cottam, *Senate Titanic Hearings*, 922.

39 US Senate, *Titanic Disaster Report*, 16–17.

40 'Capt. Rostron Explains Wireless Censorship,' *New York American*, 6 May 1912.

BIBLIOGRAPHY

Abbreviations used in the notes for archives consulted:

BHC: Bolton History Centre, Bolton.

CPL: Crosby Public Library, Liverpool.

GLL: Guildhall Library, Aldermanbury, London.

IWM: Imperial War Museum, Lambeth Road, London.

LMA: London Metropolitan Archives, Northampton Road, London.

LRO: Liverpool Record Office, Central Library and Archives, Liverpool.

MMM: Merseyside Maritime Museum, Albert Dock, Liverpool.

MHA: Maritime History Archive, Memorial University, St John's, Newfoundland.

NAK: National Archives (Public Records Office), Kew, Richmond, Surrey.

SAO: Southampton Archives Office, South Block, Civic Centre, Southampton.

SJL: Special Collections and Archives, Sydney Jones Library, Liverpool University.

SLA: Southampton Library and Archives, Civic Centre, Southampton.

WHS: West End Local History Society, West End, Southampton.

BOOKS

Aldred, John. *A Brief History of Canon Slade School, 1855–2005.* Bolton, Eng.: McGrath Regional Publications, Ltd., 2005.

Aylmer, Gerald. *R.M.S. Mauretania: The Ship and Her Record.* 1934. Reprint with additional text: Stroud, Gloucestershire: Tempus Publishing, Ltd., 2000.

Ballard, Robert. *The Discovery of the Titanic: Exploring the Greatest of All Lost Ships.* Toronto: Madison Press Books, 1887.

Barczewski, Stephanie. *Titanic: A Night Remembered.* New York: Hambledon and London, 2004.

Barratt, Nick. *Lost Voices from the Titanic: The Definitive Oral History.* New York: Palgrave Macmillan, 2010.

Beesley, Lawrence. *The Loss of the SS Titanic: Its Story and Its Lessons.* 1912. Reprint, Boston: Houghton Mifflin, 2000.

Bisset, Sir James. *Commodore: War, Peace and Big Ships.* London: Angus and Robertson, 1961.

Bisset, Sir James. *Sail Ho! My Early Years at Sea.* New York: Criterion Books, 1958.

Bisset, Sir James. *Tramps and Ladies: My Early Years in Steamers*. London: Angus and Robertson, 1959.

Booth, John and Sean Coughlan. *Titanic: Signals of Disaster*. Westbury, Wiltshire, UK: White Star Publications, 1993.

Brinnin, John Malcolm. *The Sway of the Grand Saloon: A Social History of the North Atlantic*. New York: Delacorte Press, 1971.

Britten, Sir Edgar. *A Million Ocean Miles*. 1936. Reprint, Wellingborough, Eng.: Patrick Stephens, 1989.

Brode, Tony. *The Southampton Blitz*. 1977. Reprint, Southampton: Itchen Printers, Ltd., 1978.

Bryceson, Dave. *The Titanic Disaster as Reported in the British National Press, April–July 1912*. New York: W. W. Norton, 1997.

Butler, Daniel Allen. *The Other Side of the Night: The Carpathia, the Californian and the Night the Titanic Was Lost*. Drexel Hill, PA: Casemate, 2009.

Carse, Robert. *A Cold Corner of Hell: The Story of the Murmansk Convoys, 1941–1945*. Garden City, NY: Doubleday, 1969.

Conway's All the World's Fighting Ships, 1860–1905. London: Conway Maritime Press, Ltd., 1979.

The Cunard Express Liners Lusitania and Mauretania. 1907. Reprint, *Ocean Liners of the Past, No. 2. in a series of reprints from 'The Shipbuilder,'* Greenwich, CT: New York Graphic Society, Ltd., 1970.

The Cunard Turbine-Driven Quadruple-Screw Atlantic Liner 'Mauretania.' 1907. Reprint, Wellingborough, Eng.: Patrick Stephens Ltd., 1987.

Davie, Michael. *Titanic: The Death and Life of a Legend*. New York: Alfred A. Knopf, 1987.

Diggle, Capt. E. G. *The Romance of a Modern Liner*. London: Sampson Low, Marston & Co., Ltd., 1930.

Duffield, Allison E. (comp.). *Tracing Your Family History, Merchant Navy*. London: Imperial War Museum, 2005.

Eaton, John P. and Charles A. Haas. *Titanic, Destination Disaster: The Legends and the Reality*. New York: W. W. Norton, 1987.

Eaton, John P. and Charles A. Haas. *Titanic: Triumph and Tragedy* (2nd ed.). New York: W. W. Norton, 1995.

Evans, R. A. *Mersey Mariners*. Birkenhead, Merseyside: Countyvise Limited, 1997.

Fox, Stephen. *Transatlantic: Samuel Cunard, Isambard Brunel and the Great Atlantic Steamships*. New York: Perennial, 2004.

Gawler, Jim. *Lloyd's Medals, 1836–1989: A History of Medals Awarded by the Corporation of Lloyd's*. Toronto: Hart Publishing, 1989.

Gilbert, Sir Martin (intro.). *The Straits of War: Gallipoli Remembered*. Phoenix Mill, Gloucestershire, UK: Sutton Publishing Co., 2000.

Gracie, Archibald. *The Truth about the Titanic*. New York: M. Kennerley, 1913.

Grattidge, Harry. *Captain of the Queens: The Autobiography of Captain Harry Grattidge, Former Commodore of the Cunard Line*. New York: E. P. Dutton and Co., 1956.

Heyer, Paul. *Titanic Legacy: Disaster as Media Event and Myth*. Westport, CT: Praeger Publishers, 1995.

Hickey, Michael. *Gallipoli*. London: John Murray, 1995.

Holy Bible, King James Version.

Hurd, Sir Archibald. *A Merchant Fleet at War*. London: Cassell and Co., Ltd., 1920.

Hurd, Sir Archibald. *The Merchant Navy, vol. 1: History of the First World War*. London: John Murray, 1921.

Hurd, Sir Archibald. *The Merchant Navy, vol. 3: History of the First World War*. London: John Murray, 1929.

Hyde, Francis E. *Cunard and the North Atlantic, 1840–1973: A History of Shipping and Financial Management*. London: Macmillan Press Ltd., 1975.

Hyslop, Donald, Alastair Forsyth and Sheila Jemima. *Titanic Voices*. Southampton: Southampton City Council (Amadeus Press), 2006.

Jeffery, Sydney. *The Liverpool Shipwreck and Humane Society, 1839–1939*. Liverpool: Daily Post Printers, n.d. (1939?).

Jordan, Humfrey. *Mauretania: Landfalls and Departures of Twenty-Five Years*. London: Hodder and Stoughton, 1936.

Keegan, John. *The First World War*. New York: Vintage, 2000.

Lightoller, Charles H. *Titanic and Other Ships*. London: Ivor Nicholson and Watson, Ltd., 1935.

Lord, Walter. *A Night to Remember*. 1955. Reprint, New York: Bantam Books, 1997.

Lord, Walter. *The Night Lives On: The Untold Stories and Secrets Behind the Sinking of the Unsinkable Ship – Titanic!* New York: Avon Books, 1986.

Lynch, Don and Ken Marschall. *Titanic: An Illustrated History*. New York: Hyperion/Madison Press, 1992.

Maginnis, Arthur J. *Atlantic Ferry: Its Ships, Men and Working* (3rd ed.). New York: Whittaker and Co., 1900.

Marshall, Logan. *The Sinking of the Titanic*. 1912. Reprint (Bruce M. Caplan, ed.), Bellevue, WA: Seattle Miracle Press, 1997.

Maxtone-Graham, John. *The Only Way to Cross*. 1972. Reprint: New York: Barnes and Noble Books, 1997.

McCart, Neil. *Atlantic Liners of the Cunard Line: From 1884 to the Present Day*. Wellingborough, Eng.: Patrick Stephens, 1990.

McNeil, Capt. S. G. S. *In Great Waters: Memoirs of a Master Mariner*. New York: Harcourt, Brace and Co., 1932.

Mussell, John W. (ed.). *The Medal Yearbook, 2011*. Honiton, Devon: Token Publishing, Ltd., 2011.

Padfield, Peter. *The Titanic and the Californian*. New York: John Day Company, 1965.

Parkes, O. and Maurice Prendergast. *Jane's Fighting Ships, 1919: A Reprint of the 1919 Edition of Fighting Ships*. Newton Abbot, Eng.: David and Charles Reprints, 1969.

Paterson, Sarah (comp.). *Tracing Your Family History, Army*. London: Imperial War Museum, 2006.

Plumb, J. H., et al. *The English Heritage*. St Louis, MO: Forum Press, 1980.

Ransome-Wallis, P. *North Atlantic Panorama, 1900–1976*. Shepperton, Eng.: Ian Allen Ltd., 1977.

Rasor, Eugene L. *The Titanic: Historiography and Annotated Bibliography*. Westport, CT: Greenwood Press, 2001.

Reade, Leslie. *The Ship That Stood Still: The Californian and her Mysterious Role in the Titanic Disaster*. New York: W. W. Norton, 1993.

Rostron, Sir Arthur H. *Home from the Sea*. London: Macmillan, 1931.

Rostron, Sir Arthur H. *The Loss of the Titanic* (John Booth, comp.). Melksham, Eng.: Norton Press Printing, 1991.

Rudenno, Victor. *Gallipoli: Attack from the Sea*. New Haven, CT: Yale University Press, 2008.

Smith, Ken. *Mauretania: Pride of the Tyne*. Newcastle, Eng.: Newcastle Libraries and Information Service, 1997.

Smith, Ken. *Turbinia: The Story of Charles Parsons and his Ocean Greyhound*. Newcastle, Eng.: Tyne Bridge Publishing, 2009.

Smith, Ken. *Tyne to Titanic: The Story of the Rescue Ship Carpathia*. Newcastle, Eng.: Newcastle Libraries and Information Service, 1998.

Spedding, Charles T. *Reminiscences of Transatlantic Travellers*. Philadelphia: J. B. Lippincott, 1925.

Steel, Nigel and Peter Hart. *Defeat at Gallipoli*. London: Papermac, 1995.

Stenson, Patrick. *The Odyssey of C. H. Lightoller*. New York: W. W. Norton, 1984.

Ticehurst, Brian J. *The Titanic's Rescuers: Captain Arthur Henry Rostron, the Crew of the Carpathia and the Carpathia*. Southampton: B&J Printers, 2001.

ARTICLES AND SERIALS

Axon's Commercial and General Directory of Bolton... , 1881. Little Bolton: Henry Axon, 1881.

Axon's Commercial and General Directory of Bolton, Farnworth, Kersley, Halliwell, Astley Bridge, Horwich, Turton, Ainsworth, Walkden, Westhoughton and the townships comprised in the Bolton Union (2nd ed.). Bolton, Lancashire: Henry Axon, 1885.

Gore's Directory of Liverpool and its Environs. London: Kelly's Directories, Ltd., 1891, 1894, 1896, 1898, 1899, 1901, 1904, 1905, 1907, 1908, 1909, 1911, 1912, 1913, 1915, 1916, 1918, 1921, 1922, 1923, 1925, 1927, 1931.

Kelly's Directory of Southampton and Neighbourhood, 1928–29 (36th ed.) and *1937–38* (45th edition). London: Kelly's Directories, Ltd.

Lloyd's Register of British and Foreign Shipping. London: Lloyd's, 1886–7, 1888–9, 1889–90, 1892–3, 1893–4, 1895–6, v. 1 and v. 2; 1910–11, v. 1; 1915–16, v. 2; 1924–5, v. 2; 1925–6, v. 2.

Lloyd's Weekly News. 'The Deathless Story of the Titanic: Complete Narrative with Many Illustrations,' n.d. (c. 1912), DX 949 R 1988 258, MMM.

'Lloyd's War Losses: The First World War: Casualties to Shipping through Enemy Causes, 1914–1918. A Facsimile Reprint of the Original Held at the Guildhall Library, City of London.' London: Lloyd's of London Press, Ltd., 1990, GHL.

Rostron, Arthur H. 'Rescue of the "Titanic" Survivors.' *Scribner's Monthly*, 53 (March 1913): 354–64.

Slade, Lt. Cmdr. G. H. 'A Distinguished Old Conway (Commodore Sir Arthur H. Rostron, R.D – A memory, 1929.)' *The Cadet*, (Sep 1973): 242–4; DX 949 (R), MMM.

Post Office Bolton Directory for 1876–1877. Tillotson & Son: Bolton, 1876.

Slater's Royal National Commercial Directory of Lancashire and the Manufacturing District around Manchester. Manchester: Isaac Slater: 1882.

Shipping and Mercantile Gazette and Lloyd's List. London: Lloyd's, 1887–96, 1897, 1907, 1914, 1940.

Titanic Historical Society. *Titanic Commutator* II, no. 22 (sum. 1979).

Titanic Historical Society. *Titanic Commutator* II no. 24 (win. 1979).

Westender: Newsletter of the West End Local History Society 2, no. 10 (Feb–Apr 2001).

Westender: Newsletter of the West End Local History Society 8, no. 5 (May–June 2012).

NEWSPAPERS

Appleton [WI] Post-Crescent

Bolton News

Bolton Evening News

Boston Globe, Daily and Evening editions.

Charleston [SC] Daily Mail

Columbus [OH] Dispatch

[London] *Daily Telegraph*

Davenport [IA] Democrat and Leader

Eastleigh [Hampshire] News

Hampshire Advertiser and Southampton Times

Kingsport [TN] Times

Liverpool Echo

(Liverpool) *Daily Post*

London Gazette

Manchester Guardian

Nevada State Journal (Reno)

New York American

New York Evening Post

New York Times

Oakland [CA] Tribune

Ogden [UT] Standard Examiner

Portsmouth [NH] Herald

St Louis Post-Dispatch

(Southampton) *Southern Daily Echo*

The Times (London)

Tyrone [PA] Daily Herald

Washington Post

MANUSCRIPT SOURCES

BOLTON HISTORY CENTRE, BOLTON

Bolton Evening News, 22 Jan 1999 (via clippings book B11.28): Certified copy of an Entry of Birth, Pursuant to the Births and Deaths Registration Act 1953 Registration District: Bolton. 1869. Birth in the Sub-district of Sharples in the County of Lancaster.

Bolton Journal and Guardian, 'Pictorial Bolton Series, No.XLIV, 10 Jan 1885' (booklet), B373 CHU.

'Transcriptions of the Memorial Inscriptions in the "New Ground" Part of the Church Yard of Christ Church, Walmsley, Bolton,' Bolton and District Family History Society, 1999.

GUILDHALL LIBRARY, LONDON

'Lloyd's Missing Vessels Book,' 1897–1900, case no. 2611; *Cedric the Saxon*.

'Lloyd's Weekly Confidential Index to the Movements of Allied Vessels,' microfilm reels 245–50.

IMPERIAL WAR MUSEUM, LONDON

Sgt. H. Elliot, R.A.M.C., Diary (10 July 1915 to 12 Mar 1916), Documents: Elliot, H., 99/62/1.

Fred W. Odhams, letter from Alexandria, Egypt, to his mother and sister, 7 Apr 1915, Documents: Odhams, F. W., 93/25/1.

LONDON METROPOLITAN ARCHIVES

'Lloyd's Captains' Registers,' MS18567, 34 (1880–7); MS18567, v. 44; MS18567, v. 46 (1888–95); MS18567, v. 54 (1888–95); MS18567, v. 56; MS18567, v. 69; MS18567, v. 85 (1904–11); MS18568, v. 2; MS18568, v. 6b; MS18569, v. 031; MS18569, v. 33.

MERSEYSIDE MARITIME MUSEUM, LIVERPOOL

Brown, Mildred, letter to mother written aboard RMS *Carpathia*, 17 Apr 1912, D/BRW/2.

Brown, Mildred, letter to 'Nellie' written in Montreal, c. 30 Apr 1912, D/BRW/4.

Cherry, Gladys, letter to mother written aboard RMS *Carpathia*, 17 Apr 1912, DX/1522/1.

Cherry, Gladys, letter to mother written aboard RMS *Carpathia*, 18 Apr 1912; and Cherry, Gladys, letter to mother written aboard RMS *Carpathia*, 19 Apr 1912; DX/1522/2.

'Cunard Carpathia Capacity Plan, Twin Screw R.M.S. Carpathia, General Arrangement, March 1913' (scale: 1/8 inch = 1 foot) B/CUN/8/1903.1/1/2, (1913).

HMS *Conway*: Annual Reports, D/CON/1/2–3, 1864–94 (Batch 1, Reel 1): 'School Ship "Conway". Annual Reports, 1884 to 1894.': 'Mercantile Marine Service Association, Liverpool. School Ship "Conway". Report of the Proceedings at the Distribution of Prizes, on Wednesday, July 22nd, 1885…'

HMS *Conway*: Annual Reports, D/CON/1/2–3, 1864–94 (Batch 1, Reel 1): 'School Ship "Conway". Annual Reports, 1884 to 1894.': 'Mercantile Marine Service Association, Liverpool. School Ship "Conway". Report of the Proceedings at the Distribution of Prizes, on Thursday, July 22, 1886, by His Worship the Mayor of Liverpool (Sir David Radcliffe).'

'HMS *Conway* Muster Roll,' 1883–1905, D/CON/4/2.

'HMS *Conway* Registers of Cadets,' 1884–7, Batch 2 Reel 6, D/CON/13/8.

Merseyside Maritime Museum, 1988, 258 [ephemera envelope] DX/949R. Contains: 'Copy of brief account of Capt. Rostron's career, written by his daughter, Mrs. M. E. Howman of Bristol;' Copy of hand-written account of *Titanic* rescue by Rostron, dated *Carpathia* 'At Sea April 27th 1912;' Copy of 'Report Book [Cunard] Officers, &c,' case 227; Copy of advertisement for Medallic Art Company, Danbury, CT.

MARITIME HISTORY ARCHIVE, MEMORIAL UNIVERSITY, ST JOHN'S, NEWFOUNDLAND

Camphill, 'Agreement and Account of Crew,' 17 July 1893, voyage of 19 July 1893 to 9 May 1894, Antwerp to Liverpool.

Cedric the Saxon, 'Agreement and Account of Crew,' 28 Feb 1887, voyage of 28 Feb 1887 to 15 Jan 1888, Hull to Liverpool.

Cedric the Saxon, 'Agreement and Account of Crew,' 14 Mar 1889, voyage of 16 Mar 1889 to 12 July 1890, Liverpool to Barry.

Cedric the Saxon, 'Agreement and Account of Crew,' 24 June 1895, voyage of 5 July 1895 to 29 Apr 1896, Antwerp to London.

Cedric the Saxon, 'Account of Crew and Other Particulars of a Foreign Going Ship,' voyage of 4 July 1896 to missing, London to foreign.

Red Gauntlet, 'Agreement and Account of Crew,' 10 Oct 1890, voyage of 10 Oct 1890 to 19 Aug 1891, Barry to Rouen.

Red Gauntlet, 'Agreement and Account of Crew,' 7 Sep 1891, voyage of 10 Sep 1891 to 14 Sep 1891, Rouen to Liverpool, 1, MHA.

NATIONAL ARCHIVES (PUBLIC RECORDS OFFICE), KEW, RICHMOND, SURREY

'Awards to British Seamen by Foreign Governments,' BT261/8.

Cedric the Saxon, 'Agreement and Account of Crew,' 27 Feb 1888, voyage of 29 Feb 1888 to 23 Feb 1889, Liverpool to Liverpool, BT99/1614.

Cdr. A. H. Rostron, RNR, 'Medals and Clasps Issued,' ADM 171/63.

'Medal card of Rostron, Arthur Henry,' BT351/1 image 1243; reference 122103, [British First World War Medals issued to merchant seamen].

'Medal Card of Rostron, George, Cheshire Regiment 36988 Private, Machine Gun Corps Second Lieutenant,' WO 372/17.

'Mentioned in Dispatches, 1914–18,' N–R, ADM171/193.

'Rewards Given by His Majesty's Government,' 1910–32, BT261/6.

Rostron, Arthur Henry, Royal Naval Reserve Service Record, ADM 340/120 12C.

'Sea Transport Medal,' South African War, 1899–1902, ADM 171/52.

SYDNEY JONES LIBRARY, LIVERPOOL UNIVERSITY, SPECIAL COLLECTIONS AND ARCHIVES

'Pay Register, Captains, No. 3,' Cunard Collection, D42/GM14/6.

'Register of Officers,' Case 247, William B. Cresser, Cunard Collection, D42/GM16/2.

'Register of Officers,' Case 257, Arthur Henry Rostron, Cunard Collection, D42/GM16/2.

Royden, Sir Thomas, Correspondence File, Cunard Collection, D42/C2/121.

Cunard Steamship Co., 'Ships' Movement Books,' Cunard Collection, D42/GM1: v. 3 (17 Mar 1906 through 15 Feb 1908); v. 6 (24 Dec 1911 through 22 Nov 1913); v. 7 (23 Nov 1913 through 26 June 1915); v. 8 (27 June 1915 through 10 June 1916); v. 9 (11 June 1916 through 17 Nov 1917); v. 11 (18 Nov 1917 through 26 Apr 1919).

GOVERNMENT DOCUMENTS

'Census Returns of England and Wales, 1871,' RG10 3931, folio 97, p. 5. NAK.

'Census Returns of England and Wales, 1881,' RG11 3832, folio 19, p. 31. NAK.

'Census Returns of England and Wales, 1891,' RG12 3112, folio 24, p. 19. NAK.

'Census Returns of England and Wales, 1901,' RG13 3445, folio 94, p. 31. NAK.

'Census Returns of England and Wales, 1911,' NAK.

Department of the [US] Navy, Bureau of Equipment, 'International Wireless Telegraph Convention,' Wash. DC: USGPO, 1907.

'England and Wales Birth Index, 1837–1915,' v. 8C. England and Wales Civil Registration Indexes, General Register Office, London.

'General Index. Births Registered in England and Wales,' months of: Jan–Mar 1901 (469, microfiche 4464); Jan–Mar 1903 (478, microfiche 4521); Oct–Dec 1907 (449, microfiche 4658); Jan–Mar 1915 (383, microfiche 5033). CPL.

Library of Congress, 'Catalog of Copyright Entries,' Musical Compositions, Library of Congress Copyright Office, 1912.

Photograph 01690, Digital Collection, US Library of Congress.

United States House of Representatives, 62nd Congress, 2nd Session, Report No. 830, 'Capt. Arthur Henry Rostron,' United States Congressional Serial Set No. 6132.

United States Immigration and Naturalization Service, 'Passenger and Crew Lists of Vessels Arriving at New York, New York,' *Berengaria*, 9 Oct 1926, microfilm roll T715 3956, p. 80, US National Archives, Washington, DC.

United States Immigration and Naturalization Service, 'Passenger and Crew Lists of Vessels Arriving at New York, New York,' *Carmania*, 24 Feb 1913, microfilm T715 2018, p. 122 and 13 Feb 1918, microfilm roll T715 2563, p. 270, US National Archives, Washington, DC.

United States Immigration and Naturalization Service, 'Passenger and Crew Lists of Vessels Arriving at New York, New York,' *Mauretania*, 7 Apr 1919, microfilm roll T715 2635, p. 233 and 20 Sep 1919, microfilm roll T715 2682, p. 111, US National Archives, Washington, DC.

United States Immigration and Naturalization Service, 'Passenger and Crew Lists of Vessels Arriving at New York, New York,' *Saxonia*, 3 Aug 1917, microfilm roll T715 2536, p. 42 and 3 Dec 1917, microfilm roll T715 2554, p. 147, US National Archives, Washington DC.

United States Immigration and Naturalization Service, 'Passenger and Crew Lists of Vessels Arriving at New York, New York,' *Tyrrhenia*, 5 Feb 1924, microfilm roll T715 3448, p. 37, US National Archives, Washington DC.

United States Senate, '*Titanic' Disaster Hearings before a Subcommittee of the Committee on Commerce United States Senate Sixty-Second Congress Second Session*, Washington, DC: USGPO, 1912.

United States Senate, *Titanic Disaster Report of the Committee on Commerce, United States Senate* (62nd Cong., 2nd Session, Report No. 806), Washington, DC: USGPO, 1912.

ONLINE SOURCES

BBC News, 'Street named after Carpathia's Captain Arthur H. Rostron,' 25 Nov 2011 (www.bbc.co.uk/news), accessed 5 Nov 2012.

Bolton Church Institute School War Memorial, 'Names, 1914–1918, George Rostron' (www.bolton-church-institute.org.uk), accessed 24 Oct 2012.

Bolton Church Institute, 'Family of George Rostron' (www.bolton-church-institute.org.uk/trees/rostron-g.pdf), accessed 24 Oct 2012.

Bolton School, Old Boys' Association, 'Distinguished Old Boys' (www.boltonschool.org), accessed 17 July 2013.

The Cachalots: The Southampton Master Mariners, 'Past Captains and Officers,' (www.cachalots.org.uk), accessed 7 Nov 2012.

Commonwealth War Graves Commission, 'Find War Dead,' (www.cwgc.org/find-war-dead/casualty/1637752/ROSTRON, GEORGE), accessed 9 Aug 2014.

Eastleigh Borough Council, 13 Sep 2010, 'Naming of Streets in Hedge End and West End' (www.eastleigh.gov.uk/meetings/documents), accessed 5 Nov 2012.

Encyclopedia Titanica (www.encyclopedia-titanica.org), accessed 2010–2013.

Gittins, Dave, 'Carpathia: Legends and Reality' (www.titanicbook.com/carpathia.html), accessed 24 Oct 2012.

The Halifax Explosion (www.cbc.ca/halifaxexplosion), accessed 27 Oct 2012.

'HMS Conway, 1859–1974: Britain's premier Merchant Navy school ship,' 'The Third HMS Conway – HMS Nile, 1826–1876' (www.hmsconway.org/history_third), accessed 15 July 2013.

'HMS Conway 1859–1974: Britain's premier Merchant Navy school ship,' 'Slop Chest' (www.hmsconway.org), accessed 15 July 2013.

Lancashire Online Parish Clerk Project (www.lan-opc.org.uk), accessed 25 and 29 June 2011. (Burial of Henry Rostron, 16 June 1866; marriage of James Rostron and Nancy Lever, 19 June 1867; baptism of Arthur Henry Rostron, 19 June 1869; baptism of Ethel Minnie Stothert, 13 Nov 1873; marriage of Arthur Henry Rostron and Ethel Minnie Stothert, 14 Sep 1899.)

Smith, William A., Speech of Senator William Alden Smith to the US Senate on his committee's Titanic Enquiry, 28 May 1912, Titanic Enquiry Project, www.titanicinquiry.org.

Treaty of Versailles, Part VIII, Articles 231–47 and Annex III (www.firstworldwar.com).

'The U-boat Wars, 1939–45' (www.uboat.net), accessed 29 Oct 2012.

Wreck Commissioners' Court. Scottish Hall, Buckingham Gate, 'Proceedings before the Right Hon. Lord Mersey, Wreck Commissioner of the United Kingdom … on a Formal Investigation Ordered by the Board of Trade into the Loss of the SS "Titanic",' Titanic Enquiry Project (www.titanicenquiry.org), accessed 2010–2013.

'Wreck Commissioner's Enquiry, Report on the Loss of the "Titanic" (SS),' Titanic Enquiry Project (www.titanicenquiry.org), accessed 2010–2013.

CORRESPONDENCE

Rostron, Dr Arthur John (grandson of Sir Arthur), letter to the author, 21 Oct 2011.

INTERVIEWS

Andrews, Roy, museum volunteer, West End Local History Museum and Heritage Centre, 2 July 2011.

Rostron, Dr Arthur John (grandson of Sir Arthur), National Museum of Scotland, Edinburgh, 18 July 2011.

MUSEUM EXHIBITIONS

'The First World War,' Imperial War Museum, London, 15 July 2011.

'Survival at Sea: Stories of the Merchant Navy in the Second World War,' Imperial War Museum, London, 15 July 2011.

INDEX